TEACHER'S EDITION

On Location 2

Reading and Writing for Success in the Content Areas

Thomas Bye
with John Chapman

McGraw-Hill

On Location 2 Teacher's Edition, 1st Edition

Published by McGraw-Hill ESL/ELT, a business unit of The McGraw-Hill Companies, Inc., 1221 Avenue of the Americas, New York, NY 10020. Copyright © 2005 by the McGraw-Hill Companies, Inc. All rights reserved. Permission is granted to reproduce these materials as needed for classroom use or for use by individual students. Distribution for sale is prohibited.

ISBN: 0-07-288678-1
1 2 3 4 5 6 7 8 9 QPD/QPD 11 10 09 08 07 06 05

Editorial director: Tina B. Carver
Executive editor: Erik Gundersen
Senior developmental editor: Mari Vargo
Developmental editor: Fredrik Liljeblad
Production manager: Juanita Thompson
Cover designer: Wee Design Group
Interior designer: Wee Design Group

Photo Credits

Cover Images: All cover images courtesy of the Getty Images Royalty-Free Collection except the following: cockroaches eating crackers: David Maitland/Getty Images; tropical storm: Images produced by Hal Pierce, Laboratory for Atmospheres, NASA Goddard Space Flight Center/NOAA; interview in classroom: Barbara Stitzer/Photo Edit; Frog: Royalty-Free/CORBIS; Giraffes: Royalty-Free/CORBIS; man caught in hurricane: Royalty-Free/CORBIS; California State Capitol: Focus Group/Andre Jenny/PictureQuest.

www.esl-elt.mcgraw-hill.com

TABLE OF CONTENTS

Scope and Sequence iv
Welcome to *On Location* viii
Academic Literacy: Five "Power Standards" For Success x
Best Practices: Helping Students Develop Academic Literacy xiii
Developing Academic Literacy: A Research-Based Approach xviii

Procedural Notes:
- Unit 1 .... 2a
- Unit 2 .... 20a
- Unit 3 .... 38a
- Unit 4 .... 56a
- Unit 5 .... 74a
- Unit 6 .... 92a
- Unit 7 .... 110a
- Unit 8 .... 128a
- Unit 9 .... 146a
- Unit 10 .... 164a

From the Student Book:
- Mini-Unit A: Listening and Taking Notes 182
- Mini-Unit B: Reading and Taking Notes 184
- Mini-Unit C: Reading and Summarizing 190
- Spelling and Phonics Activities 192
- ChecBrics 197
- Glossary 207
- Common Irregular Verbs 211
- Listening Script 212
- Index 217
- Text and Audio Credits 220
- Photo Credits 221

Practice Book Answer Key 222
Research Statement References 230

Scope and Sequence

Unit	Readings	Genres/ Writing Tasks	Reading Strategies	Word Work/ Spelling and Phonics
1 Can We Talk? page 2	Magazine interviews with Alex Rodriguez and Christina Vidal	Interviews	Skimming	Homophones Spelling the /ā/ sound as in *fame* and *play*
2 Animals Nobody Loves page 20	Selections from *Animals Nobody Loves* and *The Unhuggables*	Short informational reports	Taking notes Listing what you know	The suffixes *-y* and *-ing* Spelling the /ch/ sound as in *check* and *kitchen*
3 I Made It Myself! page 38	Instructions for making Halloween make-up and costumes	How-to instructions	Drawing a picture Predicting	Compound words Spelling the /ō/ sound as in *hole* and *boat*
4 Trying to Be Cool page 56	Selections from "Stupid Things I Did to Be Cool" from *Consumer Reports for Kids*	Personal narratives	Questioning the author Predicting	The suffix *-er* and *-or* in nouns Pronouncing words with the letters *gh*
5 Who Eats What? page 74	Selections about food chains from *Who Eats What?*	Explaining a process	Taking notes Making diagrams	Compound words that are animal names Spelling the /o͞o/ sound as in *food* and *blue*

Grammar	Organization	Style	Writing Conventions	Content Area Connections	Links to Literature
Wh- questions	Organizing information in an interview	Posing questions that get interesting answers	Sentence-level punctuation	Civics	Portrait poem
Subject-verb agreement with present tense verbs	Writing rich paragraphs: topic sentence and supporting sentences	Using adjectives to make writing vivid	Serial commas	Natural science	Poem "Acro-Bat," by Kenn Nesbitt
Imperatives	Organizing steps in a time sequence	Using specific words in how-to instructions	Symbols that stand for words	Consumer Economics Math	Poem "Best Mask," by Shel Silverstein
Simple past tense	Describing events in a time sequence	Writing for your audience: formal vs. informal language	Commas with *when*	Civics	Poem "Motto," by Langston Hughes
Present vs. past tense	Organizing parts of a process	Combining sentences with *that* clauses	Commas with examples	Science	Poem "Links in a Food Chain"

Scope and Sequence

Unit	Readings	Genres/ Writing Tasks	Reading Strategies	Word Work/ Spelling and Phonics
6 Real-Life Heroes page 92	True stories about rescues from *National Geographic World*	True stories	Predicting	Compound words derived from nouns and verbs plus their objects or prepositions Pronouncing words with the letters *oo*
7 Nature's Fury page 110	First- and third-person descriptions of natural disasters	Describing an event	Visualizing	Synonyms Pronouncing words with the letters *ou*
8 Drugs: The True Story page 128	Persuasive pamphlets against drugs and tobacco use	Persuasive writing	Identifying the main purpose Skimming	Prefixes that mean "not" Pronouncing words with the letters *ea*
9 I Love Jell-O®! page 146	"Reviews" of Jell-O® and oatmeal	Evaluations	Visualizing Summarizing	Antonyms Spelling the /j/ sound as in *jam* and *badge*
10 Let's Debate! page 164	Articles from *Junior Scholastic* that present debates	Debates	Identifying facts and opinions Skimming	Word families Spelling the /or/ sound as in *for* and *four*

Grammar	Organization	Style	Writing Conventions	Content Area Connections	Links to Literature
Adverbial time clauses	Organizing the action of a narrative	Writing titles and leads that grab the reader's attention	Exclamation points	Civics Health	Tall tale: "Paul Bunyan and the Gumberoos"
Review of the past tense	Describing an event	Using action-packed verbs Using similes	Sentence combining	Natural science	Myth: "The Turtle Tale"
Gerunds as subjects and objects	Organizing opinions, facts, and examples in persuasive writing	Using subheadings for clarity	Dashes	Health	Excerpts from *Go Ask Alice,* the diary of a teen drug user
Adverbial clauses of condition (*if* clauses)	Justifying an opinion with reasons, details, and facts	Using stand-out adjectives	Commas with sentence-starting adverbs	Consumer Economics Health	Review of Shel Sliverstein's *Falling Up* Poem "Tattooin' Ruth," by Shel Silverstein
Modals of persuasion	Organizing an argument	Using quoted speech to support an argument	Punctuation with quotes	Civics Health	Poem "How to Successfully Persuade Your Parents to Give You More Pocket Money," by Andrea Shavick

Welcome to On Location

How Does the Teacher's Edition Work?

The *On Location* **Teacher's Edition** is organized around each unit in the Student Book. An overview of each unit describes the lessons and identifies the standards that are addressed in each lesson. Each page from the Student Book is reproduced and accompanied by helpful notes and suggestions for use.

Each lesson has three parts—

- A **Warm Up** engages the attention of students and focuses them on the lesson objective.
- **Teaching the Lesson** provides teachers with step-by-step suggestions for actively engaging students in each activity.
- A **Wrap Up** provides lesson closure—enabling the teacher to assess student learning.

In addition to providing procedural notes and suggestions for use, each unit in the Teacher's Edition includes extra teaching tips and ideas for employing best practices, technology tips, culture notes, and tips for using the Practice Book. Opportunities for assessment and recycling are also included. Many of these useful features are accompanied by icons:

- Best Practice
- Access for All
- Using Technology
- ✓ Assessment
- ♻ Re-teaching/Recycling
- **PB** Practice Book reference

Student Book answer keys are included after the procedural notes for each lesson, and a Practice Book answer key can be found at the back of the Teacher's Edition.

Components at a Glance

The *On Location* program is organized into three levels. Book 1 enables students to meet beginning-level standards for reading, writing, and oral language. By the end of Book 1, students are able to read simple paragraphs and write well-formed, connected sentences. Book 2 enables students to meet early intermediate standards. By the end of Book 2, students are able to read simple multi-paragraph selections and write related paragraphs. Book 3 enables students to meet intermediate-level standards. By the end of Book 3, students are able to read and produce simple essays—writing that informs, explains, analyzes, and persuades.

Each **Student Book** is organized into ten engaging, task-based units, each focusing on a particular nonfiction reading and writing genre. Every reading is authentic—giving students opportunities to read a variety of real-world text selections they will encounter in school and in their lives and to produce writing in the same academic genres.

Along the way, students engage in structured listening and speaking activities that develop academic language functions, promote thinking and discussion, and build motivation.

Each unit also opens doors to academic content. Students explore topics in science, social studies, and geography, and learn essential academic vocabulary and skills to help them tackle grade-level content across the curriculum. In addition, every unit provides literature that extends the content of the readings.

The **Practice Book** provides students with the opportunity to master the reading skills, vocabulary, and grammar introduced in the Student Book while allowing them to evaluate their own writing and practice test-taking skills. Activities allow students to further explore unit topics, respond to literature selections, and discover how much they learned from the activities and writing tasks in the Student Books.

The **Audio Program** includes taped activities that develop social and academic listening skills. Each reading selection in the Student Book is accompanied by audio, providing students with the opportunity to listen to multiple speakers and various genres.

On Location **Phonics** provides systematic, explicit instruction that helps students who are new to English hear the sound patterns of their new language and use knowledge of sound-letter relationships to read and write high-frequency words and phrases that they hear and see around them. Incorporating a "fast-track" approach, this optional component enables newcomers to learn both language and content from day one. Teaching notes at the bottom of each student page make *On Location* Phonics a self-contained program.

The *On Location* program includes a powerful **Staff Development Video** to support implementation of the program. The video provides strategies for teaching reading and writing from a language arts perspective—focusing on best practices such as pre-teaching vocabulary, use of read aloud/think aloud techniques, interactive reading, modeled writing, shared writing, use of rubrics, and cooperative learning. The training video provides strategies for reading and writing in the content areas and demonstrates how *On Location* can be used effectively.

The *On Location* **Assessment System** includes a placement test, a diagnostic, end-of-unit tests, and an end-of-level test for each book. Task-specific rubrics (or "ChecBrics") help students plan, revise, and evaluate their work.

Due to the *On Location* program's emphasis on academic reading and writing, teachers can be sure that *On Location* will help their school meet Adequate Yearly Progress (AYP) targets. The *On Location* assessment system supports district accountability efforts by providing tools that enable teachers to evaluate mastery of English language development/English language arts standards.

ACADEMIC LITERACY: FIVE "POWER STANDARDS" FOR SUCCESS

If English Learners are to achieve world-class standards in the content areas, they must develop high levels of academic literacy—the language, thinking, and learning tools needed to achieve content standards across the academic curriculum. Five *On Location* Power Standards guarantee that students can compete across the academic curriculum. Organized in three levels, *On Location* benchmarks ramp students up to early advanced proficiency in English.

❶ Use listening and speaking skills and strategies to accomplish academic tasks in the content areas.

Book 1	Book 2	Book 3
■ Listen for the main idea ■ Use academic language functions—seeking information, identifying, describing, narrating, sequencing, and classifying ■ Ask and answer informational questions ■ Participate in structured whole-class, group activities ■ Give short oral presentations	■ Listen for details ■ Use academic language functions—comparing, analyzing, justifying, persuading, and evaluating ■ Initiate and answer questions that elicit explanation ■ Work with peers to complete a task or solve a problem ■ Give more extended oral presentations	■ Listen to learn ■ Use academic language functions—inferring, problem solving, and synthesizing ■ Initiate and answer questions that involve higher-order thinking ■ Participate in sustained discussion and debate ■ Give elaborate oral presentations

❷ Use decoding and word attack skills, knowledge of vocabulary, and knowledge of grammar to read fluently.

Book 1	Book 2	Book 3
■ Decode familiar words ■ Read common sight words ■ Use simple word clues to unlock meaning	■ Use knowledge of English phonemes, morphemes, and syntax to decode simple text ■ Use word attack skills to read unfamiliar words ■ Use context to figure out the meaning of new words	■ Read aloud with accuracy, correct pacing, and expression ■ Distinguish words with multiple meanings ■ Identify members of word families ■ Recognize idioms and figurative language

Power Standards

❸ Read and understand a range of academic text materials.

Book 1	Book 2	Book 3
■ Read familiar words, phrases, and short sentences ■ Answer simple factual questions ■ Identify sequence and logical order in text ■ Read and respond to literature ■ Use pictures and signpost words to predict ■ Read short connected paragraphs with guidance	■ Read simple narratives and informational texts ■ Identify the main idea and details ■ Identify patterns in text: sequence, compare/contrast, and cause and effect ■ Read and respond to literature ■ Identify the purposes of different texts ■ Use context to predict ■ Restate and summarize information ■ Use basic reading strategies to unlock meaning	■ Read a range of narrative, expository, and persuasive texts (essays) ■ Read text from the content areas ■ Follow the logical sequence of arguments in persuasive text ■ Read and respond to literature ■ Compare and contrast information ■ Use cognitive and metacognitive strategies to unlock meaning

❹ Write effectively across a variety of academic genres.

Book 1	Book 2	Book 3
■ Write three or four related sentences within a guided structure ■ Record information and ideas in categories ■ Use graphic tools to record ideas and information ■ Use the writing process	■ Produce writing that shows a simple awareness of purpose, audience, and style ■ Use graphic tools to organize ideas ■ Write a paragraph with a topic sentence and details or examples ■ Use the writing process	■ Produce writing that shows a more sophisticated awareness of purpose, audience, and style ■ Show personal voice in writing ■ Write an essay with a controlling idea that sheds light on a subject ■ Use graphic tools to show relationships ■ Use the writing process

❺ Apply the conventions of English usage orally and in writing.

Book 1	Book 2	Book 3
<ul><li>Produce subject-verb-object sentences</li><li>Produce target grammatical forms in structured activities</li><li>Spell words in sentences with controlled vocabulary</li><li>Spell familiar short vowel and sight words</li><li>Use sentence-level punctuation and capitalization</li><li>Edit writing for correctness</li></ul>	<ul><li>Produce sentences with some variation and elaboration</li><li>Accurately produce target grammatical forms in structured activities</li><li>Spell words in sentences with controlled vocabulary</li><li>Edit writing for correctness</li></ul>	<ul><li>Use complex sentences in writing with correct coordination and subordination of ideas</li><li>Use transitions to elaborate ideas</li><li>Spell frequently misspelled words</li><li>Use conventions in grade-level written work</li><li>Edit writing for correctness</li></ul>

Best Practices: Helping Students Develop Academic Literacy

The *On Location* Teacher's Editions are designed for teachers who are working to ensure that their students develop powerful reading and writing skills—teachers just like you! Each lesson in the Teacher's Edition describes an array of research-based teaching practices whose use will ensure that English Learners will master the five *On Location* Power Standards.

On Location Power Standard ❶ Use listening and speaking skills and strategies to accomplish academic tasks in the content areas.

Structured Listening—Students listen for a purpose to a taped activity, then respond by sharing with a classmate, writing a sentence, taking a position, or otherwise showing that they understand. Structured listening activities are most effective when the tape or CD is played twice—each time with a different listening prompt.

Structured Interaction—Working in pairs (**Heads Together**), small groups (**Team Talk**), or as a class (**Let's Talk**), students explore a question or topic that results in a written product—a word or sentence, a completed chart or other graphic, or some other work product.

Oral Presentation Rubrics—Before students give an oral presentation, they work together to develop a checklist-type rubric that will help them plan their presentation and that the class will use to evaluate each presentation. The rubric should include from three to five indicators related to effectiveness of the presentation, accuracy of content, and "stage presence."

On Location Power Standard ❷ Use decoding and word attack skills, knowledge of vocabulary, and knowledge of grammar to read fluently.

Fluency and expression

Shared Reading—Students share the reading of a text to develop fluency and expression. Typical shared reading activities may include *echo reading* (students echoing the words of the teacher after reading), *choral reading* (students reading at the same time as the teacher), and *partial-completion reading* (teacher reading most of the text, then pausing for students to read words or phrases).

Preteaching vocabulary: alternatives to dictionary use

Word Check—Using finger signals (thumbs up, thumbs down, thumbs sideways), students show whether they think they can define a word, have seen the word but can't define it, or have never seen the word. This strategy is used before and after a vocabulary lesson to help engage students in the study of words and to enable the teacher to assess learning.

Contextual Redefinition—Working in small groups, students attempt to define six to eight words they will encounter in a reading, using prior knowledge. They are then presented with each word used in a sentence that provides clues to the word's meaning. Students revisit and modify their definitions

Word Clues—The teacher presents challenging new vocabulary in short explanations or anecdotes that help students hear the words in context. The teacher takes care to provide examples, to paraphrase the target word, and to make explanations concrete.

Developing word-analysis and vocabulary skills

Word Study—Each unit of *On Location* includes structured word study activities which focus on the development of vocabulary, how words are formed, and spelling and phonics.

Mini-Lesson—Each short lesson focuses on a single skill, strategy, or procedure related to the reading or writing students are doing. For example, as students read, the teacher might stop to show students how knowledge of prefixes can help them understand the meaning of unfamiliar words. Mini-lessons usually include both explanation and demonstration. These lessons are most effective when students help contribute additional examples.

Word Map—A word map is a visual representation of a definition. A word map shows the category to which a word belongs, its features or properties, and examples of the term. For example, a word map might show that a reptile is an animal (category), that it is cold-blooded and covered with scales (properties), and that rattlesnakes, alligators, and crocodiles are examples. The teacher can help students create word maps on the chalkboard, using shared/interactive writing techniques.

Word Family Charts—Students fill in partially-completed charts that include word family members that are related in meaning but are different parts of speech—for example, *educate*, *educated*, and *education*.

Understanding how English grammar works

Grammar Study—Each unit of *On Location* includes a structured grammar study lesson that focuses on a rule of English grammar or on how English sentences work. These lessons include a "Listen Up" activity, which develops metalinguistic awareness.

Structured Language Practice Activities—Structured language practice—including both guided and independent practice activities—helps students produce and practice specific points of grammar or the use of functions. *Completion activities* require students to supply the target form in an oral sentence stem. *Transformation activities* require students to change a particular prompt—for example, changing the subject from singular to plural, then making other changes in the sentence.

On Location Power Standard ❸ Read and understand a range of academic text materials.

Three-Step Passage Reading—For each selection, the Teacher's Edition provides a three-step approach to help students read and understand the passage.

1. **My Turn (Read Aloud/Think Aloud)**—The teacher reads a selection aloud to students, modeling what good readers do, what readers are thinking as they read, and how they use reading strategies to unlock meaning. This step also provides an opportunity for the teacher to—

    - build background knowledge
    - note the author's purpose and audiences
    - focus on the meaning of individual words and how words are strung together to form sentences
    - note a grammar point
    - teach and model a specific reading strategy—for example, predicting what comes next

2. **Our Turn (Interactive Reading)**—Interactive reading is a collaborative reading experience guided by the teacher. Students follow along as the teacher reads, then they join in on the reading. The teacher focuses on aspects of the reading process, again modeling the use of strategies to unlock meaning. During passage reading, the teacher may comment on the selection or pose questions that cause students to engage more deeply in the meaning and language of the selection. The teacher can help students figure out the meaning of unfamiliar vocabulary as they read, using context and specific word solving skills (e.g., knowledge of roots and affixes, word relationships, etc.) and encourage students to talk about the text. The teacher can also prompt students to notice text structure, identify stylistic features, or comment on the language in the text.

3. **Your Turn (Independent Reading)**—Finally, the student tackles the text on his or her own. The direction line before each reading always provides the student with a task of some sort that will enhance student learning.

Use of graphic organizers: clusters, charts, diagrams—A graphic organizer is a visual that defines relationships among ideas, concepts, or elements of a text. Graphic organizers can be used before, during, and after reading. They can enhance readiness for learning, understanding of materials, and recall.

Graphic organizers are most often used to develop knowledge of vocabulary and key concepts; to help organize pre-reading predictions; to tap prior knowledge and organize thinking; to analyze the structure of various forms of narrative; and to organize information presented in expository text. A variety of graphic organizers is always provided in the student materials.

Checks for Understanding—Frequent checking for understanding is essential for monitoring student learning and adjusting teaching. A variety of strategies for checking for understanding is embedded throughout each unit.

- **Summarizing**—After reading a paragraph or passage, have students summarize what they have read or respond to the text. Use the summarizing Mini-Units in Books 2 and 3 to help students develop this important skill. The first activity in the Practice Book involves a re-telling or summarizing task, which gives students extra practice with this important skill.
- **Question All-Write**—The teacher interrupts students as they read to pose a written question about the passage. The teacher uses student responses to enhance discussion of the reading or reteach an important concept. The strategy also builds "wait time" into question-answer routines.
- **Outcome Sentence**—Students respond to a written sentence stem at the end of a lesson. Typical sentence stems include "I learned that _____" or "I still wonder about _____." Students then share their responses with classmates, enabling the teacher to audit student learning and to build on student responses.
- **Sentence Synthesis**—The teacher writes three or four key terms from the reading or lesson on the board. Students use these words to write a meaningful sentence (or two) that summarizes the main idea of the reading or lesson.

On Location Power Standard ❹ Write effectively across a variety of academic genres.

Use of the Writing Process—Students move through a structured process that results in a polished written product in a particular genre and shares it with an audience. Steps in the writing process include "Getting It Out," during which students select a writing topic and organize their ideas, typically using a graphic organizer of some sort; "Getting It Down," during which students develop a first draft, typically using an outline;

"Getting it Right," during which students revise and edit their writing, usually relying on the supportive feedback of peers (**Group Share**); and "Presenting It"—when students share a final draft with classmates.

Shared Writing—The teacher and students discuss, then share in the writing of a common text related to a topic under discussion, something the class has been studying, or a common class experience. The teacher is the scribe, using the board, chart paper, or an overhead transparency. The teacher can use the shared writing to model both reading and writing strategies as text is created—facilitating discussion and providing instruction in text organization, style, grammar, and conventions of print. The students are seen as writing "apprentices."

Interactive Writing—Like shared writing, interactive writing is a collaborative activity in which the teacher and students create text. Students typically share the decision about what they are going to write and also "share the pen." As in shared writing, the students are seen as writing "apprentices."

Language Experience Approach—The language experience approach (LEA) promotes reading and writing—usually some form of narrative—through the use of personal experiences and oral language. The underlying premise is that students will learn to read material that stems from their own experiences. Students generate their own reading material from their own oral language and begin to read the words they already know.

The most basic form of LEA involves the transcription of an individual student's personal experience. The experience is transcribed as the learner dictates it, without transcriber corrections to grammar or vocabulary. This technique keeps the focus on the content rather than the form of what is written. Errors are corrected later, during revising and editing stages of the writing process. With beginning students, the writing may only be several sentences long.

Modeled Writing—Modeled writing enables students to see how the teacher thinks as s/he writes. In a modeled writing episode, the teacher chooses the genre, particular focus, content, and structure. The product is the teacher's—not a product that is the result of collaboration among students. It is a well-formed piece of writing that helps students develop insights into the writing process.

Writing Frames—Writing frames provide a scaffold for students as they produce writing that follows a particular organizational pattern. The frame provides words and phrases that help guide the student's writing.

Graphic Organizers—Graphic organizers—timelines, T-charts, Venn diagrams, or concept charts—help students organize their ideas and generate support to make their writing come alive. Every unit in the Student Book provides a graphic organizer to help students "get it out." The Practice Book includes blank graphic organizers to help students move through prewriting activities.

Use of Rubrics—Students are encouraged to use task-anchored "ChecBrics," which are included at the end of the Student Book and at the end of the Practice Book to plan and polish their writing. Organized around four major facets of writing—organization, content, style, and grammar/mechanics—students "check" to make sure that they have addressed each indicator, then give themselves an overall rating. They attach the ChecBric to their writing before they put it in their portfolios.

Guided Revision—Every Writer's Workshop provides step-by-step guidance that helps students revise their writing. Focusing on key traits related to the writing task, students systematically examine their first drafts and are provided with structured guidance for additions or modifications.

Group Share—Students produce their best writing when they have a chance to "audition" their writing and receive feedback from peers before they develop a final draft.

Portfolios—Portfolios enable students to keep their best writing in one place and help the teacher conference with students. The teacher might consider creating a tabbed hanging folder for each student, kept in a colorful plastic bin in the classroom.

Notebooks—Notebooks allow students to create their own reference lists of important ideas, useful vocabulary, word formations, grammar rules, etc. Students can include definitions and sample sentences to enrich their personal reference materials.

On Location Power Standard ❺ Apply the conventions of English usage orally and in writing.

Mini-Lesson—As with word analysis and vocabulary skills, mini-lessons on oral or written conventions can be embedded in reading or writing activities that students are doing. For example, as students read, the teacher might stop to point out the use of punctuation with quotation marks. Or, as students talk, the teacher might address the appropriate use of a particular academic language function.

Interactive Editing—The teacher either dictates or presents several sentences that include problems related to capitalization, punctuation, grammar, spelling, or word choice. Students write or copy the sentences, then edit them individually or with a partner. The class then discusses the particular convention and its use.

Developing Academic Literacy: A Research-Based Approach

Thomas Bye, Ph.D.

If English Learners are to achieve rigorous *academic standards*, they must develop high levels of *academic literacy*—that is, the language, thinking, and learning tools needed to achieve content standards across the curriculum. Related to the construct of cognitive academic language proficiency (Cummins, 1981), the concept of academic literacy is broad, encompassing the listening and speaking skills students need to read and write in the content areas; strategies for comprehending, processing, and producing texts in academic disciplines and contexts; the formal rules and patterns of language; readers' and writers' purposes and roles; and knowledge of language use in a social context. *On Location* incorporates key elements of traditional literacy approaches, student-centered frameworks such as the Cognitive Academic Language Learning Approach (Chamot & O'Malley, 1994, 1999), and a socioliterate view of academic literacies (Johns, 1997), providing a genre-based approach that—

- enables students to explore the purposes, structures, and stylistic ground rules of various forms of text—within a social context;
- helps students gain insight into their own reading and writing processes as a means of taking responsibility for their own learning;
- helps students develop a toolkit of strategies for comprehending text and producing academic writing;
- helps students master the patterns, rules, and conventions of written language.

Best teaching approaches and practices, confirmed by research, provide the underpinnings for the innovative *On Location* approach.

Skills for Beginning Readers

❶ **Explicit, systematic phonemic awareness and phonics instruction helps students learn to read—provided that it helps make text comprehensible.**

On Location recognizes that many students who are new to English need to develop phonemic awareness and decoding skills if they are to read fluently. The National Reading Panel (2000) reports that teaching phonemic awareness provided value-added results for students across a range of grade levels and that systematic phonics instruction improves older students' decoding, spelling, and oral reading skills. *On Location* enables teachers to incorporate phonics instruction into a comprehensive reading program that allows for the differentiated use of phonics instruction, based on individual need—especially students who do not know how an alphabetic language like English works. Because *On Location* Phonics activities are always linked to meaningful text rather than presented as isolated rules or patterns, the direct teaching of phonics helps make selections more comprehensible—and thus helps students learn to read (Krashen, 2004; Smith, 1994). And each unit in Books 1–3 provides instruction that enables students to explore relationships between common sound/spelling patterns—promoting fluent reading and comprehension.

❷ **Reading fluency contributes to comprehension of text.**

The ability to read orally with ease, accuracy, and expression is one of several critical factors necessary for reading comprehension. According to National Reading Panel findings, structured practice in oral reading has a significant and positive impact on word recognition, fluency, and comprehension. *On Location* Phonics includes structured oral reading activities that build fluency. The Teacher's Editions for Books 1–3 provide suggestions for interactive passage reading activities that promote reading with accuracy and expression.

Reading Comprehension

On Location adopts the definition outlined by the RAND Reading Study Group (RRSG) that reading comprehension is a process of both extracting and constructing meaning involving the interaction of three elements: the reader, the text, and the activity or purpose for reading (RRSG, 2002)—within a social context. *On Location* helps teachers orchestrate these elements to ensure that English Learners develop powerful reading comprehension skills.

❶ Effective comprehension instruction is driven by clear student outcomes.

Effective teachers identify clear learning outcomes for their students, and they provide highly-scaffolded instruction to help students meet these goals. Scaffolded instruction includes explanation and modeling of the reading process and coaching in how to use the process to understand novel text (Dole et al, 1991; Hogan & Pressley, 1997; Roehler & Duffy, 1991; National Reading Panel, 2000). Every *On Location* unit incorporates a predictable, "backwards buildup" approach that enables students to produce academic writing based on models of authentic, high-quality text. Carefully designed learning activities address standards for academic literacy. Standards are identified for every lesson in the Teacher's Edition, and step-by-step suggestions show the teacher how to scaffold each activity in the Student Book.

❷ Effective reading comprehension instruction relies on the use of challenging but manageable text materials.

Effective teachers use text selections that students can read with guidance from the teacher. They consider the linguistic and cognitive demands of reading selections and scaffold reading experiences to provide all students with access to high-level text (Hiebert, 1999). *On Location* provides students with high-interest, instructional-level text that helps them read in the content areas. The Teacher's Edition provides passage reading techniques for ensuring that all students can access reading selections.

❸ Effective teachers have a repertoire of techniques for enhancing students understanding of different types of text.

Effective teachers have a repertoire of techniques for enhancing students' comprehenion of specific texts—including use of quick writes and other evidence checks; techniques for structured engagement, including cooperative learning; use of questioning strategies; and summarization (National Reading Panel, 2000; Duke & Pearson, 2002). *On Location* provides an array of interactive activities—including accountable talk—that promote comprehension and provides frequent checks for understanding throughout every lesson.

❹ Effective reading comprehension instruction activates prior knowledge and builds background.

Accomplished teachers recognize that background knowledge is a critical factor in reading for meaning, and they help activate prior knowledge before students read so that topics and concepts in reading selections are more accessible (Keene & Zimmermann, 1997). Teachers also help build background knowledge during the reading process. Every unit of *On Location* includes interactive activities that connect students to prior experiences, introduce the topic of the readings, and develop key concepts and vocabulary they will need as they tackle the readings.

❺ Effective reading comprehension instruction teaches students the processes and strategies used by expert readers.

Expert readers use an array of strategies to construct meaning before, during, and after reading. Research confirms that comprehension can be improved when students learn to use specific cognitive and metacognitive strategies and to reason strategically when they encounter difficult text (Baker & Brown, 1984; Rinehart et al., 1986; Pearson et al., 1990). English Learners, in particular, benefit from instruction that focuses on the use of cognitive and metacognitive strategies (Padron, 1992; Chamot & O'Malley, 1994).

On Location helps students use key reading strategies that researchers have identified as critical to comprehension and vary the use of strategies according to the purpose and characteristics of the genre (Cooper, 1993; Kintch, 1998; National Reading Panel, 2000). Students learn to *identify important information,* including critical facts and details; use *prediction* and *inferencing* skills; *monitor their own understanding* of text and adjust their use of strategies; practice *generating questions* as they read; and *summarize* what they have read to show understanding. And, on nearly every page, students use *graphic organizers* to organize their thinking.

❻ Vocabulary instruction increases text comprehension.

The larger the student's oral and reading vocabulary, the easier it is to make sense of text (National Reading Panel,

2000). Both direct and indirect vocabulary instruction predicts gains in reading comprehension. Researchers have also established that vocabulary and word analysis skills instruction increases the reading vocabulary of English Learners (Jimenez, 1997; Klinger & Vaughn, 2000).

On Location provides students with a variety of engaging activities for learning new vocabulary—before, during, and after reading. Students use context to define words, use new words in meaningful sentences, and engage in activities that extend content-area vocabulary.

❼ **Effective reading comprehension instruction engages students in reading across the curriculum.**

If students are to succeed, they must be able to read across a wide variety of academic genres—including narrative, descriptive, expository, persuasive, and simple literary texts. They do this through a well-planned curriculum that includes reading in the content areas (Chamot & O'Malley, 1994). *On Location* units are organized by genre, providing students with content-based reading selections across the academic curriculum.

❽ **Instruction in a variety of genres, text structures, and coherence relations improves comprehension.**

Research shows a strong relationship between text comprehension and how expository text is organized (Pearson & Fielding, 1991). Students' ability to understand the complex material in textbooks is increased when they are able to identify coherence relations in text—using words, phrases, sentences, and other markers to understand the organization and flow of ideas (Graesser et al., 2002). Every *On Location* lesson helps students explore and analyze the organizational features of the reading selections they have read, focusing on strategies the writer uses to create coherence—that is, reader-friendly text.

Developing Powerful Writers

❶ **Students learn to write by writing.**

As with reading, students learn to write through frequent in-class and out-of-class opportunities that involve writing for a variety of purposes and audiences (NCTE, 2004). *On Location* provides students with a variety of writing scenarios and tasks that enable them to explore a range of purposes, audiences, and social contexts for producing written discourse. The Practice Book provides students with extension activities that reinforce the use of new writing skills.

❷ **Reading and writing are inter-related meaning making processes.**

Students who are good readers are more likely to develop as effective writers. In order for students to write a particular type of text, it is helpful if they read the same type of text. Writing also helps students become better readers (NCTE, 2004). Further, when reading and writing occur together, evaluative thinking and taking other perspectives occurs (Tierney, 1990). In every unit, students read two or more exemplars of the type of writing they will produce. Activities cause students to engage in oral communication that uses the same academic language functions they will use in writing.

❸ **Writing in the content areas improves both academic literacy and content learning.**

When students write about topics in the content areas, they examine concepts and ideas in a subject area and develop and practice key literacy skills related to reading comprehension, vocabulary, and word attack skills. Writing across the curriculum helps students explore new concepts and take the time to process what they are learning. Writing also helps students thoughtfully explore issues, in the context of various content areas (Barr et al., 1991). Writing in the content areas also helps students move beyond the textbook, inquiring into topics as they write (Fredricks et al, 1997). *On Location* provides students with writing tasks that link to the social sciences, sciences, and, through response, to literature.

❹ **Instruction in the writing process develops effective writers.**

Researchers have explored how accomplished writers write, examining how students plan, draft, and revise their work (Emig, 1971; Graves, 1983; Calkins, 1986, 1991). Writers move back and forth among the stages of the writing process as they shape and polish their work. As students become more experienced, making the writing process their own, they become more skillful at producing academic writing. Whatever the content area or the type of writing, students can use the writing process to produce writing across the content areas. Every unit of *On Location* includes a culminating writer's workshop, which provides practice, within an interactive setting, in use of the writing process.

❺ Grammar and conventions are most effectively taught within the context of writing.

Because writing occurs in a social context, students need to learn to control the conventions established for public texts (NCTE, 2004). Experts argue for the teaching of grammar and mechanics in context (Weaver, 1996). *On Location* provides both lessons in grammar—focusing on grammar points that commonly occur in student writing—and mini-lessons that focus on written conventions.

Unit 1 Can We Talk?

Unit Overview

Section	At a Glance	Standards
Before You Begin	Students focus on interviewing.	■ Derive meaning from visual information ■ Ask and answer questions
A. Connecting to Your Life	Students write an interesting interview question.	■ Ask and answer questions
B. Getting Ready to Read	Students learn useful vocabulary and discuss the "claim to fame" of various famous people.	■ Use context to determine the meaning of unfamiliar words ■ Write sentences that describe people
C. Reading to Learn	Students read an interview with the well-known baseball player, Alex Rodriguez. PRACTICE BOOK: Students take notes on an interview with Alex Rodriguez.	■ Ask and answer questions ■ Find the main ideas and details in text ■ Draw inferences from text
D. Word Work	Students learn common words that sound the same but have different meanings. PRACTICE BOOK: Students choose the correct homophones to complete sentences.	■ Identify homophones ■ Recognize and use knowledge of spelling patterns when reading and writing
E. Grammar	Students practice forming *Wh–* questions. PRACTICE BOOK: Students use word cues to complete *Wh–* questions.	■ Produce well-formed questions
F. Bridge to Writing	Students read an interview with TV star Christina Vidal, and then identify the "stars" in their own classroom. PRACTICE BOOK: Students practice test-taking skills. PRACTICE BOOK: Students practice language functions.	■ Ask and answer questions ■ Use the social conventions of language (e.g., when interviewing someone)

Section	At a Glance	Standards
G. Writing Clinic	Students focus on the content of interesting interview questions and learn how an oral interview is organized when transcribed. PRACTICE BOOK: Students read an interview with basketball great Earl Boykins, then generate questions to ask him. PRACTICE BOOK: Students practice writing information questions.	■ Identify structural patterns found in written interviews ■ Group related ideas ■ Write well-formed declarative and interrogative sentences
H1. Writer's Workshop: Getting It Out	Students assume the role of school newspaper reporter and prepare to interview someone they know. PRACTICE BOOK: Students plan their interview questions.	■ Use the writing process: prewriting ■ Ask and answer questions ■ Listen for details and record information accurately ■ Use everyday social language
H2. Writer's Workshop: Getting It Down	Students turn their oral interview notes into written interviews.	■ Use the writing process: drafting
H3. Writer's Workshop: Getting It Right	Students check and revise their own interviews.	■ Use the writing process: revising and editing
H4. Writer's Workshop: Presenting It	Students act out their interviews with classmates.	■ Give a short oral presentation
I. Beyond the Unit	Students invite an adult from the community for a class interview. Students read a portrait poem. PRACTICE BOOK: Students write their own portrait poems.	■ Ask and answer questions ■ Listen and take notes ■ Write a brief personal letter ■ Identify the use of repetition in poetry

UNIT 1 • STUDENT BOOK, PAGE 2

BEFORE YOU BEGIN

Standards
- Derive meaning from visual information
- Ask and answer questions

- Have students read the title of the unit. Ask: *When would you say this to someone?*

- Have students look at the picture on page 3. Ask: *Who are the two people in the picture? What are they doing? What can you guess about them?*

- Have two different students read the words in the speech and thought bubbles. Ask: *What is a hobby?* Have students give examples of hobbies. Ask: *Why does Frankie think a question about hobbies is a good question?*

- **Interactive Writing** As students discuss question 3, list student-generated questions on the board. For example: *Do you go to school, Frankie? How old are you?*

Unit 1
Can We Talk?

Read...
- An interview with a famous baseball star.

- An interview with a young TV actress.

- A portrait poem by a student.

Objectives:

Reading:
- Reading magazine interviews with famous people
- Strategy: Skimming
- Literature: Responding to a poem

Writing:
- Writing down an interview
- Note-taking: Recording exact words

Vocabulary:
- Recognizing homophones: Words that sound the same but have different meanings

Listening/Speaking:
- Listening for facts
- Asking information questions

Grammar:
- Forming *Wh-* questions

Spelling and Phonics:
- Spelling the /ā/ sound as in *fame* and *play*

Frankie Morales, star of the TV show *The Adventures of Max Jones*

BEFORE YOU BEGIN

Talk with your classmates.

1. Who is in the picture?
2. What can you guess about these two people?
3. Imagine that you are there. What question would you like to ask?

Can We Talk? 3

UNIT 1 ▪ STUDENT BOOK, PAGE 4

A CONNECTING TO YOUR LIFE

Standard
- Ask and answer questions

WARM UP
- Have students look at the four photos of famous people on page 4. Have students read the captions aloud.
- Find out what students know about each person. Ask: *What do you know about Jennifer Lopez? What is special about Tiger Woods? How many Harry Potter books has J.K. Rowling written?*

TEACHING THE LESSON

🎧 1. Tuning In
- Point out the picture on page 3. Tell students they are going to listen to the young woman interview teen TV actor Frankie Morales. Then call attention to the four questions on page 4. Ask students to listen carefully and write their answers on the lines provided.
- Play the tape or CD, or read the script twice. Have students listen for answers to questions a and b the first time. Have them listen for answers to questions c and d the second time. Give students time to write their answers. Then ask students to share what they wrote with the class.

2. Talking It Over
- Have students look at the photos. Invite them to tell which person they would like to meet. Ask why they would like to meet this person.
- Ask students to write one question they would like to ask this person. Point out the sample question in the Student Book and have them write their questions on the line provided.
- 🍎 **Heads Together** Have students share the questions they wrote with a partner, then with classmates.

READING

A CONNECTING TO YOUR LIFE

🎧 **1. Tuning In** Listen to the interview with an actor. Write answers to the questions below.

  a. Why is Frankie famous? _____
  b. What is Frankie's favorite hobby? _____
  c. In real life, is Frankie a good student? _____
  d. What is Frankie's family like in real life? _____

2. Talking It Over Look at the pictures. Choose one person you would like to meet.

Write down a question you would ask him or her.
_____

Example question for Jennifer Lopez: *Where were you born?*

Jennifer Lopez, singer/actress

Tiger Woods, champion golfer

J. K. Rowling, writer (Harry Potter books)

Jaime Obregon, new kid in school

Read the title of this unit. What do you think you will learn to do in this unit? Check (✓) the correct answer.

_____ 1. how to write letters to friends
_____ 2. how to interview other people
_____ 3. how to describe other people

4 Unit 1

- Read the title of the unit aloud. Have students use finger signals to show their predictions. Have a volunteer identify and explain the correct response.

✓ WRAP UP
- Take the hot seat! Have students write, then ask you one good question. Answer students' questions.

> **TEACHING TIP** 💡 Bring in old magazines containing interviews with famous people. Add them to your classroom library.

ANSWER KEY

Tuning In: 1. a. He is a TV star. b. Golf. c. Yes, he is. d. His family isn't perfect.
Talking it Over: 2.

READING

UNIT 1 ■ STUDENT BOOK, PAGE 5

B GETTING READY TO READ

1. Learning New Words Read the sentences below. Try to guess the meanings of the underlined words.

1. Everybody knows Jennifer Lopez because she is an actress. Acting is her <u>claim to fame</u>.
2. My father told me I should work hard. That was good <u>advice</u>.
3. Tran got a job after school. He has an <u>opportunity</u> to make money.
4. Tina doesn't work for somebody else. She has her own <u>business</u>.
5. Dr. Vang is a medical doctor. Medicine is his <u>career</u>.
6. Rafael studies hard. He is <u>serious about</u> school.

Match each word or phrase on the left with the correct definition on the right.

1. claim to fame
2. advice
3. opportunity
4. business
5. career
6. be serious about

a. to care a lot about something
b. a chance to do something that will be good for you
c. the main reason a person is famous
d. a job you have trained for and will do a long time
e. an opinion about what to do or not do
f. buying and selling things

2. Talking It Over Work in a small group. Make a list of six famous people who have different careers. Write a sentence that describes each person's claim to fame. You can use the careers below or think of others.

EXAMPLE: <u>Jennifer Lopez is a movie actress</u>.

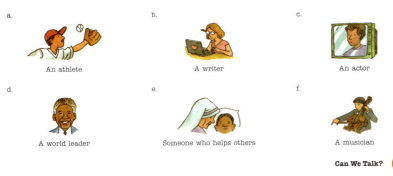

a. An athlete
b. A writer
c. An actor
d. A world leader
e. Someone who helps others
f. A musician

Can We Talk? 5

B GETTING READY TO READ

Standards
- Use context to determine the meaning of unfamiliar words
- Write sentences that describe people

WARM UP

🍎 **Heads Together** Ask students to work in pairs. Have them identify someone famous whom they admire, then share.

TEACHING THE LESSON

1. Learning New Words

- Write these words on the board: *claim to fame; advice; opportunity; business; career; be serious about*. Have students work in groups of three, trying to write a definition for each word or phrase.

- Have each small group read sentences 1–6, then revise their original definitions. Have them share out.

- Now have each group match each word to its definition, then share out. Confirm the correct answers.

- Have students revisit their original definitions, modifying them as needed.

- Have each group write a sentence for each word. Have students share out.

2. Talking It Over

- Point out the six pictures. Help students name athletes, writers, etc.

🍎 **Team Talk** Have students form groups of three to choose a person from each field and write one sentence about him or her.

🌈 **Access for All** Ask students to look at the six pictures and say what kind of skills each person must have. For example: *An athlete has to be strong and have good coordination.* As individuals name skills, ask others to show—thumbs up or thumbs down—if they have the skill.

✓ Wrap Up

🍎 **Outcome Sentence** Have students complete this sentence frame and share out:

_____ is famous for _____.

ANSWER KEY

Learning New Words: 1. c; 2. e; 3. b; 4. f; 5. d; 6. a.

Unit 1   5

UNIT 1 ■ STUDENT BOOK, PAGE 6

C READING TO LEARN

Standards
- Ask and answer questions
- Find the main ideas and details in text
- Draw inferences from text

WARM UP

- Play a matching game. One student names a sport, then calls on another student to give an example of someone who is famous for playing the sport.
- **Build Background** Tell students that they are going to read an interview with a baseball superstar, Alex Rodriguez. Note that he plays for the New York Yankees. Have students help you generate the names of other baseball players and teams.

TEACHING THE LESSON

1. Before You Read

- Ask students to look at the photo of Alex Rodriguez. Have them share what they know about him. For example: *His family comes from the Dominican Republic.*
- 🎧 **Shared Quick Write** Record students' statements about Alex Rodriguez. Ask students to use complete sentences.

🎧 2. Let's Read

- Explain that the *Q:* in an interview means *question* and the *A:* means *answer*.
- Explain that when you skim something, you look it over quickly to get the main ideas (Reading Strategy box). One way to skim an interview is to read the questions quickly.
- 🎧 **My Turn: Read Aloud/Think Aloud** Read the interview with Alex Rodriguez aloud or play the tape or CD. Model correct phrasing and fluent

---

READING

C READING TO LEARN — Interviews

READING STRATEGY
Skimming:
When you skim, you read the whole passage quickly for general meaning. You don't read every word.

1. Before You Read Look at the photo. What do you know about this baseball player?

🎧 **2. Let's Read** Skim the interview below and answer this question: Who is Alex Rodriguez? Then read the interview carefully.

WHO: Alex Rodriguez
CLAIM TO FAME: Star player for the New York Yankees. He is *featured* in *Backyard Baseball,* a video game.

Q: In *Backyard Baseball*, kids get to create their own teams. Who's on your "dream team"?
A: I like some *old-timers* like Dale Murphy and Hank Aaron. My favorite all-time player is Cal Ripken Jr.

Dale Murphy, Hank Aaron, and Cal Ripken Jr. are baseball stars from the past.

Q: What team did you *root for* when you were a kid?
A: I was born in New York, so I was a Mets *fan*.

Q: As a kid, were you the best player on the team?
A: No, because I always played with older kids.

Q: How should a kid *handle* a bad day on the field?
A: My number 1 advice is focus on academics. Keep working hard. Hard work will give you opportunities.

Q: Do you wish you had gone to college?
A: I made a promise to my mom to one day get a *degree*. I'd love to study business and *own* my *own* team.

featured—having a part in (a movie or story)
old-timer—someone from the past
root for—to want someone (like a sports team) to win
fan—a person who likes something or someone a lot
handle—to deal with

degree—proof you have finished a course of study at a school—usually a university
own^1—to have something because you bought it
own^2—belonging to a person

---

reading. As you read, stop to comment on words and ideas. For example: *A dream team is a team with the best players on it.*

- 🎧 **Our Turn: Interactive Reading** Take turns having students read the questions while you read the answers and vice-versa. Focus on the glossed words, ask questions, and make comments:

Why do you think Alex wanted to play with older kids?

What does the word "opportunities" mean? Look at the sentences before and after this sentence.

- ✓ 🎧 **Question All-Write** Have students write the answer to this question: *Why does Alex want to go to college?*
- **Build Fluency** Have different students read after you. Encourage them to copy your intonation.
- 🎧 **Your Turn: Independent Reading** Have students read the passage on their own, writing down one thing they admire about Alex. Have them share their ideas.
- 🌈 **Access for All** Have more proficient volunteers role-play the interview for classmates.

Teacher's Edition

READING

UNIT 1 ■ STUDENT BOOK, PAGE 7

3. Unlocking Meaning

❶ **Finding the Main Idea** Which sentence is true about Alex Rodriguez? Check (✓) the correct answer.

_____ 1. He is a professional baseball player.
_____ 2. He invents baseball video games.
_____ 3. He plays both baseball and basketball.

❷ **Finding Details** Choose the best ending for each sentence. Check (✓) the correct answer.

1. Alex's favorite baseball player of all time is—
   _____ a. Hank Aaron.
   _____ b. Cal Ripken Jr.
   _____ c. Dale Murphy.
2. When Alex was a boy, he rooted for—
   _____ a. the Texas Rangers.
   _____ b. the San Francisco Giants.
   _____ c. the New York Mets.
3. Alex advises young people—
   _____ a. to play football instead of baseball.
   _____ b. to play with older kids.
   _____ c. to work hard in school.
4. In the future, Alex says he would like to—
   _____ a. play for the Mets.
   _____ b. make more video games.
   _____ c. buy his own baseball team.

❸ **Think about It** Alex says he always played baseball with older kids. How do you think this helped him or hurt him? Talk with a partner.

❹ **Before You Move On** Write down one more question you would like to ask Alex.

Source: An interview with Alex Rodriguez, *TIME For Kids*, March 21, 2003. Used with permission from TIME For Kids Magazine.

Can We Talk? 7

THINK ABOUT IT

 Heads Together Ask students to work in pairs. Have them discuss the question then share their ideas.

BEFORE YOU MOVE ON

- Have students write a question they would like to ask Alex.

✓ WRAP UP

 Outcome Sentence Have students complete this sentence stem, then share with classmates:

Many people admire Alex Rodriguez because _____.

PB PRACTICE BOOK ACTIVITY

See Activity A, Revisit and Retell, on Practice Book page 1.

ANSWER KEY

Finding the Main Idea: 1.
Finding Details: 1. b; 2. c; 3. c; 4. c.

CULTURE NOTE

Point out that different cultures hold different sports in high regard. Ask students what sports people in their culture most admire, and what sports are admired in other cultures. You might wish to list the native countries of the students on the board and have them list the sports that are popular in those countries.

3. Unlocking Meaning

✓ FINDING THE MAIN IDEA

- Have students use finger signals to show you which sentence provides the best overall description of Alex.

✓ FINDING DETAILS

- Have students complete each item.
- Review the correct answers with the class. Have volunteers find the sentence in the interview that supports each answer.

Unit 1 7

UNIT 1 ■ STUDENT BOOK, PAGE 8

D WORD WORK

Standards
- Identify homophones
- Recognize and use knowledge of spelling patterns

WARM UP

- Write these sentences on the board: *She's a baseball fan. It's an electric fan.* Ask students to explain the difference between the two fans. Point out that sometimes two words with the same sound can have different meanings.

TEACHING THE LESSON

1. Word Detective

- Have students write the correct word as you read each sentence aloud. Invite volunteers to explain why they chose the word they did.

2. Word Study

- Read and discuss the definition of *homophones* (words with the same sound, but different meanings). Ask students to take turns explaining the difference between the pairs of words.

- Encourage students to start lists of homophones in their **notebooks**. Suggest that they include sample sentences to clarify the different meanings.

3. Word Play

- Point out the list of words and read them aloud. Then read the directions. Read one of the words, for example, *eye*, and write it on the board. Then ask a student to go to the board and write a word that sounds the same (*I*). Then ask different students to make up sentences using the words *I* and *eye*.

Spelling and Phonics

- Have students listen to the words. Explain that the words all contain the /ā/ sound, but that this sound is spelled

READING

D WORD WORK

1. Word Detective Many words sound the same but have different meanings. Complete each sentence. Read the sentences aloud.

1. The Yankees _____ the game.
   a. won
   b. one
2. I love my _____.
   a. ant
   b. aunt
3. Grandma can't _____ well.
   a. hear
   b. here
4. The dog has a long _____.
   a. tail
   b. tale
5. I want to _____ new clothes.
   a. by
   b. buy
6. I am _____ with my work.
   a. threw
   b. through

2. Word Study Learn more about words that sound the same but have different meanings.

Homophones are two words that have the same sound but different meanings. They can be spelled the same or differently.

EXAMPLES: Diego has a **son**.
            Diego likes the **sun**.

            Alex wants to **own** a baseball team.
            Alex uses his **own** glove.

3. Word Play Work with a partner. Think of the homophone for each word below and write it down. Then make up sentences for *both* words and write them also. You can use a dictionary.

1. four _____
2. eye _____
3. flour _____
4. be _____
5. two _____
6. no _____
7. lie _____
8. cent _____
9. our _____

SPELLING AND PHONICS:
To do this activity, go to page 192.

differently in each word. Have students think of other words with the /ā/ sound.

- Have students complete each word so that it is spelled correctly. Encourage students to use their dictionaries to check spellings.

✓ WRAP UP

- Write this sentence on the chalkboard: *Our bear cannot bear to be bare at any hour.* How many homophones can students find?

PB PRACTICE BOOK ACTIVITY

See Activity B, Word Work, on Practice Book page 2.

ANSWER KEY

Word Detective: 1. a; 2. b; 3. a; 4. a; 5. b; 6. b.

Word Play: Possible answers: 1. four/for; 2. eye/I; 3. flour/flower; 4. be/bee; 5. two/too; 6. no/know; 7. lie/lie; 8. cent/sent; 9. our/hour.

Spelling and Phonics: a. g<u>a</u>me; b. l<u>a</u>te; c. m<u>ai</u>l; d. w<u>ai</u>t; e. subw<u>ay</u>; f. st<u>ea</u>k; g. t<u>a</u>ke, br<u>ea</u>k h. t<u>a</u>stes; i. surv<u>ey</u>.

READING

UNIT 1 ▪ STUDENT BOOK, PAGE 9

E GRAMMAR — Information Questions

1. Listen Up Listen to each question. Point your thumb up 👍 if it sounds correct. Point your thumb down 👎 if it sounds wrong.

- 👍 👎 1. What is your favorite sport?
- 👍 👎 2. Who your teacher is?
- 👍 👎 3. When did you come to the U.S.?
- 👍 👎 4. Where you live?

2. Learn the Rule Information questions begin with question words like *what*, *when*, *who*, *where*, and *how*. Learn how to make information questions below, then do Activity 1 again.

INFORMATION QUESTIONS

	Question word or phrase	Main verb *be* or helping verb	Subject	Main verb + rest of sentence
1. When the main verb is *be*, it goes before the subject.	What Who	is are	your favorite food? his friends?	
2. With all other verbs, use *do*, *does*, or *did* in the question.	Where How When	does do did	he you Juan	live? like our school? come to the U.S.?
3. The object of the verb in *how many* and *how much* questions is part of the question phrase.	How many brothers	do	you	have?

3. Practice the Rule Work with a partner. Read the answers. Then write the questions. Use question words or phrases.

1. Q: *What is your favorite sport*? A: My favorite sport is soccer.
2. Q: _____? A: My best friend is Vladimir.
3. Q: _____? A: She lives in Los Angeles.
4. Q: _____? A: I came to the U.S. last year.
5. Q: _____? A: I have three sisters.
6. Q: _____? A: My favorite subject is math.

Can We Talk? 9

E GRAMMAR

Standard
- Produce well-formed questions

WARM UP

- Write these ill-formed questions on the board:

  What your favorite food is?
  Where he lives?
  How many brothers you have?

Explain that each is *incorrect*. Ask students to rewrite each correctly, then put their questions away for later. Do not correct the questions.

TEACHING THE LESSON

🎧 1. Listen Up

- Read the directions. Play the tape or CD, or read the questions twice and have students follow the directions.

2. Learn the Rule

- Have students study the chart. As you discuss each type of information question, ask students to provide examples.

- After you finish teaching the rules, repeat the Listen Up activity.

3. Practice the Rule

- Read the sample answer aloud, then call on a student to read the sample question. Practice Q&A exchanges with students.

- **Heads Together** Ask pairs of students to work together. Have them take turns generating questions and answers.

✓ WRAP UP

- Ask students to look at the questions they "corrected" in the Warm Up. Have them make further corrections and share out.

PB PRACTICE BOOK ACTIVITY

See Activity C, Grammar, on Practice Book page 3.

ANSWER KEY

Listen Up: Correct sentences: 1, 3.

Practice the Rule: 2. Who is your best friend? 3. Where does she live? 4. When did you come to the U.S.? 5. How many sisters do you have? 6. What is your favorite subject?

Unit 1 9

UNIT 1 ■ STUDENT BOOK, PAGE 10

F BRIDGE TO WRITING

Standards
- Ask and answer questions
- Use the social conventions of language (for interviews)

WARM UP

- Tell students that they are now going to read about another famous person—a young TV actress named Christina Vidal. (Her show was on for two seasons.)

TEACHING THE LESSON

1. Before You Read

Heads Together Ask students to name TV shows that they like. List all responses on the board. Invite students to describe each show briefly.

2. Let's Read

Remind students that when they skim a reading, they look it over quickly to get the main ideas (Reading Strategy box). Model how you might skim the interview by reading the questions first.

My Turn: Read Aloud/Think Aloud Read the passage aloud or play the tape or CD. Model correct phrasing and fluent reading. As you read, stop to comment on words and ideas. For example: *When people "share a dream," they have the same hopes for the future.*

Our Turn: Interactive Reading Take turns having individual students read the questions while you read the answers and vice-versa. As students read, focus on the glossed words, ask questions, and make comments:

What dream do both Christina and Taina share?

What is a high school of the performing arts?

WRITING

F BRIDGE TO WRITING
Interviews

READING STRATEGY
Skimming:
When you skim, you read the whole passage quickly for general meaning. You don't read every word.

1. Before You Read Can you think of any kids who have their own TV shows? Make a list.

2. Let's Read Read the following interview with actress Christina Vidal. Once again, *skim* the questions then read the entire interview.

The Nickelodeon TV network makes shows for kids.

WHO: Christina Vidal, 19
CLAIM TO FAME: She plays Taina Morales on the Nickelodeon TV show *Taina*.

Q: *Is Taina a lot like you?*
A: Yes, in so many ways. We share the same dreams of wanting to become a star. We're both Puerto Rican. She goes to a performing-arts high school. Growing up in New York, I traveled an hour every day to the LaGuardia High School of Performing Arts.

Q: *What's it like being one of the first Latinas to star in their own show on U.S. TV?*
A: It feels great to be a part of something that shows Latinos in a different kind of light. I'm really proud to be a Puerto Rican. I want to show people that there don't need to be any stereotypes.

Q: *You also sing on the show. How serious are you about music?*
A: I love music and acting. I want to pursue both careers. Eventually, I'd like to record an album.

Source: An interview with Christina Vidal, *TIME For Kids,* March 9, 2001. Used with permission from TIME For Kids Magazine.

dreams—hopes for the future
performing arts—music, dance, or drama
in a different kind of light—in a different way
stereotype—an idea about a person based only on their race, religion, ethnic group, etc.
acting—playing someone in a movie or show
pursue—to do or try something
eventually—one day

✓ **Question All-Write** Have students write answers to these questions:

Why is Christina proud?

What is an example of a stereotype?

What is another way to say "pursue a career"?

- **Build Fluency** Have pairs of students take turns reading the interview questions and answers.

- **Your Turn: Independent Reading** Ask students to read the gloss and explain in their own words what "stereotype" means. Elicit some common stereotypes. Then ask what it means "to be seen in a different kind of light" (not to be seen as a stereotype).

🌈 **Access for All: Reader's Theater** Have more-fluent students take turns reading the interview aloud or acting it out. Encourage students to read with expression.

10 Teacher's Edition

WRITING

3. Making Content Connections You have read interviews with two famous people. Who are the "stars" in your own class? Find out.

"Star" Search

Find someone who…	Name
1. writes poetry.	_____
2. is good at more than one sport.	_____
3. draws or paints.	_____
4. can play more than one instrument.	_____
5. has a good singing voice.	_____
6. comes from a really large family.	_____
7. likes to help other people.	_____
8. has a "superstar" personality.	_____

4. Expanding Your Vocabulary Imagine that you are interviewing someone. Read each situation and check (✓) the correct statement or question.

1. You begin the interview.
   _____ a. "Let me tell you what I think."
   _____ b. "Thank you for agreeing to talk with me."
   _____ c. "Please give me another example."

2. You want to let the person know you are interested.
   _____ a. "I don't have any more questions."
   _____ b. "How boring!"
   _____ c. "Tell me more!"

3. You want to let the person know you don't understand what they said.
   _____ a. "I disagree with you."
   _____ b. "I'm sorry. I didn't get that."
   _____ c. "I'm not sure that's right."

4. It's time to end the interview.
   _____ a. "Thank you for your time."
   _____ b. "Could you begin by telling me about yourself?"
   _____ c. "Can I ask you a few more questions?"

Can We Talk? 11

UNIT 1 ■ STUDENT BOOK, PAGE 11

interview. Ask students to look at the four situations and tell why each one is important. For example: *It's important to have a friendly beginning so that the person will feel comfortable with you.*

● **Heads Together** Ask students to work in pairs. The partners take turns thinking of other phrases they could use in each of the four situations. For example, for situation 1, they might say, *How are you today?* and for situation 2, they might say, *That's wonderful!*

● **Team Talk** Have students form groups of three or four students each. Give each student two slips of paper. Ask students to write out one question or one answer on each slip. Tell them to include a sentence or a question from each of the four situations.

■ Have groups exchange slips of paper and sort them into the correct order. Then have two people from each group take turns performing the interviews for the class.

PB PRACTICE BOOK ACTIVITY

See Activity D, Test-Taking Practice, on Practice Book pages 4 and 5.

See Activity E, Using New Vocabulary, on Practice Book page 6.

✓ WRAP UP

● **Outcome Sentence** Have students complete this sentence stem, then share:

Many people admire Christina Vidal because _____.

ANSWER KEY

Expanding Your Vocabulary: 1. b; 2. c; 3. b; 4. a.

---

3. Making Content Connections

■ Ask students what it means to be a "star." What does it mean to be a "star student"? Help students generate examples as you record them on the board. Next, compare the ideas your students have generated with the list of star qualities listed in the student book.

■ Conduct a "People Search"! Have students mingle, asking each other questions. Then have them write the name of a student next to each item on the list. Set a time limit of ten minutes.

■ Ask students to share their lists of "stars." Encourage students to give specifics. For example: *Carlos won a prize. He's the #1 surfer in the area.*

4. Expanding Your Vocabulary

■ Tell students that when they do an interview, there is a beginning, a middle (when you ask your questions), and an end. Explain that it is important to say the right things during different parts of the

Unit 1   11

UNIT 1 ■ STUDENT BOOK, PAGE 12

G WRITING CLINIC

Standards
- Identify structural patterns found in written interviews
- Group related ideas
- Write well-formed declarative and interrogative sentences

WARM UP

- Have students look once again at both selections in the Student Book. Point out that even though they are different interviews, they are the same in some ways. What do they notice? (Students might point out that both are organized the same way or that they both begin with the name of the person being interviewed, followed by the reason the person is famous, followed by the questions and answers.)

- Tell students they are going to learn how to organize an interview and how to make it interesting to read.

TEACHING THE LESSON

1. Think about It

🍎 **Let's Talk** Ask students to identify people who are usually interviewed by reporters (politicians, athletes, TV stars). Discuss why those people get interviewed while teenagers, parents, and teachers usually don't. (People like to read about people whose lives are out of the ordinary or who have accomplished something very special.)

2. Focus on Organization

- Explain that an interview begins with a *heading*, or information written at the top of the page. Have students look at the heading for Alex's interview. Have them look for the heading in Christina's interview and ask for a volunteer to read it aloud.

- Discuss the purpose of a heading.

WRITING

G WRITING CLINIC   Interviews

1. Think about It What kinds of people usually give interviews to reporters? Check (✓) the correct answers.

_____ politicians
_____ parents
_____ TV stars
_____ teenagers
_____ athletes
_____ teachers

2. Focus on Organization

❶ An interview usually has a **heading**. The heading tells the reader who the person being interviewed is and why that person is interesting. Read the heading below.

> **WHO:** Alex Rodriguez
> **CLAIM TO FAME:** Star player for the New York Yankees. He is featured in Backyard Baseball, *a video game.*

❷ The **body** of the interview has questions and answers. Match each of the following questions with the correct answer.

1. Where were you born?
2. When did you begin playing baseball?
3. Who is your favorite baseball player?
4. What's the best part about being a baseball player?
5. What's the hardest part about being a baseball player?
6. What other sports do you like?

a. My all-time favorite is Cal Ripken Jr.
b. Golf and tennis.
c. In New York City.
d. I love the fans.
e. I have to travel a lot. I hate to be away from home.
f. When I was a boy.

12 Unit 1

🍎 **Heads Together** Tell students that questions and answers come next. Have them match each answer to its question in Part 2, then share out.

- Explain that questions often ask about the person's life, their claim to fame, and their likes and dislikes. Help students generate questions for each area of focus. Prompt students: *How else could you ask about this?* Record student questions.

PB PRACTICE BOOK ACTIVITY

See Activity F, Focus on Organization, on Practice Book page 7.

WRITING

UNIT 1 ▪ STUDENT BOOK, PAGE 13

❸ Interview questions often ask about personal information, the reason the person is famous, and the person's likes and dislikes. Work with a partner. Imagine you could interview either Alex Rodriguez or Christina Vidal. What would you ask? Complete the following chart.

Personal Information	Their claim to fame	Their likes and dislikes
Where do you live?	When did you start acting?	Do you like movies?

3. Focus on Style

❶ Good interview questions make the person say more than just "yes" or "no." Which of the following questions is better? Why?

❷ Rewrite each of the following questions to make information questions. Begin your questions with words like these:

| What…? | What kind…? | Who…? | When…? |
| Where…? | How…? | How well…? | |

1. Do you like school?   _What do you like about school?_
2. Are you good at sports? _____
3. Do you have lots of friends? _____
4. Do you do your homework every night? _____
5. Do you like TV? _____
6. Do you like music? _____
7. Are your classes easy or hard? _____
8. Have you lived in the U.S. long? _____
9. Do you like living in the U.S.? _____

Can We Talk?   **13**

✓ WRAP UP

- Once again, take the hot seat. Have students count off 1–3. Have the 1s ask you a personal question; the 2s ask you about your claim to fame; and the 3s ask you about your likes and dislikes.

ANSWER KEY

Focus on Organization: Activity 2.: 1. c; 2. f; 3. a; 4. d; 5. e; 6. b.

Focus on Style: Activity 2: Possible answers: 1. What do you like about school? 2. What sports are you good at? What kinds of sports do you enjoy? 3. Who are your friends? 4. When do you do your homework? 5. What kinds of TV shows do you like? How much TV do you watch? 6. What kind of music do you like? 7. How difficult are your classes? 8. How long have you lived in the U.S.? When did you come to the U.S.? 9. What do you like about living in the U.S.?

🍎 **Heads Together** Ask students to work in pairs to complete Part 3. Have them write at least three questions in each column. When they finish, invite pairs of students to role-play their questions and answers for the class.

3. Focus on Style

- Remind students that interesting interviews ask questions that get the person talking. Ask: *Which is the better question? Why?* (Point out that the second question is better because it encourages the interviewee to give a specific list of answers instead of just saying *yes* or *no*. These answers add interesting information to the interview.)

- Ask students to rewrite each question in Part 2. Invite different students to read revised questions aloud.

📘 PRACTICE BOOK ACTIVITY

See Activity G, Focus on Style, on Practice Book page 8.

UNIT 1 ■ STUDENT BOOK, PAGE 14

H WRITER'S WORKSHOP

Standards
- Use the writing process: prewriting
- Ask and answer questions
- Listen for details and record information accurately
- Use everyday social language

1. Getting It Out
WARM UP

- Ask students to name some accomplishments that are their "claim to fame." For example: *I have a perfect 4.0 average in high school so far. I'm the top point scorer on the basketball team.*

- Tell students that they are going to choose a person to interview, organize their questions on a form, formulate questions that will get the person talking, and then conduct an actual interview.

TEACHING THE LESSON

- Tell students the first step (Part 1) involves choosing a person to interview. Remind students that the person must have some claim to fame. They must have accomplished something special.

- Point out the three pictures. Read and discuss with students the accomplishment listed under each one. Then ask students to decide who they are going to interview. Have them share with a partner.

- Review the three types of questions in the chart in Part 2. Invite different students to complete the question starters in the column called *Their claim to fame* using words that apply to the person they plan to interview. Have each student make a copy of the chart, leaving out the sample sentences.

▶ WRITING

For help with taking notes, complete Mini-Unit, Part A on page 182.

H WRITER'S WORKSHOP — Interviews

Imagine that you are a reporter for your school newspaper. You want to interview a person you know with a "claim to fame," perhaps a classmate or a family member.

1. Getting It Out

❶ Choose a person to interview. Ask yourself: What is this person's claim to fame?

on the honor roll   good at drawing   speaks four languages

(*I speak Hmong, Mien, French, and English.*)

❷ Think about good questions to ask. Make a chart. Use question words that will encourage the person to talk.

Personal information	Their claim to fame	Likes and dislikes
Where were you born?	**How** does it feel to...?	**Which** sport do you like best?
When did you come to the U.S.?	**What** is the best part about...?	**Who** is your favorite singer?

❸ Make a form like this one for taking interview notes. Write as many questions as necessary. Leave room after each question for the answers.

```
Name: _____
Reason I am interviewing this person: _____
Personal information: _____
_____
Question #1: _____?
Answer: _____
```

14 Unit 1

Then have them write questions they might ask based on the person they are interviewing and his or her claim to fame.

- Students can write their interview notes on the form in Activity H on Practice Book page 9.

PB PRACTICE BOOK ACTIVITY

See Activity H, Writer's Workshop, on Practice Book page 9.

WRITING

UNIT 1 ▪ STUDENT BOOK, PAGE 15

❹ Interview the person.

1. Find out about the person's background.

2. Ask questions about the person's claim to fame.

3. Ask other questions to learn more about the person.

4. Write down the person's exact words.

5. Thank the person for talking with you.

Can We Talk? 15

- Walk students through the interview process as it is presented in the Student Book.

🌈 **Access for All** Consider having students who are less proficient conduct their interviews with you or an instructional assistant. Provide guided practice, helping them formulate questions and record the answers. Suggest that more advanced students interview someone they have never met before who does not speak their language.

✓ WRAP UP

- You may wish to poll the class to find out who each student is planning to interview and what the person's claim to fame is. Invite the rest of the students to suggest things to ask about or even specific questions to ask

Unit 1   15

UNIT 1 ■ STUDENT BOOK, PAGE 16

H WRITER'S WORKSHOP

Standards
- Use the writing process: drafting, revising, and editing
- Give a short oral presentation

2. Getting It Down
WARM UP

- Invite volunteers to describe the interviews they conducted. Ask: *Who did you interview? What was the most interesting thing you learned about the person?*

- Explain that students will be learning to put the information they have collected into a professional-looking format so that their interviews will look like the two actual magazine interviews in this unit.

TEACHING THE LESSON

- Have students take out the interview notes they made. Walk them through the three steps in drafting the interview (Part 1).

- Have students complete the first two steps together in class.

- Ask students to complete the third step, checking the information they have written with the person they interviewed.

- Help students read Juan's interview with William (Part 2). Guide students through the speech bubble comments, asking, for example, whether students agree that Juan's questions are good ones.

- Set a deadline for the fact-checking of the interviews to be completed. Suggest that students rewrite the interview, rather than crossing things out, if any of the information needs to be changed.

WRITING

2. Getting It Down

❶ Draft your interview.

1. Write the person's name at the top of a piece of paper. Write his or her claim to fame under the name.

   WHO: William Vang
   CLAIM TO FAME: Speaks four languages

2. Carefully copy each question and answer from your note-taking sheet. Put **Q:** in front of each question and **A:** in front of each answer. Use complete sentences.

   Q: When did you come to the U.S.? How old were you?
   A: I came here when I was 40.

3. Show the person the interview. Correct any mistakes.

❷ Read part of Juan's interview with William.

MINI-LESSON
Using Punctuation: Remember to put a period (.) or exclamation point (!) at the end of statements and a question mark (?) at the end of questions.

WHO: William Vang
CLAIM TO FAME: Speaks four languages
Q: When did you come to the U.S.? How old were you?
A: I came here when I was 14.
Q: How many languages do you speak?
A: Four! I speak Hmong, Mien, French, and English.
Q: Which language you speak best?
A: I speak Hmong best! That's my native language.
Q: How did you learn to speak four languages so well?
A: I had good teachers—my family!

I came here when I was 14… not 40!

Juan puts a heading at the beginning of the interview.

Juan asks good questions.

Juan writes William's exact words.

Oops! The helping verb "do" is missing in one of the questions!

16 Unit 1

🍎 **Mini-Lesson on Conventions** Point out the use of sentence-level punctuation. Then write several examples of statements, questions, and exclamations on the board without end punctuation. For example: *Who is that, Stop talking right now,* and *I speak three languages.* Elicit from the class the type of punctuation needed for each sentence. Correct mistakes and confirm correct answers. Ask students to locate the periods, exclamation points, and question marks in Juan's interview and say how each one is used.

✓ WRAP UP

- Tell students that they will have a chance to revise their work during the next session. Have them locate the ChecBric for this unit in the Student Book or Practice Book. Have them prepare for Getting It Right by reviewing the ChecBric on their own, underlining indicators they're not sure about.

WRITING

UNIT 1 ▪ STUDENT BOOK, PAGE 17

3. Getting It Right Take a careful look at your interview. Use this guide to revise what you have written.

Ask yourself . . .	How to check . . .	How to revise. . .
1. Does my interview have a heading?	Underline the person's name and claim to fame.	Add the reason that you interviewed the person (claim to fame).
2. Did I ask good questions?	Did the person answer more than "yes" and "no"?	Ask the person follow-up questions that begin with words like *what, why, who, when,* and *how.*
3. Did I write each question correctly?	Ask a neighbor to check your questions.	Correct the word order in the question. Add a helping verb if you need to.
4. Did I record the person's exact words?	Ask the person you interviewed to read his or her answers.	Make any changes.

4. Presenting It Share your interview with others.

❶ Act out your interview with the person you talked to. If you interviewed someone from outside of class, ask a classmate to help you act out the interview.

❷ Ask for feedback on the interview.

Can We Talk? 17

---

3. Getting It Right
WARM UP

- Guide students through the ChecBric for this unit in the Student Book (p. 197) or Practice Book (p. 101). Explain that they will use the ChecBric to prepare a final draft of their writing.
- Have volunteers explain, in their own words, what each indicator in the ChecBric means.

TEACHING THE LESSON

- Have students use the information in the chart and the ChecBric to revise their work.

✓ WRAP UP

- Help students pair up with classmates to practice for their presentations.

📁 Give students time to fill out the ChecBric on Practice Book page 101. Ask them to attach it to their writing when they put it in their portfolios.

4. Presenting It
WARM UP

- It's time for students to present their interviews! Remind them that their interviews should interest the audience.
- As a class, develop a simple presentation checklist. Record ideas on the board. In addition to content and organization, focus on speaking skills, enthusiasm, involvement of audience, and length of presentation.

TEACHING THE LESSON

- Tell students to pay attention to four things as they present their interviews:
  1. Use a loud and clear voice.
  2. Read naturally and with expression.
  3. Use eye contact with partners.
  4. Act "professionally"—avoid laughter and immature behavior.
- Have pairs of students present their interviews, paying attention to the presentation checklist.
- After each presentation, have students tell the presenter what they liked about the interview.

✓ WRAP UP

🔴 **Let's Talk** Ask students what they think are the most important things to remember when interviewing someone. Write their ideas on the board. Then invite students to share the easiest and the hardest parts of the interviewing process for them.

Unit 1   17

UNIT 1 ■ STUDENT BOOK, PAGE 18

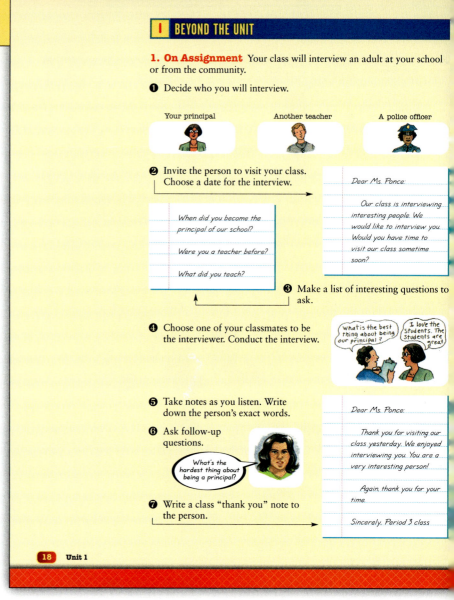

BEYOND THE UNIT

Standards
- Ask and answer questions
- Listen and take notes
- Write a brief personal letter
- Identify the use of repetition in poetry

1. On Assignment
WARM UP

■ **Heads Together** Ask students to name adults at school or in the community that they would like to know more about. List names on the board, including reasons that the student thinks the person would be interesting to interview. For example: *Mr. Hudson, the school bus driver. He plays the guitar in a rock band.*

TEACHING THE LESSON

- Have students review the names on the list. Have them discuss the pros and cons of interviewing each (*Our principal is very busy, but she would be interesting to interview*).

- Help them vote on who they want to invite to class (Part 1).

■ **Interactive Writing** Have the class cooperate in writing the invitation (Part 2). Repeat suggested sentences aloud and have the class decide whether to use them or not. Write the accepted sentences on the board. Choose a student to write the final copy.

■ **Let's Talk** Have students work in small groups to generate questions for the interview (Part 3). Each group might have a separate focus. One could ask personal information, another could ask about the person's claim to fame, and the third could make up questions about likes and dislikes. Remind students to keep in mind the person's "claim to fame." As a class, decide which questions are most interesting and write these on the board. Then decide together how to order the questions.

- Have several students (or all students) be prepared to ask one question each.

- During the actual interview, ask all students to take notes (Parts 4 and 5). Remind them to write down the exact words each person says. If possible, duplicate copies of the questions before the interview so that students can concentrate on writing just the answers.

- Encourage students to ask follow-up questions, perhaps things that didn't occur to them when they were planning the formal list of questions (Part 6).

- Have students collaborate on what to say in the thank you note (Part 7). Elicit ideas from the class and record the sentences on the board. Then help students decide how the sentences might be ordered. Have a student copy the note from the board and have each student sign it. Address it and send it to your interviewee.

18 Teacher's Edition

2. Link to Literature

🎧 **SHARED READING** A portrait poem reveals things about a person—just like an interview. Read this portrait poem written by a student. To make her poem fun to read, she tells some things about herself that are true and some things that are false!

LET'S TALK Answer the questions.

1. Which statements about Paula are probably true? Why?
2. Which statements are probably false? Why?
3. What can you say about Paula from her portrait?

JUST FOR FUN Write your own portrait poem. It should be ten lines long.

- Begin and end with "I am …"
- Write four truthful statements about yourself
- Write four "lies" about yourself. Make each one believable.

I am Paula Jones.

I am sixteen years old.
I ride wild stallions.
I collect foreign coins.
My sister has six fingers on her left hand.
My mother and I always get along.
Time has stood still for me.
My father is a spy in the CIA.

I am Paula Jones.

stallion—a male horse
CIA—Central Intelligence Agency

Can We Talk? 19

UNIT 1 ▪ STUDENT BOOK, PAGE 19

- **Build Fluency** Have volunteers read lines from the poem aloud. Encourage students to read with expression.
- 🍎 **Let's Talk** Ask students what they usually say when someone asks them to describe themselves. Why do they give this answer?
- Have students complete the Just For Fun activity.

✓ WRAP UP

- Have students read their poems aloud while their audience guesses which statements are false.

📕 PRACTICE BOOK ACTIVITY

See Activity I, Responding to Literature, on Practice Book page 10.

✓ UNIT WRAP UP

🍎 **Outcome Sentence** Have students complete this sentence stem, then share:

I enjoyed interviewing someone because _____.

🎧 2. Link to Literature

WARM UP

Have students read the poem silently. Ask what they notice about it. Tell the class that this kind of poem is called a portrait poem. Explain that a portrait is a photograph, painting, or drawing of a person. Ask the class why this poem is called a portrait poem.

TEACHING THE LESSON

🍎 **Shared Reading** Read the poem aloud as students follow along. Model oral expression and use pauses that help clearly communicate the meaning of the phrases.

- Now play the tape or CD, or read the poem again. As students listen, ask them to think about which statements are probably true and which are false and how they can tell.
- Ask the class what they can tell about Paula from reading her poem.

Unit 1   19

Unit 2 Animals Nobody Loves

Unit Overview

Section	At a Glance	Standards
Before You Begin	Students focus on the great white shark—an animal nobody loves!	■ Find information in captions ■ Dictate sentences
A. Connecting to Your Life	Students explore the reasons that people dislike or fear various animals.	■ Listen to a description ■ Write a simple sentence with a noun, a verb, and an adjective
B. Getting Ready to Read	Students learn new words for describing animals, and then rank the animals according to degree of danger.	■ Use new vocabulary in simple sentences
C. Reading to Learn	Students read a passage about the yucky cockroach! PRACTICE BOOK: Students summarize the Student Book passage.	■ Read simple paragraphs independently ■ Use reading strategies to understand text ■ Write a summary
D. Word Work	Students make adjectives from related nouns and verbs. PRACTICE BOOK: Students practice changing nouns and verbs into adjectives.	■ Use parts of words, including suffixes, to read fluently ■ Use knowledge of sound/spelling patterns to spell words
E. Grammar	Students learn the rules for subject-verb agreement. PRACTICE BOOK: Students practice subject/verb agreement.	■ Use knowledge of grammar to correct errors in speaking and writing
F. Bridge to Writing	Students read a passage about the animal people fear most—the shark! PRACTICE BOOK: Students practice taking Reading Vocabulary and Reading Comprehension tests. PRACTICE BOOK: Students practice new vocabulary.	■ Read simple paragraphs independently ■ Use reading strategies to understand text ■ Read different kinds of information and tell how they are different ■ Use a dictionary to find the meanings of new words

Section	At a Glance	Standards
G. Writing Clinic	Students learn to write a well-formed paragraph with a topic sentence and details. PRACTICE BOOK: Students practice writing a paragraph. PRACTICE BOOK: Students practice using adjectives.	■ Make an outline ■ Write a paragraph ■ Use adjectives in simple sentences
H1. Writer's Workshop: Getting It Out	Students begin writing a page for a class book on animals nobody loves. They select an animal to write about, read about the animal, and take notes. PRACTICE BOOK: Students practice categorizing information.	■ Use simple sentences ■ Read and gather facts ■ Make notes
H2. Writer's Workshop: Getting It Down	Students turn their notes into an outline, and then draft their paragraphs.	■ Make an outline ■ Use simple sentences to write a paragraph that has a topic sentence and details
H3. Writer's Workshop: Getting It Right	Students respond to each other's work as well as their own, then revise and edit.	■ Revise written work for organization and clarity ■ Edit writing for conventions
H4. Writer's Workshop: Presenting It	Students present their pages to classmates.	■ Give a short oral presentation ■ Speak so that others can understand ■ Answer questions
I. Beyond the Unit	Students make a class book of animals nobody loves. They also read a humorous poem, "Acro-Bat." PRACTICE BOOK: Students write a short response to the poem "Acro-Bat."	■ Describe the parts of books ■ Repeat and follow directions ■ Respond to a poem

UNIT 2 ▪ STUDENT BOOK, PAGE 20

BEFORE YOU BEGIN

Standards
- Find information in captions
- Dictate sentences

- Have students look at the photo on page 21. Ask: *What kind of animal do you see in the picture?*

- Have students read the title of the unit. Ask: *Is a shark an animal that people love or an animal people hate? How do you feel when you look at the photo?* Help students think of words, listing what they dictate on the board. Possibilities include *scared, afraid,* and *terrified.*

- Ask students what type of shark it is. Have a volunteer read the caption under the photo.

- **Shared Writing** Ask students what they know about sharks. Guide them in using complete sentences. Begin by modeling a sentence, writing on the board: *Sharks are very large.* Then have students add their own sentences about sharks until you have created a list. Encourage students to use what they see in the photograph. Have students read each sentence aloud.

Unit 2
Animals Nobody Loves

Read...
- A short selection about a disgusting creature: the cockroach.

- A short selection about a scary animal of the sea: the shark.

 **Link to Literature**
- "Acro-Bat," a poem by Kenn Nesbitt.

20 Unit 2

Objectives:

Reading:
- Reading an informational selection about nature
- Strategies: Taking notes, listing what you know
- Literature: Responding to a poem

Writing:
- Organizing an informational paragraph
- Writing a topic sentence and details
- Using adjectives to make writing vivid
- Making a class book

Vocabulary:
- Turning nouns and verbs into adjectives
- Learning names of types of animals

Listening/Speaking:
- Listening to descriptions
- Ranking
- Comparing animals

Grammar:
- Understanding subject-verb agreement

Spelling and Phonics:
- Spelling the /ch/ sound as in *check* and *kitchen*

A great white shark

BEFORE YOU BEGIN

Talk with your classmates.

1. Look at the picture. What do you see? How does the picture make you feel?
2. Read the caption. What type of shark is it?
3. What do you know about sharks? Help your teacher make a list.

UNIT 2 ■ STUDENT BOOK, PAGE 22

A CONNECTING TO YOUR LIFE

Standards
- Listen to a description
- Write a simple sentence with a noun, verb, and adjective

WARM UP

- Have students look at the photos. Read the name of each animal aloud. Ask for volunteers to read the names.

TEACHING THE LESSON

🎧 1. Tuning In

- Tell students that they are going to listen to a description of *one* of the animals. Play the tape or CD, or read the script twice. Give students time to write the name of the animal. Then have them hold up their papers and compare answers.

2. Talking It Over

- 🍎 **Heads Together** Explain that one photo *does not belong* with the others. Have students talk with a partner and decide which animal does not belong. Tell students to be ready to share their answer and tell *why*.

- List and tally responses on the chalkboard. Lead students to this explanation—*The dog doesn't belong because all five other animals have one thing in common: People do not like them!*

- Ask: *Why don't people like rattlesnakes?* Write the answer on the chalkboard: *People don't like rattlesnakes because their bites can kill you.*

- 🍎 **Heads Together** Have students think of one reason that most people don't like each of the other scary animals. Then have them write a sentence about each animal.

READING

A CONNECTING TO YOUR LIFE

🎧 **1. Tuning In** Listen to the description on the tape or CD. Look at the pictures below. Which one of these animals is the speaker talking about?

2. Talking It Over Work with a partner. Look at these animals. One of them does **not** belong with the others. Which animal is it? How do you know?

The five other animals share one thing: People do not *like* them! Talk about one reason that people don't like each animal. Share your reasons with your classmates.

EXAMPLE: *People don't like rattlesnakes because they can bite you.*

A spider

A dog

A rattlesnake

A cockroach

A crocodile

A rat

Read the title of this unit. What do you think this unit is probably about? Check (✓) the correct answer.

_____ 1. cute animals

_____ 2. pets

_____ 3. scary animals

- 🍎 **Shared Writing** Have students dictate the sentences they have written about each animal as you record them on the board.

- Have students look again at the title of the unit and then predict what the unit is about.

✓ WRAP UP

- Tell students that they are going to read and write about animals that people often do not like.

- Ask students to bring in a photograph of an animal that nobody loves. Show copies of magazines like *National Geographic*, explaining that students can find magazines like this in the library.

ANSWER KEY

Tuning In: A rattlesnake.

Talking It Over: The dog does not belong because it is not a dangerous or disgusting animal.

Talking It Over: 3.

READING

UNIT 2 ■ STUDENT BOOK, PAGE 23

B GETTING READY TO READ

1. Learning New Words Read the sentences below. Try to guess the meanings of the underlined words.

1. Rats eat garbage. Ugh! They are <u>disgusting</u>!
2. Crocodiles can crush other animals to death with their <u>powerful</u> jaws.
3. Rattlesnakes are <u>dangerous</u>. You can die from a rattlesnake bite!
4. A shark usually eats other fish, but if it is really hungry, it may <u>attack</u> and kill people.
5. Cockroaches can live in very hot places and very cold places. They can <u>survive</u> almost anywhere.
6. Dogs are very loving <u>creatures</u>. They usually don't bite.
7. The baseball game was <u>amazing</u>! It lasted for 18 innings.

Dogs are loving creatures.

Now, match each word on the left with the correct definition on the right.

1. disgusting
2. powerful
3. dangerous
4. attack
5. survive
6. creature
7. amazing

a. an animal
b. to try to hurt
c. able to hurt or kill
d. to stay alive
e. very unpleasant and sickening
f. very surprising and difficult to believe
g. very strong

2. Talking It Over Work in groups of three or four. Look at the animals on page 22. Rank them on the scale below. Use the new words you just learned to discuss your choices.

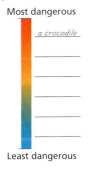

Most dangerous — a crocodile
Least dangerous

Animals Nobody Loves **23**

B GETTING READY TO READ

Standard
■ Use new vocabulary in simple sentences

WARM UP
■ Ask students to share photos of animals they have brought to class.

TEACHING THE LESSON

1. Learning New Words
■ Write the new words on the board. Have students work in groups of three, defining the words they know (or think they know). Have them share their definitions with classmates.

■ Now have students open their books to page 23. Ask for volunteers to read each pair of sentences aloud, stating what they think the underlined word means.

■ Ask students to match each word to its definition. Provide the correct answers.

■ Have students revisit the original definitions they wrote, making corrections as needed.

🌈 **Access for All** Students with strong bodily-kinesthetic intelligence may remember new words best by acting them out. Invite volunteers to pantomime words while others guess the words.

2. Talking It Over
■ Put the names of three animals on the board: *a dog*, *a cat*, and *a crocodile*.

■ Draw and label a scale like the one at the bottom of page 23. As a class, order the three animals from most dangerous to least dangerous. Explain that this activity is called "ranking"—that is, putting things in order. Examples of ranking scales include large to small and safe to dangerous.

🍎 **Team Talk** Divide students into groups of three or four. Have them draw and label a scale on a piece of chart paper. Then help students read the directions for the activity. Have groups share their charts, explaining why they ranked the animals as they did.

✓ WRAP UP
■ Ask students to talk with a partner at lunch or after school, thinking of one or two animals that are disgusting but not really dangerous. Tell them that they should be ready to share with classmates.

ANSWER KEY

Learning New Words: 1. e; 2. g; 3. c; 4. b; 5. d; 6. a; 7. f.

Unit 2   23

UNIT 2 ■ STUDENT BOOK, PAGE 24

C READING TO LEARN

Standards
- Read simple paragraphs independently
- Use reading strategies to understand text
- Write a summary

WARM UP
- Remind students that they were to have thought of one or two animals that are disgusting but not dangerous. Have pairs of volunteers share their answers, telling why the animal is disgusting.

TEACHING THE LESSON

1. Before You Read
- Focus students on the photograph. Explain that a cockroach is a very good example of an animal that is *disgusting* but not *dangerous*.

2. Let's Read
- Explain that a report tells the reader about a subject. Have students read the title and the source line and then tell you what the report is about and where it comes from.
- Discuss the boxed Reading Strategy with the class. Elicit students' ideas about what note-taking involves. Explain that students should write only words and short phrases, not complete sentences. Assure them that they should not worry about correct spelling.
- **My Turn: Read Aloud/Think Aloud** Read the passage aloud or play the tape or CD. Model the fun of reading the passage. Model correct phrasing and fluent reading. As you read, stop to comment on words. Talk with students about the ideas in the passage.

READING

C READING TO LEARN
Short Informational Reports

READING STRATEGY
Note-taking:
As you read, write down new information and interesting facts or ideas to help you remember them.

1. Before You Read Most people really dislike cockroaches. What do you know about cockroaches? Why do people think cockroaches are so *disgusting*? Talk with a partner.

2. Let's Read Read this short report of information. The selection gives interesting and important information about cockroaches. As you read, **take notes** about things that make cockroaches so amazing.

Cockroaches

Cockroaches are really yucky. They look disgusting, they crawl all over the food left out in kitchens and people have a very hard time getting rid of them. But, like them or not, cockroaches are truly amazing creatures.

Few animals are better **equipped for** life on earth than they are. They can live almost anywhere, eat almost anything, and survive for weeks on almost nothing. They can **withstand** heat waves and cold spells.

When cockroaches **scatter**, they **scurry** away on long, strong legs at nearly one **foot** per second. At the same time they flatten themselves as thin as a dime and squeeze safely through cracks and **crevices**. Cockroaches are so successful at staying alive that they have survived for more than 350 million years—since before the age of **dinosaurs**.

Source: *The Unhuggables* by Victor Waldrup, Debbie Anker, and Elizabeth Blizzard

One foot equals 30.5 centimeters.

equipped for—made for
withstand—to experience something bad without damage
scatter—to run in different directions
scurry—to move fast
crevice—a narrow opening
dinosaur—a reptile that lived millions of years ago

24   Unit 2

- Now play the tape or CD, or read the passage again. Ask students to listen for reasons that cockroaches are hard to get rid of. Then invite volunteers to share all the reasons they can remember.
- **Our Turn: Interactive Reading** Now have students help you read the passage. Read the first sentence of each paragraph yourself. Then call on individuals to read other sentences. As students read, focus on glossed words, ask questions, and make comments.
- **Your Turn: Independent Reading** Have students read the passage on their own, listing things that make cockroaches amazing.
- ✓ **Question All-Write** Have students write a sentence that answers this question: *How are cockroaches amazing?*

CULTURE NOTE
Point out that not all cultures like or dislike the same animals. For example, in parts of 17th-century India, the rat was worshipped. Encourage students to give examples from their own cultures.

24   Teacher's Edition

READING

UNIT 2 ■ STUDENT BOOK, PAGE 25

3. Unlocking Meaning

❶ **Finding the Main Idea** Which of the following sentences talks about the most important idea from the article? Check (✓) the correct answer.

_____ 1. Cockroaches are stronger than humans.
_____ 2. Cockroaches are amazing.
_____ 3. Cockroaches are very hard to get rid of.

❷ **Finding Details** Read the second and third paragraphs of the article again. Then read the sentences below. Write T for *True* and F for *False*.

_T_ 1. Cockroaches eat almost anything.
_____ 2. Cockroaches need to eat every day or they will die.
_____ 3. Cockroaches can live almost anywhere.
_____ 4. Cockroaches can't live in cold weather.
_____ 5. Cockroaches are easy to kill because they move slowly.
_____ 6. Cockroaches can move around in very tiny places.
_____ 7. Cockroaches were on Earth before dinosaurs.

❸ **Think about It** Cockroaches were on the Earth over 100 million years before dinosaurs! Dinosaurs disappeared 65 million years ago but cockroaches are still here today. Why do you think that cockroaches survived so long? Talk with a partner. Write three reasons.

350 million years ago   4,500 years ago

❹ **Before You Move On** The title of the article you just read is "Cockroaches." Read the article one more time. Can you think of a *more interesting* title for the article? Write the title, then share it with your classmates.

New Title: _____

Animals Nobody Loves **25**

THINK ABOUT IT

- Focus students on the timeline. Have them explain what the timeline says in their own words.

- Ask students to look at the passage again and find reasons why cockroaches have survived for so long. Write the reasons on the board.

- 🍎 **Heads Together** Have students work in pairs, writing three sentences about cockroaches. Encourage them to use their own words.

BEFORE YOU MOVE ON

- Have students look at the title of the reading. Point out that the title doesn't make you want to read the article. Ask: *What would be a better, more interesting title?* Have students write their own titles to share at the beginning of the next lesson.

✓ WRAP UP

- 🍎 **Outcome Sentence** Have students complete this sentence stem, then share:

Something I learned about cockroaches is _____.

PB PRACTICE BOOK ACTIVITY:

See Activity A, Revisit and Retell, on Practice Book page 11.

ANSWER KEY

Finding the Main Idea: 2.

Finding Details: 1. T; 2. F; 3. T; 4. F; 5. F; 6. T; 7. T.

Think About It: Answers will vary.

---

3. Unlocking Meaning

✓ FINDING THE MAIN IDEA

- Read each sentence aloud as students follow along. Have students hold up one finger if the main idea is the first sentence, two fingers if it is the second sentence, and three fingers if it is the third sentence.

- ✓ 🍎 **Outcome Sentence** Have students complete this sentence stem, then share:

Cockroaches are amazing because _____.

✓ FINDING DETAILS

- Ask students to read each sentence and then answer T for True or F for False. Ask for volunteers to answer each item. Have each volunteer find the sentence in the passage that supports the answer.

Unit 2   25

UNIT 2 ▪ STUDENT BOOK, PAGE 26

D WORD WORK

Standard
- Use parts of words, including suffixes, to read fluently

WARM UP

- Have students share the titles they created for the cockroaches reading. Record the titles on the board. Identify titles that have adjectives in them, or add your own title to the list.

- Underline the adjective in the title. Point out that adjectives sometimes have parts of smaller words inside them. Circle the smaller words (amaz[e], surpris[e]).

TEACHING THE LESSON

1. Word Detective

- Have students complete the activity. Check students' answers.

2. Word Study

- Help students learn the rule. List the words *taste* and *amaze* on the board. Ask: *What happens to these words when the suffix –y or –ing is added?* (They become adjectives.)

- Focus students on the rule in the starburst. Provide additional verbs that end in *e*, encouraging volunteers to add a suffix, then dictate the spelling of each word as you record.

3. Word Play

- **Heads Together** Have students complete the activity. Ask volunteers to share their answers.

Spelling and Phonics

- Tell students that three words in the passage have the same sound, but the sound is spelled differently each time: *cockroa__ch__*, *__k__itchen*, and *__c__reature*. Have students complete each incomplete word. Encourage them to use their dictionaries.

READING

D WORD WORK

1. Word Detective Sometimes you can guess what a word means by looking for a smaller word or part of a word inside the longer one. The underlined words below are adjectives. Find the smaller words or parts inside the adjectives and write them down.

An adjective describes a person, place, or thing.

1. <u>dirty</u> animal
   smaller word: _dirt_
2. <u>amazing</u> creature
   smaller word: _____
3. <u>scary</u> spider
   smaller word: _____
4. <u>disgusting</u> place
   smaller word: _____

2. Word Study You can make many nouns and verbs into adjectives by adding a short ending called a suffix. Look at the words below. Circle the suffix in each adjective. *Note:* sometimes the spelling changes a little when a noun or verb is changed into an adjective.

Drop the final -e when you add the ending -y or -ing.

-y		-ing	
sugar	→ sugary	surprise	→ surprising
freak	→ freaky	annoy	→ annoying

3. Word Play Work with a partner. Write an adjective for each word below by adding –y or –ing. Then choose five of the adjectives and write one sentence for each. *Note:* Some words can take either –y or –ing, but they will have different meanings. Use a dictionary.

Usually, you add -y to nouns and -ing to verbs to make adjectives.

1. ice _icy_
2. wind _____
3. interest _____
4. scare _____
5. creep _____
6. dirt _____
7. bore _____
8. excite _____
9. salt _____
10. sleep _____
11. confuse _____
12. blood _____

Sentences:
1. _____
2. _____
3. _____
4. _____
5. _____

SPELLING AND PHONICS: To do this activity, go to page 192.

✓ WRAP UP

- **Interactive Writing** Ask the class to think of a "yucky" animal—something other than a cockroach—and then write an adjective that describes the animal. Use their adjectives to create a class "list poem" entitled, "The Yuckiest Animal on Earth."

PB PRACTICE BOOK ACTIVITY

See Activity B, Word Work, on Practice Book page 12.

ANSWER KEY

Word Detective: 1. dirt; 2. amaze; 3. scare; 4. disgust.

Word Play: 1. icy; 2. windy; 3. interesting; 4. scary; 5. creepy; 6. dirty; 7. boring; 8. exciting; 9. salty; 10. sleepy; 11. confusing; 12. bloody.

Spelling and Phonics: a. watch; b. picture; c. chimpanzee; d. beach; e. stretch; f. adventure.

UNIT 2 ■ STUDENT BOOK, PAGE 27

E GRAMMAR — Subject-Verb Agreement

1. Listen Up Listen to each sentence. Point your thumb up 👍 if it sounds correct. Point your thumb down 👎 if it sounds wrong.

- 👍 👎 1. Cockroaches is really yucky.
- 👍 👎 2. Cockroaches are amazing creatures.
- 👍 👎 3. Cockroaches lives almost everywhere.
- 👍 👎 4. A cockroach run very fast.

2. Learn the Rule Learn how to make present tense verbs agree with their subjects. After you have learned the rules, do Activity 1 again.

SUBJECT-VERB AGREEMENT WITH PRESENT TENSE VERBS

1. When the subject is a singular noun or the singular pronoun *he*, *she*, or *it*, the verb ends in –s or –es.

   A cockroach **eats** almost anything.

2. When the subject is a plural noun or the pronoun *I*, *you*, *we*, or *they*, the verb doesn't end in –s or –es.

   Cockroaches **like** to live in the dark.

3. With the verb *be*, use *is* when the subject is a singular noun or the singular pronoun *he*, *she*, or *it*. Use *are* when the subject is a plural noun or the pronoun *you*, *we*, or *they*. Use *am* when the subject is *I*.

   A cockroach **is** a yucky insect.   Cockroaches **are** yucky insects.   I **am** afraid of cockroaches.

3. Practice the Rule Read each sentence aloud. Circle the correct form of each verb.

1. Many people think spiders (is/**are**) scary creatures.
2. Many people (is/are) afraid of spiders.
3. Spiders (trap/traps) other insects in webs.
4. The black widow spider (is/are) very dangerous.
5. Rats (live/lives) everywhere.
6. Rats (spread/spreads) dirt and disease.

Animals Nobody Loves   27

E GRAMMAR

Standard
- Use knowledge of grammar to correct errors in speaking and writing

WARM UP

- Write the sentences below on the chalkboard. Tell students that all the sentences are wrong. Have students correct each sentence and save their corrections for later.

  Juan hate snakes.

  Juan and Tran both hates snakes.

  Juan and Tran is afraid of snakes.

- Explain that each sentence breaks an important rule in English—making sure that verbs agree with their subjects.

TEACHING THE LESSON

🎧 1. Listen Up

- Ask students to listen carefully. Play the tape or CD, or read the sentences in the book twice. Have students point their thumbs up if the sentence sounds correct, and down if it sounds wrong.

2. Learn the Rule

- Present and teach each rule for subject/verb agreement. As you work through each rule, have students provide additional sentences with singular subjects and plural subjects using the verb *be* and other verbs.

- After you have taught the rules, repeat the Listen Up activity. Have students look at the three sentences you wrote on the board at the beginning of the lesson. Did they write the correct forms?

3. Practice the Rule

- Have students circle the correct form of each verb.

- Call on students to read each sentence aloud, choosing the correct form of the verb in parentheses. Call on another student to agree or disagree and give reasons for agreeing or disagreeing.

✓ WRAP UP

- Have students write the rule for subject/verb agreement in their **notebooks**, using their own words. Ask them to include examples.

PB PRACTICE BOOK ACTIVITY

See Activity C, Grammar, on Practice Book page 13.

ANSWER KEY

Listen Up: Correct sentence: 2.

Practice the Rule: 1. are; 2. are; 3. trap; 4. is; 5. live; 6. spread.

Unit 2   27

UNIT 2 ▪ STUDENT BOOK, PAGE 28

F BRIDGE TO WRITING

Standards
- Read simple paragraphs independently
- Use reading strategies to understand text
- Read different kinds of information and tell how they are different
- Use a dictionary to find the meanings of new words

WARM UP
- Tell students that they are now going to read about an animal that is very *dangerous*—an animal that is feared by people around the world.
- Have students give examples of animals that people fear. Record their examples on the board.

TEACHING THE LESSON

1. Before You Read
- Focus students on the photograph. Ask: *Do you remember what type of shark this is?* (great white shark) *Where do sharks live?* (in the ocean)
- Ask students to list everything they already know about sharks before they read (Reading Strategy box).
- **Shared Quick Write** Ask: *Why are so many people afraid of sharks?* Record students' answers. Help them form complete sentences.

2. Let's Read
- **My Turn: Read Aloud/Think Aloud** Begin by reading the passage aloud. Model correct phrasing and expression and fluent reading. As you read, stop to comment on words. For example: *The word hammerhead is made up of two words, hammer and head. Why?*

WRITING

F BRIDGE TO WRITING — Short Informational Reports

READING STRATEGY
Listing What You Know: Make a list about what you already know about the topic before you read. Then you can focus on new information as you read.

1. Before You Read Work with a partner. Many people are afraid of sharks. What do you already know about sharks? List three things.

2. Let's Read Read about sharks. As you read, add one fact that you didn't know to your list.

SHARK

Can you guess what a hammerhead shark looks like? What about a tiger shark?

The shark is the most **feared** animal in the sea. Some sharks are large and dangerous. Others are just a few feet long and eat small fish. Sharks come in many different sizes, shapes, and colors. Hammerheads, tiger sharks, and mako sharks have powerful jaws and razor-sharp teeth. Some sharks can bite three hundred times harder than a human.

The most dangerous shark is the great white shark. It usually swims in the open sea. But sometimes a great white shark may attack and kill swimmers with no **warning**. It may even attack small boats. Its large, saw-edged teeth can rip through wood and even **metal**. The great white shark has a huge **appetite** and will eat any animal or person that it finds in its **path**.

A great white shark

Source: *Animals Nobody Loves* by Seymour Simon

feared—frightening to people
warning—a sign of danger
metal—a material like steel, tin, or iron
appetite—hunger
path—way

28 Unit 2

- Talk with students about the ideas in the passage.
- Now play the tape or CD, or read the script. As students listen, ask them what they think the scariest thing about a shark is. Invite volunteers to share their opinions with the class.
- **Our Turn: Interactive Reading** Have students help you read the passage. Read the first sentence of each paragraph yourself, asking students what each paragraph is going to be about. Call on individuals to read the other sentences. As students read, focus on glossed words, ask questions, and make comments.
- ✓ **Question All-Write** Say: *In paragraph 2, we learn that the great white shark has saw-edged teeth. What do "saw-edged" teeth look like? Draw a picture, then hold it up.*
- **Your Turn: Independent Reading** Have students read the passage on their own, listing facts that they didn't know.
- **Access for All** Work with small groups for whom the passage is too difficult. Paraphrase difficult vocabulary and ideas. Ask questions about each sentence.

28 Teacher's Edition

WRITING

UNIT 2 • STUDENT BOOK, PAGE 29

3. Making Content Connections You have read about two animals that nobody loves: cockroaches and sharks. Now, work with a partner. Complete the chart below.

	Cockroach	Shark
1. What does it look like?	six long legs, can be flat as a dime	
2. Where does it live?		
3. What does it do?		

4. Expanding Your Vocabulary In the chart below, find the word in each row that *does not* go with the word in capital letters. Cross it out.

An insect   A fish   A reptile   A mammal   A bird

1. INSECT	mosquito	cockroach	~~crocodile~~
2. FISH	shark	eagle	piranha
3. REPTILE	crocodile	tiger	rattlesnake
4. MAMMAL	human	mosquito	lion
5. BIRD	eagle	Superman	parrot

A mosquito   A piranha   A tiger

An eagle   A lion   A parrot

Animals Nobody Loves   **29**

3. Making Content Connections

- **Heads Together** Have students work in pairs. Ask them to complete the chart. Encourage students to look back at the two passages.
- Draw the chart on the board. As pairs of students share, record their ideas on the chart.
- As a class, discuss what you should do if you meet a shark face to face. Record students' ideas. (Best answer: If you meet a shark face to face, you should make a fist and try to punch it in the head. Often, the shark will swim away.)

4. Expanding Your Vocabulary

- Have students look at the photos, reading the name of each animal. Tell students that they are going to figure out which animals go together and which do not.

- **Think Aloud** Read the first series of words aloud. Say: *Insects have wings and their bodies have three parts.* Lead students through the thinking that will help them decide which animal doesn't belong: *A mosquito has wings and it bites you. It's probably an insect. A crocodile lives in the water, has huge teeth, and skin like a lizard. It's not an insect.* Have students complete the exercise. Encourage them to use their dictionaries to check their answers before sharing with classmates.

JUST FOR FUN

Practice animal vocabulary. Play Lingo Bingo. Divide students in groups of four. Have each group fold a piece of paper in four parts one way, then four parts the other way, making 16 squares. As you write the name of an animal on the board, have each group copy the name in any square. Provide 16 animal names. In random order, describe each animal without naming it. As each group guesses the animal, they put an X in the square. The first group with a complete row of four Xs whispers out "Lingo Bingo!"

PB PRACTICE BOOK ACTIVITY

See Activity D, Test-Taking Practice, on Practice Book pages 14 and 15.

See Activity E, Using New Vocabulary, on Practice Book page 16.

✓ WRAP UP

- **Outcome Sentence** Have students complete this sentence stem, then share out:

One thing I learned about sharks is _____.

ANSWER KEY

Expanding Your Vocabulary: 1. crocodile; 2. eagle; 3. tiger; 4. mosquito; 5. Superman.

Unit 2

UNIT 2 ■ STUDENT BOOK, PAGE 30

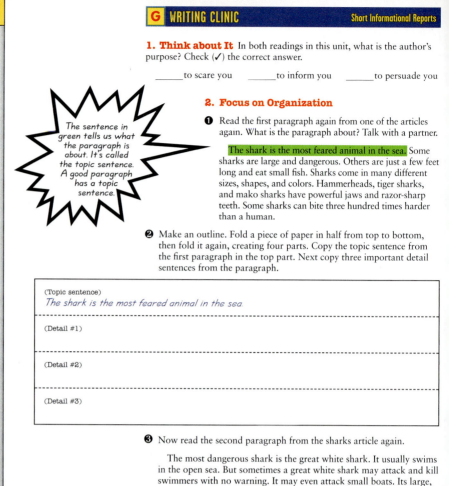

G WRITING CLINIC

Standards
- Make an outline
- Write a paragraph
- Use adjectives in simple sentences

WARM UP

- Have students look at both selections in the Student Book. Point out that both are organized, or grouped, in paragraphs. Explain that a paragraph is a group of written sentences that are about the same idea.

- Tell students that they are going to learn how to write good paragraphs—and make them interesting to read.

TEACHING THE LESSON

1. Think about It

- Remind students that when writers write something, they have both a reader and a purpose in mind. Have students tell you the purpose of both readings.

2. Focus on Organization

- Ask students to imagine that a paragraph is like a group of people. One of the sentences is a "leader" and the rest are "followers." The leader is called the *topic sentence*.

- Have students read the first paragraph again (Part 1). Ask: *What is the paragraph about?* Have students tell you why the sentence in green is the topic sentence.

- Have students make an outline, using a piece of paper folded in four parts, as shown in the Student Book (Part 2).

- Ask the class to read the second paragraph to themselves (Part 3). Answer any questions they may have.

- Have students read the second paragraph again and then outline it as shown in the Student Book. Ask for several volunteers to read their paragraphs aloud.

PB PRACTICE BOOK ACTIVITY

See Activity F, Focus on Organization, on Practice Book page 17.

WRITING

UNIT 2 ▪ STUDENT BOOK, PAGE 31

❹ Turn your paper over and use the other side to outline the second paragraph. This time, don't copy. Use your own words.

(Topic sentence)

(Detail #1)

(Detail #2)

(Detail #3)

3. Focus on Style

❶ This is a sentence that a student wrote about great white sharks. The sentence is interesting to read because it has two adjectives. Circle the adjectives.

They are large, dangerous animals.

❷ Work with a partner. Think of at least five animals that people do not like. Write the name of each animal in the correct place in the chart below.

	huge	large	small	tiny
dangerous	great white shark			
powerful				
disgusting				
scary				
annoying				mosquito

❸ Write a sentence about each animal. Use two adjectives in each sentence. Share your sentences with your classmates.

Animals Nobody Loves **31**

adjectives from the chart (Part 3). Have students share their sentences with classmates.

PB PRACTICE BOOK ACTIVITY

See Activity G, Focus on Style, on Practice Book page 18.

✓ WRAP UP

- Have students add an entry in their **notebooks** about sharks using sentences with vivid adjectives.

ANSWER KEY

Think about It: to inform you.

Focus on Style: Answers will vary.

3. Focus on Style

- Have students look again at the passage on sharks. Help them find examples of adjectives. Explain that adjectives help paint a picture. Write these two sentences on the board:

  Sharks have jaws and teeth.

  Sharks have powerful jaws and razor-sharp teeth.

  Ask: *Which sentence is more interesting? Why?*

  Have students read the sample sentence and circle the adjectives (Part 1).

- Draw a chart, as shown in Part 2. Help students think of another animal that people fear or do not like. Where does the animal belong in the chart?

- 🍎 **Heads Together** Have students list five animals that they fear or dislike and then complete their own charts (Part 2). Explain that they are to write a sentence for each animal using both

Unit 2   31

UNIT 2 • STUDENT BOOK, PAGE 32

H WRITER'S WORKSHOP

Standards
- Use simple sentences
- Read and gather facts
- Make notes

1. Getting It Out
WARM UP

- Show students a copy of Seymour Simon's book, *Animals Nobody Loves*, or a similar title that has pictures of animals and short text.

- Tell students that they are each going to make a page for a class book. Explain that the first step will be to decide what to write about and then to get their ideas down on paper.

TEACHING THE LESSON

- Have students choose an animal to write about. Remind students that the animal must be unlovable—either kind of yucky or dangerous.

- Have students look at each photo (Part 1). Focusing on each photo, ask students: *Who can give me one fact about…?* Encourage students to use complete sentences based on the information in each "fact file."

- Help students generate additional ideas for animals to write about. Record their responses on the board. Give students a few moments to select their animal. Consider tallying which animals students have chosen so that you have variety.

- **Shared Writing** Help students make notes, using a piece of paper folded in four sections, as shown in the student book (Part 2). Using the fact file for the rat and the model on page 33, help students generate rough notes on the board.

WRITING

H Writer's Workshop — Short Informational Reports

Write a book with your class called, "Creatures that Kids Love to Hate." Make a page for the book. Follow the directions below.

1. Getting It Out

❶ Begin by choosing an animal to write about. Look at the pictures below for ideas or choose another unlovable creature.

1. Spider

Important facts:
Usually harmless
Has eight legs
Spins a web to trap insects
Kills by biting and injecting poison
Usually bites people only when bothered

2. Rat

Important facts:
Small, furry mammal
Has very sharp teeth
Lives nearly everywhere in the world
Lives in garbage dumps
Lives in people's houses
Eats food that is left out
Carries fleas and can spread disease

3. Piranha

Important facts:
The most dangerous fish in the world
Has killed more humans than sharks
Is less than one foot long
Lives in rivers and streams in South America
Has razor-sharp teeth
Can eat the meat off a large animal or human in just a few minutes.

4. Skunk

Important facts:
Small mammal
Is usually peaceful
Eats insects and berries
Usually goes out only at night
Has white stripes along its back
Raises its tail to scare its enemies
Will spray bad-smelling liquid if bothered

32 Unit 2

🌈 **Access for All** Consider having students who are less proficient work on the same animal. Provide them with extra guidance. Have students who might be more advanced work on an animal that is not pictured in the Student Book. Guide them as they do their own research.

📓 **Using Technology** Help more advanced students connect to the Web sites listed in the Student Book.

✓ WRAP UP

- Have students share their notes with a partner.

> **TEACHING TIP** 💡 Depending on how large your class is, consider dividing students into teams of six to eight, each responsible for writing their own book.

32 Teacher's Edition

WRITING

UNIT 2 ▪ STUDENT BOOK, PAGE 33

❷ Print the name of your animal in capital letters at the top of a piece of paper. Fold the paper in one direction, then in the other, to make four sections. Number each section.

Write each of the following questions in one section. Then write words and ideas in each section that answer these questions:

1. What is it?
2. Where does it live?
3. What is it like?
4. Why do so many people dislike or fear it?

RAT	

1. What is it?
    a rodent
	2. Where does it live?
	    under houses
	    in attics
	    in garbage dumps
	    everywhere!

3. What is it like?
    small, furry animal
    has a long tail
    makes squeaky sounds
    runs or scurries very fast
    has sharp teeth ... can chew
        through wood and metal
    eats our food
    eats garbage
	4. Why do so many people dislike or fear it?
	    carries fleas that spread disease
	    sometimes bites people
	    gives me bad dreams!!!

 CONNECT TO THE WEB. CHECK IT OUT:

www.nationalgeographic.com/kids This site will help you learn more about creatures in nature. You will connect to National Geographic for Kids Magazine, which includes many articles about animals.

www.nwf.org/kids Web site for the National Wildlife Federation for Kids.

Animals Nobody Loves

📘 PRACTICE BOOK ACTIVITY

See Activity H, Writer's Workshop, on Practice Book page 19.

UNIT 2 ▪ STUDENT BOOK, PAGE 34

H WRITER'S WORKSHOP

Standards
- Make an outline
- Use simple sentences to write a paragraph that has a topic sentence and details
- Revise written work for organization and clarity
- Edit writing for conventions
- Give a short oral presentation
- Speak so that others can understand
- Answer questions

2. Getting It Down
WARM UP

- Remind students that they have made notes about an animal, grouped around four questions: *What is it? Where does it live? What is it like? Why do so many people dislike/fear it?*

- Have students look again at the sample notes on page 33. If they were writing a paragraph about rats, which facts would they want to include in their paragraphs? Encourage them to share and explain their ideas.

- Tell students that the next step is to turn their notes into an outline and then into a paragraph.

TEACHING THE LESSON

- Draw a blank outlining tool on the board.

- 🍎 **Shared Writing** Help students generate a topic sentence for a paragraph about rats, based on the notes they have discussed. As a class, generate a "follower" sentence about rats—a sentence containing a detail.

- Have students work with a partner to generate two more follower sentences about rats that support the topic sentence. As a class, complete the outline. Then give students time to develop their own outlines, based on their notes (Part 1).

- Focus students on Juan's paragraph (Part 2). Say: *What would Juan's outline look like? What would his topic sentence be? Which sentences contain only details?*

- Focus students on the information in the speech bubbles next to the paragraph. Ask: *What is wrong about the paragraph? Does anything need to be fixed?* Then have students turn their outlines into paragraphs.

- 🍎 **Mini-Lesson on Conventions** Point out the Mini-Lesson box and the use of commas in Juan's paragraph.

WRAP UP

- Tell students that they will have a chance to revise their work during the next session. Have them locate the ChecBric for this unit in the Student Book or Practice Book. Have them prepare for Getting It Right by reviewing the ChecBric on their own, underlining indicators they're not sure about.

34 Teacher's Edition

WRITING

UNIT 2 • STUDENT BOOK, PAGE 35

3 Getting It Right Now take a careful look at what you have written. Use this guide to revise your paragraph.

Ask yourself...	How to check...	How to revise...
1. Does my paragraph have a good topic sentence?	Underline your topic sentence.	Add a sentence that tells what your paragraph is about.
2. Do the details relate to the topic sentence?	Put a check mark (✓) in front of each sentence that gives an example or detail.	Add sentences that give examples or details.
3. Do I use adjectives to make my paragraph interesting?	Circle each adjective.	Add adjectives.
4. Does each verb agree with its subject?	Look at the chart on page 27. Does each verb follow the rules?	Correct each verb.

4. Presenting It Draw a picture of your animal—or clip a photograph from a magazine—to go with your paragraph. Share your work with your classmates.

❶ Begin by showing the picture of your animal and naming it.
❷ Read your paragraph aloud. Read slowly and speak clearly.
❸ Ask if anyone has any questions.
❹ Ask for feedback from your classmates.

Animals Nobody Loves **35**

---

3. Getting It Right
WARM UP

- Guide students through the ChecBric for this unit in the Student Book or Practice Book. Explain that they will use the ChecBric to prepare a final draft of their writing.
- Have volunteers explain, in their own words, what each indicator in the ChecBric means.

TEACHING THE LESSON

- Ask students to reread their paragraphs, imagining that they are the readers. Have them use the chart and the ChecBric to produce a second draft of their paragraphs.

WRAP UP

- Tell students that they are now ready to present their paragraphs to the class. Have them locate a photograph of their animal, or draw a picture to make their presentation more interesting.

- Give students time to fill out the ChecBric on Practice Book page 103. Ask them to attach it to their writing when they put it in their portfolios.

4. Presenting It
WARM UP

- As a class, develop a simple presentation checklist. In addition to content and organization, focus on speaking skills (poise, expression, volume, posture, eye contact), enthusiasm, use of visuals, creativity, involvement of the audience, and length of presentation.

TEACHING THE LESSON

- Tell students to pay attention to three things as they present their paragraphs:
  1. Use a loud and clear voice.
  2. Read naturally and with expression.
  3. Pause very briefly after each sentence.

- Have a volunteer read the instructions, then explain the task to classmates. Then have students present their paragraphs and photos/pictures. Model positive feedback for each presentation. Have the student who is presenting invite feedback from classmates.

✓ WRAP UP

- Ask students which animal is the most interesting and why. Write students' ideas on the board.

> **TEACHING TIP** 💡 If you have a multilevel class, you may wish to group students by level of proficiency. This will minimize anxiety and will allow you to work closely with less-proficient students.

Unit 2 **35**

UNIT 2 ■ STUDENT BOOK, PAGE 36

❙ BEYOND THE UNIT

Standards
- Describe the parts of books
- Repeat and follow directions
- Respond to a poem

1. On Assignment
WARM UP

- Show students an actual book, such as *Animals Nobody Loves.* Have a volunteer tell classmates the kind of information that is found on the cover and inside the book. Explain that they are now going to make their books, using the paragraphs they have written.

TEACHING THE LESSON

- Help students make a book of their paragraphs. Depending on the size of your class, consider dividing students into teams, each responsible for making a book. For each book, you will need:

  Four or more white pieces of 11″ × 17″ paper

  A long, sturdy needle

  Heavy thread

  Two pieces of colored poster board

  Cloth tape (the same color as the poster board or a contrasting color)

  Glue or rubber cement

  Markers

- Assign students to work on small production teams:

  Book binders

  Paragraph and picture pasters

  Cover makers

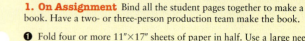

❙ BEYOND THE UNIT

1. On Assignment Bind all the student pages together to make a book. Have a two- or three-person production team make the book.

❶ Fold four or more 11″×17″ sheets of paper in half. Use a large needle to poke five holes through all the folded sheets so that they line up.

❷ Cut a 30-inch-long (one-meter) piece of thread. Thread your needle. Push the needle down through hole 1. Pull the thread through, but leave a four-inch (12-centimeter) tail so you can tie a knot later. Then go up through hole 2, down through hole 3, up through hole 4, down through hole 5, and back in the other direction. Tie and knot thread.

❸ Make the book cover. Cut two pieces of colored poster board a bit larger than the pages on all sides. Cut a strip of wide sticky tape about 16″ long. Place boards about $\frac{1}{4}$″ apart onto the sticky tape, then fold back each end of the tape to make the spine of the book sturdy.

❹ Set pages into the spine. Glue the first page onto one cover, then the last page onto the other cover.

❺ Carefully paste each picture and paragraph onto its own page. Number each page.

❻ Make a front cover for the book, showing the title, authors, and illustrators.

- Model the steps described in the book. Caution students to be careful when handling the needle.

✓ WRAP UP

- Have a "book show." Have a "publisher's rep" present each book to classmates.

TEACHING TIP 💡 Contact an elementary classroom teacher in your district. Offer to have more advanced and/or more mature students read their books to the younger elementary students.

UNIT 2 ▪ STUDENT BOOK, PAGE 37

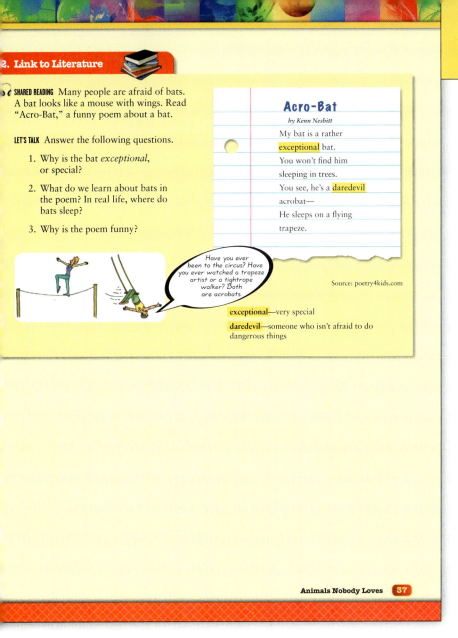

- **Build Fluency** Have students read each line aloud after you have read the line.
- **Let's Talk** Discuss questions 1, 2, and 3.

✓ WRAP UP

- Have volunteers read the poem aloud. Encourage students to read with expression.

PB PRACTICE BOOK ACTIVITY

See Activity I, Responding to Literature, on Practice Book page 20.

✓ UNIT WRAP UP

- Have students reflect upon what they learned in this unit in their **notebooks.** Consider collecting and responding to notebook entries.

2. Links to Literature

WARM UP

- Have students look at the illustration. Ask: *What do you think the poem is about?*

TEACHING THE LESSON

- **Shared Reading** Read the poem "Acro-Bat" aloud as students follow along. Model oral expression and fluency. Help students understand glossed words.
- Now play the tape or CD, or read the poem again. Ask students to listen for how many strong beats there are in each line/sentence. (Lines/sentences 1 and 3 have 4 strong beats, and lines/sentences 2 and 4 have 3. Invite students to read the lines after you, emphasizing the beats.

Unit 2   37

Unit 3 I Made It Myself!
Unit Overview

Section	At a Glance	Standards
Before You Begin	Students focus on Halloween—a fun American holiday.	▪ Derive meaning from visual information
A. Connecting to Your Life	Students talk about the kinds of parties they like and why they like them.	▪ Interact with classmates, contributing to a topic
B. Getting Ready to Read	Students learn new words and phrases to describe making or doing something simple.	▪ State simple instructions
C. Reading to Learn	Students read instructions for making fake blood and hairy moles. PRACTICE BOOK: Students write instructions in a comic strip format.	▪ Read and follow directions ▪ Sequence information
D. Word Work	Students form compound nouns. PRACTICE BOOK: Students practice using compound words.	▪ Use knowledge of compound words to determine word meaning ▪ Use knowledge of sound/spelling patterns to spell words
E. Grammar	Students form imperative sentences. PRACTICE BOOK: Students practice writing imperative sentences.	▪ Express everyday functions: giving directions, giving orders, warning, and requesting
F. Bridge to Writing	Students read instructions for making a Halloween costume. PRACTICE BOOK: Students practice taking Reading Vocabulary and Reading Comprehension tests. PRACTICE BOOK: Students practice new vocabulary.	▪ Read and follow multi-step written instructions

Section	At a Glance	Standards
G. Writing Clinic	Students examine the organization and content of "how-to" instructions. PRACTICE BOOK: Students organize recipes. PRACTICE BOOK: Students identify the functions of specific words in a set of instructions.	■ Identify the structural patterns found in procedural text ■ Use specific vocabulary
H1. Writer's Workshop: Getting It Out	Students plan instructions for something they know how to do.	■ Use the writing process: prewriting ■ Sequence information
H2. Writer's Workshop: Getting It Down	Students turn their notes into how-to instructions. PRACTICE BOOK: Students plan their how-to instructions.	■ Use the writing process: drafting ■ Use specific vocabulary
H3. Writer's Workshop: Getting It Right	Students revise and edit their own work.	■ Use the writing process: revising and editing
H4. Writer's Workshop: Presenting It	Students present their work to classmates.	■ Give a short oral presentation ■ Listen to oral presentations and take notes
I. Beyond the Unit	Students plan their own Halloween party. Students read a humorous poem by Shel Silverstein, "Best Mask?" PRACTICE BOOK: Students respond to the poem "Best Mask?"	■ Understand oral instructions ■ Read and follow written instructions (recipes) ■ Respond to a poem

UNIT 3 ■ STUDENT BOOK, PAGE 38

Unit 3

I Made It Myself!

BEFORE YOU BEGIN

Standard
- Derive meaning from visual information

- Have students look at the picture on page 39. Ask: *Why do you think he has his head in his hands?*

- Have students read the caption under the picture. Ask: *What does it mean?* Invite students who are familiar with Halloween to explain.

- Ask: *Why is Juan dressed like this? What do you know about Halloween?* Record student suggestions on the chalkboard. Focus students on the trick or treat tradition, strange costumes, pumpkins, and Halloween parties. Ask students to describe some of the costumes they have seen. Add these words (*witch, monster, ghost,* etc.) to the list.

- Ask: *Is Juan too old to wear a costume on Halloween? Do you, or other kids, dress up for Halloween? Do adults ever do this?*

Read...
- Instructions for making fake blood and hairy moles for Halloween.
- Instructions for making a scary Halloween costume.

 Link to Literature
- "Best Mask?" a poem by Shel Silverstein.

Objectives:

Reading:
- Following written instructions for making something
- Strategies: Drawing a picture, predicting
- Using illustrations to help you follow instructions
- Literature: Responding to a poem

Writing:
- How-to instructions
- Organizing steps in a time sequence
- Using exact words

Vocabulary:
- Recognizing compounds
- Learning party vocabulary

Listening/Speaking:
- Listening to instructions
- Giving oral instructions
- Giving feedback

Grammar:
- Understanding functions of imperatives

Spelling and Phonics:
- Spelling the /ō/ sound as in *hole* and *boat*

Trick or treat!

BEFORE YOU BEGIN

Talk with your classmates.

1. Look at the picture. Who do you see? Why is he holding his head?
2. Read the caption. What does it mean?
3. What do you know about Halloween? Help your teacher make a list.

I Made It Myself!

UNIT 3 ■ STUDENT BOOK, PAGE 40

A CONNECTING TO YOUR LIFE

Standard
- Interact with classmates, contributing to a topic

WARM UP

- Have students look at the picture. Ask several students to take turns sharing things you might see on Halloween.

- **Build Background** Explain that Halloween is celebrated on October 31 in the U.S., Canada, and the British Isles. Children go door to door—trick or treating. They wear costumes, beg for candy, and play pranks. Halloween traditions go back to ancient times in Britain when druids believed that evil spirits were active on that evening.

TEACHING THE LESSON

🎧 1. Tuning In

- Tell students they are going to hear a teacher talking to her students. Read aloud the three possible answers and ask: *What's the difference between telling a story, giving a lecture and showing how to do something?*

- Play the tape or CD, or read the script twice. Then ask students to circle the answer to the Tuning In question.

2. Talking It Over

- 🍎 **Heads Together** Have students work with a partner to identify each item in the picture and complete the activity. When they finish, go over the answers. Then ask students what kind of party Juan is going to.

- 🍎 **Shared Writing** Ask students to write a sentence about their favorite kinds of parties (food, clothing, and activities). Record student responses.

- Have students complete the final exercise. Call on different students to answer and tell why they think their answer is correct.

40   Teacher's Edition

READING

A CONNECTING TO YOUR LIFE

🎧 **1. Tuning In** There's a party at school tomorrow. Listen. What is the teacher doing?

    a. telling a story   b. giving a lecture   c. showing how to do something

2. Talking It Over Juan is getting ready for the party.

Work with a partner. Match the words and phrases on the right with each item in the picture. What kind of party do you think it is?

_____ 1. skull mask
_____ 2. ghost
_____ 3. tombstone
_____ 4. carved pumpkin
__a__ 5. monster mask
_____ 6. Halloween costume
_____ 7. witch's hat
_____ 8. fake teeth
_____ 9. fake blood
_____ 10. trick or-treat bag

Read the title of this unit. What do you think this unit might be about? Check (✓) the correct answer.

_____ 1. what to do if you meet a headless man
_____ 2. how to write and follow directions for making things
_____ 3. the history of American holidays

40 Unit 3

WRAP UP

- Tell students they are going to read several sets of instructions for how to make and do fun things for Halloween. Then they will practice writing instructions that tell someone else how to do something.

- Have students bring to class a set of instructions for making or doing something.

- 💻 **Using Technology** If students have access to the Internet, they can use the keyword *recipe* and the name of a dish to find instructions for how to prepare the dish.

ANSWER KEY

Tuning In: c.
Talking It Over: 1. i; 2. d; 3. c; 4. e; 5. a; 6. g; 7. j; 8. h; 9. f; 10. b.
Talking It Over: 2.

READING

UNIT 3 ■ STUDENT BOOK, PAGE 41

B GETTING READY TO READ

1. Learning New Words Read the following vocabulary words and definitions.

1. **stretch**—to make longer or larger by pulling
2. **cover**—to put something on something else
3. **mix**—to stir together
4. **place**—to put somewhere
5. **have (someone do something)**—to ask (someone to do something for you)
6. **spread**—to push a substance around on a surface
7. **roll**—to make round
8. **remove**—to take out of

Complete the sentences below with the missing vocabulary words. Then write the complete sentences in the correct order to describe how to make a pizza.

1. _Remove_ the pizza from the oven when it's bubbly.
2. _____ your dad help you understand the directions.
3. _____ the dough to make a large circle.
4. _____ the dough into a ball.
5. _____ a thin layer of tomato sauce on the dough.
6. _____ the pizza in a 450° oven.
7. _____ flour, salt, yeast, and water in a bowl.
8. _____ the sauce with shredded cheese.

2. Talking It Over Talk with a partner. Imagine that he or she is a visitor from another planet. Give instructions for making or doing something simple that you do every day.

1.
How to brush your teeth

2.
How to make a sandwich

3.
How to boil water

4.
How to give a dog a bath

5.
How to wrap a present

6.
How to . . .

I Made It Myself! 41

B GETTING READY TO READ

Standard
- State simple instructions

WARM UP

- Have students share what their instructions are for. Then have two students read their instructions aloud. Ask other students to listen for the verbs. Afterwards, ask students to name the verbs that they heard. Write them on the board.

TEACHING THE LESSON

1. Learning New Words

- List the new words on the board. Explain that these are words we often find in directions for making something.

- As you read the words aloud, ask a different student to read each definition.

- Invite students to take turns pantomiming the actions represented by the words. For example, a student might *stretch* an imaginary rubber band or *spread* butter on an imaginary slice of bread. Have other students name the actions.

- Next ask students to write each word in the correct blank. Check answers by calling on different students to read a sentence aloud.

- **Heads Together** Have students work in pairs to number the steps in the correct order. Go over their answers together.

2. Talking It Over

- **Heads Together** Have students work in pairs. Assign a different set of instructions to each pair. Tell students that they need to figure out how to teach a visitor from another planet how to do something. Have students write out their instructions.

- **Shared Writing** Tell students that you are the visitor from another planet. Have volunteers "teach" you how to brush your teeth, make a sandwich, etc. As students give their instructions, record the steps on the chalkboard.

✓ WRAP UP

- Ask students to take turns pantomiming instructions as the class guesses the task.

ANSWER KEY

Learning New Words: 1. Remove; 2. Have; 3. Stretch; 4. Roll; 5. Spread; 6. Place; 7. Mix; 8. Cover. The order is: 2, 7, 4, 3, 5, 8, 6, 1.

Talking It Over: Answers will vary.

Unit 3 41

UNIT 3 ■ STUDENT BOOK, PAGE 42

C READING TO LEARN

Standards
- Read and follow directions
- Sequence information

WARM UP

- With their books closed, ask students to think about how they might make fake blood. Ask students to share.

TEACHING THE LESSON

1. Before You Read

- Tell students to imagine that they are going to a Halloween party. Help them brainstorm possible costumes they might wear.

🎧 2. Let's Read

- Tell students they are about to read two sets of instructions.

- Have students look at the instructions. Ask: *What are the three sections in each set of instructions?* (What you need, a warning, and the directions, or steps.)

- Focusing on the Reading Strategy, explain that instructions can be confusing and that drawing each step can make them clearer.

- 🍎 **My Turn: Read Aloud/Think Aloud** Read each set of instructions aloud or play the tape or CD. As you read, stop to comment and ask questions about words. Talk with students about the steps in the instructions. For example: *The drop of green food coloring must make the red color darker.*

- Now play the tape or CD, or read the passage again. Ask students to decide which set of instructions they think would be more fun to do.

- 🍎 **Our Turn: Interactive Reading** After you read each heading (*You will need...*), call on individuals to read the ingredients/materials, the warning, and

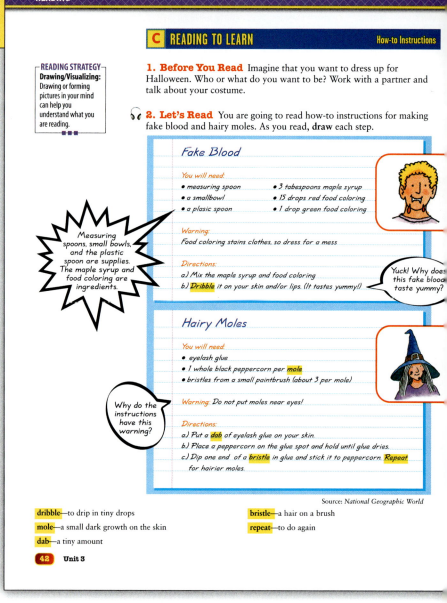

the directions. As they read, focus on the glossed words, ask questions, and make comments:

In the directions, explain the word "dribble" in your own words.
Why do you think fake blood tastes "yummy"?
Why do the instructions for Hairy Moles have this warning?

- 🍎 **Your Turn: Independent Reading** Have students read on their own. Have them choose one set of instructions and draw illustrations for each step (Reading Strategy box).

- 🌈 **Access for All** Have more proficient students work in pairs. Have them take turns closing the book and recalling the ingredients, the warning, and as many of the directions as they can remember.

CULTURE NOTE

Invite students to ask questions about Halloween and write them on the board. Then invite other students to answer. If no one knows the answer to a question, suggest that the students talk to friends and relatives, find the answer, and share it later.

READING

UNIT 3 ▪ STUDENT BOOK, PAGE 43

3. Unlocking Meaning

❶ **Identifying the Purpose** Check (✓) the phrase that explains the purpose of the instructions.

_____ 1. to warn you about the dangers of Halloween makeup

_____ 2. to explain how to make Halloween makeup

_____ 3. to teach you how to make a costume

❷ **Finding Details** Put the steps for making fake blood in the correct order.

_____ Put the blood on your skin.

__1__ Get your supplies and ingredients ready.

_____ Mix the ingredients.

Put the steps for making hairy moles in the correct order.

_____ Glue bristles to the peppercorns.

_____ Hold the peppercorn until the glue dries.

_____ Put the peppercorn on the glue.

_____ Put a tiny drop of glue on your skin.

_____ Get your supplies and ingredients ready.

❸ **Think about It** Imagine a Halloween party. Fold a piece of paper in four parts to make a chart like the one below. Write a word in each box that explains what you might see at a Halloween party.

1. costumes	3. decorations
Pirate	Jack-o'-lanterns
2. refreshments	4. games or activities
Pumpkin cookies	Bobbing for apples

❹ **Before You Move On** On Halloween, people dress up as animals, movie stars, ghosts, and other funny or scary things. Do you know about a holiday in another country that is like Halloween? Share what you know with your classmates.

I Made It Myself! **43**

---

3. Unlocking Meaning

✓ IDENTIFYING THE PURPOSE

- Ask students to identify the purpose of the instructions. Have them hold up one finger if the purpose of the reading is expressed in the first sentence, two if it is in the second, and three if it is in the third.

✓ FINDING DETAILS

- Have students order the steps for making fake blood and hairy moles.
- Have students share the captioned illustrations they made for making fake blood or hairy moles.

THINK ABOUT IT

 Team Talk Have students form groups of three or four. Read the instructions and ask each group to discuss the four aspects of a Halloween party. Then ask each student to complete the task individually. When they finish, have them share their work with the group.

▪ **Strategy Focus: Listing** Draw a large model of the four-part chart on the board. As students share out, record their ideas.

BEFORE YOU MOVE ON

▪ Ask students to share information about holidays like Halloween in other countries.

✓ WRAP UP

Outcome Sentence Have students complete the following sentence stem, then share:

_If I went trick or treating, I would dress up as a _____ because _____._

PB PRACTICE BOOK ACTIVITY

See Activity A, Revisit and Retell, on Practice Book page 21.

ANSWER KEY

Identifying the Purpose: 2.

Finding Details: First set: 3, 1, 2; Second set: 5, 4, 3, 2, 1.

Think about It: Answers will vary.

Unit 3   43

UNIT 3 ▪ STUDENT BOOK, PAGE 44

D WORD WORK

Standard
- Use knowledge of compound words to determine word meaning

WARM UP

- Hold up or point out classroom objects that are compound nouns. Ask students to name each item and write it on the board. For example: *Paper clip, light switch, workbook,* etc. Ask: *What do you notice about these words?* (They are made up of two smaller words.)

TEACHING THE LESSON

1. Word Detective

- Explain that many words in English are made up of two words—"paint" and "brush" in "paintbrush." These words are called *compound* nouns. Have students work with partners to find the smaller words in each compound.

2. Word Study

- Teach the meaning of the three terms: *closed, open,* and *hyphenated.*
- Ask students to match the examples of compound nouns with the types.
- Encourage students to start a list of compound nouns in their **notebooks**.

3. Word Play

- Have students complete the activity on their own. Then copy the chart on the board and invite students to complete one column each.

Spelling and Phonics

- Point out that the five words listed all contain the /ō/ sound, but that this sound is spelled differently in each word. Have students complete the activity.

READING

D WORD WORK

1. Word Detective Two nouns can sometimes be put together to form a new noun, called a "compound." Compound nouns have their own meaning:

paint + brush = paintbrush

You can often understand the meaning of a compound word by looking for the small words inside. Find the small words in each of the following compound words. What does each small word mean? What does each compound word mean? Talk with a partner.

tablespoon	food coloring	shower cap
eyelash	lipstick	sweatshirt
newspaper	tombstone	snowman

2. Word Study There are three types of compound words. Match the types of compound words with the correct examples. Write your answers.

Types of Compound Words	Examples
1. Closed compound (one word)	a. life jacket, home run, air conditioning
2. Open compound (two words)	b. first-class, runner-up
3. Hyphenated compound (separated by a hyphen)	c. bathroom, birthday, eyeball

SPELLING AND PHONICS: To do this activity, go to page 193.

3. Word Play Complete the chart below. Put each of the following compounds in the correct column. You can use a dictionary.

notebook	cardboard	nail clipper	hand lotion	potato chip
teaspoon	yardstick	report card	glue stick	hairbrush
hairspray	basketball	textbook	ballpoint pen	tennis racket

making things	playing sports	looking nice	doing schoolwork
cardboard			

✓ WRAP UP

- Have a contest. Write *book, ball,* and *shirt* on the board. Ask students to choose one of the words and write compound nouns using that word. Give them two minutes. See who has the longest list. Then write three lists on the board using all the answers.

PB PRACTICE BOOK ACTIVITY

See Activity B, Word Work, on Practice Book page 22.

ANSWER KEY

Word Study: 1. c; 2. a; 3. b.

Word Play: Making things: cardboard, teaspoon, yardstick, glue stick, potato chip; **playing sports:** basketball, tennis racket; **looking nice:** hairspray, nail clipper, hand lotion, hairbrush; **doing schoolwork:** notebook, report card, textbook, ballpoint pen.

Spelling and Phonics: a. sh<u>ow</u>; b. g<u>oes</u>; c. gh<u>o</u>st; d. thr<u>oa</u>t; e. sn<u>ow</u>ing; f. sl<u>ow</u>; g. c<u>o</u>ckr<u>oa</u>ch; h. wr<u>o</u>te, n<u>o</u>te; i. kn<u>ow</u>, j<u>o</u>kes; j. sh<u>ow</u>; k. c<u>o</u>de; l. d<u>ough</u>.

E GRAMMAR — Imperatives

1. Listen Up Listen to each sentence. Point your thumb up 👍 if it sounds correct. Point your thumb down 👎 if it sounds wrong.

👍 👎 1. Take out your book.
👍 👎 2. You open to page 42, please.
👍 👎 3. Turn on the oven.
👍 👎 4. Please you be quiet during the test.

2. Learn the Rule Read the following rules about imperatives. Then do Activity 1 again.

IMPERATIVES

1. Imperative sentences are used **to give directions**. Leave off the subject *you* in the sentence—start with the verb.
   Mix the maple syrup and the food coloring.

2. Imperative sentences can also be used **to give an order**. Leave off the subject *you*.
   Put down your pencils and stop writing.

3. Imperative sentences can be used **to make polite requests**. Leave off the subject *you*. Use the word *please*.
   Shut the door, please.

4. Finally, imperative sentences can be used **to warn others**. Leave off the subject *you*.
   Be careful!

3. Practice the Rule Read each sentence. Write "D" in front of the sentence if it is part of a set of directions, "O" if it is an order, "R" if it is a request, and "W" if it is a warning.

_O_ 1. Go to the office right now.
___ 2. Please pass the salt.
___ 3. Add salt and pepper to taste.
___ 4. Hand me the scissors, please.
___ 5. Cut along the dotted line.
___ 6. Be careful with the scissors.
___ 7. Discuss it with a partner.

I Made It Myself! 45

E GRAMMAR

Standard
- Express everyday functions: giving directions, giving orders, warning, and requesting

WARM UP

- Blindfold a student and lead him or her to one corner of the room. Then place several chairs in front of the student to create a maze. Ask other students to take turns using words to help the person get back to his or her seat. You might start with an example: *Take two steps forward.* Other students can give instructions such as *Turn left. Turn right. Go ahead a couple feet.* Record one or two sets of directions on the board, noting that they all begin with a verb.

UNIT 3 ■ STUDENT BOOK, PAGE 45

TEACHING THE LESSON

🎧 1. Listen Up

- Ask students to listen carefully. Play the tape or CD, or read the sentences aloud twice. Have students point their thumbs up if the sentence sounds correct, and down if it sounds wrong.

2. Learn the Rule

- As you discuss each function the imperative form can have, ask students to provide their own sentences to illustrate that function.

- Repeat the Listen Up activity. Pause after any sentences that several students get wrong this time around and ask another student to explain the error.

3. Practice the Rule

- **Think Aloud** Read the instructions. Review the example: "Go to the office right now" is an order. If it were directions, it would be about how to get there. If it were a request, it would use the word "please." If it were a warning, it would be intended to keep the person safe.

✓ WRAP UP

- Have pairs of students role-play simple situations that involve giving directions, ordering someone to do something, requesting something, or warning someone.

PB PRACTICE BOOK ACTIVITY

See Activity C, Grammar, on Practice Book page 23.

ANSWER KEY

Listen Up: Correct sentences: 1, 3.

Practice the Rule: 1. O; 2. R; 3. D; 4. R; 5. D; 6. W; 7. D/O.

UNIT 3 ■ STUDENT BOOK, PAGE 46

F BRIDGE TO WRITING

Standard
- Read and follow multi-step written instructions

WARM UP
- Read the title of the instructions. Ask: *Why did the writer use this title?*

TEACHING THE LESSON

1. Before You Read
- Have students look at the picture on page 39. How did Juan make his costume? As students dictate how the costume was made, record the predicted steps on the board. Leave the instructions on the board for later.
- Explain that using pictures to predict what you are about to learn is a powerful strategy (Reading Strategy box).

2. Let's Read
- **Heads Together** Have students work in pairs to talk about what they think happened to Juan's head.
- **My Turn: Read Aloud/Think Aloud** Read the introduction, the list of materials, and the directions aloud or play the tape or CD. As you read, stop to make comments about words and ideas.
- Play the tape or CD, or read the passage again. Have students close their books. As they listen, ask them to remember as many of the materials as they can. Have students collaborate as you write everything they remember on the board.
- **Our Turn: Interactive Reading** Have students help you read the directions. Begin by reading the first step, then have students read the remaining steps. Focus on the glossed words, ask questions, and make comments:

What is an "assistant"?

What does it mean to "head" out the door? Why is this a funny ending?

- ✓ **Question All-Write** Ask students to look again at the title. Explain that it has two meanings. Have them explain, in writing, what they think the two meanings are.
- **Build Fluency** Have pairs practice reading to each other.
- **Your Turn: Independent Reading** Have students read the passage on their own. As they read, have them compare the instructions the class generated (on the board) with the actual instructions. How are the actual instructions different?

TEACHING TIP 💡 Because these instructions are complex, consider bringing the materials to class and making the costume together.

- **Access for All** Ask less proficient students to do the Independent Reading in pairs. Have them take turns reading a step and then pausing to discuss it together.

46 Teacher's Edition

WRITING

UNIT 3 ■ STUDENT BOOK, PAGE 47

3. Making Content Connections Imagine you are going to attend a Halloween party. What kinds of costumes and make up would you see? Complete the chart below.

Character	Costume	Makeup
1. *A pirate*		
2. *A rock star*		
3. *Cleopatra*		
4. *Werewolf*		
5. Your choice: _____		

A rock star

A werewolf

4. Expanding Your Vocabulary Find the word in each row of the following chart that *does not* go with the word in capital letters. Cross out your answers. You can use your dictionary.

a. CELEBRATION	festival	custom	holiday	~~sadness~~	tradition
b. REFRESHMENTS	drinks	prize	appetizers	buffet table	pretzels
c. COSTUMES	mask	wig	makeup	clothes hanger	disguise
d. PARTY GAMES	contest	exercise	competition	prize	winner
e. DECORATIONS	banner	balloons	clothing	streamers	crepe paper

I Made It Myself!   47

---

3. Making Content Connections

■ **Heads Together** Have students work in pairs to complete the chart. Encourage them to discuss their ideas as they work.

■ Draw the chart on the board. Record as students share out.

■ With a show of hands, have students indicate their favorite costumes and makeup. Ask individuals to explain why they favor that particular item.

4. Expanding Your Vocabulary

■ Have students look at each set of words and listen as you read them aloud. Have them point their thumbs up if they know the word or down if they have never seen or heard it. When over a third of the class points thumbs down, use the word in a sentence, but do not attempt to define it. Repeat your sentences several times, providing students with time to guess at possible meanings.

■ Now explain that one word in each set doesn't fit. Begin with "celebration." Ask: *What do you think of when you see the word celebration?* Make a word web as students call out words. Talk students through each word in the set, encouraging them to define the word. Why does the word "sadness" *not* fit?

■ Have students work in pairs to find the word that doesn't fit in the other sets. Have students share out, explaining why the word doesn't fit. Discuss the meaning of unusual words (e.g., "streamers").

JUST FOR FUN

Play Party Lingo Bingo. Divide students in groups of four. Have each group fold a sheet of paper in four parts one way, then four parts the other way, making 16 squares. As you write a party word on the board, each group copies the word in any square. Provide 16 party words. In random order, talk about each word without naming it. As each group guesses the party word, they put an X in the square. The first group with a complete row of four Xs, whispers out, "Lingo Bingo!"

✓ WRAP UP

■ **Outcome Sentence** Have students complete this sentence stem, then share:

This reading taught me _____.

PB PRACTICE BOOK ACTIVITY

See Activity D, Test-Taking Practice, on Practice Book pages 24 and 25.

See Activity E, Using New Vocabulary, on Practice Book page 26.

ANSWER KEY

Expanding Your Vocabulary: a. sadness; b. prize; c. clothes hanger; d. exercise; e. clothing.

UNIT 3 ■ STUDENT BOOK, PAGE 48

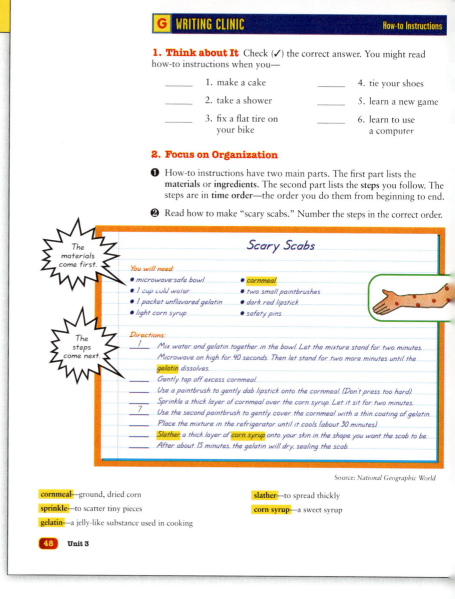

G WRITING CLINIC

Standards
- Identify the structural patterns found in procedural text
- Use specific vocabulary

WARM UP

- Have students look back at the instructions they have read. Ask them to identify the ways in which all sets of instructions are the same (e.g., *they all have a title, they list ingredients*, etc.).
- Tell students they are going to learn how to become champion writers of "how-to" instructions.

TEACHING THE LESSON

1. Think about It

- Ask students to think about the six actions or activities and tell you which ones would *not* have written directions. Discuss the answers with the class. (They would probably never read how-to instructions for tying shoes or taking a shower.) Have students tell you why these actions would not have instructions.

2. Focus on Organization

- Referring to the costume instructions on page 46, note that there are two parts. Read and paraphrase the explanation beginning "How-to instructions have..."
- Now focus students on a new set of instructions—for making "Scary Scabs." Have a volunteer tell you what a scab is. Focus first on the ingredients/materials, calling attention to the glossed words.
- Now have students read the steps. Ask students to give examples of things they *sprinkle* (salt, pepper) and things they *slather* (butter, cream cheese). Explain that *slather* means to put a lot of butter, cream cheese, etc. on something. When you use a normal amount, you use the word *spread*.
- Explain that the steps are out of order. Have students work with a partner to figure out the correct order. Have students share out.

PB PRACTICE BOOK ACTIVITY

See Activity F, Focus on Organization, on Practice Book page 27.

48   Teacher's Edition

WRITING

UNIT 3 ▪ STUDENT BOOK, PAGE 49

3. Focus on Style

❶ Look at the following first step. Suppose a set of instructions started with this:

  1. Mix ingredients together in the bowl.

What would you put in the bowl? You wouldn't know! Good how-to instructions use **specific words**. Specific words answer questions like these:

- What kind?   **chocolate** milkshake
- How much?   **one cup** of water
- How long?   for **thirty minutes**
- How?   **dribble** butter on your popcorn

❷ Work with a partner. Find examples of exact words in the scary scabs instructions. Make a list.

dark red lipstick _____ _____
_____ _____ _____

❸ Look at the underlined parts of the sentences below. Which specific question does each underlined part answer? Write the letter of a question in each blank.

Questions:
a. What kind?
b. How much?
c. How long?
d. How?

  _a_ 1. Use a <u>microwave-safe</u> bowl.
  ___ 2. Add <u>1 cup</u> of water to the gelatin.
  ___ 3. Microwave on high <u>for 40 seconds</u>.
  ___ 4. Place the mixture in the refrigerator <u>until it cools</u>.
  ___ 5. <u>Gently</u> dab lipstick onto the cornmeal.
  ___ 6. Cover the cornmeal with a <u>thin coating</u> of gelatin.
  ___ 7. <u>After about 15 minutes</u>, the gelatin will dry.

I Made It Myself! 49

✓ WRAP UP

- Write on the board the first step in a process—for example, making hot chocolate: *Put one cup of milk in a small saucepan.* Ask different students to take turns adding one step each until the hot chocolate is complete. As students add steps, point out examples of specific information they provide, and help them make general instructions more specific if necessary.

PB PRACTICE BOOK ACTIVITY

See Activity G, Focus on Style, on Practice Book page 28.

ANSWER KEY

Think about It: 1, 3, 5, 6.

Focus on Organization: 1, 5, 6, 4, 7, 2, 3, 8.

Focus on Style 2: Possible answers: microwave-safe bowl; 1 cup; 1 packet; unflavored; light corn syrup; two; dark red lipstick; for two minutes; for 40 seconds; gently; too hard; sprinkle; thick; etc.

Focus on Style 3: 1. a; 2. b; 3. c; 4. c; 5. d; 6. b; 7. c.

3. Focus on Style

- Ask students to imagine that they are following a recipe. Focus students on the sentence, "Mix ingredients together in the bowl." Ask: *What's wrong with these instructions?* Help students see that they lack specific words—words that tell what kind, how much, how long, and how (Part 1).

- Focus students on the examples. Help them generate additional examples.

  🍎 **Heads Together** Ask students to work in pairs as they complete Part 2 and write down examples of exact words from the scary scabs instructions. Record as students share out.

- Ask students to complete Part 3. Review the correct answers with the class. Encourage students to paraphrase each sentence using a non-specific wording that contrasts with the specific information given. For example: Instead of *microwave-safe bowl,* a student might say *a bowl.* In place of *a cup of water,* the student might say *some water.* Point out the importance of being specific.

Unit 3 49

UNIT 3 ▪ STUDENT BOOK, PAGE 50

WRITING

H WRITER'S WORKSHOP

Standards
- Use the writing process: prewriting
- Sequence information

1. Getting It Out
WARM UP

- Ask students to think about a time they had to follow written instructions. What did the instructions show them how to make or do? What was one good thing about the instructions? What was one problem?

- Tell students that they are now going to have the chance to write instructions for making or doing something that other people can follow.

TEACHING THE LESSON

- Begin by helping students list ideas for things they might teach others how to do or make. Which illustrated activities do students know how to do (Part 1)? Brainstorm two or three additional ideas. Encourage students to think on their own, adding to their lists.

> **TEACHING TIP** 💡 Consider using the ideas that students have generated to model each step in the planning process: making a chart like the one on page 51, selecting an activity to explain, listing ingredients/materials, and making a timeline of steps.

H WRITER'S WORKSHOP — How-to Instructions

Write how-to instructions for something you know how to do.

1. Getting It Out

❶ Decide what you will explain. Make a list of things you know how to do. Here are some possibilities.

1.
Making a pizza

2.
Doing a magic trick

3.
Juggling three balls

4.
Making a Halloween mask

5.
Making a book cover

50 Unit 3

50 Teacher's Edition

WRITING

UNIT 3 ▪ STUDENT BOOK, PAGE 51

❷ Choose two or three things on your list. Ask yourself the following questions, then decide which activity you will explain to others.
  1. How well do I know how to make or do this?
  2. How easy/hard is it to explain in words?

Here is how Lori answered these questions. Why did Lori decide to write directions for making a pizza?

Possible things to explain	How well do I know how to make or do this?	How easy/hard is it to explain this in words?
1. *Juggling three balls*	*I know how to do this.*	*Hard to teach with words.*
2. *Making a mask*	*I did this once when I was little.*	*Easy.*
3. *Making a pizza*	*I do this often. I'm good at this!*	*Easy.*

❸ Make a list of the materials or ingredients you will need. Here is Lori's list:

pizza shell	sauce	cheese
mushrooms	onions	pepperoni

❹ Plan your instructions. Think about the steps involved. Put them in **time order**. Here is the "timeline" that Lori made.

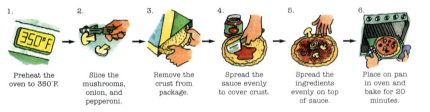

1. Preheat the oven to 350°F.
2. Slice the mushrooms, onion, and pepperoni.
3. Remove the crust from package.
4. Spread the sauce evenly to cover crust.
5. Spread the ingredients evenly on top of sauce.
6. Place on pan in oven and bake for 20 minutes.

I Made It Myself! 51

- Tell students that some things are easy to explain, while other things are more difficult. Referring to the illustrations, have students identify what would be easy to explain in words, what would be difficult to explain, and why.

- Have several volunteers share three things on their lists that they are thinking about explaining. Focus students on the two questions in the chart (Part 2): *How well do I know how to do this? How easy/hard is it to explain this in words?*

- Note that Lori has decided to make a pizza. Point to the chart that shows why Lori decided to write about making a pizza. Ask students to copy the chart on a separate piece of paper and fill in three of their own choices in the left-hand column. Then have them make notes in the chart on how well they can do each thing and how easy or hard it is to explain.

- When they finish their charts, ask students to make a choice of topic and share out their choices. Model with students how they might choose the best topic. Then have students work with a partner, discussing topic choices.

- Have students work on their own to make a list of ingredients or materials needed (Part 3). Remind them to check their lists over to be sure they haven't forgotten anything.

- Review Lori's timeline of steps (Part 4). Have students make similar timelines for their own instructions.

🌈 **Access for All** Using interactive writing, work with a small group of less proficient students to develop a common set of instructions for making something (or have an instructional assistant help). Involve students in illustrating and labeling the timeline and instructions.

✓ WRAP UP

- Have several volunteers share out their timelines.

UNIT 3 ■ STUDENT BOOK, PAGE 52

H WRITER'S WORKSHOP

Standards
- Use the writing process: drafting, revising, and editing
- Use specific vocabulary
- Give a short oral presentation
- Listen to oral presentations and take notes

2. Getting It Down

WARM UP
- Tell students that it's now time to turn their timelines into a set of instructions. Ask a volunteer or two to tell you in their own words what they think they'll need to do.

TEACHING THE LESSON
- Have students look at the planner. Ask: *What do you notice?* Explain that the planner will help them draft an actual set of instructions.
- When they finish drafting their own instructions, ask students to read Lori's instructions for making a pizza, paying attention to the comments in the speech bubbles.
- **Mini-Lesson on Conventions** Explain that symbols can take the place of words. Ask students to find the symbols in the instructions. Then write the words for these symbols on the board and have different students write the correct symbol next to each. Generate additional common symbols (e.g., ' (foot/feet), @ (at), % (percent), $ (dollar), etc.).

✓ WRAP UP
- Remind students that instructions are sometimes hard for others to follow. Ask them to think of things they might do to make sure that their instructions are clear (e.g., show them to a partner, act out the instructions step by step, check to see that the steps are in the right order, etc.).
- Tell students that they will have a chance to revise their work during the next session. Have them locate the ChecBric for this unit in the Student Book or Practice Book. Have them prepare for Getting It Right by reviewing the ChecBric on their own, underlining indicators they're not sure about.

PB PRACTICE BOOK ACTIVITY
See Activity H, Writer's Workshop, on Practice Book page 29.

WRITING

2. Getting It Down

❶ Turn your timeline into instructions. Complete the planner below.

How to _____

Materials or ingredients:
1. _____   4. _____
2. _____   5. _____
3. _____   6. _____

Warning! (Do you need to warn people about anything?) _____
_____

Directions
1. _____
2. _____
3. _____
4. _____
5. _____
6. _____

❷ Here is what Lori wrote.

Lori lists the ingredients.

How to Make a Pepperoni Pizza

Ingredients
12" pizza pan   ¼ pound mushrooms
pizza crust   1 onion
bottled sauce   1 pepperoni stick

She lists the steps in time order.

Directions
1. Preheat oven to 350°F.
2. Slice mushrooms, onion, and pepperoni.
3. Remove pizza crust from package.
4. Spread sauce evenly to cover crust.
5. Spread other ingredients evenly.
6. Place on pan in oven. Bake for 20 minutes or until brown.

She uses specific words.

MINI-LESSON
Using Symbols: Symbols are often used to stand for certain words:
12" pizza pan = 12-inch pizza pan
350° = 350 degrees

WRITING

3. Getting It Right Take a careful look at what you have written. Use this guide to help you revise your work.

Question to ask...	How to check...	How to revise...
1. Are all of the materials or ingredients listed?	Draw a line to connect each item with the step.	Add any supplies or steps you left out.
2. Did I remember all of the steps? Are the steps in time order?	Imagine that you are actually following each step that you have written.	Add a step if you need to or change the order of the steps.
3. Did I use exact language in each step?	Highlight nouns and verbs that are exact.	Replace general words with words that are exact.

4. Presenting It

1. Share your instructions with your classmates.
2. Ask for volunteers to repeat each step in your directions.
3. As you listen to others, take notes. Use a note-taking guide like this one.

Materials or ingredients needed:
1. _____ 4. _____
2. _____ 5. _____
3. _____ 6. _____

Warnings (if any): _____

Directions:
1. _____
2. _____
3. _____
4. _____
5. _____
6. _____

I Made It Myself! 53

UNIT 3 ■ STUDENT BOOK, PAGE 53

- Before they develop final drafts, have students look once again at the chart and the ChecBric.

WRAP UP

- Suggest that students practice reading their instructions aloud to a partner or family member before the next class.
- Give students time to fill out the ChecBric on Practice Book page 105. Ask them to attach it to their writing when they put it in their portfolios.

4. Presenting It
WARM UP

- As a class, develop a simple presentation checklist. In addition to content and organization, focus on speaking skills, enthusiasm, use of visuals, creativity, involvement of the audience, and length of presentation.

TEACHING THE LESSON

- Have students present their instructions. Point out the note-taking guide that students will use as they listen.

> **TEACHING TIP** Make copies of the guide so students don't have to recopy it for each presentation.

- Have students use the note-taking guide to take notes as they listen.
- Have one listener repeat each step in the presenter's directions. Were they able to follow the instructions?

✓ WRAP UP

- Ask students what they think the most important thing about giving directions is. Note each one on the board.

---

3. Getting It Right
WARM UP

- Guide students through the ChecBric for this unit in the Student Book or Practice Book. Explain that they will use the ChecBric to prepare a final draft of their writing.
- Have volunteers explain, in their own words, what each indicator in the ChecBric means.

TEACHING THE LESSON

- Have students revise their instructions, using the chart and the ChecBric.
- **Group Share** Have students share their instructions with classmates and get feedback. Ask students to think about which parts of their writing they would like others to comment on. Help them generate questions. For example: *Do you think the instructions are useful to others? Did I leave out any ingredients or materials?*

Unit 3   53

UNIT 3 ■ STUDENT BOOK, PAGE 54

▐ BEYOND THE UNIT

Standards
- Understand oral instructions
- Read and follow written instructions (recipes)
- Respond to a poem

🎧 1. On Assignment
WARM UP

- It's time to plan a class Halloween party! Ask students to name things that make a great party as you list ideas on the board. Guide them to include decorations, tasty food, and fun games.

TEACHING TIP 💡 Enlist the help of parent volunteers or instructional aides in planning and carrying out the party. Think through all of the planning steps in advance, especially materials that you will need, how food will be prepared, and how the party game will be managed as it is played.

TEACHING THE LESSON

- First, point out the series of six pictures and ask volunteers to describe what each picture shows. Then play the tape or CD twice, or read the instructions as students look at the pictures and take notes. Ask for three or four volunteers to be in charge of making a Jack-o'-lantern for the party—as well as other decorations.
- Ask students to read through the recipe. Recruit a group to make the "Eyeballs." Help the group gather the necessary materials and work together.

TEACHING TIP 💡 Enlist the help of the homemaking teacher or parent volunteers with these tasks.

- Tell students that you will also play a game called Draw and Guess. Preview the game for students, going through each step. Then assign an additional three or four students the task of assembling materials for the game.
- It's the day of the party! Have each work team of students meet with you before school (or after school the day before the party) to make sure that they have completed their tasks and are ready for the party.

■ **Using Technology** Point out the Halloween Web site in the Student Book and suggest that students go to this site and read about other kinds of Halloween decorations, foods, and games.

✓ WRAP UP

🍒 **Outcome Sentence** Have students complete this sentence stem, then share:

The most important thing about having a fun party is _____.

54 Teacher's Edition

❸ Play a party game: Draw and Guess! You will need slips of paper with Halloween words like these: *mummy, vampire, haunted house, skeleton, cobweb, witch, jack-o'-lantern, black cat, tombstone, scream, ghost, and bat.* Put the slips of paper in a bowl.

1. Choose two teams or four or five kids.
2. A player on one team takes a slip of paper out of the bowl, then draws a picture of the word.
3. His or her team tries to guess the word in two minutes or less. If they guess the word correctly, the team gets a point.
4. The other team goes next, trying to guess a word.
5. Keep playing until everyone has a chance to draw.
6. Keep score to see which team wins. Give the winners a prize!

2. Link to Literature

 SHARED READING People love to wear masks on Halloween. Read "Best Mask?" by Shel Silverstein.

LET'S TALK Answer the questions.

1. What kind of contest did the person in the poem win?
2. Why is the poem funny?
3. Have you ever won a contest? What did you do to win?

ABOUT THE AUTHOR

Shel Silverstein was born in Chicago, Illinois in 1930 and died in 1999. He wrote many fun stories and poems. Some of his most famous books are *The Giving Tree, Where the Sidewalk Ends,* and *Falling Up.*

BEST MASK?

They just had a contest for scariest mask,
And I was the wild and daring one
Who *won* the contest for scariest mask—
And (sob) I'm not even *wearing* one.

I Made It Myself! 55

UNIT 3 ■ STUDENT BOOK, PAGE 55

- Have volunteers read the poem aloud. Encourage students to read with expression.

- **Let's Talk** Help students discuss the meaning and humor of the poem. Have a volunteer tell you what the pronoun *one* in the second line refers to, then what the pronoun *one* in the last line refers to. Ask students why the speaker of the poem says that he was "wild and daring" (because he went to a mask contest without a mask on).

✓ WRAP UP

Have students draw their own "best masks," then share with classmates.

PB PRACTICE BOOK ACTIVITY

See Activity I, Responding to Literature, on Practice Book page 30.

✓ UNIT WRAP UP

- Have students reflect in their **notebooks** on what they learned to do in this unit and what they enjoyed most. Consider responding to reflections.

---

2. Link to Literature

WARM UP

- Have students look at the illustration, then the title of the poem. Ask: *What do you think the poem is about?*

TEACHING THE LESSON

- **Shared Reading** Read the poem "Best Mask?" by Shel Silverstein aloud as students follow along. Model oral expression and use pauses that help clearly communicate the meaning of the phrases. Pause slightly on the word *sob* and give the word a sobbing sound.

- Now play the tape or CD, or read the poem again. As students listen, ask them to notice the descriptive words. Then ask volunteers to identify the descriptive words (scariest, wild, daring).

Unit 3   55

Unit 4  Trying to Be Cool
Unit Overview

Section	At a Glance	Standards
Before You Begin	Students talk about a teenage boy who dyes his hair blue to try to be cool.	■ Derive meaning from visual information ■ Use descriptive adjectives
A. Connecting to Your Life	Students discuss what is cool—and very un-cool.	■ Relate personal observations and ideas
B. Getting Ready to Read	Students learn useful vocabulary and consider social group behavior.	■ Use context to determine the meaning of unknown words ■ Engage in sustained discussion with peers on a topic
C. Reading to Learn	Students read three short accounts written by kids who did "stupid things" to be cool. PRACTICE BOOK: Students write a short narrative.	■ Read personal narratives ■ Use reading strategies to unlock meaning ■ Recall major points in a story
D. Word Work	Students practice turning verbs into nouns by adding –er, -r, or -or. PRACTICE BOOK: Students practice using nouns with suffixes.	■ Use knowledge of suffixes to determine word meaning ■ Spell frequently used words correctly
E. Grammar	Students learn regular and irregular past tense verb forms. PRACTICE BOOK: Students complete sentences with past tense verbs.	■ Express past actions
F. Bridge to Writing	Students read three more stories about stupid things kids did to be cool. PRACTICE BOOK: Students practice taking Reading Vocabulary and Reading Comprehension tests. PRACTICE BOOK: Students practice new vocabulary.	■ Read personal narratives ■ Use reading strategies to unlock meaning ■ Recall major points in a story ■ Use descriptive adjectives

Section	At a Glance	Standards
G. Writing Clinic	Students learn how to organize a personal narrative. Students also learn how to write for different audiences. PRACTICE BOOK: Students examine the content of personal narratives, then write short personal narratives. PRACTICE BOOK: Students rewrite an email for a different audience.	■ Identify the structural patterns found in personal narratives ■ Identify cause and effect patterns ■ Use language register appropriate to audience
H1. Writer's Workshop: Getting It Out	Students identify something stupid or foolish they have done to write about, then plan their narrative. PRACTICE BOOK: Students write comic strip stories to plan their personal narratives.	■ Use the writing process: prewriting ■ Sequence events ■ Use dialogue to tell a story
H2. Writer's Workshop: Getting It Down	Students outline their narrative, then draft a paragraph.	■ Use the writing process: drafting
H3. Writer's Workshop: Getting It Right	Students revise and edit their own work.	■ Use the writing process: revising and editing
H4. Writer's Workshop: Presenting It	Students present their stories to classmates.	■ Give a short oral narrative presentation
I. Beyond the Unit	Students imagine that they are submitting their stories to an online magazine, and then type up their work. Students read the poem, "Motto," by Langston Hughes. PRACTICE BOOK: Students write a poem modeled on "Motto."	■ Use word-processing conventions ■ Respond to a poem ■ Write a poem based on a model

UNIT 4 ▪ STUDENT BOOK, PAGE 56

Unit 4 Trying to Be Cool

Read...
- Stories about teens who did things just to be cool when they were younger.

 Link to Literature
- "Motto," a poem by Langston Hughes.

Objectives:

Reading:
- Personal narratives
- Strategies: Questioning the author, predicting
- Literature: Responding to a poem

Writing:
- Writing a personal narrative
- Describing events in a time sequence
- Indentifying your audience: Formal vs. informal language

Vocabulary:
- Using the -er/-or suffix to form nouns from verbs
- Learning words that describe personality

Listening/Speaking:
- Listening to advice
- Comparing different groups of students
- Listening to feedback from others

Grammar:
- Using the simple past tense

Spelling and Phonics:
- Pronouncing words with the letters -gh-

BEFORE YOU BEGIN

Standards
- Derive meaning from visual information
- Use descriptive adjectives

- Have students look at the picture on page 57, and then describe the boy. Ask: *Why is his hair blue? What has he done? How do you think he feels?*

- Have students read the caption under the picture. Ask: *Why is he called "Mr. Cool"?* (He is trying to be popular or admired by his friends.)

- Have students tell you what kids often do to be cool. Record their ideas on the board. Keep your list for later.

  Access for All Encourage students with strong interpersonal intelligence (those who are especially good at understanding others' feelings) to volunteer why they think it's so important to some kids to act "cool."

Mr. Cool

BEFORE YOU BEGIN

Talk with your classmates.

1. Look at the picture. Describe the boy.
2. Read the caption. Why is the boy called "Mr. Cool"?
3. What do you know about students who try to be cool?

UNIT 4 ■ STUDENT BOOK, PAGE 58

> **A   CONNECTING TO YOUR LIFE**
>
> **Standard**
> - Relate personal observations and ideas

WARM UP

- Ask students to look at the pictures as volunteers read the captions aloud. Refer to the list that students generated of things kids do to be cool. Add the pictured actions or ideas to the class list.

TEACHING THE LESSON

🎧 1. Tuning In

- Tell students they are going to hear two girls talking. One of them has done something she thinks is very cool.
- Play the tape or CD, or read the script. Ask students to listen carefully in order to find out what Michelle has done.
- Now play the tape or CD, or read the script a second time. Ask: *What is Michelle trying to convince Lori to do? Why? Do you agree or disagree with Michelle?*
- Invite volunteers to share why they agree or disagree with Michelle.

2. Talking It Over

- 🍎 **Heads Together** Call attention to the list of ideas on the board. Have students work in pairs, rating each item on the class list from 1 to 10.
- Have students share out their ratings. Compare ratings across pairs.
- Focus students on the title of the unit. With a show of fingers, have students tell you what they think the unit is about.

READING

A   CONNECTING TO YOUR LIFE

🎧 **1. Tuning In** Listen to Michelle giving advice. Do you agree or disagree with her advice?

2. Talking It Over
Some things that kids do are cool and some things are not. Look at the pictures below. Are these things cool or uncool?

1.
Shaving your head

2.
Wearing baggy pants

3.
Being mean to friends

4.
Wearing your baseball cap backward

5.
Piercing a part of your body

6.
Carrying a book bag

Work with a partner. Complete the diagram below. Rate the things in the pictures above from 1 (very uncool) to 5 (very cool). Then add three more things.

Very uncool		Pretty cool		Very cool
1	2	3	4	5

Read the title of this unit. What do you think this unit is probably about? Check (✓) the correct answer.

_____ 1. students who are popular

_____ 2. students who did something to be cool but were sorry later

_____ 3. students who did things to stay out of the hot weather

---

WRAP UP

- Tell students they are going to read about things kids did to be cool. Then they will write their own stories.
- Ask students to ask adult members of their families about some of the things they did to be cool when they were young—and how they feel about it now. Ask students to be ready to share what they learned.

> **TEACHING TIP** 💡 Keep in mind that students may be reluctant to share embarrassing moments with classmates. Be ready to adjust the activities in this unit in such a way that students can talk about other people's experiences instead of their own, if necessary.

ANSWER KEY

Talking It Over: 2.

READING

UNIT 4 • STUDENT BOOK, PAGE 59

B GETTING READY TO READ

1. Learning New Words Read the sentences below. Try to guess the meanings of the underlined words.

1. Everybody at school likes Juan. He's a <u>popular</u> guy.
2. Matt bought an expensive new car to <u>impress</u> the girls.
3. Pedro is great at every sport. He's a real <u>jock</u>!
4. Tom decided to <u>go out for</u> wrestling this season. He always wanted to wrestle.
5. Stefan doesn't care what others think of him. He doesn't care about his <u>image</u>.
6. Most of the girls at school wear <u>brand-name</u> jeans like BAM!
7. Marisol still thinks that smoking is "<u>in</u>," but nobody thinks it's cool anymore.
8. Lots of kids do things to be cool, but it often <u>backfires</u> on them instead. They just look silly.

Complete the sentences below with the missing vocabulary words from above.

1. People who are _popular_ have a lot of friends.
2. Kids who love sports often _____ athletic teams like football or track.
3. If something is fashionable, people say it is _____.
4. _____ clothing has a name everybody knows.
5. When you want other people to like you, you might try to _____ them by wearing cool clothes or telling funny stories.
6. Someone who has a positive _____ makes a good impression on others.
7. When you try very hard to impress other people, it sometimes _____.
8. If you love playing sports, people will call you a _____.

2. Talking It Over Kids in the same social group often look the same, talk the same, and act the same. Work in a small group. Compare two different groups at your school. Complete the following chart.

	Group #1: _Jocks_	Group #2: _____	Group #3: _____
a. How do they dress?	They wear sports jerseys.		
b. How do they talk?			
c. What is their image?			

Trying to Be Cool

B GETTING READY TO READ

Standards
- Use context to determine the meaning of unknown words
- Engage in sustained discussion with peers on a topic

WARM UP

- Invite volunteers to share what adults did to be cool when they were young. Ask: *What did the person do? Why? How did s/he feel about it?*

TEACHING THE LESSON

1. Learning New Words

- Write the new words and phrases on the board. Have students work in groups of three, trying to write a definition for each word or phrase. Have them share their definitions and then set them aside for the next step.

- Have each small group read sentences 1 through 8 in their books, and then revise their original definitions. Have them share out.

- Now have groups complete each sentence, then share. Confirm the answers.

- Have students revisit their original definitions, modifying them as needed. Ask several volunteers to share changes they made in their original definitions.

- Have each group create an original sentence for each word and share them with the class.

2. Talking It Over

- **Build Background** Explain that kids sometimes belong to social groups. They talk alike, wear the same type of clothing, and try to have a certain image.

- Read the instructions and explain them. Then model the discussion that students might have in order to complete the column for Group 1. For example: *b. How do they talk?* (They talk about sports a lot.) *c. What is their image?* (They look strong. They all have girlfriends.)

- Brainstorm a list of other social groups students have noticed at school.

- **Team Talk** Divide the class into groups of three to complete the chart. Remind them that they can use the ideas the class just brainstormed.

WRAP UP

- Have students write in their **notebooks** about why kids like to belong to groups.

ANSWER KEY

Learning New Words: 1. popular; 2. go out for; 3. in; 4. Brand-name; 5. impress; 6. image; 7. backfires; 8. jock.

UNIT 4 ▪ STUDENT BOOK, PAGE 60

C READING TO LEARN

Standards
- Read personal narratives
- Use reading strategies to unlock meaning
- Recall major points in a story

WARM UP

- Ask students to revisit what they wrote about why people like to belong to groups. As volunteers share ideas, write them on the board.

TEACHING THE LESSON

1. Before You Read

🍎 **Heads Together** Have students talk with a partner, listing things kids do to impress each other. Invite volunteers to share their ideas with the class.

🎧 **2. Let's Read**

- Tell students they are about to read three examples of things kids did that they thought were cool at the time.

🍎 **My Turn: Read Aloud/Think Aloud** Play the tape or CD or read the passage aloud. Comment on unfamiliar vocabulary. Talk with students about the ideas in the passages.

🍎 **Our Turn: Interactive Reading** Now have students help you read each passage. Read the first sentence of each passage and then call on a student to read the rest. As students read, focus on the glossed words, ask questions, and make comments:

Why did kids laugh at Tom? Why didn't Robbie's friends take him back?

At the end of each passage, ask students to paraphrase each story, using their own words.

✓ 🍎 **Question All-Write** After you read Sarah's story, ask: *Do you think Sarah is a normal teenager? Why or*

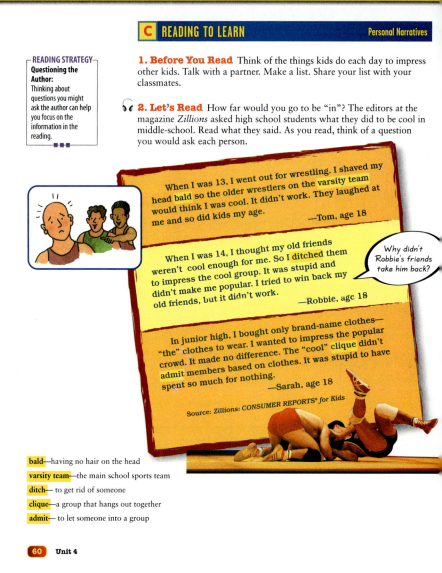

why not? Have students write one or two sentences in their notebooks and then share their responses.

- **Build Fluency** Have partners take turns reading each story aloud to each other.

🍎 **Your Turn: Independent Reading** Focus on the Reading Strategy (Questioning the Author) explaining that when you "have a conversation" with the writer, you connect to the writing.

- Have students read each of the three short passages on their own. Ask them to write at least one question they would like to ask each author. After they read, have students share their questions with the class and invite other students to suggest possible answers.

CULTURE NOTE

American culture tends to place a high value on individual expression. Teenagers have a lot of freedom in the U.S. However, they often find themselves following the crowd—trying to be like everyone else their age.

READING

UNIT 4 ■ STUDENT BOOK, PAGE 61

3. Unlocking Meaning

❶ **Finding the Main Idea** Complete the sentences. Match each phrase on the left with the correct ending on the right.

1. Tom learned that—
2. Robbie learned that—
3. Sarah learned that—

a. what you wear won't make other kids like you.
b. changing the way you look to be cool can backfire.
c. if you're not loyal to your real friends, you could end up lonely.

❷ **Finding Details** Put the following sentences in the same order that they happened in each story.

Tom's Story

_____ He shaved his head bald.
_1_ He joined the school wrestling team.
_____ The other boys laughed at him.

Robbie's Story

_____ He tried to get his friends back but they didn't want him.
_____ He dropped his old friends because he wanted new friends who were cool.
_____ The new group didn't want to be friends with him.

Sarah's Story

_____ She wore brand-name clothes to impress the popular crowd.
_____ She realized that she wasted her money.
_____ The kids in the cool clique weren't impressed.

❸ **Think about It** Talk with a partner. Decide which person—Tom, Robbie, or Sarah—did the most foolish thing and why. Share with your classmates.

❹ **Before You Move On** Read this Assyrian proverb: *Tell me your friends and I'll tell you who you are.* List the names of three of your friends. Then write two words that describe each friend. Circle the words that also describe *you*.

Trying to Be Cool   61

---

3. Unlocking Meaning

✓ FINDING THE MAIN IDEA

- Give students a few minutes to match phrases to their endings. Then ask for volunteers to read individual complete sentences.
- Review each correct response. Have volunteers read each correct response and then explain why it is correct.
- ✓ 🌰 **Outcome Sentence** Have students complete this sentence stem, and then share with classmates.

  All three stories tell _____.

✓ FINDING DETAILS

- Have students read the three sentences in each story and number each set of sentences in the correct order.
- Have volunteers read each set of sentences in the correct order.

✓ 🌰 **Sentence Synthesis** Ask students to write one or two sentences that summarize the main idea of Tom's story. (Tom shaved his head so the wrestling team would think he was cool, but they laughed at him instead.)

THINK ABOUT IT

🌰 **Heads Together** Ask pairs of students to discuss which person did the most foolish thing and *why*. Invite students to share their ideas.

BEFORE YOU MOVE ON

🌰 Ask a volunteer to read the instructions, and then explain them to classmates. Have students work individually on the task and then share out three words that describe themselves.

✓ WRAP UP

🌰 **Quick Write** Have students write a short message to one of the three kids—Robbie, Tom, or Sarah—reassuring the person that what s/he did wasn't so bad after all. Have students share their messages.

PB PRACTICE BOOK ACTIVITY

See Activity A, Revisit and Retell, on Practice Book page 31.

ANSWER KEY

Finding the Main Idea: 1. b; 2. c; 3. a.
Finding Details: Tom's story: 2, 1, 3; Robbie's Story: 3, 1, 2; Sarah's story: 1, 3, 2.
Think about It: Answers will vary.
Before You Move On: Answers will vary.

UNIT 4 ■ STUDENT BOOK, PAGE 62

D WORD WORK

Standards
- Use knowledge of suffixes to determine word meaning
- Spell frequently used words correctly

WARM UP

- Ask students to complete the following sentences orally: *Alex Rodriguez is a baseball _____. Britney Spears is a _____. (Your name) is my English _____.* Write the three completed sentences on the board (*player, singer, teacher*). Ask students what is similar about the meanings of the three words. (They describe what people do.) Ask what is similar about the spellings. (They end in *–er*.)

TEACHING THE LESSON

1. Word Detective
- Have students read each sentence, telling what each underlined word means.

2. Word Study
- Focus on the three forms of the suffix. Encourage students to start a list of *-er, -r, -or* words in their **notebooks**.

3. Word Play
- **Heads Together** Have students complete the activity in pairs. Encourage them to use their dictionaries. Have students add these words to their lists.

Spelling and Phonics
- Have students listen to the sentence and tell you what they notice about the underlined letters. (The letters *gh* are silent or have a /f/ sound.)
- Have students complete the activity. Review the answers.

READING

D WORD WORK

1. Word Detective Sometimes you can guess what a word means by looking for a smaller word inside the word. The underlined words below are nouns. Find the smaller words inside the nouns. What do the nouns mean? Write down your definitions.

1. Tom is a powerful <u>wrestler</u>.
   smaller word: _____
   definition of "wrestler": _____

2. I want to be a <u>teacher</u> when I grow up.
   smaller word: _____
   definition of "teacher": _____

3. Vincent van Gogh was a famous <u>painter</u>.
   smaller word: _____
   definition of "painter": _____

4. Justin Timberlake is a <u>singer</u>.
   smaller word: _____
   definition of "singer": _____

5. Who is your favorite <u>actor</u>?
   smaller word: _____
   definition of "actor": _____

6. Maria is the best <u>player</u> on the team.
   smaller word: _____
   definition of "player": _____

2. Word Study You can make many verbs into nouns by adding the suffix *-er, -r,* or *-or.* Look at the sentences below. Underline the suffixes.

-er/-r/-or = a person who does (something)	
skate	Michelle Kwan is a beautiful **skater**.
act	Tom Cruise is a handsome **actor**.
golf	Tiger Woods is an amazing **golfer**.

3. Word Play Work with a partner. For each of the following verbs, write a noun that means "someone who…" Then make a sentence using each noun.

1. write _____
2. bake _____
3. read _____
4. visit _____
5. interview _____
6. fight _____
7. work _____
8. drive _____
9. dance _____

SPELLING AND PHONICS:
To do this activity, go to page 193.

✓ WRAP UP

- Write these words on the board: *partn<u>er</u>, neighb<u>or</u>, oth<u>er</u>*. Have students talk with a partner about why the underlined letters are NOT suffixes, and then share. (When the underlined letters are removed, the remaining letters do not form a word.)

PB PRACTICE BOOK ACTIVITY

See Activity B, Word Work, on Practice Book page 31.

ANSWER KEY

Word Detective: 1. wrestle; 2. teach; 3. paint; 4. sing; 5. act; 6. play.
Word Play: 1. writer; 2. baker; 3. reader; 4. visitor; 5. interviewer; 6. fighter; 7. worker; 8. driver; 9. dancer.
Spelling and Phonics: Silent *gh:* taught, caught, straight, height, neighbor, high, night, eight, thought, through, light, might, bought, right; *-gh* sounds like /f/: cough, laugh, tough, enough.

READING

UNIT 4 • STUDENT BOOK, PAGE 63

E GRAMMAR — Simple Past Tense

1. Listen Up When you tell a story, you usually use the simple past tense. Listen to each sentence. Point your thumb up 👍 if it sounds correct. Point your thumb down 👎 if it sounds wrong.

👍 👎 1. We both leaved our books at school.
👍 👎 2. Juan was late for school.
👍 👎 3. Tran fix a sandwich for lunch.
👍 👎 4. Lourdes turned her homework in late.
👍 👎 5. Parveen catched a cold.
👍 👎 6. I didn't went to the party.

2. Learn the Rule Learn how to form the past tense. Then do Activity 1 again.

THE SIMPLE PAST TENSE

Use the simple past tense to describe an action or event that took place at a specific time in the past.

1. Regular verbs add *–ed* or sometimes *–d* to form the simple past tense.
   Maria calls her sister once a week. She **called** her last night.

2. Irregular verbs have simple past tense forms that can be very different from the present tense. Check the dictionary if you're not sure.
   Sometimes I leave my books at home. This morning I **left** them on the bus!

3. When the simple past tense sentence is negative, use the auxiliary verb *did + not*. Do not change the main verb.
   I usually don't eat breakfast. I **didn't eat** breakfast this morning.

Many common verbs are irregular in the simple past tense: be (was/were), have (had), come (came), go (went), give (gave), take (took), speak (spoke), write (wrote).

3. Practice the Rule Write the simple past tense form of each verb below. Underline the irregular verbs.

draw *drew*   see _____   read _____
help _____   go   _____   want _____
eat   _____   hear _____   run   _____
listen _____   speak _____   walk _____
like _____   do   _____   drink _____

Trying to Be Cool **63**

E GRAMMAR

Standard
- Express past actions

WARM UP

- Have students watch as you perform a series of actions. For example you might open the door and close it. After each action, ask, *What did I do?* (You opened/closed the door.) Correct any incorrect past tense forms as necessary and write them on the board.

- Circle the *–ed* endings of the words on the board. Point out that some other past tense verbs don't have that ending. Explain that students will be learning about the different forms of the simple past tense in this lesson.

TEACHING THE LESSON

🎧 1. Listen Up

- Play the tape or CD or read the sentences aloud. Have students point their thumbs up if the sentence sounds correct, and down if it sounds wrong.

2. Learn the Rule

- Focusing on the explanations and examples, teach students the past tense forms. Call attention to the starburst. For more irregular verbs, see page 211.

- 🍒 **Think Aloud** Review the rules and lead students through the thinking process. For example: *I take my sister to school every day. How do I make the past tense? "I taked my sister to school yesterday" doesn't sound right. I'll check the Irregular Verbs List. The past tense of "take" is "took." I took my sister to school yesterday.*

- Repeat the Listen Up activity.

3. Practice the Rule

- Have students complete the activity and share out.

- Have students write their own sentences for three verbs in each column and then share their sentences with classmates.

✓ WRAP UP

- Write sentences with correct and incorrect past tense forms on the board. Include irregular verbs. Have students identify and correct errors.

PB PRACTICE BOOK ACTIVITY

See Activity C, Grammar, on Practice Book page 33.

ANSWER KEY

Listen Up: Correct sentences: 2, 4.

Practice the Rule: <u>drew</u>, helped, <u>ate</u>, listened, liked, <u>saw</u>, <u>went</u>, <u>heard</u>, <u>spoke</u>, <u>did</u>, <u>read</u>, wanted, <u>ran</u>, walked, <u>drank</u>.

Unit 4 **63**

UNIT 4 ▪ STUDENT BOOK, PAGE 64

F BRIDGE TO WRITING

Standards
- Read personal narratives
- Use reading strategies to unlock meaning
- Recall major points in a story
- Use descriptive adjectives

WARM UP

- Ask students to recall the things Tom, Robbie, and Sarah did. Tell students they are going to read three more stories about things kids did to be cool.

TEACHING THE LESSON

1. Before You Read

- **Heads Together** Ask students to tell a partner something they did to impress others when they were younger.
- **Shared Quick Write** Have students share as you write what they did on the board. Guide them in the use of past tense verb forms. Underline the past tense verbs in each sentence.

2. Let's Read

- Read the title of each story. Thinking aloud, predict what the first two stories are about (Reading Strategy box). Ask a volunteer to predict what the third story is about.
- **My Turn: Read Aloud/Think Aloud** Read the three passages aloud or play the tape or CD. Model correct phrasing and fluent reading. As you read, stop to comment on words.
- Now play the tape or CD or read the passages again. Ask students to think about whether or not the predictions were correct. Ask volunteers to share responses. Talk about the effects of a good title.
- Call attention to the starburst note on idioms. Provide several other

WRITING

F BRIDGE TO WRITING — Personal Narratives

READING STRATEGY
Predicting: When you predict, you use things like pictures and titles to help you guess what you're going to read about.

1. Before You Read You are going to read three more stories about stupid things that kids did to be cool. What is one thing you did when you were younger to impress other kids? Share your story with a partner.

2. Let's Read Each story has a title. As you read, use the titles to **predict** what the stories are about.

"Jump on the bandwagon" is an idiom. You have to learn the meaning of the whole phrase to understand it, not just the individual words.

Jumped on the cuffed-pants bandwagon
When I was 13, the "cool" kids **cuffed** their pants. I **jumped on the bandwagon** even though most of my pants were a little too short anyway. When I cuffed them, they barely covered my calves. I looked goofy, but at least I had cuffs!
—Jeremy, age 18

Permed my hair
Perms were **all the rage** in fourth grade. So I got my long, straight, beautiful hair **transformed** into a short, layered, curly bob. The 'cool' girls were doing weird things with their hair—crimping it, feathering and teasing bangs into a **tortured imitation** of a celery stalk. It totally **backfired** on me. I looked like a 9-year-old with 60-year-old hair.
—Tara, age 17

Tara makes her story interesting by using a lot of adjectives and unusual verbs, like transformed and backfired.

Dyed my hair bright orange
When I was 12, it seemed like all the "in" girls had blonde hair. So I used a lightener, and my nice brown hair turned bright orange! I looked like **Raggedy Ann** and felt really stupid.
—Julie, age 19

Source: Zillions: CONSUMER REPORTS® for Kids

cuff—to turn up the bottom of pant legs
jump on the bandwagon—to do what is popular with most people at the moment.
perm—to make hair curly using a chemical treatment
all the rage—very popular
transform—to change completely
tortured imitation—a bad copy
Raggedy Ann—a type of doll with bright red-orange hair

64 Unit 4

---

examples—each with the verb "jump"—*jump down your throat* (yell at someone), *jump the gun* (start before it's time, start a race before the starting gun fires).

- **Our Turn: Interactive Reading** Have students help you read each passage. Take turns with students reading a sentence or two aloud. After each of the stories, ask these three questions: *What did s/he do? Why did s/he do it? How did s/he feel about it later?*

As students read Jeremy's story, have them try to visualize what he looks like in his short pants and describe what they see.

- **Build Fluency** Read each short narrative aloud and then have students read after you.
- **Your Turn: Independent Reading** Have students read the passages on their own. Ask them to write down the lessons that the kids learned. Have students share out.

WRITING

UNIT 4 • STUDENT BOOK, PAGE 65

3. Making Content Connections Work with a partner. From the stories you have read, choose the three students you think did the stupidest things to be cool. Check (✓) their names. Summarize their stories by completing the chart below.

For help with summarizing, complete Mini-Unit, Part C on page 190.

- ☐ Tom
- ☐ Robbie
- ☐ Sarah
- ☐ Jeremy
- ☐ Julie
- ☐ Tara

Name	What they did	Why they did it	What they learned

4. Expanding Your Vocabulary

❶ Everybody has an image. The adjectives below describe a person's image. Match each word on the left with the word on the right that means the same thing or almost the same thing.

1. popular
2. mean
3. carefree
4. intelligent
5. immature
6. conceited
7. silly

a. stuck-up
b. childish
c. smart
d. well-liked
e. dumb
f. easygoing
g. nasty

❷ Is your own image of yourself the same as the image others have of you? Ask three classmates or family members how they would describe you. Complete the following chart.

How I describe myself:	How others describe me:

Trying to Be Cool **65**

- Have trios of students complete the matching activity. Try to include a student in each trio who probably knows the meaning of some of the words. Review the answers with the class. Then ask each trio to write a sentence using a *positive* word and a sentence using a *negative* word. Have them share their sentences.

- Read the words again, asking students to give you the same hand signals. If anyone points his or her thumb sideways, ask another student to define the word.

- Ask students to complete the first column of the chart with words they think describe them. Then have them ask at least three classmates or family members to choose words that they think describe the student and have students write these in the second column.

- Invite students to share their lists with classmates. Encourage them to think about why the other people might have different views of them than they have of themselves.

Access for All Encourage students with artistic talent to illustrate "image" words and then share the pictures with classmates.

PB PRACTICE BOOK ACTIVITY

See Activity D, Test-Taking Practice, on Practice Book pages 34 and 35.

See Activity E, Using New Vocabulary, on Practice Book page 36.

WRAP UP

- Have students write what they have learned about themselves in their notebooks.

ANSWER KEY

Expanding Your Vocabulary: 1. d; 2. g; 3. f; 4. c; 5. b; 6. a; 7. e.

3. Making Content Connections

- **Heads Together** Have a volunteer read the instructions. Explain the task to the class. Have students work in pairs, choosing the three kids they think did the stupidest things, and then working together to complete the chart.

- Copy the chart on the board. Identify the three teens that students believe did the stupidest things. Ask students to share information from their charts as you record.

4. Expanding Your Vocabulary

- Ask a volunteer to say what the word *image* means (what you think about yourself or what others think about you).

- Read the list of words, each of which could describe a person. As you read each word, have students point their thumbs up if they know what the word means, sideways if they have seen the word but are not sure what it means, and down if they have never seen the word.

Unit 4 65

UNIT 4 ▪ STUDENT BOOK, PAGE 66

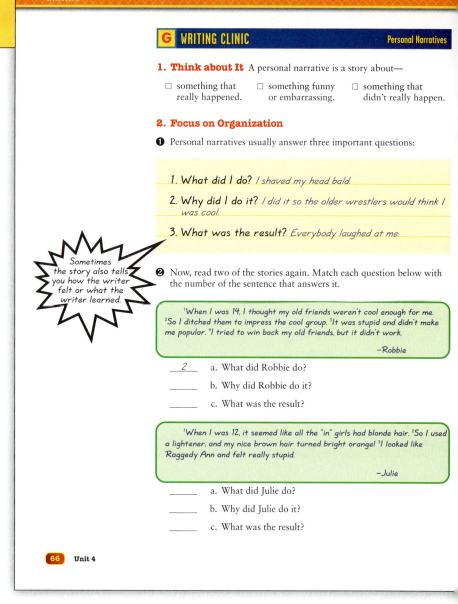

G WRITING CLINIC

Standards
- Identify the structural patterns found in personal narratives
- Identify cause and effect patterns
- Use language register appropriate to audience

WARM UP

- Ask students to think once again about the stories they have read. Ask: *What do all of the stories have in common?* (They're all about people who did things to be cool. They're all about the people who wrote the stories.)

TEACHING THE LESSON

1. Think about It

- Explain that *narrative* is another word for *story*. Ask students to provide examples of other types of narratives (novels, television shows, movies). Have them check what they think a *personal narrative* is.

- Tell students that the first response is correct, and then have them tell you why.

2. Focus on Organization

- Review the three important questions in Part 1, focusing on the examples. Noting the comment in the starburst, ask students how this writer might have felt or what he might have learned. (He might have felt foolish or embarrassed. He might have learned that changing himself to please others doesn't work.)

- Read the instructions for Part 2 and remind students to write their answers in the Student Book. Point out the superscripts that number the sentences in each paragraph. Tell students to use these sentence numbers to answer the questions.

- Review the correct answers with the class.

PB PRACTICE BOOK ACTIVITY

See Activity F, Focus on Organization, on Practice Book page 37.

66 Teacher's Edition

WRITING

3. Focus on Style

❶ The people who read what you write are called your audience. Choose the statement that describes the audiences for the stories on pages 60 and 64. Check (✓) the correct answer.

_____ 1. They're other students.
_____ 2. They're adults.
_____ 3. They're young children.

❷ Pretend that you wrote two letters about your family vacation—one to a friend, the other to a teacher. Take out a piece of paper. Write *To a Friend* on one side and *To a Teacher* on the other. Then write each sentence below on the correct side of the paper.

1. a. My family always takes really cheap vacations.
   b. My family always takes inexpensive vacations.
2. a. We usually go on vacation in June, when the weather is warm and sunny.
   b. We usually take off in June, when it's nice and hot out.
3. a. We stay clear of any trip that means getting on a plane—my parents are really tightwads!
   b. To save money, my parents prefer taking driving trips.
4. a. My parents drag me along. The idea of me staying at home alone freaks them out.
   b. My parents insist that I come along since they don't want to leave me at home without supervision.
5. a. This year, we piled into our funky old van and drove to a weird place called Water World.
   b. This year, the family climbed into our van and drove to Water World, a popular vacation destination.
6. a. Our vacation was very enjoyable. I can hardly wait for next summer to come!
   b. It turned out that I actually had an OK time. I guess I might agree to go along next summer.

You usually use formal language when you're talking to adults (like your teacher) or to people you don't know.

Trying to Be Cool 67

UNIT 4 • STUDENT BOOK, PAGE 67

- Read and discuss the directions for Part 2 and do the first item on the board with the class. Point out that *inexpensive* is a more formal way of saying *cheap*.

- 🍎 **Heads Together** Have students complete the activity in pairs. Review the correct answers by having one student read all the *To a Friend* sentences in sequence. Then have another student read all the *To a Teacher* sentences. Help students discuss why each sentence is appropriate for one audience or the other.

- Have volunteers recount the story—first where the audience is a teacher, then where the audience is a friend—as though they're talking to the person.

PB PRACTICE BOOK ACTIVITY

See Activity G, Focus on Style, on Practice Book page 28.

✓ WRAP UP

- Have students take turns making statements using either very formal language or very informal language. Have each student call on a classmate to rephrase the sentence using the opposite type of language. For example: Student A: *That movie sucked!* Student B: *That movie was terrible.*

ANSWER KEY

Focus on Organization 2: Robbie: 2, 1, 3 Julie: 2, 1, 3.

Focus on Style 1: 1.

Focus on Style 2: To a Friend: 1. a; 2. b; 3. a; 4. a; 5. a; 6. b. To a Teacher: 1. b; 2. a; 3. b; 4. b; 5. b; 6. a.

---

3. Focus on Style

🍎 **Let's Talk** Read the directions for Part 1. Ask: *What do you usually think of when you hear the word "audience"?* (A group of people in a movie theater.) Explain that most movies are aimed at a particular audience—children, teens, young adults, or older adults. Have students give examples of different movies. Ask: *What makes a movie good for one audience but not another?* (What it is about, the characters, the language.) Explain that people who read your writing are also an audience and that writers have to keep that audience in mind when writing.

- Have students identify the audience for the stories they have just read (other kids). Have students look back at the narratives and tell you what kind of language is used in them (formal or informal), identifying examples of words and phrases (*cool, ditched them, stupid*). If necessary explain the difference between formal and informal language.

Unit 4 67

UNIT 4 ▪ STUDENT BOOK, PAGE 68

H WRITER'S WORKSHOP

Standards
- Use the writing process: prewriting
- Sequence events
- Use dialogue to tell a story

1. Getting It Out
WARM UP

- Remind students that each of the stories they have read come from an article published in *Zillions*, a magazine for kids.

- Ask students to imagine that they are writing a class article about the same topic—silly things they did when they were younger. Explain that they will each contribute a story to the article.

TEACHING THE LESSON

- Have students remember something they did that was stupid or foolish. Caution students that they should select a memory they would be willing to share with others. Explain that the questions in Part 1 will help them choose what they want to write about.

- **Modeled Writing** Think of an example from your own past. Model responses to each of the five questions, thinking aloud as you write what you remember on the board.

- Have students write down their memories as they respond to each question. Move around the room offering suggestions and language support as needed.

- Invite volunteers to share their memories.

- Point out the cartoon frame and have a student read the words in the thought bubble and speech bubble aloud. Explain that students will turn their memories into a series of cartoon frames that tell their stories.

WRITING

H WRITER'S WORKSHOP   Personal Narratives

Your class will write a magazine article about dumb things students did when they were younger. Write a paragraph for the article that tells about something *you* did.

1. Getting It Out

❶ Begin by thinking of something you did that was stupid. Maybe you did it to be cool. Or maybe you just did it. Think about these important questions:

1. What did you do?
2. Why did you do it?
3. What was the result?
4. How did you feel about it?
5. Did you learn a lesson?

❷ Plan your story. Make a comic strip that shows what happened. Each square of a comic strip is called a frame. Look at the sample frame below.

68 Unit 4

---

68 Teacher's Edition

WRITING

UNIT 4 ▪ STUDENT BOOK, PAGE 69

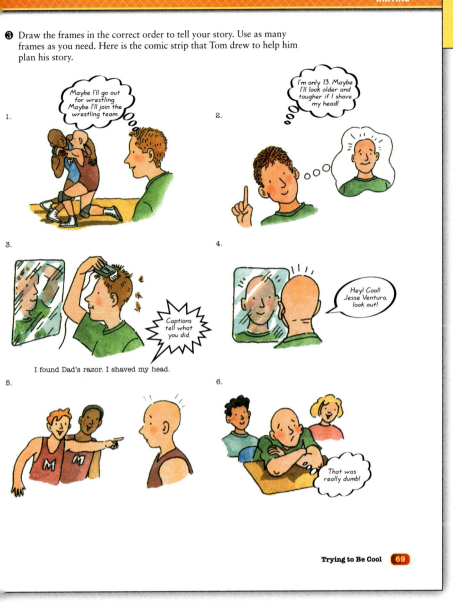

passages that describe awkward things that have happened to others. You may wish to screen stories and then have selected students share what they have found.

WRAP UP

- Ask two or three students to share their comic strips with classmates. Explain that during the next class session students will turn their comic strips into narratives.

> **TEACHING TIP** 💡 Before asking students to share personal stories, remind the class that they must respect other people's feelings. If there are stories that students might feel uncomfortable sharing with others, have them share their work only in writing and only with you.

- Have students read Tom's comic strip account aloud. Help students identify the various ways that information is communicated in the comic strip (the sequence of the pictures, captions, speech bubbles, and thought bubbles).

- Have students use the frames on Practice Book page 39 to create their cartoons.

- 🌈 **Access for All** Have students who need more instruction or support work in a small group with a teaching assistant, adult volunteer, or peer tutor. Have the group choose one student's story, then construct the story as a group, using the cartoon format.

📘 PRACTICE BOOK ACTIVITY

See Activity H, Writer's Workshop, on Practice Book page 39.

- **Using Technology** Suggest that students use the Internet to explore other people's embarrassing moments. The key words *embarrassing teen moments* will lead them to collections of short

Unit 4   69

UNIT 4 ■ STUDENT BOOK, PAGE 70

H Writer's Workshop

> **Standard**
> - Use the writing process: drafting, revising, and editing
> - Give a short oral narrative presentation

2. Getting It Down
WARM UP
- Have one or two more students share their comic strips. Help students see how each comic strip answers the five questions from page 68.

TEACHING THE LESSON
- Have students turn their comic strips into outlines, using the planner in Part 1.
- Have a volunteer read Julie's story to the class. Note the comments in each speech bubble.
- Ask students to think about the language Julie uses: *Is it formal or informal?*
- Have students draft their stories.

WRAP UP
- Have students prepare for Getting It Right by reviewing the ChecBric for this unit on their own, underlining indicators they're not sure about.

3. Getting It Right
WARM UP
- Guide students through the ChecBric for this unit. Explain that they will use the ChecBric to prepare a final draft of their writing.

WRITING

2. Getting It Down

❶ Turn your comic strip into an outline. Use this planner.

> Julie's story is written in a friendly style. It's like she's talking to the reader.

1. What I did: _____
2. Why I did it: _____
3. The result: _____

> Julie tells **what she did**. She tells **why she did it**. She describes **the result**.

❷ Now turn your outline into a paragraph. Here is what Julie wrote:

> When I was 13, I **thought I was really fat**. So I **went on a diet**. **I lost ten pounds, but it didn't make me popular. It just made me hungry.** All I did was worry about my weight, so I **am** no fun to hang out with. So instead of dieting, I switched to jogging. I'm much happier now!

> Ooops! The **verb** is in the present tense!

MINI-LESSON
Commas with *When*: If a sentence starts with *when*, use a comma to separate the two parts of the sentence: *When you finish,* put everything away.

3. Getting It Right Now take a careful look at what you have written. Use this guide to revise your story.

Questions to ask...	How to check...	How to revise if you need to...
1. Did I tell what I did?	Underline the sentence that tells what you did.	Add details so that the reader knows what you did.
2. Did I tell why I did it?	the sentence that explains why.	Add details that tell the reader your reasons for doing what you did.
3. Did I tell what happened as a result?	Put a star (★) in front of the sentence that tells what the result was.	Add a sentence that describes the result.

TEACHING THE LESSON
- Have students use the information in the chart and the ChecBric to revise their work.
- 🍎 **Group Share** Have students share their stories in groups of four or five. Have them give each other feedback on their stories and then make revisions as necessary.
- 🍎 **Mini-Lesson on Conventions** Point out the Mini-Lesson box. Ask volunteers to write sentences with *when* on the board.

WRAP UP
- As students revise, suggest that they look for ways to make their descriptions more lively. Can they use words to help their audience picture the situations?
- 📁 Give students time to fill out the ChecBric on Practice Book page 107. Ask them to attach it to their writing when they put it in their portfolios.

WRITING

UNIT 4 ■ STUDENT BOOK, PAGE 71

4. Presenting It Share your story with your classmates.

1. Show your comic strip to your classmates. Then read your story aloud. Read slowly and speak clearly.
2. Ask if anyone else ever did the same thing. Ask what happened.
3. Ask for feedback from your classmates.

Trying to Be Cool 71

- Have other students take notes as they listen to each story. Consider having a volunteer retell each story after it is presented.

- After each presentation, have other students tell the presenter what they liked about the story. Encourage students to ask questions.

 Using Technology If possible, offer to record individual presentations using audio or video equipment. This provides strong motivation for careful preparation. Also, watching the playback privately, students can monitor their own presentation style and language use.

✓ WRAP UP

- Ask students to write in their **notebooks** about the most memorable or interesting personal narrative they encountered in this unit, explaining why it was memorable or interesting.

4. Presenting It
WARM UP

- It's time for students to present their stories! Remind them that their stories should engage, or interest, the audience.

- As a class, develop a simple presentation checklist. In addition to content and organization, focus on speaking skills (poise, expression, volume, posture, eye contact), enthusiasm, use of visuals, creativity, involvement of the audience, and length of presentation.

TEACHING THE LESSON

- Tell students to pay attention to two things as they present:

  1. Use a loud and clear voice.
  2. Use eye contact to keep your audience interested.

  Write these guidelines (and others you may have) on the board.

Unit 4   71

UNIT 4 ■ STUDENT BOOK, PAGE 72

BEYOND THE UNIT

Standards
- Use word-processing conventions
- Respond to a poem
- Write a poem based on a model

1. On Assignment

WARM UP

- Ask students to share the reasons the Internet is useful. What would people miss out on if they couldn't go online?
- Ask students what Web sites they visit regularly. You might wish to list them on the board. Then invite them to tell the class about the kind of content each site contains.

TEACHING THE LESSON

- Discuss the Web site shown in the Student Book. Read the menu of links to "Real Life Stories" aloud and ask students to raise their hands to show which link their story relates to.

- 🍎 **Heads Together** Have students form groups based on the link that relates to their narrative. If some groups are larger than four, split them up.

- Have students take turns reading their stories to their group. Encourage the group to come up with a variety of possible titles for each narrative and work together to choose the best one.

- Have students type their stories at home or in the computer lab and bring in enough copies for each person in the class.

- Give each student a packet of stories.

- 💻 **Using Technology** If time and resources are available in your school, you may be able to have students' work published on a local Web site.

BEYOND THE UNIT

1. On Assignment Imagine that you and your classmates have been asked to submit your stories to kidzstories.com, an online magazine for kids.

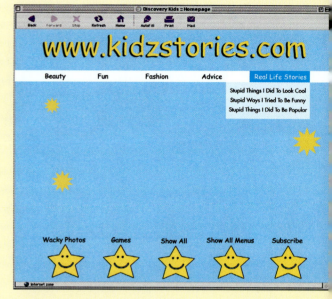

Read the menu of links to "Real Life Stories."

❶ Form a group with classmates who wrote stories related to the same link.

❷ Reread your story aloud to your group. As a group, make up a good title for your story.

❸ Using a computer, type your story, then print out enough copies for each person in class.

❹ Collect a story from each of your classmates. Imagine that you are reading their stories on the Web!

Ask local administrators about the possibility of displaying students' work in this manner.

✓ WRAP UP

🍎 **Outcome Sentence** Have students complete this sentence stem, then share:

The Internet is useful because _____.

2. Link to Literature

SHARED READING Read the poem by famous American poet Langston Hughes. What kind of language does he use?

LET'S TALK Answer the questions.

1. What can you tell about the speaker in the poem?
2. What is the speaker's motto in your own words?
3. What is your own motto? Write it down then share with your classmates.

ABOUT THE AUTHOR

Langston Hughes was born in Joplin, Missouri, in 1902 and died in 1967. He was famous for writing stories and poems that gave people an idea about true African-American culture.

dig—to like or understand someone or something
jive—jazz music or insincere talk
motto—what somebody believes
in return—by other people

Motto
Langston Hughes

I play it cool
And dig all jive.
That's the reason
I stay alive.

My motto,
As I live and learn,
is: Dig And Be Dug
In Return.

This is how jazz musicians talk.

Source: *The Collected Poems of Langston Hughes* by Langston Hughes

Trying to Be Cool 73

UNIT 4 ■ STUDENT BOOK, PAGE 73

2. Link to Literature

WARM UP

- Have students look at the illustration. Who do they see? Do any students listen to jazz? Do they like it? How do jazz musicians talk? Tell students that the poem, "Motto," will help them understand how jazz musicians talk.

TEACHING TIP Play a song from a jazz CD.

TEACHING THE LESSON

- Read the poem, "Motto," by Langston Hughes aloud to the class. Ask students what a *motto* is (a short saying that states a basic personal belief). For example: *All great achievements require time*—Maya Angelou.

- Discuss glossed words. Help students use each one in an original sentence. For example: My motto is "Live for today." I dig Mexican food. I think most pop stars talk a lot of jive. Be nice to me and I'll be nice to you in return.

- Now play the tape or CD twice. The first time, ask students to clap along with the rhythm of the poem. After the second time, ask volunteers to point out the rhyming words. If necessary, explain what rhyming means.

- **Shared Reading** Read the poem aloud as students follow along. Model fluency and expression, using pauses to help clearly communicate the meaning of the phrases. Have volunteers read the poem aloud. Encourage them to read with expression.

- **Let's Talk** Use the questions to lead a discussion of the poem.

- Have students write their own mottoes.

✓ WRAP UP

- **Outcome Sentence** Have students complete this sentence stem, then share:

  My motto is _____ because _____.

PB PRACTICE BOOK ACTIVITY

See Activity I, Responding to Literature, on Practice Book page 40.

✓ UNIT WRAP UP

- Have students write in their **notebooks** about what they have learned about themselves and others in this unit.

Unit 4 73

Unit 5 Who Eats What?
Unit Overview

Section	At a Glance	Standards
Before You Begin	Students begin to explore what they know about the food chain.	■ Derive meaning from visual information
A. Connecting to Your Life	Students identify animals and plants in the food chain.	■ Share information and ideas
B. Getting Ready to Read	Students learn useful vocabulary and discuss the transfer of energy in nature.	■ Use context to understand the meaning of unfamiliar words ■ Use complete sentences to express ideas about a topic
C. Reading to Learn	Students read and learn about the food chain. PRACTICE BOOK: Students complete a flow chart, then describe a food chain.	■ Identify cause and effect patterns in text
D. Word Work	Students explore compounds with adjectives. PRACTICE BOOK: Students practice forming compound words.	■ Use knowledge of compound words to determine word meaning ■ Identify sound/spelling relationships
E. Grammar	Students focus on when the present tense and the past tense are used. PRACTICE BOOK: Students decide whether to use the present or past tense.	■ Use verb tenses correctly
F. Bridge to Writing	Students read about how the killing of Pacific sea otters had a serious impact on the food chain. PRACTICE BOOK: Students practice taking Reading Vocabulary and Reading Comprehension tests. PRACTICE BOOK: Students write a paragraph using new vocabulary.	■ Use background knowledge to predict ■ Identify cause and effect patterns in text ■ Use a diagram to express information found in text

Section	At a Glance	Standards
G. Writing Clinic	Students use a flow diagram to show relationships in the food chain. PRACTICE BOOK: Students draw flow diagrams to illustrate food chains. PRACTICE BOOK: Students combine sentences using the relative pronoun *that*.	■ Identify cause and effect patterns in expository text ■ Combine short related sentences to form complex sentences
H1. Writer's Workshop: Getting It Out	Students plan articles they are to write about food chains on land or in the sea.	■ Use the writing process: prewriting ■ Create a diagram that conveys information accurately ■ Write a short article that explains a process
H2. Writer's Workshop: Getting It Down	Students turn their flow diagrams into an outline. Then they use the outline to write the first draft of an article. PRACTICE BOOK: Students practice creating a flow diagram based on an outline.	■ Use the writing process: drafting ■ Use an outline to organize writing
H3. Writer's Workshop: Getting It Right	Students review and revise their articles.	■ Use the writing process: revising for accuracy, organization, and clarity
H4. Writer's Workshop: Presenting It	Students present their articles to their classmates and take notes on each other's presentations.	■ Give an oral presentation that explains a process ■ Organize ideas logically ■ Use notes to summarize ideas given in presentations by others
I. Beyond the Unit	Students imagine that they are forest animals, explaining why they are important to the environment. Students read a poem called "Links in a Food Chain." PRACTICE BOOK: Students make a flow diagram to illustrate the poem, "Links in a Food Chain."	■ Use the research process ■ Give a short oral presentation ■ Respond to a poem

UNIT 5 ■ STUDENT BOOK, PAGE 74

Unit 5

Who Eats What

BEFORE YOU BEGIN

Standard
- Derive meaning from visual information

- Point to the picture and the caption on page 75.
- Have students describe what they see happening in the picture. Record their ideas on the board, using complete sentences.
- Focus on the caption. Have a volunteer explain why the caption is amusing. Ask other students to give the picture a different caption.
- Ask students why animals eat each other.
- Draw a T-chart on the board. Label the left-hand column, "What do we know?" Label the right-hand column, "What do we wonder about?" Ask: *Why do animals eat other animals?* Record student responses in the left-hand column. Copy the chart on a large piece of paper or an overhead transparency to use later in the unit. Make sure there is enough room for additional information to be added.

Read...
- A selection about the food chain.

- A report about sea otters disappearing off the west coast of North America.

 Link to Literature
- A poem called "Links in the Food Chain."

74 Unit 5

Objectives:

Reading:
- Following the explanation of a process
- Understanding cause and effect
- Strategies: Taking notes, making a diagram
- Literature: Responding to a poem

Writing:
- Explaining a process
- Making a flow diagram
- Combining sentences with *that* clauses

Vocabulary:
- Using specific terminology
- Learning names for ocean plants and animals

Listening/Speaking:
- Listening to a poem
- Giving examples
- Giving feedback

Grammar:
- Using the present vs. past tense

Spelling and Phonics:
- Spelling the /oo/ sound as in *food* and *blue*

74 Teacher's Edition

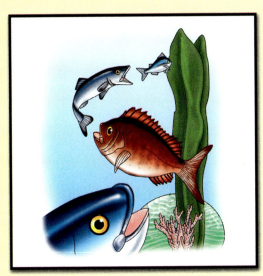

Dinnertime

BEFORE YOU BEGIN

Talk with your classmates.

1. Look at the picture. Describe what you see.
2. Read the caption. Think of another caption for the picture.
3. Why do animals eat other animals?

Who Eats What? 75

UNIT 5 ▪ STUDENT BOOK, PAGE 76

A CONNECTING TO YOUR LIFE

Standard
- Share information and ideas

WARM UP

- Ask: *Do you enjoy playing sports? Going to the mall? Going to the movies?* Tell students that to do these things, their bodies need energy, or strength. Ask: *Where does that energy come from?* Record their ideas.

- **Build Background** Explain that humans—like all other animals—get their energy from the food they eat, and that energy is passed from animal to animal through the food chain. Tell students that they are going to learn what a "food chain" is and how it works.

TEACHING THE LESSON

🎧 1. Tuning In

- Point out the box with the numbers 5–1 and the word "flower" after the 1. Tell students that they are going to listen to a poem twice. The first time they listen, have them record the names of each animal they hear, from *bottom to top*. (For example, the first animal they will hear named is a bug. They should write *bug* next to the 2.)

2. Talking It Over

- **Heads Together** Explain that the animals in each pair are related, or connected to, each other. Read the question aloud: *What kind of relationship does each pair of creatures have?* Have students talk with a partner to answer the question. Have them write their answers on a sheet of paper.

- Invite volunteers to share their answers. Compare responses.

READING

A CONNECTING TO YOUR LIFE

🎧 **1. Tuning In** Look at the numbered box to the right. Listen to the poem. List each animal in order as you hear its name. How is each animal on your list related to the animal or plant *below* it?

5. _____
4. _____
3. _____
2. _____
1. *flower*

2. Talking It Over Work with a partner to answer the question below. Then compare your answer with your classmates' answers.

Question: What kind of relationship does each pair of creatures in this chart have?

Answer: _____

1. Cat/Mouse
2. Spider/Fly
3. Caterpillar/Leaf
4. Bird/Caterpillar
5. Shark/Tuna
6. Human/Chicken

Think again about the answer to the question. What do you think this unit is about?

_____ 1. how plants and animals depend on each other to live
_____ 2. what you will see when you visit the zoo
_____ 3. how mean animals can be to each other

76 Unit 5

- Refer students to their numbered lists in "Tuning In." Ask volunteers to tell you which animals go on which numbered blank. Discuss how the plant and animals are related.

- Ask students what they predict the unit will be about.

✓ WRAP UP

- Have students revisit the T-chart they began to construct, adding to the "What do we wonder about?" column. Then have students generate questions they would like answered. Once again, save the chart for later.

ANSWER KEY

Tuning In: 1. flower; 2. bug; 3. bird; 4. snake; 5. fox. Each animal on the list eats the one below it.

Talking It Over: Possible answer: The bigger animal eats the smaller one.

Talking It Over: 1.

76 Teacher's Edition

READING

UNIT 5 ▪ STUDENT BOOK, PAGE 77

B GETTING READY TO READ

1. Learning New Words Read the sentences below. Try to guess the meanings of the underlined words.

1. Here is the <u>chain</u> of events: Juan made a face, the teacher saw him, she gave him detention.
2. A healthy breakfast gives me <u>energy</u> and strength.
3. Smoking can make you very ill. It <u>causes</u> cancer.
4. It's important to take care of the land, the water, the air, the plants, and the animals—they are all part of our <u>environment</u>.
5. Children can't survive without someone to take care of them. They <u>depend on</u> their parents.

Children depend on their parents.

Now match each word on the left with the correct definition on the right.

1. chain   a. a source of power or strength
2. energy   b. the natural world around us
3. cause   c. a sequence of closely connected things
4. environment   d. to need and rely on
5. depend on   e. to make something happen

2. Talking It Over Work with a partner. Think about these living things. How are they related to each other?

1.   2.  3.   4.
A squirrel   A grasshopper   A hawk   Grass

CONNECT TO THE WEB. CHECK IT OUT.
Visit the Smithsonian National Zoological Park at www.si.edu/natzoo
Go to the American Library Association's "Great Web Sites for Kids" for links to animal web sites at www.ala.org

Who Eats What?   77

B GETTING READY TO READ

Standards
- Use context to understand the meaning of unfamiliar words
- Use complete sentences to express ideas about a topic

WARM UP
- Ask students to think about the meat in a hamburger. Ask: *Where does the energy in that food come from?* (From eating grass.) *Where does the grass get its energy?* (From the sun and water.) Explain that these are all examples of the food chain.

TEACHING THE LESSON

1. Learning New Words
- Write the new words on the board. Have students work in groups of three, trying to write a definition for each word or phrase. Have them share their definitions and set them aside for the next step.
- Have students open their books, read sentences 1–5, and revise their original definitions. Have them share again.
- Now have groups match each word to its definition and then share out. Confirm the correct answers.
- Have students revisit their original definitions one more time, modifying them as needed. Ask volunteers to share changes they made.
- Have each group write an original sentence for each word. Have students share out.

2. Talking It Over
- **Heads Together** Read the directions aloud and have students work in pairs to complete the activity.
- Review students' responses.

✓ WRAP UP
- Brainstorm with students a short list of other animals not mentioned in the unit and then discuss together what each one depends on for energy.

ANSWER KEY
Learning New Words: 1. c; 2. a; 3. e; 4. b; 5. d.

Talking It Over: Possible answers: Grasshoppers eat grass, and hawks eat squirrels.

Unit 5   77

UNIT 5 ■ STUDENT BOOK, PAGE 78

C READING TO LEARN

Standard
- Identify cause and effect patterns in text

WARM UP

- Have the class revisit the T-chart, this time focusing on the list of things they would like to learn about the food chain. Invite students to add to the chart.

TEACHING THE LESSON

1. Before You Read

🍎 **Heads Together** Have students work in pairs. Have them choose an animal and list all the things it eats. Have volunteers share out.

🎧 **2. Let's Read**

♻️ Explain that taking notes can help you understand and remember what you read (Reading Strategy box). Tell students to use single words and short phrases as they take notes.

🍎 **My Turn: Aloud/Think Aloud** Read the article aloud or play the tape or CD one paragraph at a time. Model correct phrasing and fluent reading and stop to comment on vocabulary and ideas.

- **Build Fluency** Read the first sentence of a paragraph. Ask students what they think the rest of the paragraph will say.

🍎 **Our Turn: Interactive Reading** Have students help you read the passage. Read the first sentence of each paragraph yourself. Call on individuals to read other sentences. As students read, focus on glossed words, ask questions, and make comments.

✓ **Question All-Write** Ask: *Why are human beings at the top of the food chain? How are plants different from other living things?* Have students write one- or two-sentence responses and share out.

🍎 **Your Turn: Independent Reading** Have students read the passage on their own, taking notes on each animal and what it eats.

🍎 **Heads Together** After they have read, have students compare the notes they have taken with a partner's. Invite them to make changes or additions based on their partner's notes.

CULTURE NOTE

Be aware of personal or religious beliefs about food, and be sensitive to these beliefs during class discussions. For example, eating pork may be objectionable to some students. Some students may be vegetarians and opposed to eating meat.

READING

C READING TO LEARN   Explaining a Process

1. Before You Read Talk with a partner. Write the name of an animal. Make a list of the things it eats.

For help with taking notes, complete Mini-Unit, Part B on page 184.

READING STRATEGY
Note-taking:
As you read, you can write down interesting facts or ideas to help you remember them.

🎧 **2. Let's Read** You are going to read information about the food chain. As you read, **take notes**. Write down the name of each animal and what it eats.

Who Eats What?

¹ A **caterpillar** is eating a leaf on an apple tree. Later the caterpillar is spotted by a **wren**. It becomes part of the wren's dinner. Still later the wren is eaten by a **hawk**. Leaf, caterpillar, wren, and hawk are all linked. Together they form a food chain. Each is a link to the chain.

² The hawk is the top of the food chain because no other animal attacks and eats hawks. The animal at the top of a food chain is always the last eater—the one nobody else eats. Suppose you eat an apple off the tree. That makes you part of a short food chain—the apple and you. You are the top of the food chain. Or suppose you drink a glass of milk. Now you are the top of a slightly longer food chain. The milk came from a cow, and the cow ate the grass. So this chain is grass, cow, you.

³ Food is the **fuel** our bodies need. Food keeps us alive. It gives us the energy we need to grow, move, and do many other things. The same thing is true for caterpillars, wrens, hawks—for all animals. All must find or catch the foods they need.

⁴ Every living thing you see is part of at least one food chain. All these food chains begin with green plants. Green plants are the only living things that can make their own food. They are the only living things that do not need to eat something else.

⁵ Green plants take energy from sunlight. They use it to make food out of water and air.

⁶ All animals depend on green plants for food, even animals that don't eat plants. Hawks, for example, do not eat green plants. But the hawk ate the wren that ate the caterpillar that ate the leaf of a green plant. And so the hawk is linked to green plants through the food chain. It needs the plants as much as the caterpillar does.

Source: Who Eats What? Food Chains and Food Webs by Patricia Lauber

This is called a flow diagram.

caterpillar—an early stage of a butterfly; like a hairy worm
wren—a type of tiny bird
hawk—a type of meat-eating bird similar to an eagle
fuel—something that helps create energy

READING

UNIT 5 ▪ STUDENT BOOK, PAGE 79

3. Unlocking Meaning

❶ **Finding the Main Idea** Which of the following statements says what the reading selection is mostly about? Check (✓) the correct answer.

_____ 1. All animals need food to live.

_____ 2. Animals are linked to other animals and plants through the food chain.

_____ 3. Some animals eat both plants and other animals.

❷ **Finding Details**

1. Number the following events in the correct order.

_____ Hawks eat wrens.

_____ Caterpillars eat leaves.

_____ Wrens eat caterpillars.

2. Read the sentences below. Write T for *True* and F for *False*.

_F_ 1. Animals at the bottom of the food chain are safe from other animals.

_____ 2. Human beings are at the bottom of the food chain.

_____ 3. Food gives our bodies energy.

_____ 4. All food chains begin with insects.

_____ 5. Green plants take their energy from the soil.

_____ 6. All animals eat some type of green plants.

_____ 7. All animals are linked to green plants through the food chain.

❸ **Think about It** Talk with a partner. Imagine that there are no more green plants on earth. What would happen to hawks? Why?

❹ **Before You Move On** Work in a small group. Make a "food chain" for the ingredients in a cheeseburger.

1. Make a list of the ingredients in a "typical" cheeseburger.
2. Circle one ingredient.
3. Write what the ingredient depends on for energy.
4. Draw a food chain for the ingredient. Include yourself at the top of the food chain.

Who Eats What? **79**

3. Unlocking Meaning

✓ FINDING THE MAIN IDEA

■ Read each statement aloud as students follow along. Have students identify the main idea using finger signals.

■ As you review the answer, point out that sentence 1 is too general and 3 is too specific. Sentence 2 is correct because each paragraph of the reading describes an aspect of the food chain.

✓ **Sentence Synthesis** Ask students to write one sentence that summarizes the main idea of the reading selection. (Living things near the top of the food chain use the energy of living things lower down on the chain.)

✓ FINDING DETAILS

Heads Together Have students work individually to complete the activities. Have them share and compare their responses.

THINK ABOUT IT

Heads Together Have pairs of students discuss what would happen to hawks if there were no more green plants on earth. Have volunteers share.

BEFORE YOU MOVE ON

Team Talk Have students work in small groups to create a food chain for one of the ingredients in a cheeseburger.

Shared Writing As groups share their food chains, have the class help you record their ideas in sentence form to create simple paragraphs.

✓ WRAP UP

Outcome Sentences Write these sentence stems on the board:

I learned that _____.

I still wonder about _____.

Have students think back to the reading, complete each sentence and then share out as you make additions to the T-chart the class has created.

PB PRACTICE BOOK ACTIVITY

See Activity A, Revisit and Retell, on Practice Book page 41.

ANSWER KEY

Finding the Main Idea: 2.

Finding Details 1: 3, 1, 2.

Finding Details 2: 1. F; 2. F; 3. T; 4. F; 5. F; 6. F; 7. T.

Think about It: Possible answer: First the insects would die without green plants to eat; then the birds that eat insects would die; then hawks would die without small birds to eat.

Before You Move On: Answers will vary.

Unit 5 **79**

UNIT 5 ■ STUDENT BOOK, PAGE 80

D WORD WORK

Standards
- Use knowledge of compound words to determine word meaning
- Identify sound/spelling relationships

WARM UP

- Write the following two lists of words on the board: List 1: *green, crying, cloudy* List 2: *sky, plants, baby*. Ask students to make two-word combinations that make sense (green plants, crying baby, cloudy sky). Point out that we can make the meaning of a word more specific by adding another word in front of it.

TEACHING THE LESSON

1. Word Detective

- Have students complete the activity. Explain that each compound has a word in it that will help them match the name to its picture.
- Review the correct answers with the class.

2. Word Study

- Refer students to the chart. Ask: *Where do saltwater crocodiles live? What does a hammerhead shark look like? What does a killer whale do?*

3. Word Play

- Refer students to the photo of the golden retriever. Ask what the word "golden" describes. Have students complete the activity and then share out. Review the answers.

Spelling and Phonics

- **Heads Together** Have students listen to the words and say what they notice about the red letters. (The sound /o͞o/ is spelled in different ways.)
- Have students complete each word. Go over the answers.

READING

D WORD WORK

1. Word Detective Match each name with a picture.

- _e_ 1. golden retriever
- ___ 2. black bear
- ___ 3. praying mantis
- ___ 4. vampire bat
- ___ 5. rattlesnake
- ___ 6. yellow jacket
- ___ 7. German shepherd
- ___ 8. hammerhead shark

a.  b.  c.   d.

e.  f.   g.   h.

SPELLING AND PHONICS: To do this activity, go to page 194.

2. Word Study You can make some nouns more specific by adding another word. For example, many animals have names that explain where they come from, what they look like, or what they do.

WHERE IT COMES FROM OR LIVES	WHAT IT LOOKS LIKE	WHAT IT DOES
saltwater crocodile	hammerhead shark	killer whale

3. Word Play Make a chart like the one in Activity 2. Look at the animal names in Activity 1. Decide what each name tells you and put it in the correct place on the chart. Some animals may fit in more than one place.

✓ WRAP UP

- Write the following words on the board: *cat, bear, tree*. Ask students to choose one word and then add other words to make the meaning more specific. Give them two minutes to complete the activity. Write the responses on the board as students volunteer them.

PB PRACTICE BOOK ACTIVITY

See Activity B, Word Work, on Practice Book page 42.

ANSWER KEY

Word Detective: 1. e; 2. f; 3. g; 4. d; 5. a; 6. h; 7. c; 8. b.

Word Play: Where It Comes From: German shepherd; **What It Looks Like:** golden retriever, black bear, praying mantis, vampire bat, rattlesnake, yellow jacket, hammerhead shark; **What It Does:** praying mantis, rattlesnake (golden retriever, vampire bat also acceptable).

Spelling and Phonics: a. shamp<u>oo</u>; b. st<u>ew</u>; c. scr<u>ew</u>; d. bl<u>ue</u>; e. r<u>u</u>de; f. gl<u>ue</u>; g. st<u>u</u>dent; h. gr<u>ou</u>p; i. m<u>o</u>ve; j. z<u>oo</u>; k. s<u>oo</u>n; l. y<u>ou</u>.

E GRAMMAR — Present Tense vs. Past Tense

1. Listen Up Listen to each sentence. If it describes something that is always or usually true, hold up one finger. If it is about something that happened in the past, hold up two fingers.

1. Caterpillars eat leaves.
2. The wren ate the caterpillar for dinner.
3. All food chains begin with green plants.
4. Green plants take energy from sunlight.
5. The spider caught the fly in its web.
6. Hawks do not eat green plants.

2. Learn the Rule Read these rules for when to use the present and past tenses, then do Activity 1 again.

PRESENT TENSE VS. PAST TENSE

1. When you want to talk about things that are always or usually true, use the *present tense*.

   Most cats **eat** mice.   The sun **comes** up every morning.

2. When you want to talk about an event that happened in the past, use the *past tense*.

   The cat **ate** the mouse that it **caught** under the house.   We **saw** a full moon last night.

3. Practice the Rule Complete each sentence below with the correct form of the verb in parentheses.

1. Many animals (eat/ate) ____eat____ plants for their food.
2. Plants (use/used) _____ energy from the sun.
3. The hawk was hungry. He (eats/ate) _____ the mouse.
4. Food (gives/gave) _____ our bodies energy.
5. The shark (attack/attacked) _____ the swimmer. It tore him in two.
6. In the early 1800s, cowboys (kill/killed) _____ nearly all the buffalo.
7. Wrens (are/were) _____ one of a hawk's favorite foods.
8. Hawks never (eat/ate) _____ plants. They only eat animals.

Who Eats What? 81

E GRAMMAR

Standard
- Use verb tenses correctly

WARM UP

- Write these incorrect sentences on the board:

  I go to bed at 10:00 last night.
  I usually went to bed by 9:00.

  Have students identify and correct each error, explaining the correction.

UNIT 5 ■ STUDENT BOOK, PAGE 81

✓ TEACHING THE LESSON

1. Listen Up

- Play the tape or CD, or read the sentences twice. Have students hold up one finger if a sentence describes something that is always true, and two fingers if it describes the past.

2. Learn the Rule

- Read each rule and ask a volunteer to explain it in his or her own words. As you discuss each tense, ask students to help make additional sentences that relate to their own lives. For example, *I go to school early every day. Yesterday I went to school at 7:30.*

- Repeat the Listen Up activity. Revisit any sentences that students get wrong.

3. Practice the Rule

- Read the directions and have students complete the activity. Suggest that students ask themselves the question: *Is this something that happens every day, or is it something that happened in the past?*

- Have students share their completed sentences.

✓ WRAP UP

- Write several base forms of verbs on the board and ask students to take turns making pairs of statements using the present and past tenses. For example, *I study every night. Last night I studied for three hours.* Possible verbs: study, get up, have biology class, play soccer, etc.

PB PRACTICE BOOK ACTIVITY

See Activity C, Grammar, on Practice Book page 43.

ANSWER KEY

Listen Up: Always true: 1, 3, 4, 6; Past: 2, 5.
Practice the Rule: 1. eat; 2. use; 3. ate; 4. gives; 5. attacked; 6. killed; 7. are; 8. eat.

UNIT 5 ▪ STUDENT BOOK, PAGE 82

F BRIDGE TO WRITING

Standards
- Use background knowledge to predict
- Identify cause and effect patterns in text
- Use a diagram to express information found in text

WARM UP
- Refer to the T-chart the class created at the start of the unit. What do they know about the food chain? What do they wonder about?
- Tell students that one thing *you* wonder about is what would happen if the chain were somehow broken. Add this question to the T-chart.

TEACHING THE LESSON

1. Before You Read
🍎 **Heads Together** Have students work in groups to discuss effects on the food chain if wrens, caterpillars, or green plants disappeared. (Without the wrens, there would be too many caterpillars. They would eat up the green plants. Many of the caterpillars and other insects wouldn't have enough food. There would be less food for the birds.)

🎧 **2. Let's Read**
- Have students look at the flow diagram on page 78. Tell them that they are going to make a flow diagram as they read (Reading Strategy box).
- 🍎 **My Turn: Read Aloud/Think Aloud** Read the passage aloud or play the tape or CD. Model correct phrasing and fluent reading. As you read, stop to comment on unfamiliar vocabulary. Talk with students about the ideas in the passage.

READING

F BRIDGE TO WRITING — Explaining a Process

1. Before You Read Look again at the flow diagram on page 78. What do you think might happen if the wren disappeared from the food chain? What would happen to the caterpillars? What would happen to the green plants?

READING STRATEGY
Making Diagrams: Making a diagram can help you understand what happened to someone or something in a story or an article.

🎧 **2. Let's Read** This article describes what happened when people killed so many sea otters that they almost disappeared completely. As you read, **make a diagram** that shows what happened to the otter.

Why do you think the kelp, eagles, harbor seals, and fish disappeared?

Humans often make changes in food chains. Then they find that one change causes other changes. That was what happened when hunters killed nearly all the Pacific sea otters.

² The otters lived off the west coast of North America. They lived in beds of giant seaweed, called kelp. Every year thousands of otters were killed for their fur. By the early 1900s almost none were left. But as the otters disappeared, so did beds of kelp. And so did eagles, harbor seals, and fish. What had happened? The answer lay in the kelp.

³ Kelp is a green plant at the start of many food chains. It is eaten by tiny animals that are eaten by bigger animals that are eaten by fish. The fish are food for eagles and seals, as well as people.

⁴ Kelp is also eaten by spiny animals called sea urchins. In eating, they may cut off stems at the seafloor. The kelp then floats away.

⁵ Sea urchins are one of the foods otters like best. But when hunters killed the otters, there was no one to eat the urchins. The urchins destroyed the kelp beds.

⁶ Once the hunting stopped, the otters made a comeback. They ate sea urchins, and the kelp began to do well. When the kelp did well, the fish came back—and so did the eagles, seals, and fishermen.

Sea otters are still endangered. What do you think that means?

Source: *Who Eats What? Food Chains and Food Webs* by Patricia Lauber

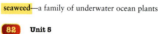

seaweed—a family of underwater ocean plants   **destroy**—to put an end to

82 Unit 5

🍎 **Our Turn: Interactive Reading** Read each paragraph aloud. Then call on a student to read it again. After the student's reading, pause to discuss what has just been read. Review the paragraph, focusing on the glossed words, asking questions, and making comments.

- **Build Reading Fluency** Have pairs of students take turns reading paragraphs aloud to each other.

✓ 🍎 **Question All-Write** Ask: *Why did the eagles, harbor seals, and fish disappear? What do you think the word "spiny" means? What do the words "make a comeback" mean?* Have students write one or two sentences for each question and share their responses.

🍎 **Your Turn: Independent Reading** Have students read the passage again, this time by themselves and then complete this sentence stem:
The sea otters made a comeback because _____.

- Then have students create flow diagrams and share them.

82 Teacher's Edition

READING

3. Making Content Connections Work with a partner. Complete the chart below.

	On land	In the sea
a. Give an example of an animal at the top of a food chain.		
b. Give an example of a plant at the bottom of a food chain.		
c. Name an animal that eats only plants.		
d. Name an animal that eats other animals.		

4. Expanding Your Vocabulary Food chains in the sea are hard to study because the plants and animals live underwater. Match the words and phrases in the box with each item in the picture.

_____ 1. kelp   _____ 7. squid
_e_ 2. mackerel   _____ 8. tuna
_____ 3. octopus   _h_ 9. anchovy
_____ 4. killer whale _____ 10. seal
_____ 5. red algae   _g_ 11. sea lion
_____ 6. krill   _____ 12. herring

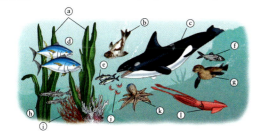

Who Eats What? 83

UNIT 5 ■ STUDENT BOOK, PAGE 83

- Talk about what you see in the picture as you share the correct answers. For example, pointing to the sea lion, you might say: *This animal looks a lot like a seal. But it has little ears and it's also a lot bigger than a seal. It's called a sea lion.* Then have students check their answers.

JUST FOR FUN

Practice animal vocabulary. Play Lingo Bingo. Divide students in groups of four. Have each group fold a piece of paper in four parts one way and then four parts the other way, making 16 squares. Provide 16 animal names. As you write the name of each animal on the chalkboard, each group writes the name in any square on their paper. In random order, describe each animal without naming it. As each group guesses the animal, they put an X in the square. The first group with a complete row of four Xs whispers out, "Lingo Bingo!"

PB PRACTICE BOOK ACTIVITY

See Activity D, Test-Taking Practice, on Practice Book pages 44 and 45.

See Activity E, Using New Vocabulary, on Practice Book page 46.

3. Making Content Connections

● **Heads Together** Remind students that they have read about two food chains—one on land and one in the sea. Explain that they are now going to examine how they are the same and how they are different. Have students work in pairs to complete the chart.

● **Interactive Writing** Copy the chart on the board. Ask volunteers to come to the board and help complete the chart. Encourage different students to fill in a variety of examples.

4. Expanding Your Vocabulary

- Have students cover the top half of the page with a piece of paper, allowing only the pictured sea plants and animals to show. How many plants and sea creatures can they name? Record as they name plants or animals.

- Now have students write the letter of each animal in the picture next to its name.

✓ WRAP UP

● **Outcome Sentences** Write these sentence stems on the board:

I learned that _____.

I still wonder about _____.

Have students think back to the reading about sea otters, complete each sentence, and then share out as you revisit the T-chart the class has created, making additions.

ANSWER KEY

Expanding Your Vocabulary: 1. a; 2. e; 3. k; 4. c; 5. i; 6. j; 7. l; 8. d; 9. h; 10. b; 11. g; 12. f.

UNIT 5 ■ STUDENT BOOK, PAGE 84

G WRITING CLINIC

Standards
- Identify cause and effect patterns in expository text
- Combine short related sentences to form complex sentences

WARM UP

- Ask students to revisit the flow diagram on page 78. Point out that a diagram shows us a *process*, a series of steps. For example this diagram shows us that hawks eat wrens and that wrens eat caterpillars. A flow diagram is also a way of explaining something. Tell students that they can also explain a process by writing about it.

TEACHING THE LESSON

1. Think about It

- Ask: *In which magazine would you find an article about the food chain—or any other scientific process?* Have students tell you why such an article wouldn't appear in the first two magazines. Have them suggest titles of other magazines in which you might find information about the natural world.

2. Focus on Organization

- Have students reread the paragraph and then look at the flow diagram (Part 1). Tell students that the flow diagram presents the same information as the paragraph. Have a volunteer explain why. Point out that the order of items in the diagram, however, is not necessarily the same as the order in which they are mentioned in the paragraph.

- **Interactive Writing** Draw the second diagram on the board (Part 2). Have students help you fill in the missing information between sea otters and kelp. Then ask volunteers to come to the board and help complete the diagram. Have each one tell you in his/her own words why the diagram looks like it does.

- Have students work independently to complete the diagram in Part 3. Review the correct answers with the class at the end.

PB PRACTICE BOOK ACTIVITY

See Activity F, Focus on Organization, on Practice Book page 47.

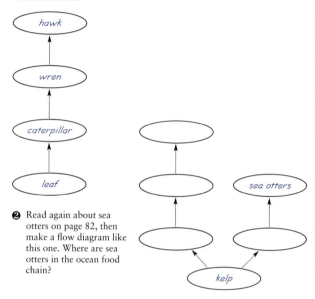

WRITING

G WRITING CLINIC — Explaining a Process

1. Think about It You would probably find a magazine article about the food chain in—

☐ Mad ☐ Teen People ☐ Science and Nature

2. Focus on Organization

❶ Reread the first paragraph.

   A caterpillar is eating a leaf on an apple tree. Later the caterpillar is spotted by a wren. It becomes part of the wren's dinner. Still later the wren is eaten by a hawk. Leaf, caterpillar, wren, and hawk are all linked. Together they form a food chain. Each is a link to the chain.

This **flow diagram** shows how the food chain works. Flow diagrams use lines and arrows to show how things happen. Look at the diagram. What does a hawk eat?

❷ Read again about sea otters on page 82, then make a flow diagram like this one. Where are sea otters in the ocean food chain?

84 Unit 5

84 Teacher's Edition

WRITING

UNIT 5 • STUDENT BOOK, PAGE 85

3 What happened when the sea otters disappeared? Complete the following diagram.

1. Hunters killed almost all the sea otters.
   ↓ so...
2. There were no sea otters to eat the _____.
   ↓ so...
3. There were so many sea urchins that they destroyed the _____.
   ↓ so...
4. Tiny sea animals didn't have _____ to eat.
   ↓ so...
5. Bigger fish didn't have _____ to eat.
   ↓ so...
6. Eagles and seals didn't have _____ to eat, so they disappeared.

3. Focus on Style

1 Writers sometimes combine two sentences when they have the same noun. The new sentence has a clause with the relative pronoun *that*.

The hawk ate the **wren**.   The **wren** ate the caterpillar.

The hawk ate the **wren that** ate the caterpillar.

This is like a "sentence chain!"

2 Combine each pair of the following sentences to make one sentence.

1. The cat ate the mouse.   The mouse ate the cheese.
   The cat ate the mouse that ate the cheese.
2. The dog chased the cat.   The cat ate the rat.
   _____
3. The wren ate the caterpillar.   The caterpillar ate the leaf.
   _____
4. The hawk ate the wren.   The wren ate the caterpillar.
   _____

Who Eats What?   **85**

- Have students combine each pair of sentences on their own. Review correct answers.

PB PRACTICE BOOK ACTIVITY

See Activity G, Focus on Style, on Practice Book page 48.

✓ WRAP UP

- Make a statement describing a meat that you like to eat. For example, *I love hamburgers*. Ask different students to create an oral food chain starting with your statement. For example, S1: *Hamburgers come from cows*. S2: *Cows eat grass*. S3: *Grass needs sunlight*. When the chain ends, have a student start another one.

ANSWER KEY

Think about It: Science and Nature

Focus on Organization 2: Left side: (kelp) tiny sea animals, bigger sea animals, fish; **Right side:** (kelp) sea urchins, sea otters.

Focus on Organization 3: 2. sea urchins 3. kelp 4. kelp 5. tiny sea animals 6. fish.

Focus on Style 2: 1. The cat ate the mouse that ate the cheese. 2. The dog chased the cat that ate the rat. 3. The wren ate the caterpillar that ate the leaf. 4. The hawk ate the wren that ate the caterpillar.

3. Focus on Style

- Copy the first pair of sentences on the board. Circle the object of the first sentence and the subject of the second sentence. Point out that these two words are exactly the same. Explain that when the object in the first sentence and the subject in the second sentence are the same, we can substitute the word *that* for the subject of the second sentence.

- Explain that writers often combine sentences to provide variety in their writing. Too many short sentences in a row can become boring. Writers also sometimes combine sentences to save space or to emphasize the connections between the subject of the first sentence and the subject of the second.

- 🍒 **Shared Quick Write** Ask students to make up original sentences like the example in the book. As they dictate, record the pairs of sentences on the board. Then call on volunteers to dictate combined sentences as you write.

Unit 5   **85**

UNIT 5 ■ STUDENT BOOK, PAGE 86

WRITING

H Writer's Workshop — Explaining a Process

Imagine that *Kids Discover* magazine has invited your class to write short articles about the food chain.

1. Getting It Out

❶ Learn more about food chains on land and in the sea. Check out these fact files. Find food chains. Choose one food chain to write about.

Fact file: Animals on land

Animal	What it eats
1. beetle	flowers, leaves, fruit
2. cricket	leaves
3. snail	leaves
4. chipmunk	berries, acorns, snails, crickets
5. rabbit	tree bark, vegetables
6. weasel	rabbits, mice
7. coyote	rabbits, sheep
8. hawk	chipmunks, smaller birds

Fact file: Animals in the sea

Animal	What it eats
1. krill	algae, kelp, sea lettuce
2. anchovy	algae, kelp, sea lettuce
3. herring	algae, kelp, sea lettuce
4. squid	krill
5. tuna	krill, anchovies, herring, sardines
6. sea lion	herring
7. shark	tuna, mackerel
8. killer whale	sea lions

A cricket   A snail   A rabbit   A weasel

❷ Use a large sheet of paper and colored markers. Draw a flow diagram that shows the food chain you have chosen. Use arrows to show who eats what. IMPORTANT: Save your flow diagram for later.

Here is a diagram that Zaida drew to show a food chain in the ocean:

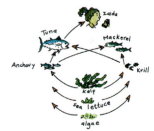

86 Unit 5

H Writer's Workshop

Standards
- Use the writing process: prewriting
- Create a diagram that conveys information accurately
- Write a short article that explains a process

1. Getting It Out
WARM UP

- Ask students to look over the fact files on this page. Explain that they'll be discovering food chains within these charts, making flow charts, and writing about food chains.

TEACHING THE LESSON

- Tell students that they will first decide on a food chain to write about (Part 1). Have them review the fact files to choose a food chain.

  Access for All Encourage more advanced students to gather information on their own for another food chain, either on land or in the sea. Help them use the Internet as a resource—pointing out the *Connect to the Web* note on page 87.

  Let's Talk Have a volunteer read the instructions for Part 2 and then explain the task to classmates. Have another volunteer explain what Zaida's flow diagram tells us. Then encourage other students to add information. For example: *The plants are at the bottom of the food chain. Small sea animals eat them.* Be sure that someone explains why Zaida is at the top of the food chain.

- Make sure each student has a large piece of paper and access to colored markers. Have each student draw a flow diagram based on the land or sea animal they have chosen to write about.

 Using Technology Show students how to download and print images from Internet Web sites. They can use these images in their diagrams.

✓ **Question All-Write** Have each student write a one-sentence response to each question in Part 3 on the reverse side of their flow diagrams.

✓ WRAP UP

- Invite volunteers to share their written responses to the three questions.

86 **Teacher's Edition**

WRITING

UNIT 5 ■ STUDENT BOOK, PAGE 87

 CONNECT TO THE WEB. CHECK IT OUT.

For information about food chains, go to the Forest Service Web Site at www.fs.fed.us

❸ Think about why your food chain is important. Ask yourself questions like these:

1. Where do I fit into this food chain?
2. How do all animals connect to green plants?
3. What would happen if one animal or plant disappeared from this food chain?

2. Getting It Down

❶ Turn your flow diagram into words. Use the outline below.

1. Lead sentence: _____
2. Description of the food chain
   a) At the bottom of the food chain: _____ (1)
   b) Who eats (1): _____ (2)
   c) Who eats (2): _____ (3)
   d) Who eats (3): _____ (4)
3. What is important to understand about the food chain: _____

Who Eats What? **87**

H WRITER'S WORKSHOP

Standards
- Use the writing process: drafting
- Use an outline to organize writing

2. Getting It Down
WARM UP

- Have students show their flow diagrams to their partners, explaining what the flow diagram says.
- Tell students that it's time to write their articles—turning their diagrams into outlines and their outlines into first drafts.

TEACHING THE LESSON

- Have students look at the outline. Explain that the first step is to develop a lead sentence. Tell students that a lead sentence "shakes hands" with the reader. The lead sentence can set the scene. Explain that a lead sentence is often a topic sentence, but not always.

 Shared Writing Ask students to look again at Zaida's flow diagram on page 86. Help students generate various possible lead sentences based on the information in the flow diagram.

- Now have students read the lead sentence in Zaida's article on page 88. Note that Zaida's lead sentence is also a good topic sentence.

- Now help students complete part 2(a) of the outline. Then help them with 2(b). Explain that line 2(b) will be about the animal that eats the plant or animal above (1). The animal on line 2(c) eats the animal above (2), etc.

- Have a volunteer read Zaida's article aloud. Encourage students to comment on the strengths they see in the article, as you record. Save your list for the next workshop session.

- Now give students time to draft their own articles, based on their outlines.

WRAP UP

- Tell students that they will have a chance to revise their work during the next session. Have them locate the ChecBric for this unit in the Student Book or Practice Book. Have them prepare for Getting It Right by reviewing the ChecBric on their own, underlining indicators they're not sure about.

PB PRACTICE BOOK ACTIVITY

See Activity H, Writer's Workshop, on Practice Book page 49.

Unit 5   87

UNIT 5 ■ STUDENT BOOK, PAGE 88

WRITING

❷ Turn your outline into a short article. Here is what Zaida wrote.

> *The article has a good lead sentence.*
>
> All sea creatures eat other sea creatures and plants to survive. Algae and plants like sea lettuce and kelp are at the bottom of the food chain. Many types of fish and animals such as krill and anchovy eat sea plants.
>
> *The information is accurate and matches Zaida's flow diagram.*
>
> Larger fish, like tuna and mackerel, eat the smaller animals and fish that eat sea plants.
>
> *Zaida uses combined sentences with words like* that.
>
> And who eats the tuna? The next time you eat at a seafood restaurant, check out the menu! You might find tuna there!
>
> *The ending is clever. Zaida shows how human beings are part of the food chain! That's important to understand.*

MINI-LESSON
Using Commas: Put commas around examples:
Correct: Huge fish, like sharks, eat tuna.
Incorrect: Huge fish like sharks eat tuna.

3. Getting It Right Take a careful look at what you have written. Use these questions to help you review and revise your work.

Questions to ask...	How to check...	How to revise...
1. Did I name each plant or animal in the food chain?	Circle each animal. Then draw a line to what it eats.	Add any information that is missing.
2. Did I describe the food chain accurately?	Look up each animal in the encyclopedia or the Fact File to check what it eats.	Correct the information, if necessary.
3. Did I put the information in the right order?	Check to see that the information in your article matches your outline.	Correct the information, if necessary.
4. Did I show that I understand why the food chain is important?	Underline the part that shows that you thought about the food chain.	Add a sentence or two that shows your own thoughts about the food chain.

88 Unit 5

H WRITER'S WORKSHOP

Standards
- Use the writing process: revising for accuracy, organization, and clarity
- Give an oral presentation that explains a process
- Organize ideas logically
- Use notes to summarize ideas given in presentations by others

3. Getting It Right
WARM UP

- Guide students through the ChecBric for this unit in the Student Book or Practice Book. Explain that they will use the ChecBric to prepare a final draft of their writing.

- Have volunteers explain, in their own words, what each indicator in the ChecBric means.

TEACHING THE LESSON

- Ask students to revisit Zaida's article, noting the comments in each speech bubble. As you review the comments on Zaida's article, ask students to comment on each. For example ask: *Why is Zaida's lead sentence a good one?* (It's clear. It states the main idea of the paragraph.)

- 🍎 **Mini-Lesson on Conventions**
Explain that we often put commas around material that can be removed from a sentence without losing the main idea of the sentence. For example, if you remove the words *like sharks* from the sentence, you still have a true statement: *Huge fish eat tuna.*

- Have students use the information in the chart and the ChecBric to revise their work.

🍎 **Group Share** Have students share their stories in groups of four or five. Have students give each other feedback on their articles and then make revisions.

WRAP UP

- Tell students that they are now ready to present their articles to the class. Suggest that they reread their work aloud several times so that they will feel more comfortable when they present it to the class.

- 📁 Give students time to fill out the ChecBric on Practice Book page 109. Ask them to attach it to their writing when they put it in their portfolios.

WRITING

UNIT 5 ■ STUDENT BOOK, PAGE 89

4. Presenting It Present your article to your classmates. Take notes as you listen to other students.

❶ Plan your presentation. Look at the checklist.
❷ Begin by showing your classmates the flow diagram you made to show the food chain.
❸ Read your article aloud.
❹ Invite your classmates to ask questions.
❺ Ask for feedback from your classmates on your presentation.

Presentation Checklist

☐ The information is accurate.
☐ The information that is presented flows well.
☐ The flow diagram is carefully drawn and labeled and is easy to understand.
☐ The speaker uses a loud, clear voice.
☐ The speaker pauses briefly after each idea.
☐ The speaker looks up at the audience from time to time.

❻ As you listen to each presentation, take notes. Use a note-taking guide like this:

Animal	What it eats
krill	algae, kelp

What is important to understand about the food chain:

❼ Using your notes, volunteer to describe your classmate's presentation about food chain in your own words.

Who Eats What? 89

4. Presenting It

WARM UP

- It's time for students to present their articles! Determine order of presentation, alternating between land food chains and ocean food chains.

- As a class, develop a simple presentation checklist. In addition to content and organization, focus on speaking skills (poise, expression, volume, posture, eye contact), enthusiasm, use of visuals, creativity, involvement of the audience, and length of presentation.

> **TEACHING TIP** Since all or most students will have used one of the two fact files to prepare their articles, you might have students present in small groups to avoid repetition.

TEACHING THE LESSON

- Before students present, help them review the Presentation Checklist. Remind them to pause briefly after each idea and to look at the audience from time to time.

- Have a volunteer read and explain the directions.

- Have students give their presentations, following the steps outlined in the directions.

> **TEACHING TIP** Invite students to display their articles and illustrations on a bulletin board in the classroom.

WRAP UP

- Have students revisit the T-chart they made at the beginning of the unit. Add a third column: *What we learned*. Help students identify what they learned as you record their words on the board.

> **TEACHING TIP** Coordinate with a teacher in another area of the curriculum to develop a common writing assignment that involves explaining a process.

Unit 5

UNIT 5 ■ STUDENT BOOK, PAGE 90

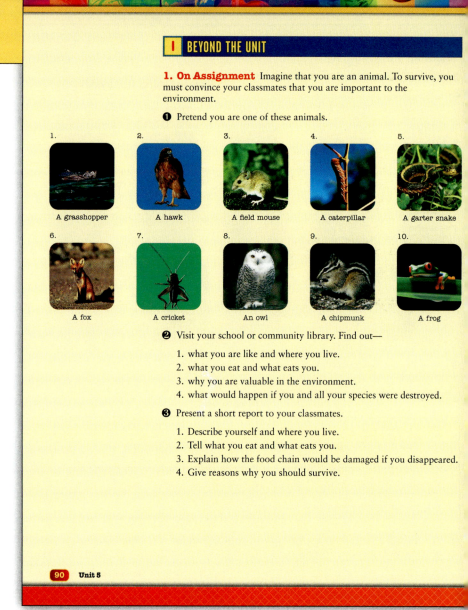

❶ BEYOND THE UNIT

Standards
- Use the research process
- Give a short oral presentation
- Respond to a poem

1. On Assignment
WARM UP

- Write the word *environment* on the board. Use the word in a sentence. *Our environment is not as clean as it was 100 years ago.* Now have a volunteer define the word in his or her own words. For example, *The environment is the land, air, and water all around us.* Have another volunteer make up another sentence that uses the word.

- Now have students look at the pictures and try to give one reason why each animal is important to the environment.

- Explain that all of the animals are important for the environment in some way. Tell students that they are going to choose an animal and present a report on its importance to the environment.

TEACHING THE LESSON

- Have each student choose an animal.

  Access for All Have students work with a partner on this activity, pairing less proficient students with more proficient students.

- Review the questions in Part 2. For question 1, ask students to find out what the animal looks like, what its personality is like (shy, aggressive, intelligent, etc.), and what its habits are (it sleeps all day). For question 3, encourage students to think about ways in which the animal improves the soil, the water, or the life of other animals and humans. For question 4, ask them to think of several possible effects their disappearance might have on other species.

- Arrange to take students to the library. Help them ask the librarian for help. Teach them how to use the catalog to find information sources.

TEACHING TIP 💡 Contact your school or community librarian in advance to arrange a class visit. Explain that students will need help identifying research tools and how to use them. Remind the librarian that your students are English Learners and that they will need to have information presented in a "sheltered" manner.

- For Part 3, remind students that they are to play the part of the animal as they report. Remind them to use "I" as they talk. For example: *I'm a hawk. I'm a very powerful bird.* Have them give their short reports.

- After each report, encourage other students to ask questions.

✓ WRAP UP

Outcome Sentence Have students complete this sentence stem, and then share:
Through my research, I learned that _____.

90   Teacher's Edition

UNIT 5 ■ STUDENT BOOK, PAGE 91

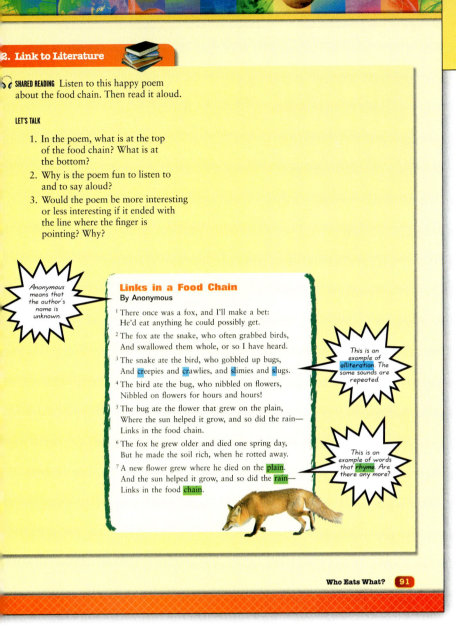

- Now play the tape or CD or read the poem again. Ask students to raise their hands each time a new animal is mentioned. Invite a student to recite the chain from memory. Then have students identify examples of rhyme in the poem.

- Have volunteers read the poem aloud. Encourage students to read with expression.

- **Let's Talk** Use the questions to lead a discussion of the poem. Help students discover what is at the top and bottom of the food chain. Lead them to understand that the lively rhythm of the lines and the use of amusing words like *creepies* and *crawlies* add to the reader's enjoyment. Ask several students to share their answers to question 3. Some may think it is more interesting not to end the poem after stanza 5 because it demonstrates the fox's place at the bottom as well as the top of the food chain.

✓ WRAP UP

- **Outcome Sentence** Revisit the "Jack's house" sentences. Write this sentence stem on the board:

  This is the dog that _____.

  Have students complete the stem, then share out.

PB PRACTICE BOOK ACTIVITY

See Activity 1, Responding to Literature, on Practice Book page 50.

✓ UNIT WRAP UP

- Have students reflect upon what they learned in this unit in their **notebooks**. Consider collecting and responding to entries.

2. Link to Literature

WARM UP

- Write these sentences on the board:

  This is the house that Jack built.
  This is the rat that lived in the house that Jack built.
  This is the cat that ate the rat that lived in the house that Jack built.

  Explain that this is an example of a "chain" sentence: It can get longer and longer by combining it with another sentence.

- Tell students that they are going to read a "chain" poem.

- **Shared Reading** Read the poem "Links in a Food Chain" aloud or play the tape or CD as students follow along. Model fluency and expression, using pauses to help communicate meaning. Discuss the starbursts. Invite students to give other examples of *alliteration*.

Unit 5   91

Unit 6 Real-Life Heroes

Unit Overview

Section	At a Glance	Standards
Before You Begin	Students talk about a life-threatening attack by an alligator.	■ Derive meaning from visual information
A. Connecting to Your Life	Students identify dangerous situations when others needed help.	■ Give a short narrative of personal experience
B. Getting Ready to Read	Students learn useful vocabulary and share stories of danger.	■ Use context to determine the meaning of unfamiliar words ■ Retell a narrative
C. Reading to Learn	Students read about a young girl who saves a man's life. PRACTICE BOOK: Students retell the story in the Student Book.	■ Identify sequences of events in narratives
D. Word Work	Students learn to form compound words. PRACTICE BOOK: Students match words to make compounds and then use them to complete sentences.	■ Use knowledge of compound words to determine the meaning of unfamiliar words ■ Use knowledge of sound/spelling patterns to spell familiar words
E. Grammar	Students learn how to use adverbial clauses with *when*, *while*, *before*, and *after*. PRACTICE BOOK: Students use adverbial clauses to combine sentences.	■ Use adverbial clauses to express time-when relationships
F. Bridge to Writing	Students read another story about "real-life heroes." PRACTICE BOOK: Students practice taking Reading Vocabulary and Reading Comprehension tests. PRACTICE BOOK: Students practice new vocabulary.	■ Make and confirm predictions about events in a story ■ Identify the elements of a story

Section	At a Glance	Standards
G. Writing Clinic	Students analyze what makes a story exciting to read. PRACTICE BOOK: Students identify lead, action, and ending sentences. PRACTICE BOOK: Students practice writing titles and leads for stories.	■ Identify structural patterns found in narratives ■ Write a story that engages the audience
H1. Writer's Workshop: Getting It Out	Students take notes as they listen to stories about people who rescued others. PRACTICE BOOK: Students practice listening and taking notes.	■ Use the writing process: planning a story ■ Listen and take notes
H2. Writer's Workshop: Getting It Down	Students turn their interview notes into an outline for a story.	■ Use the writing process: drafting a story with a beginning, middle, and end ■ Use an outline to organize writing
H3. Writer's Workshop: Getting It Right	Students revise and edit their stories.	■ Use the writing process: revising for organization and style
H4. Writer's Workshop: Presenting It	Students read their stories to their classmates.	■ Read a story aloud with fluency and expression
I. Beyond the Unit	Students choose a "Citizen of the Month" and hold an award ceremony in class. Students also read a special kind of story, "Paul Bunyan and the Gumberoos." PRACTICE BOOK: Students respond to "Paul Bunyan and the Gumberoos," then write a tall tale of their own.	■ Read and respond to a tall tale

UNIT 6 ▪ STUDENT BOOK, PAGE 92

BEFORE YOU BEGIN

Standard
- Derive meaning from visual information

- Have students look at the picture on page 93. Ask: *What do you think is happening?* Encourage students to "tell" the story by looking at the picture.

- Have students read the caption. Ask: *What is the difference between an "attack" and a "rescue"?* (An attack is an attempt to harm someone and a rescue is an attempt to save someone from harm.) Ask a volunteer to make up a sentence using the verb "attack." Then have another volunteer make up a related sentence using the verb "rescue."

- Ask students what they would do in this situation if a friend were being attacked by an alligator. Guide students to include such ideas as *make a lot of noise to scare the alligator, hit the alligator on the nose, pull the girl to safety,* and *call for help.*

- 🍎 **Heads Together** Have students imagine that they are writing a newspaper story about this incident. Have one student write a *headline* for the story, the other student write a *lead sentence* for the story—one that grabs the reader's attention.

Unit 6 Real-Life Heroes

Read...
- A story about a young girl who saved a man in danger.

- A story about four boys who survived a bear attack.

 **Link to Literature**

- "Paul Bunyan and the Gumberoos," a story by Steven Kellogg.

92 Unit 6

Objectives:

Reading:
- Reading stories about real-life heroes
- Identifying elements of plot
- Strategy: Predicting
- Literature: Responding to a tall tale

Writing:
- Writing a true adventure story
- Taking interview notes
- Writing titles and leads

Vocabulary:
- Forming compounds that come from sentences
- Learning words for accidents and emergencies

Listening/Speaking:
- Listening to real-life stories
- Comparing stories
- Interviewing others

Grammar:
- Using adverbial time clauses

Spelling and Phonics:
- Pronouncing words with the letters -oo-

---

92 Teacher's Edition

Attack and rescue!

BEFORE YOU BEGIN

Talk with your classmates.

1. Look at the picture. What is the animal in the picture?
2. Read the caption. What do you think is happening?
3. What would you do in this situation?

Real-Life Heroes

UNIT 6 ■ STUDENT BOOK, PAGE 94

A CONNECTING TO YOUR LIFE

Standard
- Give a short narrative of personal experience

WARM UP

🍎 **Heads Together** Ask students to look at the pictures. Ask if anyone has ever been in a situation like these. If so, invite the student to describe the details to the class.

TEACHING THE LESSON

🎧 1. Tuning In

- Tell students they are going to listen to a story about a girl who rescued her friend from an alligator attack.

- ✓ 🍎 **Question All-Write** Play the tape or CD, or read the script. Have students write a sentence that summarizes what happened. Have them share their sentences.

- Play the tape or CD, or read the script a second time. Ask students to listen to how the speaker, Amanda, makes her story *interesting*.

2. Talking It Over

- Have students work in pairs to talk about what appears to be happening in each picture. Have them match each headline to the correct picture on the page.

- Have students share out, explaining why each headline matches its picture.

- 🍎 **Heads Together** Assign one of the stories to each pair. Again, have students talk briefly about what is happening in their story. Then have them write a sentence that predicts how the story turned out (that is, a conclusion)—using their imagination. Have them share their conclusions. Tell them to save their conclusions for later.

READING

A CONNECTING TO YOUR LIFE

🎧 **1. Tuning In** Listen to Amanda's story. Write what happened in one sentence. Think of a time that you or someone you know was in a dangerous situation. Talk with a partner

2. Talking It Over Match the headlines with the pictures.

Headlines are usually in the present tense.

____b____ 1. Boy Saves Girl in Boating Accident
_____ 2. Local Girl Rescues Child Who Falls in Underground Tank
_____ 3. Girl Saves Drowning Pet; Pulls Animal from River.
_____ 4. Teen Drives Bus to Safety
_____ 5. Boy Pulls Child from Railroad Tracks; Tragedy Avoided
_____ 6. Seventh-grader Aids Tornado Victim

a.    b.

c.    d.

e.    f.

What do you think this unit is about? Check (✓) the correct answer.

_____ 1. kids who were afraid to help
_____ 2. kids whose pictures were in the newspaper
_____ 3. kids who saved other people's lives

- Have students look at the pictures again. Then ask them to predict what the unit is about.

✓ WRAP UP

🍎 **Outcome Sentence** Write this sentence stem on the board:

Each of the pictures tells a story about _____.

Have students share their sentences.

> **TEACHING TIP** 💡 Be aware that some students from other countries may have experienced rescue situations when they left their home countries to come to the U.S. Although their stories may be compelling, students may not be ready to share them with classmates.

ANSWER KEY

Talking It Over: 1. b; 2. d; 3. f; 4. a; 5. e; 6. c.
Talking It Over: 3.

94   Teacher's Edition

READING

UNIT 6 • STUDENT BOOK, PAGE 95

B GETTING READY TO READ

1. Learning New Words Read the following vocabulary words and definitions.

1. **save a life**—to stop someone from dying
2. **hero**—someone who is very brave, especially who risked his/her life
3. **rescue**—to save from danger
4. **stay calm**—to avoid getting too excited
5. **emergency**—a serious situation that needs immediate action
6. **first aid**—emergency help for an injured person
7. **paramedic**—someone trained to give medical help in an emergency
8. **tragic**—causing terrible destruction or death

Complete the sentences below with the new vocabulary words.

1. Ashley dialed 911. "This is a(n) _emergency_," she cried. "My baby brother fell into the swimming pool!"
2. When you _____, you often get your name in the paper.
3. Tom jumped into the lake to _____ his dog.
4. Boy Scouts and Girl Scouts are trained to give _____.
5. The _____ saved Mr. Johnson's life when he had a heart attack.
6. Tran escaped from the burning car. He avoided a(n) _____ accident.
7. If you see an accident, don't cry. Try to _____.
8. That firefighter saved my life. He is a(n) _____!

2. Talking It Over Can you remember a time when you or someone you know was in danger? What happened? Tell a partner. Be ready to share your partner's story with your classmates.

Real-Life Heroes **95**

B GETTING READY TO READ

Standards
- Use context to determine the meaning of unfamiliar words
- Retell a narrative

WARM UP

- Have students sit with the partners they worked with for Lesson A. Have the pairs share the conclusions they wrote about the pictures on page 94 with the class.

TEACHING THE LESSON

1. Learning New Words

- Write the new words on the board. Remind students that they have already seen some of these words. Have students work in groups of three, trying to write a definition for each word or phrase. Have them share their definitions, then set them aside for the next step.

- Have students open their books. Have each small group read the definitions, then compare them with their own original definitions. Have them share which words they originally defined incorrectly.

- Now have groups complete each sentence, using the correct word. Confirm the correct answers.

- Have each group create an original sentence for each word. Have students share out.

2. Talking It Over

- **Heads Together** Have students work in pairs and take turns telling each other about a situation in which they, or someone they know, was in danger. Suggest that they rehearse their stories with their partners once or twice, then call on volunteers to share stories with their classmates.

✓ WRAP UP

- Invite volunteers to retell their classmates' stories. Have other students fill in any important ideas that are left out.

ANSWER KEY

Learning New Words: 1. emergency; 2. save a life; 3. rescue; 4. first aid; 5. paramedic; 6. tragic; 7. stay calm; 8. hero.

UNIT 6 ▪ STUDENT BOOK, PAGE 96

C READING TO LEARN

Standard
- Identify sequences of events in narratives

WARM UP

- Write the word *predict* on the board and ask students where they usually hear that word. (It's used a lot in weather forecasts and to discuss the outcomes of sports events.) Explain that students are going to learn to predict to improve their reading.

TEACHING THE LESSON

1. Before You Read

♻ Tell students that when you *predict*, you use clues in the reading to guess what will happen (Reading Strategy box). Explain that even if predictions are not correct they give the reader something to focus on while reading. The reader may also change his or her predictions several times during the course of a single reading.

🍎 **Heads Together** Have students talk with a partner about what they think will happen in the story, based on the picture. Invite volunteers to share.

🎧 2. Let's Read

🍎 **My Turn: Read Aloud/Think Aloud** Read the article aloud one paragraph at a time. Model correct phrasing and fluent reading.

- Play the tape or CD, or read the passage. Stop at the end of each paragraph to comment on words and ideas. At the end of the story ask students to raise their hands if their predictions were correct. Have students explain how the picture helped them make their predictions.

🍎 **Our Turn: Interactive Reading** Read the first sentence of each paragraph. After the first sentence of

---

READING

C READING TO LEARN   True Stories

READING STRATEGY
Predicting:
When you predict, you use clues in the reading to try to guess what will happen. This makes the reading easier to understand.

1. Before You Read Look at the picture that goes with the following story. Before you read, **predict** what happened. Tell the story in your own words. Talk with a partner.

🎧 **2. Let's Read** You are going to read a true story about Ashley Makale, an average teen who became a real-life hero. After you read the first sentence, stop and try to predict what will happen.

Calm under Pressure

¹ When Ashley Makale took a **Red Cross** baby-sitting class, she had no idea the skills she learned would someday save a life. But that's exactly what happened. Ashley was baby-sitting for neighbor Barry Becker's three-month-old daughter and five-year-old son while Becker worked at home. When Becker ran to stop his dog from chasing a cat in the backyard, he crashed through a sliding-glass door.

(Compare the first sentence in the story and the last sentence. What do you notice?)

² **Fast call.** Ashley saw Becker fall and rushed to his side. He had deep gashes in his knee and foot. Becker was losing so much blood that Ashley knew she had to get help and stop the bleeding fast. Holding the baby, Ashley ran to the phone and dialed 911. Then she used a towel to apply pressure to Becker's knee while she **reassured** the children. Paramedics soon arrived. After several surgeries, Becker began long-term **physical therapy** to use his leg again.

(Notice how the details make the story interesting.)

³ **Real lesson.** Ashley was honored by the Los Angeles County Sheriff's Department for her actions. "I didn't know everyone would think this was such a big deal," Ashley says. "That baby-sitting class taught me to stay calm in an emergency, and that's just what I did."

Source: *National Geographic World*

pressure—(1) urgent problems; (2) pressing hard on something
Red Cross—an organization that helps injured people or disaster survivors
reassure—to give comfort
physical therapy—special treatment for injuries to the body

---

paragraph 1, note how the lead sentence sets the scene. Then call on individuals to read other sentences. As students read, focus on glossed words, ask questions, and make comments.

- **Build Fluency** Have pairs of students take turns reading paragraphs aloud to each other.

🍎 **Your Turn: Independent Reading** Have students read the passage on their own, taking notes. Have them jot down each thing that happened in *time order*. Have them keep their notes for later.

🌈 **Access for All** Have students with linguistic intelligence turn the story into a skit, then act it out.

🌈 **Access for All** When asking questions about a reading passage, tailor each question to the ability level of the student you are addressing. For example, less proficient students do better with *Yes/No* questions or other questions requiring one-word answers. Intermediate level students can handle *Wh-* questions. Save open-ended and critical thinking questions for more advanced students.

READING

UNIT 6 ▪ STUDENT BOOK, PAGE 97

3. Unlocking Meaning

❶ **Finding the Main Idea** Which of these sentences tells the most important idea from the article? Check (✓) the correct answer.

_____ 1. Glass doors are very dangerous.
_____ 2. A girl took a baby-sitting class from the Red Cross.
_____ 3. A girl saved a man's life by staying calm during an emergency.

❷ **Finding Details** Number the sentences in the order that they happened in the story.

_1_ Ashley took a baby-sitting class.
_____ Ashley tried to stop Becker's bleeding.
_____ Becker ran through a sliding-glass door.
_____ The paramedics arrived.
_____ Ashley saw that Becker was bleeding a lot.
_____ The Sheriff's Department honored Ashley.
_____ Becker fell and Ashley ran to his side.
_____ Ashley called 911 to report the emergency.

❸ **Think about It** What do you think happened **after** the paramedics arrived? Number the following sentences in the order you think they happened.

_____ The paramedics drove Becker to the hospital.
_____ The paramedics gave Becker first aid.
_____ Becker had surgery.
_____ The paramedics put Becker in the ambulance.
_____ Becker spent several days in the hospital.

❹ **Before You Move On** People who do brave things sometimes receive a special certificate to honor them. Design a certificate to honor Ashley. Use the certificate to the right as an example. Explain what she did on the certificate.

Real-Life Heroes 97

---

that note-taking can help them understand and remember a story.

THINK ABOUT IT

- Ask volunteers to read sentences aloud. Clarify the meaning of any new words. Then read the directions and have students complete the activity. Review the correct answers with the class.

BEFORE YOU MOVE ON

- **Heads Together** Read and explain the directions. Help students think of various forms of recognition that people might receive (e.g., student of the month award; athletic trophy).

- Have students work in pairs to design a certificate for Ashley.

✓ WRAP UP

- Have pairs of students share what they have written on their certificates.

PB PRACTICE BOOK ACTIVITY

See Activity A, Revisit and Retell, on Practice Book page 51.

ANSWER KEY

Finding the Main Idea: 3.
Finding Details: 1, 6, 2, 7, 4, 8, 3, 5.
Think about It: 3, 1, 4, 2, 5.

---

3. Unlocking Meaning

✓ FINDING THE MAIN IDEA

- Ask students to identify the statement that best tells what the story is about. Have them tell you why each statement is or is not the main idea. (The first sentence is true but it is a general statement. The second sentence contains a single detail.)

- Tell students to imagine that "Calm Under Pressure" is an episode of a TV show, *Real-Life Heroes*. Have them write a one-sentence "blurb" about the episode for the TV section of the newspaper.

✓ FINDING DETAILS

- Have students number the sentences in the correct chronological order. Have a volunteer read his or her sequence of sentences aloud. Ask: *Does everyone agree? Why or why not?* Then have students compare the sequence of sentences with their own notes. Ask who took accurate notes and who did not. Remind students

Unit 6 97

UNIT 6 ■ STUDENT BOOK, PAGE 98

D WORD WORK

Standard
- Use knowledge of compound words to determine the meaning of unfamiliar words

WARM UP

- Hold up several objects that are compounds (history book, paper clip, eyeglasses). Write the name of each on the board. Ask: *What do you notice about the names of these objects?* (They are all made up of smaller words.) Have students see how many other objects in the room with two-word names they can identify.

TEACHING THE LESSON

1. Word Detective

- Have students match the compounds with their meanings. Review the correct answers with the class.

2. Word Study

- Read and discuss how compounds are formed: *verb + direct object* and *verb + object of a preposition*, focusing on each pair of example sentences.
- Write these sentences on the board and ask students to identify the direct object or object of a preposition in each. Guide them in forming compounds.
  1. *Mr. Lee teaches English.* (direct object—He's an <u>English teacher</u>.)
  2. *It's a lace for a shoe.* (object of prep.—It's a <u>shoelace</u>.)

3. Word Play

- **Team Talk** Have students form compounds with a partner. Review the sentences with the whole class.

Spelling and Phonics

- Have students listen as you read each word.

READING

D WORD WORK

A frying pan

1. Word Detective Match each compound word in the left-hand column with its correct meaning on the right.

1. baby-sitter   a. a place where you can catch a bus
2. life-saving   b. a machine for cutting grass
3. frying pan   c. someone who cares for a young child
4. dishwasher   d. saving someone's life
5. bus stop   e. something you use for cooking
6. lawnmower   f. a machine for washing dishes

2. Word Study Many compounds are made from a verb + a noun. You can often figure out what a compound means by making a sentence that explains it. Notice that the noun and verb switch places in many compounds.

SPELLING AND PHONICS:
To do this activity, go to page 194.

VERB + NOUN (DIRECT OBJECT)	
1. A barber gives **haircuts**.	A barber **cuts** **hair**.
2. The president gave me a **handshake**.	The president **shook** my **hand**.
VERB + NOUN (OBJECT OF A PREPOSITION)	
3. They're **machine-made**.	The toys were **made** by a **machine**.
4. John is a **factory worker**.	John **works** in a **factory**.

3. Word Play Read the sentences on the left. Complete each sentence on the right with a compound word.

1. Ana makes dresses.   Ana is a <u>dressmaker</u>.
2. We both like riding on horseback.   We both like horseback _____.
3. The furniture is made by hand.   The furniture is _____ made.
4. The cowboys on TV are fighting with guns.   The cowboys on TV are having a gun _____.
5. Ms. Sanchez makes pizza.   Ms. Sanchez is a pizza _____.

98 Unit 6

- Have students write each word in the correct column and share.

✓ WRAP UP

- Have students make a list of "spelling demons" in their **notebooks**. They should include examples of the three different types of compound words—open compounds, closed compounds, and hyphenated compounds.

PB PRACTICE BOOK ACTIVITY

See Activity B, Word Work, on Practice Book page 52.

ANSWER KEY

Word Detective: 1. c; 2. d; 3. e; 4. f; 5. a; 6. b.

Word Play: 1. dressmaker; 2. (horseback) riding; 3. hand (made); 4. (gun) fight; 5. (pizza) maker.

Spelling and Phonics: took: cook, cookie, good, look, foot; **blood:** flood; **balloon:** cool, moon, pool, school; **door:** floor, poor.

READING

UNIT 6 ▪ STUDENT BOOK, PAGE 99

E GRAMMAR — Adverbial Time Clauses

1. Listen Up Listen to each sentence. Point your thumb up 👍 if it sounds correct. Point your thumb down 👎 if it sounds wrong.

👍👎 1. After he put on his seat belt, he got in the car.

👍👎 2. The Chang family was eating dinner when the doorbell rang.

👍👎 3. Wipe your feet on the mat before you walk in the house.

👍👎 4. I was playing basketball while I fell and broke my arm.

2. Learn the Rule Read the following rules for adverbial time clauses, then do Activity 1 again.

ADVERBIAL TIME CLAUSES

When, while, before, and after link one event to another event. Clauses that start with these words are called adverbial time clauses. An adverbial clause can come before or after a main clause.

when	(at the specific point that something else happened) When Clause: first event Main Clause: second event	When Becker fell, Ashley ran to his side. Ashley ran to Becker's side when he fell.
while	(at the same time that a longer continuing event was happening) While Clause: continuing event Main Clause: short event	While I was eating, the phone rang. The phone rang while I was eating.
before	(before something else happened) Before Clause: second event Main Clause: first event	Before you arrived, I cleaned the house. I cleaned the house before you arrived.
after	(after something else happened) After Clause: first event Main Clause: second event	After we ate dinner, I washed the dishes. I washed the dishes after we ate dinner.

3. Practice the Rule Complete the following sentences. Use *when*, *while*, *before*, or *after*.

1. I was watching TV ___when___ the phone rang.
2. _____ the alarm went off, I jumped out of bed.
3. The alarm went off _____ I was sleeping.
4. _____ I took a shower, I got dressed.
5. I ate breakfast _____ I left for school.
6. Mary turned on the radio _____ she got into the car.
7. My parents came home _____ I was taking a nap.

Real-Life Heroes   **99**

E GRAMMAR

Standard
- Use adverbial clauses to express time-when relationships

WARM UP

- Write the words *before*, *after*, *when*, and *while* on the board and ask students to repeat each one after you. Then ask students to watch carefully as you perform these actions: 1. Stand by your desk and put on your coat. 2. Whistle or hum a song while you slowly walk around your desk. 3. As you sit down in your desk chair, take off your coat. 4. Close your eyes and sit still for a minute or two. Then write these sentence frames on the board and ask students to help you complete them.

  1. _____ *I walked around the desk, I put on my coat.* (before)
  2. _____ *I was walking around my desk, I whistled.* (while)
  3. _____ *I sat down, I took off my coat.* (when)
  4. *I closed my eyes* _____ *I sat down.* (after)

TEACHING THE LESSON

🎧 1. Listen Up

- Play the tape or CD, or read the sentences twice. Have students follow the directions.

2. Learn the Rule

- Present the rules for the use of adverbial time clauses. As you discuss each type of clause, ask students to provide additional sentences that illustrate how each rule works.

- Point out that we use a comma after an adverbial clause when it comes at the beginning of a sentence.

- Do the Listen Up activity again.

3. Practice the Rule

- Have students complete the activity, then share out.

✓ WRAP UP

- Write the sentences below on the board. Ask volunteers to explain each error and correct it. Add more sentences for more practice.

  1. *I always brush my teeth before I get up in the morning.* (after)
  2. *Peter had a bad dream before he was sleeping last night.* (while)

PB PRACTICE BOOK ACTIVITY

See Activity C, Grammar, on Practice Book page 53.

ANSWER KEY

Listen Up: Correct sentences: 2, 3.

Practice the Rule: 1. when; 2. When; 3. while; 4. After; 5. before; 6. after; 7. while.

Unit 6   **99**

UNIT 6 ▪ STUDENT BOOK, PAGE 100

F BRIDGE TO WRITING

Standards
- Make and confirm predictions about events in a story
- Identify the elements of a story

WARM UP

- Have students look at the picture. Ask them what they would do if a friend was being attacked by a bear. Write their responses on the board.

TEACHING THE LESSON

1. Before You Read

- Ask if anyone has ever gone camping in the woods. Ask what kinds of things could go wrong. Have them share with a partner, then share with the class as you record.

2. Let's Read

- Have students look at the picture, title, and subheadings of the reading. What do they predict will happen in the story? Have them talk with a partner, then share.

- Tell students that when you *predict*, you can use information like pictures, titles, and subheadings to guess what a story is about (Reading Strategy box). Explain that predicting gives the reader something to focus on while reading.

- **My Turn: Read Aloud/Think Aloud** Read the story aloud. Model correct phrasing and fluent reading. As you read, stop to comment on words and ideas.

- Now play the tape or CD, or read the passage twice. As students listen, ask them to think about what they would have done if they had been there.

- **Our Turn: Interactive Reading** Now have students help you read the passages. Take turns with students reading a few sentences at a time. After

READING

F BRIDGE TO WRITING
True Stories

1. Before You Read This story is about a camping trip. Think of one or two problems you might have on a camping trip. Share them with a partner.

2. Let's Read Look at the picture and read the title and the subheadings of the following story. **Predict** what the story is about. Talk with a partner.

READING STRATEGY
Predicting:
When you predict, you use things like pictures and titles to help you guess what you're going to read about.

"BEAR-LY" IN TIME

1 Every summer brothers Joey and Ryan L'Heureux and their cousins Jonathan and Kerry look forward to Boy Scout camp. But last year's camping trip with fellow Scout Matt Murphy almost turned tragic.

Why is the first paragraph a good lead?

2 **TEAMWORK.** One morning the boys heard something outside their tents. "When I looked out, I saw a black bear crashing into Matt's tent—with Matt inside!" says Joey. Kerry and Joey ran to get Matt's dad while the other boys tried to distract the bear. The bear dragged Matt and his tent down a ravine.

The quoted words make the story a lot more exciting to read.

3 **RACE FOR HELP.** When Matt's dad arrived, he was able to chase the bear up a tree while Jonathan and Ryan pulled Matt out of the tent. Then Jonathan ran to the camp's first aid station to call for help. The other boys stayed with Matt until the paramedics arrived. Though he had scalp wounds and cuts requiring 195 stitches, Matt is fine today.

4 **REWARD.** The four L'Heureux boys received the Boy Scouts' Lifesaving Award Honor Medal. "Matt needed our help," says Jonathan, "and we did what we had to do."

Source: *National Geographic World*

distract—to make someone pay attention to something else

ravine—a deep, narrow valley

---

each paragraph, pause to discuss. Focus on the glossed words, ask questions, and make comments.

✓ **Sentence All-Write** Have students write one or two sentences summarizing the story. Have them share out.

- **Build Fluency: Echo Reading** Ask different students to read each line aloud after you. Practice reading for fluency.

- **Your Turn: Independent Reading** Now have students take notes as they read the story on their own, recording events in time order. Create a class timeline on the board.

- **Access for All** Students with strong linguistic intelligence may enjoy acting out the story for the class. Students with strong artistic intelligence can draw pictures to illustrate key events in the story.

WRITING

UNIT 6 ▪ STUDENT BOOK, PAGE 101

3. Making Content Connections Work with a partner. Compare the two stories you have read in this unit. Then complete the following chart, using your own words.

	Calm Under Pressure	"Bear-ly" in Time
1. Who are the people in the story? Circle the name of the hero or heroes.		
2. Where did the story happen?		
3. What happened? What was the emergency?		
4. What actions did the hero or heroes take?		
5. How did the story end?		

4. Expanding Your Vocabulary Match the emergency on the left with the correct action to take on the right. You can use your dictionary to look up the underlined words.

_f_ 1. You sprain your ankle.   a. Read the <u>label</u> for what to do.

____ 2. Your little sister drinks liquid soap, thinking that it's milk.   b. Take the person to the <u>emergency room</u>.

____ 3. Your mother cuts her hand.   c. Apply a thin layer of <u>antibiotic</u> cream.

____ 4. Your friend is bitten by a strange dog that has no collar.   d. Apply <u>pressure</u> to the wound with a clean cloth.

____ 5. Your brother falls and scrapes his knee.   e. Gently scrape out the <u>stinger</u> with a blunt object (like a credit card).

____ 6. You are stung by a bee.   f. Apply a cold <u>compress</u>.

Real-Life Heroes **101**

---

3. Making Content Connections

🍎 **Heads Together** Have pairs of students compare the two stories and complete the chart together.

🍎 **Interactive Writing** Copy the chart on the board. Invite volunteers to fill in the cells of the chart until it is complete.

🌈 **Access for All** Have more-proficient students work in small groups, altering the events of a story. Have them rewrite the story so that it has a different ending. Have them share with the class.

4. Expanding Your Vocabulary

- Write the vocabulary words on the board. As you write and say each word, have students point their thumbs up if they know what the word means, point their thumbs sideways if they're not sure, and point their thumbs down if they have never seen the word.

- Ask volunteers who pointed their thumbs up to define the word, then use it in a sentence. Encourage other students to refine or clarify definitions, as needed.

- Now have students work with a partner, matching each problem with the correct solution. Have students share their matches.

✓ 🍎 **Sentence All-Write** Have students write a sentence using each word. Have volunteers dictate their sentences as you record and help them make corrections.

PB PRACTICE BOOK ACTIVITY

See Activity D, Test-Taking Practice, on Practice Book pages 54 and 55.

See Activity E, Using New Vocabulary, on Practice Book page 56.

✓ WRAP UP

🍎 **Outcome Sentence** Have students imagine that they are to award the L'Heureux boys a certificate for bravery. Have them complete this stem, and then share:

The Boy Scouts of America recognizes the L'Heureux brothers because they _____.

ANSWER KEY

Making Content Connections: Calm Under Pressure: 1. (Ashley) Becker 2. in a home 3. A man was badly cut. 4. She calmed the children. She stopped the bleeding. She called 911. 5. The man had surgery and recovered; **"Bear-ly" in Time:** 1. Joey, Ryan, Jonathan, Kerry, Matt's (dad), Matt 2. on a camping trip in the woods 3. A bear attacked Matt. 4. Kerry and Joey ran to get Matt's dad. Jonathan and Ryan tried to distract the bear. Matt's dad chased the bear up a tree. 5. Matt was fine in the end.

Expanding Your Vocabulary: 1. f; 2. a; 3. d; 4. b; 5. c; 6. e.

Unit 6   **101**

UNIT 6 ■ STUDENT BOOK, PAGE 102

G WRITING CLINIC

Standards
- Identify structural patterns found in narrative
- Write a story that engages the audience

WARM UP

- Have students look back at the stories they have read. Ask: *What makes both of them interesting to read?* List students' ideas (*dangerous situations, good beginnings, exciting action*, etc.).

TEACHING THE LESSON

1. Think about It

- Ask students to think about where they might read true stories.

2. Focus on Organization

- Ask a volunteer to read the first paragraph. Then read or paraphrase the comment to the left of the paragraph. Explain that a good story has an exciting lead.

- Now have pairs of volunteers alternate in reading each successive paragraph and its comment to the left. As students work through the selection, add additional explanations and ideas to help clarify each point. For example, after the first comment you might say: *How can we tell what is going to happen?* (We have the words "would someday save a life.") After the third comment you might ask: *What words describe the action?* (fall, rush, losing blood, stop the bleeding, holding, ran, dialed, used a towel, apply pressure, reassured the children)

- Explain that a good ending is as important as a good beginning. Have students imagine how "Calm under Pressure" would read if the story ended with the sentence, "Paramedics soon

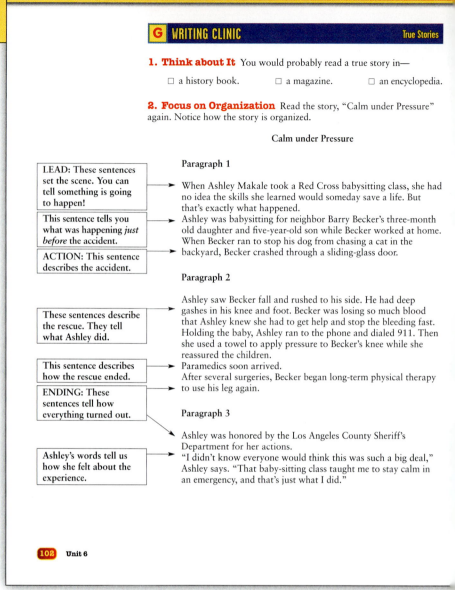

arrived." Ask: *As a reader, how would you feel?* (They would want to know how things turned out.)

- Explain that ending a story with a quote is a good way to make it interesting. Have them look once again at the endings for both stories. Have them read the quotes. How do the quotes make the reader feel? (They make the reader feel as though everything turned out all right.)

PB PRACTICE BOOK ACTIVITY

See Activity F, Focus on Organization, on Practice Book page 57.

WRITING

UNIT 6 • STUDENT BOOK, PAGE 103

3. Focus on Style

❶ Interesting stories often have creative titles. Look again at the titles of each reading. Explain how the title relates to the story.

Example: *Calm under Pressure*—Ashley didn't panic in an emergency and she saved a man's life.

❷ For each story on the left, choose the best title from the column on the right. Work with your classmates.

1. A boy saves his brother, who is trapped under the bed when a twister hits.	a. On the Right Track
	b. Tornado Terror
2. A boy rescues a girl in a boating accident.	c. Help! I'm Drowning!
3. A girl rescues a child from a fast-approaching train.	d. It's a Boy!
4. A girl rescues a child who falls into an underground cave.	e. It's Cold and Dark Down Here!
5. A boy stops a school bus that is out of control.	f. Step on the Brake!
6. A boy helps his mother give birth to a baby because she can't get to the hospital.	

A railroad track

Stepping on the brake

❸ Good stories also have leads that set the scene for what is going to happen. Match each lead on the left to the best title on the right.

1. The sky turned black. Tim heard a roar. It was a twister!	a. On the Right Track
2. Doctors learn to deliver babies in medical school. But Vincent Cho learned how before the eighth grade!	b. Tornado Terror
	c. Help! I'm Drowning!
3. When the bus driver slumped over the wheel of the bus, Danny Johnson knew he had to act—and act fast!	d. It's a Boy!
4. "I'm being sucked into the ground!" screamed Ana.	e. It's Cold and Dark Down Here!
5. Most summer days, Juan and his friends spend their time boating on Lake Wobegon.	f. Step on the Brake!
6. Shannon Smith's heart stopped when she heard the train's roar and the child's screams.	

Real-Life Heroes **103**

3. Focus on Style

- Explain that an unusual and interesting title builds interest in the story at the same time that it tells what the story is about. Read the example in Part 1 aloud and invite students to tell why it works well. Then ask students to work with a partner as they explain how the title of the second story, "'Bear-ly' in Time," relates to the story. Have students share and discuss. (The word "bear" refers to the animal that attacked Matt and it's also part of the word "bear-ly"—which means "almost not" when it is spelled "barely." So the title means that they almost weren't able to save Matt in time.)

- Call on a different student to match each title to its story (Part 2). Ask them to "think aloud" as they answer. For example: *For item 3, I looked for titles that have something to do with trains or children.*

- Explain that the beginning of a story is called a lead (Part 3). Ask: *Why is a good lead important?* Have them read each lead on the left. Ask: *What do these leads do?* (They set the scene. They help tell the story.)

- 🍎 **Heads Together** Have students work in pairs, matching each lead to its story. Ask volunteers to share out, explaining why each lead and story matches.

📘 PRACTICE BOOK ACTIVITY

See Activity G, Focus on Style, on Practice Book page 58.

✓ WRAP UP

- 🍎 **Outcome Sentences** Have students complete these stems in their **notebooks**. Have them share out.

  A good title is important because _____.

  One way to write a good lead is to _____.

  One way to write a good ending is to _____.

ANSWER KEY

Think about It: a history book, a magazine.

Focus on Style 1: The word "bear-ly" is like the word *barely* which means *almost didn't*. It indicates that in the story the boys almost didn't move fast enough to save their friend. The word "bear-ly" is also a reference to the bear that injured Matt.

Focus on Style 2: 1. b; 2. c; 3. a; 4. e; 5. f; 6. d.

Focus on Style 3: 1. b; 2. d; 3. f; 4. e; 5. c; 6. a.

UNIT 6 ■ STUDENT BOOK, PAGE 104

H WRITER'S WORKSHOP

Standards
- Use the writing process: planning a story
- Listen and take notes

🎧 1. Getting It Out
WARM UP

- Ask if anyone knows what an interview is. Have volunteers explain. Ask students if they have ever seen an interview on TV. Ask volunteers to describe interviews they've seen.

TEACHING THE LESSON

- Tell students that they will be listening to two interviews and taking notes on both of them (Part 1). Explain that they will write their stories using the notes from the second interview. If necessary, have students complete Mini-Unit, Part A on page 182.

- 🌈 **Access for All** Have less proficient students work in pairs or small groups, with guided support from an instructional aide, volunteer, or peer tutor. Encourage more proficient students to conduct their own interviews, developing different stories.

- Have a volunteer read the five questions aloud, paraphrasing each (Part 2). If students stumble over *incident*, help them clarify the meaning, then use the word in a sentence.

- Play the tape or CD, or read the script once all the way through (Part 3). Ask some general comprehension questions such as: *Who was the hero?* (a girl named Karla) *What was the dangerous situation in this story?* (Her dog almost drowned.) *Where did the events happen?* (in Karla's back yard)

WRITING

For help with taking notes, complete Mini-Unit, Part A on page 182.

H WRITER'S WORKSHOP — True Stories

Imagine that you have been asked to write a story for a book called *Kids Did It! Real-Life Heroes*.

1. Getting It Out

❶ You will listen to two interviews with people who helped others in danger. Take notes. You will use your notes from the second interview to write your story.

❷ Read the interview questions.

Interview Questions
1. Who was involved?
2. Where did the incident happen?
3. What happened?
4. How did everything turn out?
5. How did you feel?

🎧 ❸ Listen to the first story. Practice taking notes.

- Have students write the five interview questions on a separate piece of paper, leaving space between each. Then have them listen to the story a second time, taking notes. Pause after each exchange so that they have time to take notes.

- 🌈 **Access for All** Consider having students who have difficulty comprehending rapid spoken English read the script as they listen to the interview. Then have them complete the note-taking and writing steps along with the rest of the students.

WRITING

UNIT 6 • STUDENT BOOK, PAGE 105

4 Here are the notes that Stefan took. Compare your notes with his.

Story #1: Interview Questions

1. Who was involved? *Karla Pierce and family members, dog Tucker.*
2. Where did the incident happen? *In my backyard, which has a stream running behind it.*
3. What happened? *My family was having a barbecue in backyard with friends. Suddenly, someone shouted that our dog Tucker had fallen in the stream. The stream was moving really fast. I rushed to the edge of the stream and could see that Tucker was in trouble. He was fighting the current and kept hitting rocks. So I stretched out on the bank (it was really slippery!) and hooked my foot around a tree. I reached out over the water and grabbed Tucker by the paw. I pulled him out of the water. (He weighs 100 pounds.)*
4. How did everything turn out? *We were both cold, muddy, and wet but were OK.*
5. How did you feel? *I was really scared. I knew that if I didn't do something, Tucker might drown. Sometimes you have to try your hardest and not give up, you know.*

5 Now listen to the second story. Take notes. Use Stefan's notes as an example. You will use these notes to write your real-life story.

Real-Life Heroes **105**

PB PRACTICE BOOK ACTIVITY

See Activity H, Writer's Workshop, on Practice Book page 59.

- Read each interview question aloud and invite different students to read their notes aloud. Then read the notes in the Student Book. Ask students to compare what they wrote with what Stefan wrote (Part 4). Help them discover any key facts that they have omitted.

- Have students use the form on Practice Book page 59 to complete Part 5. Play the tape or CD, or read the script and have students take notes on the interview form. Pause after each exchange so students have time to take notes. Repeat the entire interview, as needed.

✓ WRAP UP

🍒 **Outcome Sentence** Have students complete this stem:

Aaron Wallace is a hero because _____.

> **TEACHING TIP** Encourage students to compare notes with a partner.

Unit 6   105

UNIT 6 ▪ STUDENT BOOK, PAGE 106

H WRITER'S WORKSHOP

Standards
- Use the writing process: drafting a story with a beginning, middle, and end, and revising for organization and style
- Use an outline to organize writing
- Read a story aloud with fluency and expression

2. Getting It Down
WARM UP

- It's time for students to draft their stories! Explain that in this lesson students will be using their notes to create an outline. They will then use the outline to write a complete first draft of their story.

TEACHING THE LESSON

- Have students look at the outline (Part 1). Ask: *What are the four main parts of a story?* (title, lead, action, and ending)

- 🍎 **Shared Writing** Tell students that, as a class, you are all going to practice making an outline using the story, "Dog Catcher." Use Stefan's notes from page 105 as the source for the outline.

- As the class develops the outline, have students reflect on the starburst comment. What other comments would they add?

- Tell students that they are now going to turn their own notes into an outline, then use their outlines to draft their stories (Part 2).

- Give students time to draft their stories.

- 🍎 **Mini-Lesson on Conventions** Have a volunteer read the note in the Mini-Lesson box, explaining it in his or her own words. Ask students to locate the exclamation points in "'Bear-ly' In

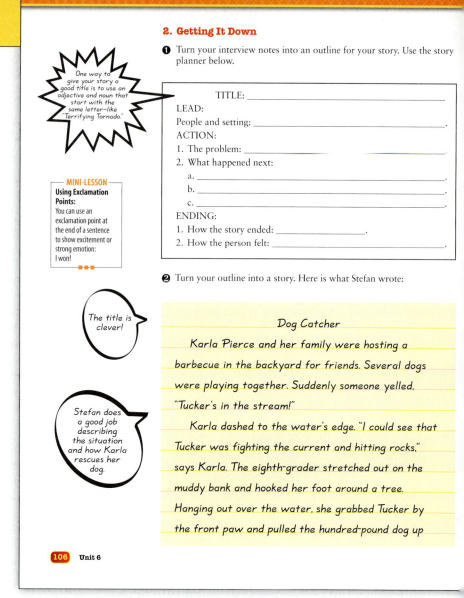

Time" and in Stefan's story. Tell students that they should not *overuse* exclamation points.

WRAP UP

- Tell students that they will have a chance to revise their work during the next session. Have them locate the ChecBric for this unit in the Student Book or Practice Book. Have them prepare for Getting It Right by reviewing the ChecBric on their own, underlining indicators they're not sure about.

3. Getting It Right
WARM UP

- Guide students through the ChecBric for this unit. Explain that they will use the ChecBric to prepare a final draft of their writing.

- Have volunteers explain, in their own words, what each indicator in the ChecBric means.

WRITING

UNIT 6 • STUDENT BOOK, PAGE 107

the steep bank. Though muddy, wet, and cold, both were unharmed.

"At the time, I wasn't scared. I knew if I didn't do something, Tucker might drown," says Karla. "Sometimes you have to try your hardest and not give up."

> The ending is strong. Karla shares the lesson she learned.

3. Getting It Right Now take a careful look at what you have written. Use these questions to help you revise your story.

Questions to ask...	How to check...	How to revise...
1. Does my story have a strong lead?	Underline the sentence(s) that set(s) the scene.	Add words that explain what was happening just before the problem occurred.
2. Did I describe the problem?	Put two stars (★★) before the sentence that describes the problem.	Add words that describe the problem.
3. Did I say what happened in time order?	Put a star (★) before each event.	Add sentences that explain what happened in time order?
4. Did I describe how the problem was solved?	Put a wavy line under the sentence that says how the problem was solved.	Add a sentence that describes how the problem was solved.
5. Does my story have an exciting ending?	Highlight the ending.	Add a sentence that says how everything turned out. Add a quote that describes a lesson learned or how someone felt.

4. Presenting It Read your true story to your classmates.

❶ Begin by giving a brief introduction to the story. Say the names of the people involved in the story and where it took place.

❷ Share the title.

❸ Read your story slowly and clearly. Whenever a person in the story talks, say their words just the way they would say them in real life.

Real-Life Heroes **107**

TEACHING THE LESSON

- Have students use the information in the chart and the ChecBric to revise their work.
- **Group Share** Have students share their stories in groups of four. Have students give each other feedback on their stories, then make revisions.

WRAP UP

- Tell students that the next step is to be sure they are fully prepared to present their stories to the class. Suggest that they practice reading them to a partner or a family member.

- 📁 Give students time to fill out the ChecBric on Practice Book page 111. Ask them to attach it to their writing when they put it in their portfolios.

4. Presenting It
WARM UP

- It's time for students to present their stories! Remind them that their stories should engage, or interest, the audience.

- As a class, develop a simple presentation checklist. In addition to content and organization, focus on speaking skills, enthusiasm, use of visuals, creativity, involvement of the audience, and length of presentation.

- **Build Fluency** Give students time to read their stories aloud to a partner, focusing on reading aloud naturally and with expression. Using Stefan's story, model fluent reading for students, focusing especially on dialogue.

> **TEACHING TIP** 💡 Since most or all stories will be based on the same taped passage, consider having students present in small groups, to help avoid repetition.

TEACHING THE LESSON

- Tell students that you want them to pay attention to three things as they present their stories:
  1. Use a loud and clear voice.
  2. Read naturally and with expression.
  3. Use eye contact to keep your audience interested.

- Have a volunteer read the instructions aloud, then explain the presentation task to their classmates.

- Have students present their stories, following the instructions and your presentation checklist.

✓ WRAP UP

- **Let's Talk** Invite students to talk about the two stories in Writer's Workshop. Which one did they like better? Why?

Unit 6   107

UNIT 6 ■ STUDENT BOOK, PAGE 108

BEYOND THE UNIT

Standard
- Read and respond to a tall tale

1. On Assignment
WARM UP
- Discuss: *Does your school give awards to students? What kinds of awards can students receive?*
- Ask a volunteer to read the steps aloud, then explain the task to classmates. Ask students to look at the picture of Paul Bunyan and say what they think the story will be about.

TEACHING THE LESSON
- **Shared Writing** Have students imagine that they are advising your school's principal on the qualities that a Citizen of the Month should have. Have students dictate ideas, telling what kind of person they think should get this honor as you record their ideas on the board (Part 1).
- Invite students to nominate a classmate as Citizen of the Month. Have students refer to the qualities they have listed (Part 2).

> **TEACHING TIP** 💡 If you are concerned that feelings might be hurt, consider having students give you their nominations in writing, telling why they are nominating the person. Read over their nominations silently, on your own, then announce the names of the two or three people that most students have selected.

- Develop a simple ballot, then have students vote (Part 3). Count the votes and announce the winner.
- Have students make a certificate for the winner (Part 4). They can use the certificate on page 97 as a model.

BEYOND THE UNIT

1. On Assignment Choose a "Citizen of the Month" for your class. Have an award ceremony to honor that person.

❶ As a class, brainstorm the qualities that a Citizen of the Month should have.

❷ Nominate a classmate. Explain why you are nominating that person.

❸ If more than one person is nominated, make a ballot with the top three names. Vote for the Citizen of the Month.

❹ Choose a classmate with good writing to make a Certificate of Honor for the chosen person.

❺ Have an award ceremony. Congratulate the winner! Tell the winner why he or she won.

- Have a student congratulate and present the award to the winner (Part 5). Then invite other students to add their own congratulations.

✓ WRAP UP
- Have students design their own "Citizen of the Month" certificate for themselves.

2. Link to Literature

UNIT 6 ▪ STUDENT BOOK, PAGE 109

SHARED READING All cultures have stories about fictional heroes who did great things. Paul Bunyan is a famous fictional hero in an American story. According to the story, Paul Bunyan and his giant blue ox, Babe, created the Grand Canyon and the Black Hills of South Dakota! Read about one of Paul Bunyan's adventures. As you read, look for examples of **exaggeration** (making something seem bigger, stronger, or better than it really is).

LET'S TALK

1. Write down an example of exaggeration.
2. What is the effect of exaggeration on the story?
3. All cultures have legends. Do you know a story about a legendary hero?

ABOUT THE AUTHOR

Steven Kellogg was born in Norwalk, Connecticut in 1941. He started writing when he was a young boy, and has written almost 90 books.

Paul Bunyan and the Gumberoos

1. At seventeen, Paul grew a fine beard, which he combed with the top of a pine tree.
2. By this time, other **settlers** were beginning to crowd into the Maine woods. Paul felt an urge to move on. He said good-bye to his parents and headed west.
3. Paul wanted to cross the country with the best **lumbering crew** available. He hired Ole, a celebrated **blacksmith**, and two famous cooks, Sourdough Slim and Creampuff Fatty. Then he signed up legendary lumbermen …
4. On the far slopes of the **Appalachian Mountains**, several of Paul's men were **ambushed** by a gang of underground **ogres** called **Gumberoos**.
5. Paul grabbed the camp dinner horn and blew a thunderous note into the Gumberoos' cave, determined to blast the meanness right out of them.
6. To Paul's **dismay**, the Gumberoos responded by snatching the entire crew. A wild, rough-and-tumble **rumpus** began inside the den.
7. When the **tussle** was over, the Gumberoos needed six weeks to untangle themselves. They disappeared **into the depths of the earth**, and they've never been heard from again.

Source: *Paul Bunyan* by Steven Kellogg

settler—someone who moves into a new region
lumbering crew—workers who cut down trees
blacksmith—someone who makes things with iron
Appalachian Mountains—a chain of mountains running from Canada to Alabama
ambush—to make a surprise attack
ogre—a monster that often eats people
Gumberoos—made-up creatures
dismay—disappointment
rumpus/tussle—a fight
into the depths of the earth—deep under the ground

Real-Life Heroes 109

2. Link to Literature

WARM UP

- Tell students that many cultures have myths in which larger than life characters accomplish unbelievable tasks. American folk heroes include John Henry, Annie Oakley, and especially, Paul Bunyan, who according to legend created the Grand Canyon, the Black Hills of South Dakota, and Puget Sound in Washington.

TEACHING THE LESSON

- Make sure students understand that Paul Bunyan was not a real person and that the stories about him are not based on any real person's accomplishments. Point out where the Grand Canyon and South Dakota are on a wall map. Ask students to describe what is special about the Grand Canyon (it's extremely wide and deep) and the Black Hills (they're tall, beautiful mountains). Again, explain that Paul Bunyan is given credit in tall tales for creating both.

- **Shared Reading** Play the tape or CD, or read the story "Paul Bunyan and the Gumberoos" aloud as students follow along. Ask simple comprehension questions as you read or stop the tape to ask questions. For example: *Where did Paul Bunyan start his adventures? What kind of work did he plan to do? Why did Paul blow his horn into a cave? What happened to the Gumberoos?*

- Now play the tape or CD, or read the story a second time. This time, have students listen for exaggerations, or statements that couldn't possibly be true.

- **Let's Talk** Use the questions to lead a discussion of the story. Help students find an example of an exaggeration in the first paragraph (Paul using the top of a pine tree to comb his beard). Have them find other examples in the tale. Ask: *What is the effect of exaggeration on the story?*

- Explain that all cultures have legends. Ask: *What larger-than-life heroes are there in your home culture?*

✓ WRAP UP

- **Outcome Sentence** Have students complete this sentence stem, then share:

  Paul Bunyan was _____.

PB PRACTICE BOOK ACTIVITY

See Activity 1, Responding to Literature, on Practice Book page 60.

✓ UNIT WRAP UP

- Have students reflect in their **notebooks** on what makes a really great story.

Unit 6 109

Unit 7 Nature's Fury
Unit Overview

Section	At a Glance	Standards
Before You Begin	Students discuss an earthquake disaster.	■ Derive meaning from visual information
A. Connecting to Your Life	Students focus on natural disasters and talk about which they fear most.	■ Listen to, then retell a narrative ■ Write a short personal narrative
B. Getting Ready to Read	Students learn useful vocabulary and focus on the sights and sounds of a natural disaster.	■ Use context to determine the meaning of unfamiliar vocabulary ■ Use sensory language
C. Reading to Learn	Students read an exciting story about a boy who lives through a twister. PRACTICE BOOK: Students retell the Student Book story from the third-person point of view.	■ Recognize first- and third-person point of view in narratives ■ Use reading strategies to unlock meaning ■ Locate details
D. Word Work	Students learn that different words can mean the same thing or almost the same thing. PRACTICE BOOK: Students rewrite a short eyewitness account, using synonyms.	■ Recognize synonyms ■ Use knowledge of sound/spelling patterns to spell familiar words
E. Grammar	Students review the correct forms for regular and irregular past tense verbs. PRACTICE BOOK: Students rewrite sentences using correct past tense verb forms.	■ Express past events
F. Bridge to Writing	Students read an eyewitness account of the 1906 earthquake in San Francisco. PRACTICE BOOK: Students practice taking Reading Vocabulary and Reading Comprehension tests. PRACTICE BOOK: Students practice new vocabulary.	■ Recognize first-person point of view in an eyewitness account ■ Use reading strategies to unlock meaning

Section	At a Glance	Standards
G. Writing Clinic	Students consider what makes an eyewitness account exciting. PRACTICE BOOK: Students make an events timeline. PRACTICE BOOK: Students choose the correct words to complete similes.	- Identify the structural patterns found in narratives - Use sensory language - Recognize figurative language: similes
H1. Writer's Workshop: Getting It Out	Students contribute to a class book of eyewitness accounts. They begin by recalling the sights and sounds of the event. PRACTICE BOOK: Students describe a disaster, then develop a timeline.	- Use the writing process: prewriting
H2. Writer's Workshop: Getting It Down	Students draft their accounts.	- Use the writing process: drafting - Use outlines to draft writing
H3. Writer's Workshop: Getting It Right	Students revise their work, developing a final draft.	- Use the writing process: revising for organization and style
H4. Writer's Workshop: Presenting It	Students present their eyewitness reports to classmates.	- Present an oral narrative
I. Beyond the Unit	Students assume the role of TV reporter, preparing and delivering a short news story. Students also read an origin tale about earthquakes, "The Turtle Tale." PRACTICE BOOK: Students respond to "The Turtle Tale."	- Provide a description - Read and respond to an origin tale

UNIT 7 ▪ STUDENT BOOK, PAGE 110

Unit 7 Nature's Fury

Read...
- A terrifying description from "Twister: Winds of Fury."

- A firsthand account of the San Francisco earthquake in 1906.

Link to Literature
- "The Turtle Tale," a myth about why earthquakes happen.

110 Unit 7

Objectives:
Reading:
- Reading first- and third-person descriptions of events (natural disasters)
- Strategy: Visualizing
- Literature: Responding to a myth

Writing:
- Describing an event: An eyewitness account
- Writing paragraphs with a topic sentence and facts
- Using action-packed verbs
- Using similes

Vocabulary:
- Recognizing synonyms
- Learning sensory words

Listening/Speaking:
- Listening to an eyewitness report
- Comparing two disasters

Grammar:
- Reviewing the past tense

Spelling and Phonics:
- Pronouncing words with the letters -ou-

BEFORE YOU BEGIN

Standard
- Derive meaning from visual information

- Write the title of the unit on the board. Ask students to think about the word "nature." Have them point their thumbs up if they know what the word means, point their thumbs sideways if they have seen the word but are not sure what it means, and point their thumbs down if they have never seen the word. Ask volunteers who pointed their thumbs up to define the term, then to use it in a sentence. (Nature is the part of the world not made by humans—plants, animals, mountains, etc.)

- Focus on the word "fury," having students define the term (anger, rage), then use it in a sentence. What does the title "Nature's Fury" refer to? Record student predictions.

- Now have students look at the photo on page 111, without reading the caption. Ask: *What do you see? Why is the ground cracked?*

- Have a volunteer read the caption aloud, then explain what an earthquake is.

- Ask if anyone in class has ever lived through an earthquake. What was it like? Record student responses on the board. Underline adjectives that describe what the person saw, what the person heard, and how the person felt.

- Have a volunteer imagine that s/he is a television reporter, covering the earthquake disaster pictured. Have the volunteer provide a description, using words and phrases students have generated.

- ✓ **Sentence All-Write** Help students list other examples of "Nature's fury"—including *hurricane*, *flood*, *wildfire*, *tornado*, and *tsunami*. Tell students to choose one disaster, then complete a stem like this, describing the disaster:

A hurricane is _____.

Have students save their sentences.

110 Teacher's Edition

Earthquake!

BEFORE YOU BEGIN

Talk with your classmates.

1. Look at the picture. What do you see?
2. Read the caption. Why is the ground cracked?
3. Were you or someone you know ever in an earthquake? What was it like?

UNIT 7 ▪ STUDENT BOOK, PAGE 112

A CONNECTING TO YOUR LIFE

Standards
- Listen to, then retell a narrative
- Write a short personal narrative

WARM UP

- Have students share their sentences from Before You Begin as they look at the pictures. As they share, find out what they know about each type of natural disaster.

TEACHING THE LESSON

🎧 1. Tuning In

- Tell students that they are going to listen to descriptions of three natural disasters. Have students fold a sheet of paper in three parts. Play the tape or CD, or read the script. As students listen, have them write the name of each disaster in one section of their papers, then share (hurricane, earthquake, flood).

- Play the tape or CD, or read the script a second time. For each disaster, have students write words and phrases that describe each disaster. Have students share out, as you record.

2. Talking It Over

- 🍎 **Heads Together** Have students work in pairs to discuss the situation they are most afraid of and why.

- Invite volunteers to share out.

- **Build Background** At this point, provide a brief explanation of common disasters: *Earthquake, Hurricane, Flood, Wildfire, Tornado, Tsunami.*

- Encourage students to write one or two sentences about a personal experience with a natural disaster. Invite volunteers to share.

- Once again, read aloud the title of the unit. Have students use finger signals to tell you what this unit is probably about.

READING

A CONNECTING TO YOUR LIFE

🎧 **1. Tuning In** Listen to the survivors of some natural disasters talk about the events. Look at the pictures below. What type of disaster is each person describing?

2. Talking It Over Work with a partner. Look at the photographs below. Which natural disaster would you fear most? Give one or more reasons.

Can you remember a natural disaster in your own life or one you heard about? Write one or two sentences that explain what happened.

EXAMPLE: *I lived through an earthquake. The house shook. Dishes fell off the shelves.*

1.
An earthquake

2.
A hurricane

3.
A flood

4.
A wildfire

5.
A tornado

6.
A tsunami

Read the title of this unit. What do you think this is probably about? Check () the correct answer.

_____ 1. what to put in a disaster survival kit

_____ 2. what it is like to experience a natural disaster

_____ 3. what scientists are doing to predict natural disasters

✓ WRAP UP

🍎 **Outcome Sentence** Have students complete this stem, then share:

I learned that _____ is dangerous because _____.

- Ask students to talk to a family member or neighbor about a natural disaster they have experienced and find out what it was like. Tell students they'll share their stories during the next class period.

TEACHING TIP 💡 Students can use the Internet to find out more about natural disasters. Have them go to http://www.fema.gov and click on "FEMA for Kids." They can test their knowledge by going to http://www.disasterrelief.org/ and clicking on "The Online Disaster Quiz."

ANSWER KEY

Talking it Over: 2.

READING

UNIT 7 ▪ STUDENT BOOK, PAGE 113

B GETTING READY TO READ

1. Learning New Words Read the sentences below. Try to guess the meanings of the underlined words.

1. Every building was destroyed by the earthquake. The <u>demolished</u> buildings were just dust.
2. The buildings all fell down. There was nothing but piles of <u>rubble</u>.
3. The walls of our house fell, then the roof. The entire house was <u>flattened</u>.
4. The wind blew hard, then stopped. We were glad when it <u>subsided</u>.
5. The earthquake was very powerful. When the first <u>shock</u> hit, it knocked me out of bed!
6. As usual, I got up at 7, took a shower, and ate breakfast. It was a <u>normal</u> morning.
7. Suddenly, we heard a terrible <u>rumble</u> from the ground. That sound told us it was an earthquake!

Now match each word on the left with the correct definition on the right.

1. demolished   a. typical or usual
2. rubble   b. a strong jolt
3. flatten   c. a deep, rolling sound
4. subside   d. completely destroyed
5. shock   e. to die down or become less
6. normal   f. to knock down to the ground
7. rumble   g. crumbled rock, bricks, etc.

2. Talking It Over Imagine that you lived through a disaster. Work with a partner. Choose one disaster. Talk about what it was like then complete the following chart.

	What did you see?	What did you hear?	How did you feel?
1. Earthquake	I saw houses falling down.	I heard …	I felt …
2. Tsunami			
3. Hurricane			

Nature's Fury **113**

B GETTING READY TO READ

Standards
- Use context to determine the meaning of unfamiliar vocabulary
- Use sensory language

WARM UP

- Have students quickly share their "interviews" with family members or neighbors about disasters. What did they learn?

TEACHING THE LESSON

1. Learning New Words

- Write the new words on the board. Have students work in groups of three, trying to write a definition for any three of these words or phrases. Have them share their definitions, then set them aside for the next step.

- Now have students open their books. Have a volunteer read each sentence aloud. Ask: *What does the underlined word mean?* Encourage groups who have defined the word to offer various definitions. Do not correct or comment.

- Now have each trio match each word to the definition. Have them compare their original definitions with the definitions in the book. Have them correct their original definitions, then share out which words they originally defined incorrectly.

- Have each trio create an original sentence for each word, writing each on a piece of paper. Have students share out.

2. Talking It Over

- Have a volunteer look at the chart, read the instructions, then explain the task to classmates.

- 🍫 **Heads Together** Have students complete the activity in pairs.

- 🍫 **Interactive Writing** Draw the chart on the chalkboard. Have volunteers complete the chart.

✓ WRAP UP

- Have students choose two words they have learned in this lesson, then write a sentence that uses both. Have volunteers share sentences.

ANSWER KEY

Learning New Words: 1. d; 2. g; 3. f; 4. e; 5. b; 6. a; 7. c.

Unit 7

UNIT 7 ▪ STUDENT BOOK, PAGE 114

C READING TO LEARN

Standards
- Recognize first- and third-person point of view in narratives
- Use reading strategies to unlock meaning
- Locate details

WARM UP

- Remind students that tornadoes and hurricanes are sometimes confused. Ask for a volunteer to explain the differences. Have students look at the title and ask: *Is this reading about a hurricane or a tornado?*

TEACHING THE LESSON

1. Before You Read

- **Heads Together** Have students look at the source line below the reading. Have a volunteer tell you another name for a tornado (twister). Have someone tell you why tornadoes are sometimes called twisters.

🎧 2. Let's Read

- Tell students that they are about to read a narrative about a tornado. Tell them to visualize as they read and think about which part of the story is the most exciting.
- Tell students that when you *visualize*, you create pictures in your mind (Reading Strategy box). Ask how visualizing can be helpful to a reader (helps with understanding).
- **My Turn: Read Aloud/Think Aloud** Begin by reading the passage aloud. Model correct phrasing and fluent reading. Comment as you read. Explain that the first paragraph of this story is told from the *third-person point of view*. The writer is not part of

the story. The rest of the story is told from the *first-person point of view*. The writer is part of the story.

- ✓ **Sentence All-Write** After reading paragraph 2, have students write a sentence that predicts what will happen next. Have volunteers share their predictions.

- **Our Turn: Interactive Reading** Read the first sentence of each paragraph. Then call on individuals to read other sentences. As students read, focus on the glossed words, ask questions, and make comments.

- **Build Fluency** Have pairs of students read alternate paragraphs. Encourage them to read with expression.

- **Your Turn: Independent Reading** Have students read the passage on their own. Ask them to decide which of the things that happened to Carson would scare them the most. Invite volunteers to share with the class.

READING

C READING TO LEARN — Describing an Event

1. Before You Read You are going to read a description of a tornado. Look at the source at the bottom of the reading. What do you think another name for a tornado is?

☐ twister ☐ hurricane ☐ wildfire

READING STRATEGY
Visualizing: Forming pictures in your mind can help you understand what you are reading.

🎧 **2. Let's Read** As you read, **visualize** what's happening in the story. What would be the most frightening part?

I Survived a Tornado!

1. For Carson Birch of Hesston, Kansas, it started as "just a normal evening" in 1990, when he was 7 years old.
2. My mom and four sisters and I were all sitting around eating pancakes and getting ready to go to a school program. Then we heard **sirens** going off. We looked out one window, and the sky was totally clear. But my mom looked out the other direction and it was really black.
3. We decided to go down to the basement, where my bedroom was. Then the electricity went out, and my mom got scared. We got onto my **bunk beds**, covered up with cushions from the couch, and all sang a **hymn**.
4. You could hear this rumbling noise, like a big train, It got louder and louder and louder. We couldn't even hear ourselves sing. And all of a sudden, in a second, it stopped. The tornado was gone.
5. We went upstairs and tried the door to the kitchen, but it wouldn't open. The ceiling had fallen in on the kitchen! The door to the garage was open, so we went outside. Some of the houses were gone. There were just cement **slabs** with people coming out of them, from down in their basements. Pretty soon my dad got home from his store, which had been flattened. It's amazing that in our whole town no one died from the tornado. I remember seeing a car up in a tree, But the strangest thing was that a week after the tornado I was in a park and found a half-broken Nintendo game that said "Birch" on it. It was ours! The tornado had carried it clear across town.
6. After that we wore shirts that said "*I SURVIVED THE BIG ONE*." Now I'm 14, and the tornado is the only thing I can remember about the first grade!

Source: "Twister: Winds of Fury," from *National Geographic World*

siren—a piece of equipment on police cars and fire engines that makes very loud warning sounds

bunk beds—two beds that are attached, one on top of the other

hymn—a religious song

slab—a thick piece of something hard, like cement

114 Unit 7

---

114 Teacher's Edition

READING

UNIT 7 ▪ STUDENT BOOK, PAGE 115

3. Unlocking Meaning

❶ **Finding the Main Idea** Which of the following statements is the main idea of the story? Check (✓) the correct answer.

_____ 1. Tornadoes are scarier than earthquakes.
_____ 2. Tornadoes can be both dangerous and destructive.
_____ 3. Tornadoes move round and round.

❷ **Finding Details** Number the sentences below in the order that they happened in the story.

_____ Carson's mother saw that part of the sky is black.
_____ The family heard a loud rumbling noise.
__1__ Carson and his family were eating dinner.
_____ The tornado moved on.
_____ Sirens went off.
_____ Carson remembers the tornado.
_____ Carson and his family went down to the basement.
_____ The family learned their home was damaged.
_____ Carson's father came home.
_____ Carson found his Nintendo game in the park.

❸ **Think about It** Based on the reading, what are two important safety rules to follow during a tornado? Check (✓) the best answers.

_____ 1. Go to the basement or a room on the lowest floor.
_____ 2. Get in your car and try to run away from the tornado.
_____ 3. Get up on the roof of your house.
_____ 4. Move away from windows.

❹ **Before You Move On** The Fujita Scale measures the force of tornadoes in **miles per hour** (MPH). Read the following descriptions, then decide which type of tornado hit Rob's farmyard.

Fujita Scale		
F-0	Gale (40–72 MPH)	damages chimneys
F-1	Moderate (73–112 MPH)	peels off shingles
F-2	Significant (113–157 MPH)	rips off roofs
F-3	Severe (158–206 MPH)	flips over cars
F-4	Devastating (207–260 MPH)	destroys houses
F-5	Incredible (261–318 MPH)	carries buildings far away

Nature's Fury 115

3. Unlocking Meaning

✓ FINDING THE MAIN IDEA

- Read each statement. Have students use finger signals to tell you which statement best describes the main idea of the story. Have students tell you why the other statements are not the main idea. (The main idea must in some way summarize the most important message of the reading passage and statements 1 and 3 don't do this.)

✓ FINDING DETAILS

- Ask students to number the sentences in the book to show the order in which the events happened.

- Draw a sample vertical timeline on the board with ten tick marks, each representing an event in the story. Write the first event next to the topmost tick mark. Ask students to complete a similar timeline on their papers. Have volunteers read aloud the events in the correct order.

THINK ABOUT IT

- **Team Talk** Working in small groups, have students select two safety rules, based on information in the reading. As a class, review responses.

BEFORE YOU MOVE ON

- **Think Aloud** Model the thinking process you use as you review the Fujita Scale. For example: *F-0 is a gale. It just damages chimneys. The storm Rob saw was stronger than that. It picked up a truck.* Then have volunteers read the other descriptions along the Fujita Scale the same way—until they conclude that F-4 is the correct response. Have a volunteer explain why.

✓ WRAP UP

- Remind students that the story starts with the third-person point of view, and continues with the first-person point of view. Have a volunteer explain in his/her own words what this means.

PB PRACTICE BOOK ACTIVITY

See Activity A, Revisit and Retell, on Practice Book page 61.

ANSWER KEY

Before You Read: twister.
Finding the Main Idea: 2.
Finding Details: 3, 5, 1, 6, 2, 10, 4, 7, 8, 9.
Think about It: 1, 4.
Before You Move On: F-4 Devastating.

Unit 7   115

UNIT 7 ▪ STUDENT BOOK, PAGE 116

D WORD WORK

> **Standards**
> - Recognize synonyms
> - Use knowledge of sound/spelling patterns to spell familiar words

WARM UP

- Write these pairs on the board:

  big : huge   small : little

  Have students tell you what each pair of words has in common. Tell students that you can make your writing better by using just the right word.

TEACHING THE LESSON

1. Word Detective

- Have students complete the activity. Review the correct answers.

2. Word Study

- Referring to the examples, explain that the word *silent* in the first sentence indicates that there was no sound at all. The word *quiet* in the second sentence indicates that there may be some noise, but not a lot.

- Have students generate pairs of sentences with synonyms, identifying differences in shades of meaning.

3. Word Play

- 🍎 **Heads Together** Have students complete the activity in pairs, then share with classmates.

Spelling and Phonics

- Read each word aloud. What do students notice about them? (The letters *ou* are pronounced differently in each word.)

- Have students complete the activity on their own, then share.

READING

D WORD WORK

1. Word Detective Match the words in the left column with the words on the right that mean the same (or almost the same) thing.

1. noisy	a. boom
2. bang	b. blow up
3. dark	c. loud
4. throw	d. black
5. fear	e. twist
6. swirl	f. peaceful
7. explode	g. toss
8. quiet	h. be afraid

2. Word Study Words that mean the same thing are called *synonyms*. Knowing synonyms can help you choose just the right word. Synonyms usually have slightly different meanings. Depending on the sentence, you might prefer to use one word rather than another.

> SPELLING AND PHONICS:
> To do this activity, go to page 195.

silent	Two minutes later, all was <u>silent</u>.
quiet	I need a <u>quiet</u> place to study.

3. Word Play Work with a partner. Find a more interesting synonym for each underlined word. You can use a dictionary or a thesaurus.

1. We heard a <u>loud</u> noise.
2. Clouds were <u>turning</u> in the sky.
3. The tornado <u>touched</u> the ground.
4. Windows <u>broke</u>.
5. The winds <u>pulled</u> off the roof.
6. We were <u>afraid</u>.

✓ WRAP UP

- Write these words on the board: *tough, stubborn*. Have students use the words to complete these sentence stems, then share:

  I would say that I'm _____.
  My parents would say that I'm _____.

  Point out that depending on who or what you are talking about, synonyms can take on different meanings.

PB PRACTICE BOOK ACTIVITY

See Activity B, Word Work, on Practice Book page 62.

ANSWER KEY

Word Detective: 1. c 2. a 3. d 4. g 5. h 6. e 7. b 8. f

Word Play: Answers will vary.

Spelling and Phonics: found: cloud, pound, ground, around, count, out; **thought:** cough; **touch:** country, enough; **group:** through, youth, soup.

UNIT 7 ■ STUDENT BOOK, PAGE 117

E GRAMMAR — Review: Simple Past Tense

1. Listen Up Listen to each sentence. Point your thumb up 👍 if it sounds correct. Point your thumb down 👎 if it sounds wrong.

👍👎 1. We heared the sirens go off.
👍👎 2. It began to rain and hail.
👍👎 3. The wind blowed hard.
👍👎 4. We went down to the basement.

2. Learn the Rule Learn how to use the past tense. After you have learned the rules, do Activity 1 again.

THE SIMPLE PAST TENSE

1. Use the simple past tense to describe an action or event that took place at a specific time in the past. Form the simple past tense of regular verbs by adding –ed or -d.	Suddenly the sky turn<u>ed</u> black. Thunder roll<u>ed</u> and lightening flash<u>ed</u>.
2. Remember that many common verbs are irregular: come (came), go (went), be (was/were), have (had), and make (made). Check the dictionary if you are not sure.	Right: The windows blew in. Wrong: The windows ~~blowed~~ in.

3. Practice the Rule Look at this Pennsylvania boy's eyewitness report. Complete the sentences with the past tense forms of the verbs in the box.

say   notice   get   come   appear
~~look~~   know   be   run   jump

My Tornado Story

It started as a regular day. I _looked_ out the window and _____ dark, black clouds. I _____ to myself, "OK—it's nothing to worry about." Ten minutes later, a thunder cloud _____ in the distance. The wind _____ stronger and was coming from the southeast at about 45 to 50 miles per hour. I _____ really worried.
It started to hail and rain really hard. I saw a funnel. I _____ what that meant: it was a tornado! The clouds swirled around. The tornado _____ closer! I _____ outside and _____ into a ditch about five feet deep. I'm thankful I'm alive after that close call!

Nature's Fury **117**

E GRAMMAR

Standard
- Express past events

WARM UP

- Write two lists of verbs on the board. List 1: *talk, dance, lift*. List 2: *think, choose, sit*. Invite students to make up sentences using the past tense of the words in List 1. Correct the sentences as necessary and elicit that all these are regular verbs ending in –ed. Repeat the activity with List 2 and elicit that these are irregular verbs with a variety of different forms.

TEACHING THE LESSON

🎧 1. Listen Up

- Read each sentence, or play the tape or CD twice. Have students follow the directions. Note to yourself how many students responded incorrectly for each item.

♻ 2. Learn the Rule

- Review the spelling and pronunciation of the regular past tense forms as well as irregular past tense forms for common verbs.
- Write the following verbs on the board and ask students to write a past tense sentence for each: *fly, go, blow, run, begin, hide, know, be*. Encourage students to suggest corrections for classmates' sentences as necessary. Then repeat the Listen Up activity.

♻ 3. Practice the Rule

- Have a volunteer read the directions, then explain the task to classmates. Have students complete the activity, then share.

✓ WRAP UP

- Write the base forms of ten regular and ten irregular verbs on slips of paper. Place them in a shoebox. Have students take turns pulling a slip out of the box, then using the verb in a sentence in the past tense.

PB PRACTICE BOOK ACTIVITY

See Activity C, Grammar, on Practice Book page 63.

ANSWER KEY

Listen Up: Correct sentences: 2, 4.
Practice the Rule: looked, noticed, said, appeared, got, was, knew, came, ran, jumped.

Unit 7   **117**

UNIT 7 • STUDENT BOOK, PAGE 118

WRITING

F BRIDGE TO WRITING

Standards
- Recognize first-person point of view in an eyewitness account
- Use reading strategies to unlock meaning

WARM UP

- Explain that students are going to read an account of a deadly earthquake that nearly destroyed San Francisco in 1906, written by a man who lived through the event.

- **Build Background** Explain that a terrifying earthquake struck San Francisco on April 18, 1906. It was the worst natural disaster in U.S. history. It may have measured 8.25 on the Richter scale. The quake started fires that burned for three days. 25,000 buildings were destroyed, 250,000 people were left homeless, and as many as 700 people were killed.

TEACHING THE LESSON

1. Before You Read

- Write the word *eyewitness* on the board. Ask students to look at the two words in this compound and explain in their own words what they mean. Help them understand that an *eyewitness* is someone who was present at an event and saw it with their own eyes.

- Invite students to give short descriptions of important events to which they were eyewitnesses.

🎧 2. Let's Read

♻ Tell students that they will need to visualize as they read. Remind students that when you *visualize*, you create pictures in your mind about what you are reading (Reading Strategy box). Ask why visualizing is useful.

F BRIDGE TO WRITING — Describing an Event

1. Before You Read An eyewitness is someone who sees something happen. Have you ever been an eyewitness to an event? What did you see?

READING STRATEGY
Visualizing: Forming pictures in your mind can help you understand what you are reading

🎧 **2. Let's Read** On April 18, 1906, a terrible earthquake hit San Francisco. Thomas Jefferson Chase was walking to work. This is his eyewitness account. As you read, **visualize** Chase's journey.

> ¹ The morning was clear and bright, not a breath of air was stirring. The city was asleep. The time was 5:18, morning of April 18th, 1906…
> ² I usually walked down Folsom to First, [then] to Market Street to eat before going to work.
> ³ I had reached about halfway to Howard on the west side of First Street when I heard a low distant rumble. … I stopped and listened. Then it hit.
> ⁴ Power and **trolley** lines snapped like threads. The ends of the power lines dropped to the pavement …, writhing and hissing like reptiles. Brick and glass showered about me.
> ⁵ Buildings along First Street from Howard to Market crumbled like card houses. One was brick. Not a soul escaped. … The dust hung low over the rubble in the street.
> ⁶ [When] this shock stopped, I crossed over to the east side of the street. As soon as I reached the curb a second shock hit. This was harder than the first. I was thrown flat, and the **cobblestones** danced like corn in a popper. More brick and glass showered down on the sidewalk.
> ⁷ As soon as it subsided, I started for Howard Street. By the time I reached the corner, a third shock hit. I was under the old Selby Shot Tower. I expected to see it go but it didn't. The flagpole on the building whipped and snapped like the popping of a whip.
> ⁸ I started down Howard for the Ferry. Looking down First Street through the dust of demolished buildings a wisp of black smoke was rising through the dust. …
> ⁹ [When I finally reached the Embarcadero], the entire south wall of the Ferry Building was out. It crashed down into the Bay. The waves were lazily lapping at the **pilings** as if nothing had happened.

Source: sfmuseum.org

Square brackets [] tell you that these are not the writer's words.

Marks like these … tell you that words have been left out.

This story is told in the first person. The narrator is telling a story about himself.

trolley—a streetcar
cobblestone—a paving stone
piling—a heavy beam that supports a building at the water's edge

118 Unit 7

- 🍎 **My Turn: Read Aloud/Think Aloud** Read the introductory paragraph and directions aloud. Then read the story, or play the tape or CD. As you read, stop to make comments and ask questions about words. Ask whether this story is told from the first- or third-person point of view.

- Call attention to the descriptive language in the story. For example, in paragraph 4, the power lines are "writhing and hissing" and in paragraph 7, the flagpole "whipped and snapped."

- Call attention to and explain the starbursts.

- 🍎 **Our Turn: Interactive Reading** Have students help you read the selection. Take turns with students reading a paragraph aloud. Pause to discuss as students read. Focus on the glossed words, ask questions, and make comments.

- ✓ 🍎 **Question All-Write** After reading paragraph 7, have students write a sentence that answers this question: *What did Chase expect to happen that didn't?*

WRITING

UNIT 7 ■ STUDENT BOOK, PAGE 119

3. Making Content Connections You have read about two kinds of disasters that can strike. Work with a partner. Complete the chart below.

	Tornado	Earthquake
1. What sights and sounds do you hear?	dark sky	
2. What kind of damage can it cause?		
3. Why is it so dangerous to people?		

4. Expanding Your Vocabulary

❶ Your writing can be more exciting to read if you use verbs that are "action packed":

Everyday verb: Juan *got* under the table.
Action-packed verb: Juan *leaped* under the table.

❷ Rewrite the sentences below. Use an "action-packed" verb from the box. Make sure you put the new verbs in the past tense.

| snap | ~~jump~~ | swirl | sway |
| crash into | rip off | tumble over | shatter |

1. Juan <u>got</u> under a table. _____ *jumped* _____
2. The clouds <u>moved round and round</u> in the sky. _____
3. The winds <u>took off</u> the roof from the house. _____
4. The buildings <u>moved back and forth</u>. _____
5. The skyscraper <u>fell</u>. _____
6. The bridge <u>broke</u> in two. _____
7. The car <u>hit</u> the tree. _____
8. The windows <u>broke</u> into tiny pieces. _____

Nature's Fury **119**

4. Expanding Your Vocabulary

- Have a volunteer read both sentences (Part 1). Which is more interesting? Why? Explain that "action packed" verbs help the reader visualize the story.

- **Heads Together** Have a volunteer read the instructions, then explain the task to classmates (Part 2). Have pairs complete the activity, then share out.

- Use this activity as an opportunity to help students understand what a thesaurus is and how it works.

PB PRACTICE BOOK ACTIVITY

See Activity D, Test-Taking Practice, on Practice Book pages 64 and 65.

See Activity E, Using New Vocabulary, on Practice Book page 66.

✓ WRAP UP

- Remind students that the account they have read is told from the *first-person* point of view. Have students now imagine that they are news reporters. Assign each student a paragraph from the reading. Have students rewrite their paragraphs from the *third-person* point of view, then share.

ANSWER KEY

Expanding Your Vocabulary: 1. Juan jumped under the table. 2. The clouds swirled in the sky. 3. The winds ripped off the roof from the house. 4. The buildings swayed. 5. The skyscraper tumbled over. 6. The bridge snapped in two. 7. The car crashed into the tree. 8. The windows shattered into tiny pieces.

- **Build Fluency** Have pairs of students practice reading alternating paragraphs with fluency and expression.

- **Your Turn: Independent Reading** Have students read the report on their own. Ask them to list favorite words and phrases that help create vivid mental pictures.

- 🌈 **Access for All** Have students with artistic talent or spatial intelligence illustrate Chase's account or draw a map of Chase's route. Have students with linguistic intelligence write a short newspaper account of the earthquake.

3. Making Content Connections

- **Heads Together** Have a volunteer read the directions, then explain the task. Give pairs of students time to complete the chart.

- **Interactive Writing** Draw the chart on the board. Have volunteers fill in the chart.

Unit 7   119

UNIT 7 ▪ STUDENT BOOK, PAGE 120

G WRITING CLINIC

Standards
- Identify the structural patterns found in narratives
- Use sensory language
- Recognize figurative language: similes

WARM UP
- Have students think about the descriptions they have read. Ask: *What makes them interesting?* List students' ideas (good descriptions, good beginnings, exciting action, etc.).

TEACHING THE LESSON

1. Think about It
- Ask students what they want a reader or listener to feel when they describe an exciting event. Help students understand that an exciting story or eyewitness account makes readers feel like they were there.

2. Focus on Organization
- Explain that a description of an event—whether it is told in the first person or in the third person—has three parts. Have students look at the diagram in Part 1, then tell you what those three parts are (opening, body, ending).
- Explain that the introduction sets the scene—telling *where* and often *when*. Have a volunteer read the first paragraph of "I Survived a Tornado!" on page 114 aloud, then identify the words that tell where and when.
- Explain that the introduction to a story is important not only because it sets the scene but also because it captures the reader's attention and creates interest. Explain that you can make your introduction even more interesting by hinting to the reader that a problem is about to occur. Have

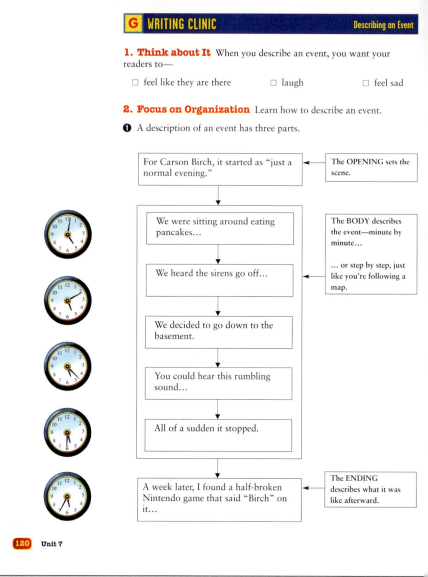

students find the words in "I Survived a Tornado!" that tell that something bad is about to happen.

- Tell students that the body of the narrative comes next. Here is where we read a "moment-by-moment" description of what happened. Have students read the story map of events. What do they notice? (The events are in exact time order.)

- Finally, explain that an effective narrative has a conclusion, or an ending. The writer once again describes the setting, often using sensory language.

- For Part 2, have a volunteer read the directions, then explain the task. Have students make diagrams, or maps, that show the organization of Chase's story.

🌈 **Access for All** Have less-proficient students work with partners on the mapping task.

PB PRACTICE BOOK ACTIVITY

See Activity F, Focus on Organization, on Practice Book page 57.

WRITING

UNIT 7 ▪ STUDENT BOOK, PAGE 121

❷ Reread the eyewitness report of the San Francisco earthquake. Make your own "map" that shows how each event happened.

3. Focus on Style

❶ A good description provides details about how things look, sound, feel, taste, or smell. Reread the description of the earthquake. Make a chart like this one. Include as many sights, sounds, feelings, tastes and smells as you can in the chart.

sight	sound
writhing like reptiles	low, distant rumble
feel	**taste/smell**
Not a breath of air was stirring....	no examples

❷ The writers of both readings in this unit use figurative language—words and phrases that "paint a picture" for the reader. These sentences all use *similes*. Similes compare two things that are not usually compared to each other.

 The word *like* tells you that a simile follows.

1. Mud and grass swirled up *like* smoke from a bonfire.
2. Power and trolley lines snapped like threads.
3. Cobblestones danced like corn in a popper.
4. The clouds bubbled at the top like boiling milk.
5. Buildings crumbled like card houses.

❸ Make up your own similes. Complete each of the following sentences.

1. The huge clouds spun like _____.
2. The tornado moved toward us like _____.
3. The earthquake made a noise like _____.
4. The building shook like _____.
5. The dishes in the cupboard rattled like _____.
6. The breaking windows sounded like _____.
7. The bridge collapsed like _____.

Nature's Fury **121**

- Tell students that writers often use similes to create vivid descriptions (Part 2). A simile is a word picture that compares one thing to another. Ask: *What are mud and grass compared to in the first sentence?* (They're being compared to smoke from a bonfire.) Ask: *How is the mud and grass like smoke?* (The mud and grass are rising in the air and swirling around like smoke.) Continue with the other sentences.

- Point out the use of the word *like* in similes. Explain that *like* means *the same as* in this situation. Invite students to read sentences aloud.

- 🍎 **Heads Together** Have pairs of students generate their own similes, then share (Part 3).

🅿🅱 PRACTICE BOOK ACTIVITY

See Activity G, Focus on Style, on Practice Book page 68.

✓ WRAP UP

- 🍎 **Outcome Sentence** Have students complete this sentence stem, then share:

  A really exciting eyewitness account describes _____.

ANSWER KEY

Think about It: feel like they are there.

Focus on Style 1: Possible answers:
sight: writhing like reptiles, clear and bright, brick and glass showered about me, dust hung low over the rubble, the flagpole...whipped and snapped, a wisp of black smoke was rising, the waves were lazily lapping; **feel:** Not a breath of air was stirring, I was thrown flat, Then it hit; **sound:** low, distant rumble, hissing like reptiles.

---

3. Focus on Style

🍎 **Team Talk** Have a volunteer read the directions for Part 1, then explain the task to classmates. Explain that writers make their descriptions come alive by using sensory language, or language that appeals to the senses—what something looks like, what it sounds like, what it feels like, and what it tastes or smells like.

- Have students look again at the story map for "I Survived a Tornado!" identifying examples of sensory language.

- Give students time to complete their charts, then share out as you record.

- Write these sentences on the board:

  Power and trolley lines snapped like threads.
  Cobblestones danced like corn in a popper.

  Have students tell you why these sentences are interesting. Have them look for other examples of interesting sentences in Chase's account.

Unit 7 **121**

UNIT 7 ▪ STUDENT BOOK, PAGE 122

H Writer's Workshop

Standard
- Use the writing process: prewriting

1. Getting It Out
WARM UP

- Tell students that the class will be writing a collection of eyewitness accounts of natural disasters for a book entitled, "Mother Nature's Anger." Have a volunteer explain the meaning of the title of the collection. Help students understand that the term "Mother Nature" is a common way for Westerners to picture the forces of nature in a friendly way.

TEACHING THE LESSON

- Have students imagine that they are eyewitnesses to one of the four natural disasters pictured—hurricane, flood, wildfire, or tornado (Part 1). Have them jot down words and ideas that come to mind as they look at each picture. After several minutes, have students share, as you record.

> **TEACHING TIP** 💡 Students can use the Internet to find out more about natural disasters. Have them go to http://www.fema.gov and click on "FEMA for Kids." The can also get information on current natural disasters worldwide at http://www.angelfire.com/on/predictions/.

- Have students choose a natural disaster to write about—one that is pictured or one they have actually experienced (Part 2). Have them complete the chart, then list the sights, sounds, and feelings they associate with the disaster. Students can use the chart on Practice Book page 69.

122 **Teacher's Edition**

WRITING

H Writer's Workshop — Describing an Event

Imagine that your class is writing a book called "Mother Nature's Anger." You will write an eyewitness account that describes an event.

1. Getting It Out

❶ Imagine what it would be like to live through a natural disaster. As you look at the following photos, what images come into your mind?

❷ Choose one natural disaster to write about. What words describe what it is like? Complete the chart below with words that describe the feelings, sounds, and sights of the event.

	Looked like...	Sounded like...	Felt like...
1.			
2.			
3.			

122 Unit 7

- Invite several volunteers to share the contents of their charts with the class. Encourage students to listen to the ideas of others, then add to their own charts.

WRITING

UNIT 7 • STUDENT BOOK, PAGE 123

❸ Maria decided to write about an earthquake. She recreated the event in "slow motion":

1.
2.
3.

❹ Here is what Maria wrote about an earthquake. Add to her chart below.

Looked like...	Sounded like...	Felt like...
1. Trees started to shake.	I heard a rumble.	I felt the ground under me move.
2. I saw cracks in the roads.	The rumble got louder—like a jet engine.	The shaking knocked me to the ground.
3. Cars turned over. Buildings fell down.	It was deathly quiet.	

Nature's Fury

WRAP UP

- Explain that during the next workshop session students will use the charts they created to help them draft their accounts.

PB PRACTICE BOOK ACTIVITY

See Activity H, Writer's Workshop, on Practice Book page 69.

- Ask students what they think the term *slow motion* means. Explain and use pantomime to show that it involves presenting something slower than it actually happens in real life. Have students focus on Maria's recreation of an earthquake, describing each phase.

- Review Maria's eyewitness chart with the class. Ask them to use their imaginations to add to the chart. Review the added information with the whole class.

- As a class, turn Maria's chart into an events timeline on the board. Then have students use the form on Practice Book page 69 to complete timelines relating to the natural disasters they have chosen to write about.

  Access for All Have an aide, adult volunteer, or peer tutor work with less-proficient students. Have them work as a group to create a single eyewitness account or their own individual accounts.

Unit 7   123

UNIT 7 ▪ STUDENT BOOK, PAGE 124

H WRITER'S WORKSHOP

Standards
- Use the writing process: drafting and revising for organization and style
- Use outlines to draft writing
- Present an oral narrative

2. Getting It Down
WARM UP

- It's time for students to draft their eyewitness accounts! Explain that in this lesson students will be using the chart to create an outline. They will then use the outline to write a complete first draft of their story.

TEACHING THE LESSON

- Have students look at the outline (Part 1). Ask: *Besides the title, what are the main parts of the account?* (Before the event [opening], description of the event [body], and after the event [ending]).

- 🍎 **Shared Writing** Tell students that, as a class, you are all going to practice making an outline using Maria's account (Part 2). Use Maria's draft as the source for the outline. Begin with the title, then move to the opening, the body, and the ending. Use partial sentences.

- Tell students that they are now going to work in the opposite direction—turning their notes into an outline, then using their outlines to draft their eyewitness accounts.

- Give students time to develop their outlines. Check their work to make sure that they are ready to move on to the next step—drafting their eyewitness accounts.

- Review Maria's story with the class and have students compare what she wrote in the story with her chart

---

WRITING

2. Getting It Down

❶ Use your diagram to make an outline of the event.

```
               Title: _____
1. Before the event: _____
2. The event:
   A. What happened: _____
      Sights: _____
      Sounds: _____
      Other sensations: _____
   B. What happened: _____
      Sights: _____
      Sounds: _____
      Other sensations: _____
3. After the event: _____
```

❷ Turn your outline into a paragraph or two. Here is what Maria wrote:

> It was a day like any other day. I was walking home from school. I was at the top of Potrero Hill, where I could see the city below. Suddenly, I heard a low rumble. Trees started to sway. I felt the ground under my feet begin to shake. It was an earthquake!
>
> The shaking became more violent. Cracks opened up in the roads, buildings began to crumble like cookies, and cars veered off the road like pieces on an overturned chessboard. The roar grew louder, like a huge jet flying over the city.
>
> After 30 long seconds, the shaking stopped. A picture of deadly destruction lay before me—toppled buildings, huge cracks in the earth, and cars thrown about like a child's toys.

MINI-LESSON
Combining Sentences: When several short sentences are combined into one, they are separated by commas:
Cracks opened up the roads, buildings began to crumble, and cars veered off the road.

❸ Evaluate Maria's eyewitness account:
1. Copy the sentences that set the scene.
2. Copy the sentences that describe what happened during the earthquake.
3. Copy examples of figurative language.
4. Copy the sentences that describe what it was like right after the earthquake ended.

124 Unit 7

(Part 3). How did she change things when she wrote the report? What kinds of details did she add?

- Have students count off 1–4. Have 1s copy the sentences that set the scene. Have 2s copy the sentences that describe the event. Have 3s copy the examples of figurative language. Have 4s copy the conclusion. Have students share.

- 🍎 **Mini-Lesson on Conventions** Point out the Mini-Lesson box and ask students to locate the commas in Maria's story. Ask different students to read the sentences with commas in them aloud, allowing a pause for each comma to help make the meaning of the sentence clearer.

WRAP UP

- Tell students that they will have a chance to revise their work during the next session. Have them locate the ChecBric for this unit in the Student Book or Practice Book. Have them prepare for Getting It Right by reviewing the ChecBric on their own, underlining indicators they're not sure about.

UNIT 7 • STUDENT BOOK, PAGE 125

3. Getting It Right Take a careful look at what you have written. Use these questions to help you review and revise your work.

Questions to ask…	How to check…	How to revise…
1. Do I set the scene?	Underline the sentences that set the scene.	Add a sentence or two that says what was happening right before the disaster hit.
2. Does my report make the reader feel they were there?	Ask a neighbor if your report helps them imagine the event.	Add more details. Use action-packed verbs that show, not tell.
3. Do I use sensory language?	Circle the words and phrases that relate to the senses.	Add more sensory details. Describe the sights and sounds of the event.
4. Do I use figurative language?	Draw a box around words that are examples of figurative language.	Add a simile or two to your report.
5. Does my ending describe the aftermath?	Draw a wavy line under the ending.	Add a sentence that describes the scene or tells how people felt after the event.

4. Presenting It Share your eyewitness report with your classmates.

❶ Read the title of your report.

❷ Begin by reading the part that sets the scene. Read clearly and calmly.

❸ Next read your description of the disaster. Use your voice to express the excitement of the event.

❹ Ask your classmates for feedback on your report.

Nature's Fury **125**

3. Getting It Right

WARM UP

- Guide students through the ChecBric for this unit in the Student Book or Practice Book. Explain that they will use the ChecBric to prepare a final draft.
- Have volunteers explain, in their own words, what each indicator in the ChecBric means.

TEACHING THE LESSON

- Have students use the chart and the ChecBric to revise their work.
- **Group Share** Have students share their eyewitness accounts in groups of four or five and give each other feedback on their articles, then make revisions.

WRAP UP

- Ask students to rehearse their eyewitness accounts on their own, whispering aloud as they read.
- 📁 Give students time to fill out the ChecBric on Practice Book page 113. Ask them to attach it to their writing when they put it in their portfolios.

4. Presenting It

WARM UP

- It's time for students to present their stories! Remind them that their stories should engage, or interest, the audience.
- As a class, develop a simple presentation checklist. Focus on content, organization, speaking skills, enthusiasm, etc.

TEACHING THE LESSON

- Tell students that you want them to pay attention to three things as they present their stories:
  1. Use a loud and clear voice.
  2. Read naturally and with expression.
  3. Use eye contact to keep your audience interested.
- Have a volunteer read the instructions aloud, then explain the presentation task to their classmates.
- Have students present their eyewitness accounts, following the instructions and your presentation checklist. Encourage listeners to ask questions.

✓ WRAP UP

- Ask students to reflect in their **notebooks** about the eyewitness report that they enjoyed listening to the most. What made it stand out from the others?

Unit 7   125

UNIT 7 ■ STUDENT BOOK, PAGE 126

❙ BEYOND THE UNIT

Standards
- Provide a description
- Read and respond to an origin tale

1. On Assignment
WARM UP

- Ask students how many watch the news each night on television. When there is some sort of disaster, point out that a reporter is usually on the scene, describing what happened. Tell students that they will have the opportunity to be reporters!

TEACHING THE LESSON

- Ask students to study the picture in Part 1, jotting down notes. (They should include the damaged roof, the overturned cars, the broken windows, the uprooted trees, and the other things that were left behind by the tornado.)

- Have students develop a lead for their stories, relying on the examples (Part 2).

- Explain the "Four C's" of good television reporting (Part 3).

  Be current means to report the latest information.

  Be correct means to report the information accurately.

  Be concise means say what you have to say in as few words as possible.

  Be clear means to make sure that your ideas are easy to understand.

- Give students time to develop their news stories. Remind them that they have 45 seconds. Encourage students to rehearse their presentations, as a partner times them.

- Have students present their stories (Part 4). Time each presentation.

❙ BEYOND THE UNIT

1. On Assignment Imagine that a tornado has hit your town! You are reporting live from the scene for your school's cable TV program, Channel 55 Eyewitness News. You will have a 45-second spot to tell your story.

❶ Look over the scene. Take notes on the damage.

❷ Figure out how you will start your story. Your lead must grab the attention of your viewers, or they will switch the channel!

a.   b.

c.

❸ Write your story. Describe the destruction. Use sensory details. Keep in mind the "Four Cs" of good news stories:

Be current.   Be correct.   Be concise.   Be clear.

❹ Present your story to your class. Speak slowly, calmly, and clearly. Look into the camera!

TEACHING TIP 💡 Students who are somewhat shy may find it very difficult to speak in front of the whole class. They may benefit more from presenting the news to a small group of students.

UNIT 7 ■ STUDENT BOOK, PAGE 127

Link to Literature

A myth is a very old story about why the world is the way it is.

SHARED READING Different cultures try to explain nature in different ways. Read this myth about earthquakes.

LET'S TALK

1. Find examples in this myth that make it fun to read.
2. In many myths, who are the main characters?
3. Do you know a myth about the Earth that you can share?

Great Spirit—God
straw—dried wheat stems
restless—not able to keep still
beast—a wild animal
argue—to disagree with someone
every once in a while—sometimes

The Turtle Tale

¹ Long, long ago, before there were people, there was hardly anything in the world but water. One day, Great Spirit looked down from heaven. He decided to make a beautiful land. But where could he begin? All he saw was water. Then he spotted a giant turtle. Great Spirit decided to make the beautiful land on the turtle.

² But one turtle was not big enough. The land Great Spirit wanted to make was very large. So he called out, "Turtle, hurry and find your six brothers." …. After six days, turtle had found her six brothers. "Come," she said, "Great Spirit wants us."

³ Great Spirit called down. "Turtles! Form a line, all of you—head to tail, north to south…. What a beautiful land you turtles will make! Now listen! It is a great honor to carry this beautiful land on your backs. So you must not move!"

⁴ The turtles stayed very still. Great Spirit took some straw from his supply in the sky. He spread it out on the turtles' backs. Then he took some soil and patted it down on top of the straw.

⁵ Great Spirit cleaned his hands on a fluffy white cloud. Then he went to work, shaping mountains and valleys, and lakes, and rivers. When he was finished he looked at the beautiful land he had made. Great Spirit was very pleased. But soon trouble came. The giant turtles grew restless. They wanted to stretch their legs. "I want to swim east," said one. "This beast goes east." "West is best. I'll swim toward the setting sun," said another.

⁶ The turtles began to argue…. One day, four of the turtles began to swim east. The others began to swim west. The earth shook! …. But after a minute, the shaking stopped. The turtles had to stop moving because the land on their backs was so heavy…. When they saw that they could not swim away, they stopped and made up.

⁷ Every once in a while, though, the turtles argue again. Each time they do, the earth shakes.

Source: *California Geology Magazine*

Nature's Fury 127

🎧 2. Link to Literature

WARM UP

■ Explain that most cultures pass stories down as part of their tradition. Such stories are called folk tales. One type of folk tale—the origin tale—explains natural events.

TEACHING THE LESSON

■ **Shared Reading** Read the story "The Turtle Tale" aloud or play the tape or CD as students follow along. Model oral expression and use pauses that help clearly communicate the meaning.

■ Ask different students to read each paragraph of the story. After each paragraph, pause to make comments and ask questions:

After paragraph 1: *Where did the Great Spirit create the beautiful land?*
After paragraph 2: *Why did the Great Spirit ask the turtle to look for her six brothers?*
After paragraph 3: *Why were the turtles not supposed to move?*
After paragraph 4: *What did the Great Spirit use to make the land?*
After paragraph 5: *Why did trouble arrive?*
After paragraph 6: *What happened when the turtles moved?*

■ **Let's Talk** Ask students what aspects of the story make it interesting and enjoyable. Have them identify the main characters; elicit that they are animals, not humans. Invite students to share other traditional stories about the Earth that they are familiar with.

✓ WRAP UP

■ **Outcome Sentence** Have students complete the following sentence stem, and then share:

When the turtles argue, _____.

PB PRACTICE BOOK ACTIVITY

See Activity I, Responding to Literature, on Practice Book page 70.

✓ UNIT WRAP UP

■ **Outcome Sentence** Have students complete this stem:

In this unit, I learned to _____.

Have them share their outcome sentences.

Unit 7   127

Unit 8 Drugs: The True Story

Unit Overview

Section	At a Glance	Standards
Before You Begin	Students discuss the dangers of drinking and driving.	■ Derive meaning from visual information
A. Connecting to Your Life	Students answer questions about drugs and tobacco.	■ Respond to consumer and public documents
B. Getting Ready to Read	Students learn useful vocabulary and explore the harmful effects of drugs.	■ Participate in focused discussion of a topic
C. Reading to Learn	Students read a brochure that details the risks of drug use. PRACTICE BOOK: Students plan a drug education poster.	■ Identify the purpose of a reading selection ■ Identify main ideas and supporting details in text
D. Word Work	Students learn prefixes meaning "not." PRACTICE BOOK: Students add the correct negative prefix to each word in a list and then use the new words to complete sentences.	■ Use knowledge of prefixes to determine the meaning of unfamiliar vocabulary ■ Use knowledge of sound/letter relationships to spell words
E. Grammar	Students learn how to use gerunds as subjects and objects in sentences. PRACTICE BOOK: Students practice using gerunds as subjects.	■ Identify and correctly use phrases
F. Bridge to Writing	Students read a fact sheet about smoking. PRACTICE BOOK: Students practice taking Reading Vocabulary and Reading Comprehension tests. PRACTICE BOOK: Students practice new vocabulary related to the effects of drugs, tobacco, and alcohol.	■ Identify a thesis and arguments

Section	At a Glance	Standards
G. Writing Clinic	Students explore ways of using writing to persuade others. PRACTICE BOOK: Students identify reasons and supporting facts/details to use in an outline for a drug education speech. PRACTICE BOOK: Students practice using subheadings.	■ Identify the structural features of persuasive text
H1. Writer's Workshop: Getting It Out	Students learn how to organize information for a brochure to convince teens not to use drugs. PRACTICE BOOK: Students organize their ideas for a drug education brochure.	■ Use the writing process: prewriting
H2. Writer's Workshop: Getting It Down	Students turn the information they organized into a detailed outline. Then they use the outline to write the first draft of a brochure.	■ Use the writing process: drafting
H3. Writer's Workshop: Getting It Right	Students revise and edit their own work.	■ Use the writing process: revising
H4. Writer's Workshop: Presenting It	Students present their brochures to their classmates and take notes on each other's work.	■ Give an oral presentation that persuades
I. Beyond the Unit	Students write a skit designed to convince others not to use drugs. Students also read excerpts from the diary, *Go Ask Alice*, written by a girl who died from drugs. PRACTICE BOOK: Students write a short reflection on the positive effects a friend has had on their lives.	■ Plan and give a short dramatic presentation ■ Respond to literature

UNIT 8 ■ STUDENT BOOK, PAGE 128

BEFORE YOU BEGIN

Standard
- Derive meaning from visual information

- Ask students to look at the picture on page 129, without reading the headline. Ask: *What happened?* Have them look at the title of the unit. Invite them to speculate on the cause of the accident. Encourage other students to add their own ideas. For example: *I think the driver was drinking beer.*

- Ask a volunteer to read the headline. Ask: *What can happen when you drink and drive?*

- Ask students to share what happens when you drink alcohol. List students' ideas. Save the list for the Unit Wrap Up.

- **Build Background** Tell students that drunk driving is one of the leading causes of auto accidents in the U.S. According to figures released by Mothers Against Drunk Driving (MADD), 41 percent of all traffic deaths are related to alcohol. In fact, more than 500,000 Americans are injured annually in crashes involving alcohol.

Unit 8
Drugs: The True Story

Read...
- Pamphlets that persuade you that drugs and tobacco are dangerous.
- Facts about common drugs and tobacco—and why people who use them take such big risks.

 Link to Literature
- A selection from *Go Ask Alice*, the real diary of a fifteen-year-old who died from drugs.

128 Unit 8

Objectives:

Reading:
- Reading informational text that persuades
- Identifying the elements of persuasive text (opinion statements, reasons, facts, and examples)
- Strategies: Identifying the main purpose, skimming
- Literature: Responding to a diary entry

Writing:
- Writing persuasively
- Supporting a position with facts and examples
- Using questions to guide and organize writing

Vocabulary:
- Learning prefixes that mean "not": *non-, il-, in-, dis-*
- Learning words that describe the effects of drugs and tobacco

Listening/Speaking:
- Listening to dialog
- Comparing two places
- Giving feedback

Grammar:
- Using gerunds as subjects and objects

Spelling and Phonics:
- Pronouncing words with the letters *-ea-*

BEFORE YOU BEGIN.

Talk with your classmates.

1. Look at the picture. What happened?
2. Read the headline. Why did the accident happen?
3. What do you know about drinking beer and alcohol?

Drugs: The True Story

UNIT 8 ■ STUDENT BOOK, PAGE 130

A CONNECTING TO YOUR LIFE

Standard
- Respond to consumer and public documents

WARM UP

- Have students look at the pictures on this page. Ask students to take turns telling what each picture shows.

TEACHING THE LESSON

1. Tuning In

- Tell students they are going to hear a conversation between two teenage girls. Play the tape or CD, or read the script once and ask a student to explain what Amy is trying to do.

- Have students listen a second time and write down at least two of the arguments Amy uses to try to convince Maria to have a beer.

- **Heads Together** Have students work in pairs to think of other reasons Maria could give for not wanting to use alcohol. Have students share out.

2. Talking It Over

- **Heads Together** For Part 1, point out the three pictures again. Ask students to write a sentence giving one reason that using drugs, alcohol, or tobacco can be dangerous. Then have them share their ideas with a partner.

- For Part 2, ask: *Do you know the facts about drugs and tobacco?* Have students complete the activity with a partner.

- Have students share their responses, explaining why they answered one way or the other. Explain that you will review the correct answers later.

- Ask students to look again at the title of the unit. Have students hold up one, two, or three fingers to show what they think the main focus of the unit is.

130   Teacher's Edition

READING

A CONNECTING TO YOUR LIFE

1. Tuning In Listen. What is Amy trying to do? Check (✓) the correct answer.

_____ 1. She's explaining to Maria why alcohol is dangerous.
_____ 2. She's trying to make Maria drink alcohol.
_____ 3. She's telling Maria why they shouldn't drink alcohol.

2. Talking It Over

❶ Write one reason that using drugs, alcohol, or tobacco can be dangerous. Share your reason with a partner.

 alcohol   drugs   tobacco

❷ Here are some possible facts about alcohol, drugs, and tobacco. Talk with a partner. Decide which statements *might* be true and which *might* be false. Circle your answers.

True False	1. About 3,000 kids start smoking every day.
True False	2. Most teens (over 80 percent) do NOT use tobacco.
True False	3. Nearly half of all teens have tried an illegal drug at least once.
True False	4. Smoking causes almost 90 percent of all lung cancer.
True False	5. Illegal drugs are always dangerous.
True False	6. Most hard drug (cocaine, heroin) users started with marijuana.
True False	7. If you're caught with a drug, you could go to jail.

❸ Read the title of this unit. What do you think is the main idea of the unit? Check (✓) the correct answer.

_____ 1. Many kids don't know the names of drugs.
_____ 2. Many kids don't understand that drugs can be harmful.
_____ 3. Many kids don't know people who take drugs.

130   Unit 8

✓ WRAP UP

Outcome Sentences Have students complete the following sentence stems and then share out:

One thing I know about _____ is that _____.
A question I have is _____.

> **TEACHING TIP** Avoid preaching to students that they should never use alcohol, drugs, or tobacco. Instead, try to elicit their feelings about these substances and invite them to learn more about the negative effects of these substances.

ANSWER KEY

Tuning In: 2. She's trying to make Maria drink alcohol.

Talking It Over 2: 1. True; 2. True; 3. True; 4. True; 5. True; 6. True; 7. True.

Talking It Over 3: 2.

READING

UNIT 8 • STUDENT BOOK, PAGE 131

B GETTING READY TO READ

1. Learning New Words Read the sentences below. Try to guess the meanings of the underlined words.

1. Even one beer changes the way you see or do things. It <u>affects</u> your behavior.
2. Tobacco can cause many problems with your body. It is harmful to your <u>health</u>.
3. Smoking can make your lungs weak and sick. It can <u>damage</u> them.
4. Smoking kills people. That's 100% true—it's a <u>fact</u>!
5. People who <u>abuse</u> drugs are foolish.
6. Tran is telling Stefan not to smoke. He is trying to <u>persuade</u> him that smoking is bad.
7. Using certain drugs can kill you—they can be <u>fatal</u>.

Complete the sentences below with the new vocabulary words.

1. Tobacco can make you sick. It is very bad for your ___health___.
2. A _____ is something that is completely true.
3. When one thing _____ something else, it means that one thing causes a change in the other.
4. Something that causes death is _____.
5. It can _____ your eyes if you look directly at the sun.
6. When you use something in a way it should not be used, you _____ it.
7. When you try to _____ someone, you give them good reasons for doing—or *not* doing—something.

2. Talking It Over Work in a small group. Draw a chart like this one and complete it. Talk about the ways that harmful drugs affect people's lives.

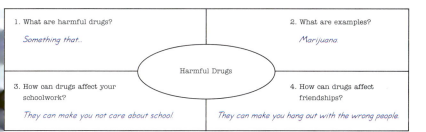

Drugs: The True Story **131**

B GETTING READY TO READ

Standard
- Participate in focused discussion of a topic.

WARM UP

🍎 **Let's Talk** Invite students to take turns sharing with the class any information they have about problems caused by illegal drugs. They can cite examples from TV shows, things they have read, or the experiences of friends and family members.

🍎 **Shared Writing** Ask students to dictate sentences about some of the situations they just described. Write the sentences on the board and discuss them. Explain new vocabulary as needed. Then invite different students to read each of the sentences aloud.

TEACHING THE LESSON

1. Learning New Words

- Write the new words on the board. Have students work in groups of three, trying to write a definition for each word. Have them share their definitions and then set them aside.

- Now have students open their books. Have a volunteer read each sentence or pair of sentences aloud. Ask: *What does the underlined word mean?* Encourage students to offer definitions. Do not correct or comment.

- Now have each trio complete the sentences. Have students share.

- Have trios revisit and revise their original definitions. Ask volunteers to share which words they redefined.

2. Talking It Over

- Have a volunteer read the directions and then explain the task to classmates. Model possible answers for each quadrant of the chart.

- 🍎 **Team Talk** Divide the class into groups of four and have them complete the activity together. Ask them to come up with at least three ideas for each section of the chart.

- 🍎 **Interactive Writing** Copy the chart on the board and then have volunteers complete each quadrant.

✓ WRAP UP

🍎 **Outcome Sentence** Have students imagine that they are advising a younger brother or sister about drugs. Have them complete the sentence stem and save it for later:

You shouldn't try drugs because _____.

ANSWER KEY

Learning New Words: 1. health; 2. fact; 3. affects; 4. fatal; 5. damage; 6. abuse; 7. persuade.

Unit 8 **131**

UNIT 8 ▪ STUDENT BOOK, PAGE 132

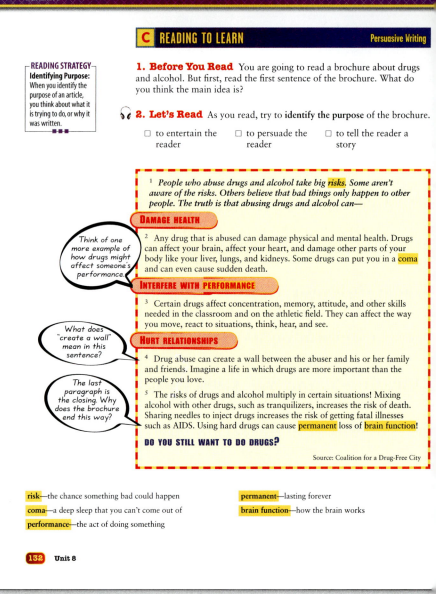

C READING TO LEARN

Standards
- Identify the purpose of a reading selection
- Identify main ideas and supporting details in text

WARM UP
- Have students share their sentences that begin, "You shouldn't try drugs because _____." Write them on the board. Explain that when you advise someone, you try to persuade them that they should or shouldn't do something. Explain that these sentences are all *reasons* for an opinion—that you shouldn't try drugs.

TEACHING THE LESSON

1. Before You Read
- Tell students that they are about to read a brochure. Explain that a brochure is a small booklet that gives information about something.
- Tell students that when you identify the purpose of a reading, you try to figure out why the writer wrote it (Reading Strategy box). Ask why this might be helpful.

🎧 2. Let's Read
- Ask students to try to identify the purpose of the brochure as they read.
- **🍎 My Turn: Read Aloud/Think Aloud** Begin by reading the passage aloud. Model correct phrasing and fluent reading. As you read, stop to comment on words and ideas. After you read, ask students what the brochure's purpose is.
- **🍎 Our Turn: Interactive Reading** Now have students help you read the passage. Read the first sentence of each paragraph yourself. Then call on individuals to read other sentences. As students read, focus on glossed words, ask questions, and make comments. Discuss the speech bubble comments next to each paragraph.
- ✓ **🍎 Question All-Write** Have students write a sentence that explains why drugs and alcohol are dangerous.
- **Build Fluency** Have pairs of students take turns reading alternate paragraphs and then summarizing what each says.
- **🍎 Your Turn: Independent Reading** Have students read the passage on their own. Ask students to write a sentence that identifies the best reason the brochure gives for not using drugs. Have students share their sentences.

CULTURE NOTE
Elicit from students what they know about the attitude toward drug use in other cultures. For example, in some Muslim countries, alcohol is illegal. In Malaysia, those who use illegal drugs can be put in prison and drug sellers can be executed.

READING

UNIT 8 ▪ STUDENT BOOK, PAGE 133

3. Unlocking Meaning

❶ **Finding the Main Idea** Choose the best title for the brochure. Check (✓) the correct answer.

_____ 1. Don't Drink Alcohol!

_____ 2. Beware! Drugs Are More Dangerous Than Alcohol!

_____ 3. The Facts about the Risks of Drugs and Alcohol

❷ **Finding Details** Match each of the following statements with the paragraph it is in.

__3__ Drugs can affect how you do in school.

_____ It can be dangerous to mix alcohol and drugs.

_____ Many people don't understand how dangerous drugs are.

_____ Drug abuse can break a family apart.

_____ Drugs can kill you.

_____ Hard drugs can destroy your brain.

_____ Diseases like AIDS can be spread by sharing needles.

_____ Drugs can affect how you think about your life.

❸ **Think about It** Work in a small group. Make a poster to persuade younger kids not to try tobacco, drugs or alcohol. Use the information in the brochure, as well as facts you already know

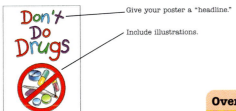

Give your poster a "headline."

Include illustrations.

Overall Rating

☆☆☆ I'm totally convinced!

☆☆ I'm pretty convinced.

☆ I'm not convinced.

❹ **Before You Move On** Put your posters on the wall. Take a "gallery walk." Rate each poster, then vote on the best poster.

Drugs: The True Story **133**

3. Unlocking Meaning

✓ FINDING THE MAIN IDEA

- Have students choose the best title for the brochure. Have them explain why their chosen title is best.

- ✓ **Sentence Synthesis** Write the following words on the board: *health, performance, relationships.* Have students write one sentence, using all three words, that explains why kids should say "no" to drugs.

✓ FINDING DETAILS

- Read and explain the directions and have students complete the activity.

- Review the correct answers. If there are differences of opinion, ask a student to first read the sentence and then read the similar information from the related paragraph in the reading.

THINK ABOUT IT

- Focus students on the poster. Explain that posters, like brochures, can also persuade. Ask: *What is the message of this poster?*

- Have a volunteer read the instructions and then explain the task to classmates.

- **Team Talk** Form groups of three or four students each and hand out poster-making materials. Remind students to look back at the brochure for ideas and ask them to add at least two new ideas of their own.

BEFORE YOU MOVE ON

- Have students rate each other's posters. Encourage them to point out positive aspects of each other's work such as catchy headlines, clever illustrations, and short, clear sentences.

✓ WRAP UP

- Have students write about the dangers of drug abuse in their **notebooks**. Suggest that they list at least five possible problems it can cause.

PB PRACTICE BOOK ACTIVITY

See Activity A, Revisit and Retell, on Practice Book page 71.

ANSWER KEY

Finding the Main Idea: 3.

Finding Details: 3, 5, 1, 4, 2, 5, 5, 4.

UNIT 8 ▪ STUDENT BOOK, PAGE 134

D WORD WORK

Standards
- Use knowledge of prefixes to determine the meaning of unfamiliar vocabulary
- Use knowledge of sound/letter relationships to spell words

WARM UP

- Write the prefix *non-* and the word *smoker* on the board. Elicit a definition of a smoker and then ask students what a *nonsmoker* is. Have students give examples of other words that begin with *non-* (nonfat, nonstop, nondairy, nonstick).

TEACHING THE LESSON

1. Word Detective

- Have students complete the activity. Review the correct answers.

2. Word Study

- Discuss the negative prefixes and the examples with the class. Ask students to explain each one in their own words.

3. Word Play

- **Heads Together** Have students do the activity in pairs. Encourage them to discuss each item as they complete it. Review the answers.

Spelling and Phonics

- Have students listen to the words and tell you what they notice about the letters *ea* in each word. (They are pronounced differently.)
- Have students complete the activity. Review the correct answers.

READING

D WORD WORK

1. Word Detective Match the word on the left with the correct definition on the right. What do you think the **boldfaced** parts of the words mean?

1. **non**smoker   a. to not like someone or something
2. **il**legal   b. not having many friends
3. **dis**like   c. not finished
4. **un**popular   d. against the law
5. **in**complete   e. someone who doesn't smoke cigarettes

2. Word Study Prefixes change the meaning of words. All of these common prefixes mean "not."

Prefix	Examples
non-	**non**drinker, **non**member, **non**sense
il-, in-, im-, ir-	**il**legal, **in**complete, **im**polite, **ir**regular
dis-	**dis**honest, **dis**loyal
un-	**un**believable, **un**important

3. Word Play Complete the sentences below. Use a prefix from the box below. You can use your dictionary.

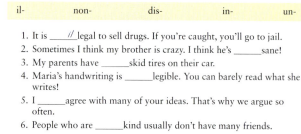

1. It is __il__ legal to sell drugs. If you're caught, you'll go to jail.
2. Sometimes I think my brother is crazy. I think he's _____ sane.
3. My parents have _____ skid tires on their car.
4. Maria's handwriting is _____ legible. You can barely read what she writes!
5. I _____ agree with many of your ideas. That's why we argue so often.
6. People who are _____ kind usually don't have many friends.

SPELLING AND PHONICS: To do this activity, go to page 195.

✓ WRAP UP

- Divide the class into two teams. Teams take turns calling out a negative prefix and the other team has to write a word on the board with the prefix. Encourage team members to work together. Allow them to use dictionaries if necessary.

PB PRACTICE BOOK ACTIVITY

See Activity B, Word Work, on Practice Book page 72.

ANSWER KEY

Word Detective: 1. e; 2. d; 3. a; 4. b; 5. c.

Word Play: 1. illegal; 2. insane; 3. nonskid; 4. illegible; 5. disagree; 6. unkind.

Spelling and Phonics: health: dead, ready, bread, headache; **great:** steak, break; **tea:** beneath, creature, real, cheap, increase, deal.

READING

E GRAMMAR — Gerunds as Subjects and Objects

1. Listen Up Listen to each sentence. Point your thumb up 👍 if it sounds correct. Point your thumb down 👎 if it sounds wrong.

👍👎 1. Abuse drugs can be dangerous.
👍👎 2. Stefan is unhappy about getting braces.
👍👎 3. Quit cigarettes is hard for most people.
👍👎 4. Paul's father quit smoke.

2. Learn the Rule Look at the chart below. After you have learned the rules, do Activity 1 again.

GERUNDS
1. A gerund is the *-ing* form of a verb used as a noun. Don't confuse it with the present progressive tense.
Gerund: **Playing** tennis is fun.   Present progressive: *Is she* **playing** *tennis now?*
2. A gerund can be the subject of a sentence.
Playing basketball is fun.   **Smoking** can make you feel dizzy.
3. A gerund can be the object of the verb.
Juan likes **playing** basketball.   Lori's father quit **smoking** last year.
4. A gerund can be the object of a preposition.
Tran is interested in **playing** basketball.   Our parents don't approve of **smoking**.

3. Practice the Rule Each of the following sentences contains one or more errors. Cross out the error. Then rewrite each sentence correctly.

1. ~~Ride~~ with a drunk driver is dangerous.   *Riding with a drunk driver is dangerous.*
2. The boy enjoys play basketball.   ____
3. Drink and drive is illegal.   ____
4. Use drugs can damage your health.   ____
5. Try to quit drugs is usually difficult.   ____
6. My brother tried to stop smoke last year.   ____
7. Alice dislikes do her homework.   ____
8. Javier quit use drugs.   ____

Drugs: The True Story   **135**

E GRAMMAR

Standard
- Identify and correctly use phrases

WARM UP
- Write these sentences on the board:

  Play basketball is fun.   Playing basketball is fun.

  Have a volunteer or two identify which sentence is correct. Underline the *-ing* form, explaining that this is called a gerund.

TEACHING THE LESSON

🎧 1. Listen Up
- Ask students to listen carefully. Then play the tape or CD, or read the sentences twice. Have students follow the directions.

UNIT 8 • STUDENT BOOK, PAGE 135

2. Learn the Rule
- Teach students how gerunds can be used as subjects, objects of verbs, and objects of prepositions.

> **TEACHING TIP** Briefly contrast a verb in the present progressive tense with the same root verb used as a gerund. Point out that gerunds never follow any form of the verb *be*:
>
> Graciela *is* <u>eating</u> ice cream. (verb—present progressive form)
>
> Graciela likes <u>eating</u> ice cream (gerund—object of verb)

- Repeat the Listen Up activity.

3. Practice the Rule
- Ask students to read each incorrect sentence carefully, write the corrected form of the sentence, and then share it with the class.

✓ WRAP UP
- Say several sentences in which a gerund is used as an object and ask students to make up a related sentence in which the same gerund is used as a subject. For example: *I hate washing dishes.* (*Washing dishes is a drag.*)

PB PRACTICE BOOK ACTIVITY

See Activity C, Grammar, on Practice Book page 73.

ANSWER KEY

Listen Up: Correct sentence: 2.

Practice the Rule: 1. Riding...; 2. ...playing...; 3. Drinking and driving...; 4. Using; 5. Trying...; 6. ...smoking...; 7. ...doing...; 8. ...using...

Unit 8   **135**

UNIT 8 ▪ STUDENT BOOK, PAGE 136

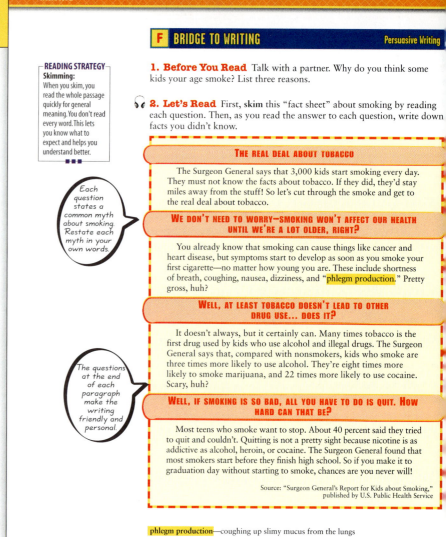

F BRIDGE TO WRITING

Standard
- Identify a thesis and arguments

WARM UP

🍎 **Quick Write** Ask students to write one or two sentences that tell what they know about the dangers of tobacco. Have students share their sentences as you record. Save the sentences for later.

TEACHING THE LESSON

1. Before You Read

🍎 **Heads Together** Ask students to work in pairs to discuss why they think some teens smoke. Possible answers: *to look cool, to appear grown up, to go along with friends.*

- Tell students that they are going to read a brochure, written by the Surgeon General of the U.S., to persuade kids not to smoke.

- **Build Background** Explain that the Surgeon General is the official U.S. spokesperson on public health.

🎧 2. Let's Read

♻️ Remind students that when you skim, you read quickly to get the general meaning before you read (Reading Strategy box). Ask why this might be useful.

- Ask students to skim and explain what the general focus of the passage is. (It's about the health effects of tobacco and how difficult it is to quit smoking.)

- 🍎 **My Turn: Read Aloud/Think Aloud** Read the passage aloud. Model correct phrasing and fluent reading. As you read, stop to comment on words and ideas.

- 🍎 **Our Turn: Interactive Reading** Take turns having individual students read a paragraph each. As students read, focus on the glossed words, ask questions, and make comments.

✓ 🍎 **Question All-Write** Ask students to write one or two sentences for each of these questions: *Why do you think tobacco is the first drug most teens use? Why is it hard to quit smoking?*

- **Build Fluency** Ask students to take turns reading a line aloud after you have read it. Break down long sentences into smaller parts.

🍎 **Your Turn: Independent Reading** Have students read the passage again, this time by themselves.

✓ 🍎 **Sentence Synthesis** Write these words on the board: *tobacco, disease, addictive*. Have students write a sentence about what they have learned, using all three words.

136 Teacher's Edition

3. Making Content Connections Work with a partner to summarize the reading. What are some common ideas that people have about substances like drugs, alcohol, and tobacco that are false or untrue? What are the facts? Complete the chart below based on the readings and your own experiences.

For help with summarizing, complete Mini-Unit, Part C on page 190.

	Common misunderstandings	Facts
Drugs and alcohol		
Tobacco		

4. Expanding Your Vocabulary The words and phrases in the box describe some common effects of drugs and alcohol. Discuss the meanings of the words with a partner. Use the words to complete the chart below.

blurred vision	intoxication	bloodshot eyes	feeling dizzy
cancer	coughing	confusion	bad breath
lack of coordination	heart attack	nausea	suffocation

Drugs	Alcohol	Tobacco
	intoxication	

Drugs: The True Story 137

WRITING

UNIT 8 ▪ STUDENT BOOK, PAGE 137

🍒 **Heads Together** Ask students to work in pairs. Have them complete the chart in their books and then share with classmates.

📘 PRACTICE BOOK ACTIVITY

See Activity D, Test-Taking Practice, on Practice Book pages 74 and 75.

See Activity E, Using New Vocabulary, on Practice Book page 76.

✓ WRAP UP

- Have students revisit their responses to the questions on page 130. Have them answer the questions again, noting which of their responses have changed. Have students share. Note that not all of the questions are answered in the readings.

ANSWER KEY

Expanding Your Vocabulary: Answers will vary. Point out that all 12 effects can be present when hard drugs are used. The common effects of drug use include *lack of coordination, bloodshot eyes, and confusion*. The common effects of alcohol misuse often include *intoxication, bloodshot eyes, lack of coordination,* and *nausea*. The common effects of tobacco use often include *feeling dizzy, cancer, coughing, bad breath,* and *heart attack*.

---

3. Making Content Connections

🍒 **Heads Together** Have a volunteer read the instructions and then explain the task to classmates. Have students look back at the brochures they have just read, discussing myths and facts. Have them complete the chart in their books. If necessary, have students complete Mini-Unit, Part C on page 190.

🍒 **Interactive Writing** Make a copy of the chart on the board. Ask several pairs of students to report their findings to the class. Have volunteers help complete the chart using student responses. As they do this, invite others to ask questions and make comments on what they are hearing.

4. Expanding Your Vocabulary

- As you introduce each new word or phrase, use it in a sentence. For example: *If I don't wear my glasses, I have blurred vision.* Ask students to use their own words to explain each term and/or to pantomime such items as *dizzy, lack of coordination,* and *nausea*.

Unit 8   137

UNIT 8 ■ STUDENT BOOK, PAGE 138

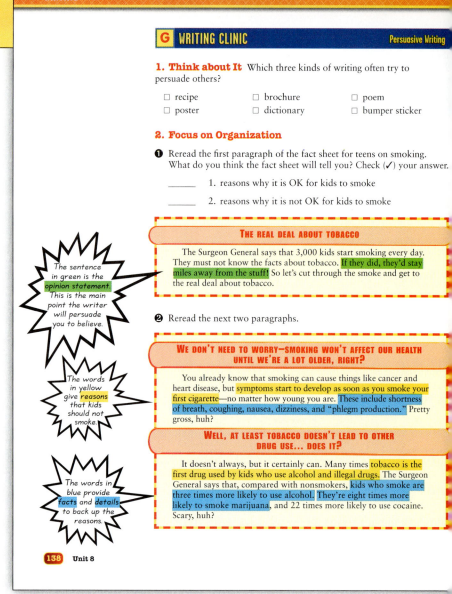

G WRITING CLINIC

Standard
- Identify the structural features of persuasive text

WARM UP

- Ask students to think about the two brochures they have read. Which one is more convincing, or persuasive? Encourage students to share their opinions, explaining why.

TEACHING THE LESSON

1. Think about It

- Remind students that they have learned that brochures are often meant to persuade others. Have students help identify other types of writing that persuades (posters, advertisements, bumper stickers). Help students describe specific examples of each type of persuasive writing. For example: *A travel poster might show a couple on a Florida beach and say, "Leave the cold and snow behind! Come to Florida this winter." A persuasive bumper sticker might say, "A vote for Smith is a vote for lower taxes!"*

2. Focus on Organization

- Have students read the introductory paragraph and identify the message that underlies the opinion statement (Part 1). Have students explain the answer.

- Write this sentence on the board:

  Kids shouldn't smoke.

  Explain that this is an opinion statement. It tells what the speaker (or writer) believes. Help students generate additional opinion statements related to alcohol and drugs. For example: *People who use drugs are ruining their futures.*

- Help students tackle the next two paragraphs (Part 2). Point out the phrases highlighted in yellow. Explain that reasons are statements that support the opinion statement. Have them look back at the final paragraph in the brochure, identifying the sentences that contain the reason. (Most teens who smoke want to stop. About 40 percent said they tried to quit but couldn't.)

- Finally, help students identify facts and details that support each reason. Point out the phrases highlighted in blue.

PB PRACTICE BOOK ACTIVITY

See Activity F, Focus on Organization, on Practice Book page 77.

WRITING

UNIT 8 ▪ STUDENT BOOK, PAGE 139

❸ Read more about smoking. Make a chart like this. Write the reasons kids should not smoke on the left side. Write facts, examples, and details on the right side. Use your own words.

Reasons Kids Shouldn't Smoke	Facts and Examples
Kids who smoke do not do as well in school as kids who do not.	

Kids who smoke think they're cool. Are they?

Only if by "cool" you mean kids who probably aren't doing very well in school. The Surgeon General found that students with the highest grades are less likely to smoke than those with the lowest grades. Tobacco use is highest among drop-outs, lowest among college students.

Kids who smoke have lower self-images. They look to smoking because they think it will give them a better image—cooler, maybe, or more attractive, or more popular. And because their self-image is low, they don't have the confidence to say no when someone wants them to use tobacco.

drop-out—a kid who leaves school
look to—to turn your attention to
self-image—how you see yourself

3. Focus on Style Brochures often use subheadings to help organize the information. When you are writing to persuade other people, questions can be a good way to highlight each main point you want to make. Match the questions on the left to the correct main point on the right.

1. Is it harmful to smoke when you're young?
2. Does tobacco use lead to other drugs?
3. Is it hard to quit?

a. Because smoking is addictive, it is very difficult to stop.
b. Smoking at any age is harmful.
c. Tobacco is often the first drug used by kids who later use alcohol and illegal drugs.

Drugs: The True Story **139**

- Have students match each reason statement to its subhead.
- Have students write their own subhead for the paragraph, using a question. Have students share out their questions as you record them on the board.

📘 PRACTICE BOOK ACTIVITY

See Activity G, Focus on Style, on Practice Book page 78.

✓ WRAP UP

- Have students look once again at the first reading—on the harmful effects of drugs and alcohol. Have them turn the three headings into questions.

ANSWER KEY

Think about It: poster, brochure, bumper sticker.

Focus on Organization 1: 2.

Focus on Organization 3: Reasons kids shouldn't smoke: Kids who smoke do not do as well in school as kids who do not. **Facts and examples:** Kids who don't smoke have higher grades. Tobacco use is highest among drop-outs and lowest among college students.

3. **Focus on Style:** 1. b; 2. c; 3. a.

- Have a volunteer read the instructions for Part 3 and then explain the task to classmates.
- **Heads Together** Have students read the excerpt and then complete the chart—sifting out reasons and supporting facts or details. Encourage students to paraphrase each reason.

3. Focus on Style

- Remind students that both brochures organize information under subheadings. Explain that subheadings do two things: they highlight each reason for the reader and they help the reader understand the information by breaking it into categories, or chunks.
- Have students revisit both brochures. Ask: *How are the subheads different in the two brochures?* (The first brochure uses phrases. The second brochure asks the reader questions.)

UNIT 8 ■ STUDENT BOOK, PAGE 140

H Writer's Workshop

Standard
- Use the writing process: prewriting

1. Getting It Out
WARM UP

- Ask students to recall conversations, TV shows or reading material in which someone was trying to persuade them to do something or believe something. Ask them what kinds of information did *not* help persuade them. (Threats? Commands? Scare tactics? Exaggeration?) Explain that this lesson will help them learn to use solid reasons, facts, and details to make their writing as persuasive as possible.

TEACHING THE LESSON

- Tell students that they will be learning some facts about three different types of drugs. Explain that they will choose one of these drugs as the topic for a brochure that they will write intended to discourage teens from using the drug.

- Have each student choose one of the three topics. Tell them that they can either draw their own charts or use the blank chart on Practice Book page 79.

> **TEACHING TIP** 💡 You may wish to have some students who have chosen the same topic work in pairs or small groups. That way they can help each other sort out the reasons, facts, and details they will include on their outlines.

🌈 **Access for All** Have more advanced students generate their own inquiries and information, rather than relying on the fact sheets.

WRITING

H WRITER'S WORKSHOP — Persuasive Writing

Write a brochure for teens on drugs or alcohol. It should convince other teens that drug and alcohol use is dangerous and foolish.

1. Getting It Out

❶ Begin by learning the facts.

Facts about Alcohol
- ✓ Affects your brain (loss of coordination, slow movement, confusion, fuzzy vision, blackouts).
- ✓ Affects your body (damages organs, can cause cancer).
- ✓ Affects self-control (you don't behave like yourself, can lead to risky behaviors).
- ✓ Can kill you (causes many teen traffic deaths, too much can lead to coma or even death).
- ✓ More dangerous for teens to drink than adults (harms growing bodies and minds, teens who drink are more likely to become alcoholics later).
- ✓ It is illegal to buy or carry alcohol if you are under 21.

Facts about Inhalants
- ✓ Affect your brain (cause an instant high, can destroy your brain before you know it).
- ✓ Affect your heart (force the heart to beat out of control, starve the body of oxygen).
- ✓ Damage other parts of the body (cause you to vomit, cause nosebleeds, destroy muscles).
- ✓ Can cause sudden death the first time you use them (from choking, heart attacks, suffocation).

Facts about Marijuana
- ✓ Many teens believe it's not harmful, but it is.
- ✓ Affects your brain (makes it hard to remember, can make you "see things," makes it hard to think, makes it hard to do things like drive, play sports, or read).
- ✓ Affects your body (makes your heart beat fast, can cause lung cancer).
- ✓ Affects your attitude (can make you not care about things, can make it hard for you to learn).
- ✓ Illegal in every state (you could go to jail).
- ✓ Most kids who use hard drugs (like cocaine or heroin) begin by using marijuana.
- ✓ Hard for many people to quit.

self-control—the ability to control what you say and do
inhalant—a drug you inhale, often fumes from products like glue or paint thinner
oxygen—the air you breathe to stay alive

140 Unit 8

WRITING

UNIT 8 ▪ STUDENT BOOK, PAGE 141

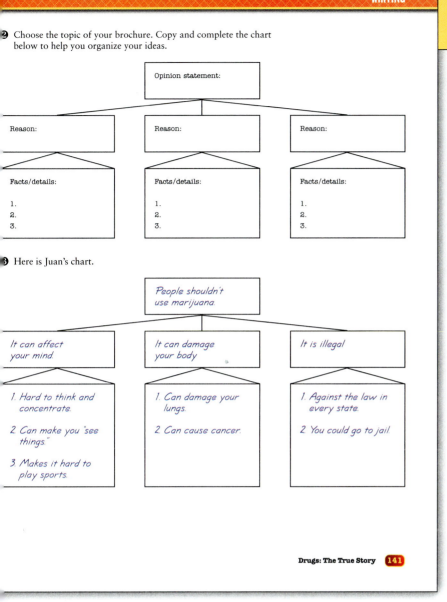

PB PRACTICE BOOK ACTIVITY

See Activity H, Writer's Workshop, on Practice Book page 79.

- Explain that Juan's chart will give students ideas about how to complete their own charts. Focus on Juan's chart, pointing out how each set of facts and details supports the reason above it. Then have students complete their charts on their own.

> **TEACHING TIP** 💡 Suggest that students check their spelling carefully while doing their charts since it will help them avoid errors in their outlines and brochures.

WRAP UP

- Survey the class to see what students plan to write about. Ask students to name their topics and read their opinion statements aloud.

UNIT 8 ▪ STUDENT BOOK, PAGE 142

H WRITER'S WORKSHOP

Standards
- Use the writing process: drafting, revising
- Give an oral presentation that persuades

2. Getting It Down
WARM UP

- Explain that in this lesson students will be using their charts to create an outline. They will then use the outline to write a complete first draft of their brochures.

TEACHING THE LESSON

- Have students take out their completed charts. Review how each part of the chart is turned into part of the outline on this page (Part 1).

- **Interactive Writing** Model the process of turning the chart into an outline. Copy the outline on the board. Using Juan's chart, help students fill in the outline.

- Next, show how the outline you have made is turned into a first draft. Map it to the sample text that Juan has written (Part 2).

- **Mini-Lesson on Conventions** Point out the Mini-Lesson box and have students locate the em dash in Juan's text. Ask students what kind of information follows this em dash (a list of examples).

- **Let's Talk** Now ask students to evaluate Juan's composition, using the six criteria (Part 3).

WRAP UP

- Tell students that they will have a chance to revise their work during the next session. Have them locate the

---

WRITING

2. Getting It Down

❶ Use your diagram to make an outline for your brochure.

Title: _____
Opinion statement: _____
1. Reason: _____
   a. Fact/example/detail: _____
   b. Fact/example/detail: _____
2. Reason: _____
   a. Fact/example/detail: _____
   b. Fact/example/detail: _____

MINI-LESSON
Using Dashes: Use a dash (—) in a sentence when you want the reader to notice information:
Eat healthy foods—fruit, vegetables, and fish.

❷ Turn your outline into several short paragraphs. Here is what Juan wrote:

> **Marijuana Madness**
> Many teens think that marijuana is not harmful. They couldn't be more wrong! Using marijuana is foolish, and it can be dangerous.
> Marijuana can affect your brain. It can make it hard to think clearly and to concentrate on what you're doing. That means you're unable to do things that require concentration—fun things like driving a car, shooting hoops, or reading a really good book. It can even make you think you're seeing things that aren't there!
> Marijuana can also harm your body. It can weaken your body and make it harder to fight diseases. It can damage your lungs and even cause lung cancer.
> That's probably why marijuana is illegal in all 50 states. Is it really worth going to jail just for a marijuana cigarette?

❸ Look at what Juan wrote. Did he leave anything out that would make his brochure even better? Use the following chart to check.

_____ 1. Has a title.	_____ 4. Gives at least two reasons.
_____ 2. Has an opinion statement.	_____ 5. Provides facts and details.
_____ 3. Uses subheadings.	_____ 6. Has a strong conclusion.

ChecBric for this unit in the Student Book or Practice Book. Have them prepare for Getting It Right by reviewing the ChecBric on their own, underlining indicators they're not sure about.

WRITING

UNIT 8 ▪ STUDENT BOOK, PAGE 143

3. Getting It Right Take a careful look at what you have written. Use these questions to help you review and revise your work.

Questions to ask . . .	How to check . . .	How to revise . . .
1. Does my introduction state my opinion?	Ask a neighbor to find the opinion statement in your introduction.	Add a sentence that clearly states your opinion.
2. Do I use subheadings with questions to help organize the information?	Put a star (★) in front of each subheading.	Add subheadings. Use short phrases or questions.
3. Do I give at least two reasons to support my opinion?	<u>Underline</u> each reason.	Add one or more reasons.
4. Do I provide facts and details to support each reason?	Circle each fact or detail.	Add facts to support your reasons.

4. Presenting It Read your brochure to your classmates. Take notes on a chart like the one below as you listen to other students. Give each student's presentation an overall rating.

Reasons	Facts and Details

Overall Rating
- ☆☆☆ Very convincing
- ☆☆ Convincing
- ☆ Not convincing

Drugs: The True Story **143**

3. Getting It Right

WARM UP

- Guide students through the ChecBric for this unit. Explain that they will use the ChecBric to prepare a final draft of their writing.
- Have volunteers explain, in their own words, what each indicator in the ChecBric means.

TEACHING THE LESSON

- Have students use the chart and the ChecBric to guide the revision of their work.
- **Group Share** Have students share their brochures in groups of four or five to give each other feedback on their compositions, then make revisions.

WRAP UP

- Suggest that students get feedback on their completed brochures from a friend or family member.
- 📁 Give students time to fill out the ChecBric on Practice Book page 115. Ask them to attach it to their writing when they put it in their portfolios.

4. Presenting It

WARM UP

- It's time for students to share their brochures with the class! Determine the order of presentation in order to vary the topics so that you don't have three or four presentations in a row on the same topic.
- As a class, develop a simple presentation checklist. Focus on content, organization, speaking skills, enthusiasm, use of visuals, etc.

TEACHING THE LESSON

- Ask students to make a note-taking chart and take notes on each presentation. For each brochure, have them list at least one example of a reason followed by related facts and details.
- After each presentation, have students rate each other using the Rating Scale. Then ask them to give each other positive feedback. Review some examples of reasons and related facts and details for each presentation. Then invite students to ask about anything they didn't understand and to comment on each other's presentations.

✓ WRAP UP

- Ask students to vote for the most persuasive of the brochures presented in class. Have the student who wrote the brochure read it aloud again. Invite comments on why it is so convincing.

Unit 8 **143**

UNIT 8 ■ STUDENT BOOK, PAGE 144

I BEYOND THE UNIT

Standards
- Plan and give a short dramatic presentation
- Respond to literature

1. On Assignment
WARM UP

- Ask students what might take place during Drug Prevention Week at their school (drug prevention posters in the halls, brochures, and special lessons on avoiding drug abuse).

TEACHING THE LESSON

- Form groups of four or five students. Have a volunteer read the instructions, then explain each step of the task to classmates.

- Discuss the first step (Part 1). Remind students that a story always has characters, a problem that needs to be solved, and a setting where the action takes place. Elicit examples of characters, problems and settings that students might use in their skits.

- ♲ Elicit what a timeline is (Part 2). (A listing of events in the order they actually happened). Ask students to think about the three major parts of their stories that will appear on their story timelines—the beginning, the middle, and the end. Suggest that they make a numbered list of the steps the characters will go through as they try to solve the problem. Ask students to think about what kind of ending they plan to use—a happy ending, an exciting ending, or an unhappy ending. Ask students to share examples of each type of ending.

- Read the sample script aloud (Part 3). Point out the use of the colon after each speaker's part. Remind students that even though they will be writing the words down, they need to keep the language informal. The characters need to sound as if they are real people talking with their friends.

- Ask students to think carefully about what they are trying to communicate through their skits (Part 4). Have students edit their scripts by reading them aloud a few lines at a time and using the three editing questions to revise them.

- Have students make a chart with these column headings: *Clear message? Convincing? Real people and words?* Have students take notes on these aspects of each skit as it is presented (Part 5).

- After each group performs its skit, invite students to comment and ask questions about it. They can use the notes they took as a guide.

✓ WRAP UP

Outcome Sentence Have students complete this sentence stem, then share:

The best part of our skit was _____.

I BEYOND THE UNIT

1. On Assignment Imagine that it is Drug Prevention Week at your school. Your class has to write and act in an anti-drug skit (a short play). Work in groups of four or five.

❶ Decide on the characters, a problem, and a place for the action.

❷ Brainstorm your story. Make a story timeline.
  ☐ Think about the opening part. How will you first tell the audience about the main problem?
  ☐ Think about the middle. How will the main characters try to solve the problem?
  ☐ Think about the ending. How will everything end?

❸ Now write a script. Write the words that each character will say. Make your characters sound like they are really talking naturally.

> *Donna: Here...have a cigarette! Smoking is cool!*
> *Juan: Are you crazy? Smoking is very uncool!*

❹ Edit your script.
  ☐ What is the message you want others to get from your skit? Is your message clear?
  ☐ Will your skit convince the audience?
  ☐ Do your characters and the dialog (the words your characters say) like people really talk?

❺ Perform your skit.

2. Link to Literature

SHARED READING *Go Ask Alice* is the true story of a teenager's slide into the world of drugs. It is based on the actual diary of a fifteen-year-old drug user. Read two entries from Alice's diary.

April 6

... I'm really going to try to make kids see that getting into drugs simply isn't worth [it]. Sure, it's great and **groovy** going on **trips**. I will never be able to say it isn't. It's exciting and colorful and dangerous, but it isn't worth it! It simply isn't worth it! Every day for the rest of my life I shall dread weakening again and becoming something I simply do not want to be! I'll have to fight it every day of my life...

April 19

Cripes! It's started again! I met Jan downtown and she asked me to a "party" tonight. None of the kids think I'm going to really stay off, because most of those who have been busted before are just being more careful and **discreet**. When I told Jan, "No, thanks," she just smiled. It scared me to death. She didn't say anything at all. She just smiled at me like, "We know you'll be back." I hope not. Oh, I really hope not.

Source: *Go Ask Alice*

---

groovy—a word used in the 1960s meaning "cool"

trip—an experience someone has when taking an illegal drug

discreet—careful not to tell information that you want to keep secret

LET'S TALK

1. How does Alice feel about drugs?
2. How hard is it for kids to get off of drugs, once they have started?
3. Who is probably right—Alice or her friend Jan?
4. Talk with a partner. Which is more persuasive—a brochure about drugs or a real-life story like *Go Ask Alice*?

Drugs: The True Story 145

UNIT 8 ▪ STUDENT BOOK, PAGE 145

- Now have a volunteer read the second excerpt aloud. Pose questions as the student reads—

  "Cripes!" is an old-fashioned expression that shows that someone is upset. Have you ever heard anyone say this?
  Why do you think the word "party" is in quotation marks? What is going to happen at this "party"?
  What do you think happens when someone gets "busted"? Can you tell from the other sentences in the paragraph?
  Why do you think Jan's smile scared Alice to death?

- **Let's Talk** Use the questions to lead a discussion of the two selections. Ask students what Alice's attitude toward drugs is. *Does she think it's easy for kids to quit taking drugs? Do you think Alice will stay off drugs or not?*

PB PRACTICE BOOK ACTIVITY

See Activity I, Responding to Literature, on Practice Book page 80.

✓ WRAP UP

- Have students discuss which would be more likely to convince kids not to use drugs—a true story or a pamphlet with anti-drug information in it.

✓ UNIT WRAP UP

- Revisit the class-generated list from Before You Begin. Have students add to it as you record their responses. Have them make similar lists for drug and tobacco use.

- **Outcome Sentence** Have students complete this short sentence frame in their **notebooks** and then share.

  I am convinced that _____ because _____.

---

2. Link to Literature

WARM UP

- Elicit or explain that when you keep a diary, you record and reflect, or think about, important things that happen in your life. Explain that sometimes diaries are considered to be literary works—for example, *The Diary of Anne Frank*.

- Tell students that they are going to read parts of *Go Ask Alice*, a famous diary of a girl who abused drugs.

- **Shared Reading** Play the tape or CD or read the first selection aloud to the class, as students follow along. Model fluency and expression. Tell students that Alice wrote her diary in the 1970s. Have students find word clues in the entries to support this. (Use of *groovy, trips, cripes*)

- Ask: *Why does Alice believe that "Drugs aren't worth it?"* Have students find evidence.

Unit 8   145

Unit 9 I Love Jell-O®

Unit Overview

Section	At a Glance	Standards
Before You Begin	Students consider the popular American dessert Jell-O®.	■ Use descriptive words
A. Connecting to Your Life	Students analyze and rate various kinds of foods.	■ Use language that evaluates
B. Getting Ready to Read	Students learn useful vocabulary and explore foods that taste good but are not good for you vs. foods that are good for you.	■ Relate ideas and observations
C. Reading to Learn	Students read a "review" of Jell-O® written by a teenager. PRACTICE BOOK: Students "interview" the teenager who wrote the review of Jell-O®.	■ Identify an author's argument and supporting reasons or details
D. Word Work	Students learn words that mean the opposite of each other. PRACTICE BOOK: Students complete analogies using antonyms.	■ Use knowledge of antonyms to determine word meaning ■ Use knowledge of sound/spelling patterns to spell words
E. Grammar	Students learn how to use *if* clauses to describe something that may or may not happen in the future. PRACTICE BOOK: Students complete conditional sentences.	■ Use complex sentences to express condition ■ Recognize shades of meaning among words
F. Bridge to Writing	Students read a food review that focuses on oatmeal. PRACTICE BOOK: Students practice taking Reading Vocabulary and Reading Comprehension tests. PRACTICE BOOK: Students practice new vocabulary.	■ Identify an author's argument and supporting reasons or details ■ Analyze and evaluate an argument and support ■ Use descriptive words

Section	At a Glance	Standards
G. Writing Clinic	Students learn how to organize a critical review. They also learn to use "stand-out adjectives" in their writing. PRACTICE BOOK: Students analyze the structure of a review. PRACTICE BOOK: Students rewrite sentences using stand-out adjectives.	■ Develop a well-formed argument ■ Use descriptive words
H1. Writer's Workshop: Getting It Out	Students assume the role of food reviewer for the local newspaper, and then plan their reviews. PRACTICE BOOK: Students generate a word web and write about their favorite food.	■ Use the writing process: prewriting ■ Develop a multi-paragraph composition that develops an argument and provides supporting details
H2. Writer's Workshop: Getting It Down	Students outline and draft their reviews.	■ Use notes and outlining to organize writing ■ Use the writing process: drafting
H3. Writer's Workshop: Getting It Right	Students revise their reviews.	■ Use the writing process: revising and editing for clarity and organization
H4. Writer's Workshop: Presenting It	Students present their reviews to their classmates.	■ Give a short oral presentation
I. Beyond the Unit	Students read and write short newspaper reviews. Students read a review of Shel Silverstein's book of poetry, *Falling Up*, and the poem "Tattooin' Ruth." PRACTICE BOOK: Students write a letter to the reviewer of the book *Falling Up*.	■ Read a response to literature ■ Respond to a humorous poem

UNIT 9 ■ STUDENT BOOK, PAGE 146

Unit 9
I Love Jell-O®!

BEFORE YOU BEGIN

Standard
- Use descriptive words

- Have students look at the picture. Ask: *What do you think Jell-O® is made of? Do you think it's good for you?*

- **Shared Writing** Write several words or phrases on the board that describe Jell-O® (e.g., jiggly, sweet). Help students generate other descriptive words or phrases as you record on the board.

- Point out that the ® symbol that follows Jell-O® means that the name of the product belongs to the company that makes it.

Read...
- A review of one guy's favorite fizzy treat.

- An explanation of why a gooey breakfast can be delicious.

Link to Literature

- A review of the book *Falling Up*, by Shel Silverstein and "Tattooin' Ruth," a poem from that book.

Objectives:

Reading:
- Evaluation: Reading food reviews
- Strategies: Visualizing and summarizing
- Literature: Reading a book review

Writing:
- Evaluation: Writing reviews
- Justifying an opinion
- Using stand-out adjectives

Vocabulary:
- Recognizing antonyms
- Using descriptive adjectives

Listening/Speaking:
- Listening to descriptions
- Comparing two things
- Stating and justifying an opinion

Grammar:
- Using adverbial clauses of condition (*if* clauses)

Spelling and Phonics:
- Spelling the /j/ sound as in *jam* and *badge*

146   Unit 9

146   Teacher's Edition

UNIT 9 ■ STUDENT BOOK, PAGE 147

Sparkling Grape Jell-O®

BEFORE YOU BEGIN

Talk with your classmates.

1. Look at the picture. What do you see? Help your teacher make a list.
2. Read the caption. What is the name of the product?
3. Have you ever eaten Jell-O®? What is it like? If not, what do you think it would be like from the picture?

I Love Jell-O®!

UNIT 9 ■ STUDENT BOOK, PAGE 148

A CONNECTING TO YOUR LIFE

> **Standard**
> ■ Use language that evaluates

WARM UP

■ Ask students to write about their favorite food—perhaps on the board—then identify the food and say something about it. For example: *Pizza is my favorite food.*
I have it for lunch every day.

TEACHING THE LESSON

🎧 1. Tuning In

■ Tell students they are going to hear people describing the food in the six pictures. Ask them to listen carefully and decide which food each person is talking about. Play the tape or CD, or read the script. As each food is described, have students write the speaker's number above the food being described.

2. Talking It Over

■ Ask: *Who eats in the school cafeteria? What food do you like a lot? What food don't you like so much? Why?*

■ Tell students that they are going to rate, or give their opinions about, cafeteria food. Copy the chart on the board and complete it with your own choice of food as a model.

🍎 **Heads Together** Ask students to work in pairs to complete the rating chart.

■ Have students move around the room and find classmates who chose the same food. Have them compare their ratings, then share.

■ Read the title of the unit aloud. Then have a student read the question and the three possible answers. Ask the class which answer is correct and why.

READING

A CONNECTING TO YOUR LIFE

🎧 **1. Tuning In** Listen to the descriptions. Match the speakers with the pictures.

a. Speaker Number ___

b. Speaker Number ___

c. Speaker Number ___

d. Speaker Number ___

e. Speaker Number ___

f. Speaker Number _1_

2. Talking It Over On the chart below, write the name of a food you eat in the school cafeteria. Rate the food by circling a number for each question.

Find a classmate who rated the same food. Compare your ratings.

Name of food:	Rating				
	Excellent	Very good	Good	Fair	Poor
1. How does it look?	4	3	2	1	0
2. How does it taste?	4	3	2	1	0
3. How does it smell?	4	3	2	1	0
5. How much does it cost?	4	3	2	1	0
6. Is it good for you?	4	3	2	1	0

Read the title of this unit. What do you think this unit is probably about? Check (✓) the correct answer.

_____ 1. foods that begin with "J"

_____ 2. foods that people love

_____ 3. foods that can make you ill

WRAP UP

■ Tell students they are going to learn some useful new vocabulary and then compare different kinds of foods.

> **TEACHING TIP** 💡 Display several newspaper advertisements, magazine advertisements, and posters advertising food products. Ask students to study them and make lists of the words used to describe each type of food. Have them look up any new words in the dictionary.

ANSWER KEY

Tuning In: a. 6; b. 2; c. 4; d. 5; e. 3; f. 1.
Talking It Over: 2.

B GETTING READY TO READ

1. Learning New Words Read the sentences below. Try to guess the meanings of the underlined words.

1. I am completely sure that you will like the restaurant. I <u>guarantee</u> you will love the food.
2. This apple tastes so sweet and juicy! It's <u>delicious</u>.
3. Eating fruit has many <u>benefits</u>! It tastes good, it fills you up, and it's good for you.
4. Juan loves all cookies, but chocolate chip and peanut butter cookies are his <u>favorites</u>.
5. There are many <u>varieties</u> of pizza on the menu: mushroom, pepperoni, four-cheese, and deluxe.
6. The food in the cafeteria gives your body lots of good things. It is <u>nutritious</u>.

Now match each word on the left with the correct definition on the right.

1. nutritious   a. tasting good
2. guarantee   b. a positive result
3. favorite   c. having things that keep you healthy
4. delicious   d. something someone likes best
5. benefit   e. to promise
6. varieties   f. different types

2. Talking It Over Work in groups of three or four.

- List ten foods you all eat. Complete the chart below. Put each food in the correct column. Which column has the longest list? Why?

Foods that taste good, but are not good for you	Foods that are good for you
candy bars	

- Choose one of the foods. Make a poster that makes others want to eat it.

I Love Jell-O®! 149

UNIT 9 ■ STUDENT BOOK, PAGE 149

TEACHING THE LESSON

1. Learning New Words

- Write the new words on the board. Have students work in groups of three, trying to write definitions for any three words on the list. Have them share, then set aside, their definitions.

- Have students open their books. Ask them to take turns reading sentences 1–6 at the top of the page aloud. After each student reads, ask other students to explain what they think the underlined word means.

- Have students complete the activity and share.

- Have students revisit their initial definitions, rewriting them as needed.

2. Talking It Over

- **Think Aloud** Model the information that you might use in each column. For example: *I love ice cream. I know it isn't really good for me, but it tastes so good! I eat broccoli a lot because it's good for me.*

- **Team Talk** Divide the class into groups of three or four and have the groups complete the activity together. Ask them to list ten foods that everyone in the group eats. Then have them write the name of each food on the chart. Ask them to discuss which list is longer and why. Invite groups to share their findings with classmates.

✓ WRAP UP

- Have students think once again about the charts that each group made. What are the similarities from group to group? Do most students like to eat foods that are good for you or foods that are not good for you?

ANSWER KEY

Learning New Words: 1. c; 2. e; 3. d; 4. a; 5. b; 6. f.

Talking It Over: Answers will vary.

B GETTING READY TO READ

Standard
- Relate ideas and observations

WARM UP

- Invite students to take turns describing foods that are good for them and foods they like to eat.

- **Shared Writing** Ask students to dictate sentences about some of the foods they just described. For example: *A salad is good for you because it has a lot of vitamins.* Write the sentences on the board and discuss them. Explain new vocabulary as needed. Then invite different students to read each of the sentences aloud.

UNIT 9 ■ STUDENT BOOK, PAGE 150

C READING TO LEARN

Standard
- Identify an author's argument and supporting reasons or details

WARM UP

- Ask students if they have ever noticed reviews in the newspaper—restaurant reviews, movie reviews, video game reviews. Have them listen as you read the food review below. Does the reviewer like Mama's Pizza?

> **Mama's Pizza**
> Lotsa mozzarella makes a monster pizza pie! The crust is thin and crisp, the sauce is red, sweet, and tangy, and there's plenty of cheese on the top. We give Mama an A+ for her pizza!

- Tell students that they are going to read a review of Jell-O®, written by a teenager and published in Teen Ink, an online magazine written by and for teenagers.

TEACHING THE LESSON

1. Before You Read

- **Heads Together** Ask students to discuss with partners foods they thought they would hate but ended up loving. Call on volunteers to share their experiences with a partner.

🎧 2. Let's Read

♻ Remind students that when you *visualize* something you are reading about, you form pictures of it in your mind (Reading Strategy box). This helps you understand and remember what you read.

- **My Turn: Read Aloud/Think Aloud** Read the passage aloud, modeling correct phrasing and fluent reading. As you read, stop to comment on each note in the speech bubbles next to the reading.

READING

C READING TO LEARN *Evaluation*

READING STRATEGY
Visualizing: Forming pictures in your mind can help you understand what you are reading.

1. Before You Read Do you remember a time when you thought you wouldn't like something, but you loved it when you ate it? Share this experience with a partner.

🎧 **2. Let's Read** Read the following selection. It is a review of a common dessert, Jell-O®. As you read, **visualize** what it would be like to eat Sparkling Grape Jell-O® for the first time.

Jell-O®   by Casey D.

> *This is an effective opening. Casey's words m[ake] you want to ke[ep] reading.*

¹There are two loves in my life. One is my dog, Sammie. The other is Sparkling Grape Jell-O®. I can't begin to tell you how wonderful it is, but I'll try to describe what makes it so special.

² The first time I tried Sparkling Grape Jell-O®, I was sick with **strep throat** and had to stay home from school. My mom went to the store and brought back a pint of **Ben and Jerry's** and two packets of Jell-O®, one cherry, which is boring, and Sparkling Grape. **Normally**, I hate Jell-O®, but my mom made the Sparkling Grape with **carbonated** water. Several hours later, she put a bowl in front of me. **Cautiously**, I took a tiny spoonful and the amazing taste of **Concord** grapes with an **explosion** of bubbles went down my throat. From then on I was **hooked**. Now, I eat Sparkling Grape Jell-O® as often as possible. I still haven't gotten tired of that cool, **tingly** feeling every time I put a spoonful in my mouth.

³ I guarantee a great meal if you add Sparkling Grape Jell-O® to your menu. It is **refreshing**, exciting, and delicious!

> *Casey's closing paragraph mak[es] you want to tr[y] Sparkling Gra[pe] Jell-O!*

Source: teenink.com

strep throat—an illness that causes a very sore throat
Ben and Jerry's—a popular brand of ice cream
normally—usually
carbonated—liquid having many tiny bubbles
cautiously—very carefully, to avoid danger
Concord—a type of sweet, purple grape
explosion—a sudden burst
hooked—liking something a lot
tingly—slightly stinging
refreshing—making someone feel pleasant and less tired or hot

150 Unit 9

- **Our Turn: Interactive Reading** Have students help you read the passage. Read the first sentence of each paragraph yourself. Then call on individuals to read other sentences. As students read, focus on glossed words, ask questions, and make comments:

  Has anyone ever had strep throat? What did it feel like?

- **Your Turn: Independent Reading** Have students read the passage on their own, trying to figure out what Casey likes best about Jell-O® and why.

CULTURE NOTE

Some people make fun of others who eat Jell-O®. Note that sometimes, one group of people will look down on others because of the foods they eat. Explain that this behavior is impolite.

🌈 **Access for All** Have students with linguistic intelligence turn Casey's review into a TV commercial, then act it out. Have those with artistic intelligence make a magazine advertisement for sparkling grape Jell-O®.

150 Teacher's Edition

READING

UNIT 9 ■ STUDENT BOOK, PAGE 151

3. Unlocking Meaning

Finding the Main Idea Casey wrote his review mostly because he wants to do what? Check (✓) the correct answer.

_____ 1. compare Sparkling Grape Jell-O® to cherry Jell-O®

_____ 2. explain how to make Sparkling Grape Jell-O®

_____ 3. convince other people to try Sparkling Grape Jell-O®

Finding Details Reread the selection on Jell-O®. Which of the following reasons does Casey give for loving Sparkling Grape Jell-O®? Check (✓) the correct answers.

_____ 1. His dog Sammie loves it.

_____ 2. It is delicious.

_____ 3. It is purple instead of red, like cherry.

_____ 4. It feels good when you eat it.

_____ 5. You can eat it with a spoon.

_____ 6. The bubbles give it a tingly feeling.

_____ 7. It is made from grapes, his favorite fruit.

Think about It Work in groups of three or four.

1. Decide on three foods that everyone in the group likes a lot.
2. List at least four reasons that you like each food. Complete the chart below.
3. Share your chart with your classmates. Did other groups describe the same foods?

Food #1	Food #2	Food #3

Before You Move On Give Casey's review a more interesting title—one that would make you really want to read the review.

I Love Jell-O®! **151**

3. Unlocking Meaning

✓ FINDING THE MAIN IDEA

- Ask students to think on their own about why Casey wrote his review. Help students see how statements 1 and 2 are off the mark.

- ✓ **Sentence Synthesis** Write these words on the board: *wonderful, taste, tingly*. Have students use these words in a sentence that summarizes why Casey loves Jell-O®.

✓ FINDING DETAILS

- Explain that several of the sentences make statements that are not part of the story. Have students do the activity. Then have students identify the sentences that do contain facts from the story and those that don't as they share out.

THINK ABOUT IT

- **Team Talk** Have students form groups of three or four. Have them read the instructions, and then explain in their own words what they are going to do in their groups. As a class, choose one food and model the process.

- Have the groups take turns sharing their charts with the class. Name a food from one chart and write it on the board. Then have the various groups take turns writing their reasons under the name. Discuss each addition with the class. Repeat this process for two or three foods. Then briefly review the responses for other foods orally with the class.

BEFORE YOU MOVE ON

- Brainstorm alternative titles for Casey's review with the class. (Possible answers: *The Love of My Life, Grape Heaven.*)

✓ WRAP UP

- Name a familiar food and challenge the class to think of ten words to describe it. Write their responses on an overhead transparency or on chart paper. Save the list.

PB PRACTICE BOOK ACTIVITY

See Activity A, Revisit and Retell, on Practice Book page 81.

ANSWER KEY

Finding the Main Idea: 3.

Finding Details: 2, 4, 6.

Unit 9

UNIT 9 ■ STUDENT BOOK, PAGE 152

D WORD WORK

Standard
- Use knowledge of antonyms to determine word meaning

WARM UP

- Display the list of words and phrases that students generated in the previous Wrap Up activity. Ask volunteers to say words or phrases that mean the opposite of items on this list. For example: *hot and sweet vs. cool and sour.*

TEACHING THE LESSON

1. Word Detective

🌰 **Heads Together** Read the directions and have students complete the activity. Review the correct answers.

2. Word Study

- Ask for volunteers to explain what antonyms are. Go over the examples.

3. Word Play

🌰 **Heads Together** Read the directions and have students complete the activity. Have students share their answers and sentences. Compare the different antonyms used.

Spelling and Phonics

- Have students listen to the words and tell you what they notice. (They all have the /j/ sound, but it's spelled in four different ways.)
- Have students complete the activity. Review the answers.

✓ WRAP UP

- Play a game of opposites. Students take turns saying a word and calling on a classmate to say another word that means the opposite. If a student answers incorrectly, the first student calls on another. Students who answer correctly present a new word and ask a classmate to come up with its opposite.

PB PRACTICE BOOK ACTIVITY

See Activity B, Word Work, on Practice Book page 82.

ANSWER KEY

Word Detective: 1. d 2. f 3. e 4. a 5. c 6. b.

Word Play: Answers will vary.

Spelling and Phonics: a. Tan<u>g</u>erines; b. ba<u>dg</u>e; c. sausa<u>g</u>e; d. <u>j</u>am; e. oran<u>g</u>e <u>j</u>uice; f. <u>g</u>iraffe.

152   Teacher's Edition

READING

D WORD WORK

1. Word Detective Match each word on the left with the word on the right that means the opposite or almost the opposite.

1. boring	a. ordinary
2. wonderful	b. warm
3. tiny	c. carelessly
4. special	d. exciting
5. cautiously	e. huge
6. cool	f. terrible

boring

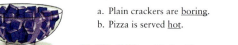
exciting

2. Word Study An antonym is a word with a meaning opposite (or almost opposite) that of another word. Do the Word Detective activity again, using your dictionary. Look at the following examples of antonyms.

a. Plain crackers are <u>boring</u>.   Sparkling Grape Jell-O® is <u>exciting</u>.
b. Pizza is served <u>hot</u>.   Jell-O® is served <u>cold</u>.

3. Word Play Work with a partner. Think of the opposite of each word or phrase in the chart below. Write pairs of sentences using both words. You can use your dictionary.

1. sweet	2. good for you	3. expensive	4. soft
sour			
5. frozen	6. thick (crust)	7. delicious	8. best

1. Ice cream is sweet. Lemons are sour.
2. _____
3. _____
4. _____
5. _____
6. _____
7. _____
8. _____

SPELLING AND PHONICS: To do this activity, go to page 196.

152 Unit 9

READING

UNIT 9 ▪ STUDENT BOOK, PAGE 153

E GRAMMAR — *If* Clauses

1. Listen Up Listen to each sentence. Point your thumb up 👍 if it sounds correct. Point your thumb down 👎 if it sounds wrong.

👍👎 1. If it will rain tomorrow, you will need an umbrella.

👍👎 2. If the doorbell rings, I will answer the door.

👍👎 3. If Rosa will win the race, she will win a prize.

👍👎 4. If you work hard, you will be successful.

2. Learn the Rule Learn how to express what will happen if something else happens. Then do Activity 1 again.

ADVERBIAL CLAUSES OF CONDITION (*IF* CLAUSES)

1. An *if* clause in a sentence talks about something that may or may not happen (a **possible condition**). The main clause identifies a possible **result**.

   If you are late for school, you will get detention.

2. Use the present tense in an *if* clause, even though the clause refers to a time in the future.

   Right: If I **am** still sick tomorrow, I **will** stay home from school.   Wrong: If I will still be sick tomorrow, I will stay home from school.

3. Practice the Rule Work with a partner. Match each condition with the correct result.

CONDITION	RESULT
1. If Juan wins the tennis tournament,	a. his teeth will fall out.
2. If Juan misses the bus,	b. he won't get his allowance.
3. If Juan wins the lottery,	c. he will sleep over at Matt's house.
4. If Juan eats too many sweets,	d. he will be late to school.
5. If Juan gets straight A's,	e. he will take home a trophy.
6. If Juan's parents give him permission,	f. he will be named "Student of the Month."
7. If Juan doesn't do his chores,	g. he will buy his parents a new house.

I Love Jell-O®! 153

E GRAMMAR

Standards
- Use complex sentences to express condition
- Recognize shades of meaning among words

WARM UP

- Hold a breakable item in front of you and pretend that you are about to drop it. Then write the words *if* and *will* on the board. Hold up the item again and ask students to use the words *if* and *will* to explain what might happen. Accept partial answers or partly correct answers and rephrase them correctly: *If you drop it, it will break.*

TEACHING THE LESSON

🎧 1. Listen Up

- Have students close their books and ask them to listen carefully. Play the tape or CD, or read the questions aloud twice. Have students follow the directions.

2. Learn the Rule

♻ Briefly review the adverbial time clauses in Unit 6. Remind students of the difference between the main clause and the subordinate clause in those sentences. Explain that an *if* clause is another kind of subordinate clause which is teamed up with a main clause.

- Use the explanations and examples to show students how *if* clauses are formed. Point out the comma that always follows an introductory *if* clause. Have students note that if the clauses are reversed, a comma is not used as a separator.

- Repeat the Listen Up activity.

3. Practice the Rule

🌰 **Heads Together** Have students work in pairs to complete the activity. Review the answers.

✓ WRAP UP

- Have students take turns presenting an *if* clause and calling on different classmates to complete it. There may be several correct completions for each sentence. For example: If clause: *If I don't come to school tomorrow, . . .* Main clause: *I won't have to take the test, I can sleep late, the teacher will be angry.* Monitor and correct errors.

PB PRACTICE BOOK ACTIVITY

See Activity C, Grammar, on Practice Book page 83.

ANSWER KEY

Listen Up: Correct sentences: 2, 4.

Practice the Rule: 1. e; 2. d; 3. g; 4. a; 5. f; 6. c; 7. b.

Unit 9   153

UNIT 9 ■ STUDENT BOOK, PAGE 154

F BRIDGE TO WRITING

Standards
- Identify an author's argument and supporting reasons or details
- Analyze and evaluate an argument and support
- Use descriptive words

WARM UP
- Time to read another review—this time for *oatmeal*. Ask a volunteer to explain what oatmeal is.

TEACHING THE LESSON

1. Before You Read
- Have students list their favorite breakfast foods. As students share their favorite breakfast foods, list them on the board. Explain new vocabulary items as necessary.

🎧 2. Let's Read
- Focus students on the strategy of summarizing (Reading Strategy box). As a class, generate one good sentence that summarizes the first paragraph. If necessary, have students complete Mini-Unit, Part C on page 190.

- 🍒 **My Turn: Read Aloud/Think Aloud** Read the review aloud. Model correct phrasing and fluent reading. As you read, stop to comment on words. For example: *What do you think "handy" means?* ("easy" or "convenient") Comment on ideas in the passages. For example: *When I eat oatmeal, I do the same thing as Keith—I add stuff like raisins and nuts.*

- 🍒 **Our Turn: Interactive Reading** Now have students help you read the passages. Take turns with students reading a few sentences at a time. After each reading, pause to discuss what has

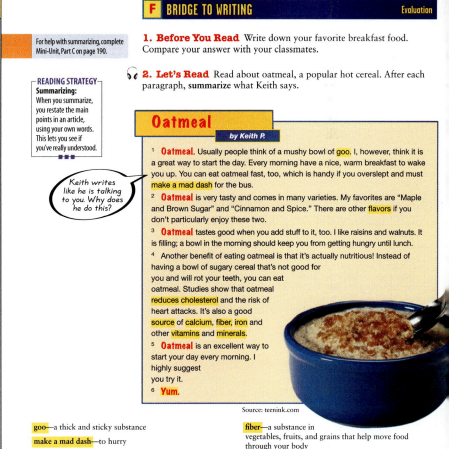

just been read. Focus on the glossed words, ask questions, and make comments:

What do you think of the idea of eating oatmeal for breakfast every single day?
Show me what a "mad dash" looks like.
What does "tasty" mean? (delicious, good tasting)
What is the opposite of tasty? (tasteless, bland, terrible tasting)
What is another way to say "nutritious"? (good for you, healthy)

- **Build Fluency** Have students read after you, line by line.

- 🍒 **Your Turn: Independent Reading** Have students read the review on their own. Have them write a summary for each paragraph and share their summaries with the class.

- 🌈 **Access for All** Have students with linguistic intelligence write a list poem about oatmeal. Have students with artistic talent making a drawing or a bumper sticker.

154 Teacher's Edition

WRITING

UNIT 9 • STUDENT BOOK, PAGE 155

3. Making Content Connections You have read two food reviews. Now, work with a partner. Compare the reviews. Complete the chart below.

	Casey's Review	Keith's Review
1. What reasons does the author give for liking the food?	It is fun to eat because it has bubbles in it.	
2. In your opinion, what is the best reason the author gives for eating the food?		
3. Based on the review, would you try the food? Why or why not?		

4. Expanding Your Vocabulary Work in groups of three or four. Think of a food you all love. Complete the chart below. Use the words and phrases in the box, or use different words. You can use your dictionary to find different words.

salty	crispy	golden	crunchy
covered with	bubbling hot	full of	satisfied
frosty	chewy	sweet	delicious
enormous	sour	content	spicy

Some words might go in more than one place in the chart.

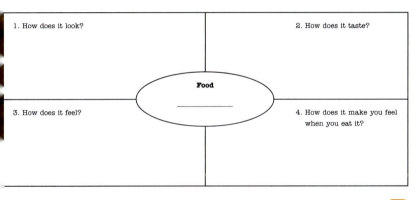

1. How does it look?
2. How does it taste?
3. How does it feel?
4. How does it make you feel when you eat it?

Food _____

I Love Jell-O®! 155

3. Making Content Connections

■ **Heads Together** Ask students to work in pairs to compare the two reviews and complete their charts together. Invite several volunteers to read their answers to the class.

■ Focus special attention on how each writer makes the reader want to try the food. Help students identify strategies that each writer uses to convince others.

4. Expanding Your Vocabulary

■ **Team Talk** Have students work in small groups. First have them choose a food they all love. Then have them work together to fill in their charts.

■ Have students look back at the reviews that Casey and Keith wrote and notice how the boys made use of descriptive words like those in the box. Invite students to take turns reading some of these descriptive sentences aloud to the group.

■ Provide dictionaries so that students can look up any words they aren't sure of. When they finish their charts, invite each group to read its chart to the class.

JUST FOR FUN

Play an add-on game. One student names and describes a food in a single sentence. For example: *I love sweet, ice-cold tea.* The second student repeats the first sentence and adds to it. For example: *I like a hot, juicy hamburger with my sweet, ice-cold tea.* See how many additions students can make without forgetting anyone's contribution.

PB PRACTICE BOOK ACTIVITY

See Activity D, Test-Taking Practice, on Practice Book pages 84 and 85.

See Activity E, Using New Vocabulary, on Practice Book page 86.

✓ WRAP UP

■ Have students list any new words they have learned in this section in their **notebooks.** Suggest that they add a sentence showing the correct use of each word.

ANSWER KEY

Making Content Connections: Answers will vary.

Expanding Your Vocabulary: Answers will vary.

Unit 9

UNIT 9 ▪ STUDENT BOOK, PAGE 156

G WRITING CLINIC

Standards
- Develop a well-formed argument
- Use descriptive words

WARM UP

- Ask students to look back at the two reviews they have just read. Ask: *In what ways are the two reviews the same? What do you notice about both?* (For example, students might say that both use lots of adjectives, that both are about foods, etc. Accept all student ideas.)

TEACHING THE LESSON

1. Think about It

- Ask: *Where do we find food reviews?* Have students tell you why you wouldn't find reviews in a textbook, book of recipes, or collection of short stories.

2. Focus on Organization

- 🍎 **Think Aloud** Alternate between reading sentences in the text and reading the speech bubble comments (Part 1). As you read the comments, add additional explanations and ideas to help clarify each point. For example, when pointing out Keith's opinion statement, you can ask students to make up some other opinions people might have about oatmeal. They can add additional reasons for liking or not liking oatmeal.

- Give special attention to the reasons that Keith provides. Have students find other reasons, as you record.

- When you discuss the note on the reviewer's "voice," explain that this term has more than one meaning. It does not mean just the sound of a person when they are speaking. "Voice" also refers to what happens when a

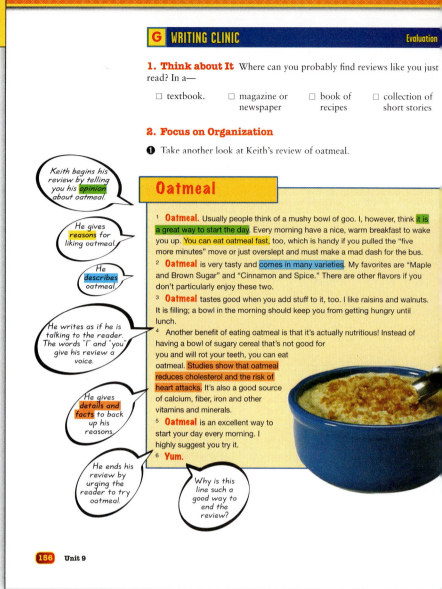

writer's words begin to have a personal connection for you. You hear the writer's "voice."

- Ask students to point out additional examples of details and facts in the review.

- Focus on how Keith ends his review. Why is his one-word comment so effective? Why does he make the word a separate paragraph?

PB PRACTICE BOOK ACTIVITY

See Activity F, Focus on Organization, on Practice Book page 87.

WRITING

❷ Good reviews give lots of reasons, details, and facts. Find the reasons, details, and facts that Keith gives for eating oatmeal. Complete the chart below.

Qualities/Characteristics	Reasons	Details/Facts
1. convenience	You can eat oatmeal fast.	This is handy if you overslept.
2. taste		
3. satisfaction		
4. health benefits		

3. Focus on Style

❶ Reviews often use **stand-out adjectives** to describe.
  1. Usually people think of a **mushy** bowl of goo.
  2. It's handy if you have to make a **mad** dash for the bus.

❷ Imagine the perfect slice of pizza. Match the adjectives to the traits below.

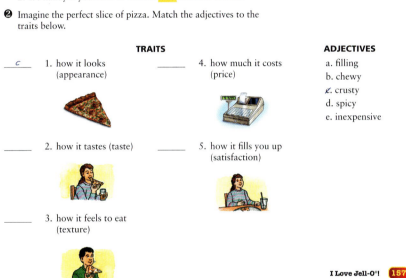

TRAITS

_c_ 1. how it looks (appearance)
___ 2. how it tastes (taste)
___ 3. how it feels to eat (texture)
___ 4. how much it costs (price)
___ 5. how it fills you up (satisfaction)

ADJECTIVES
a. filling
b. chewy
c. crusty
d. spicy
e. inexpensive

I Love Jell-O®!   157

🍇 **Heads Together** Write the words *qualities, characteristics, reasons, details,* and *facts* on the board (Part 2). Assign each word to a pair of students and have them come up with their own definition. Review the definitions with the class.

- Ask volunteers to explain in their own words what the words in the *Qualities/Characteristics* column mean. Then ask a student to read the sample *Reason* on the chart aloud. Have another student read the sentence from Keith's review that supports this reason. Repeat this activity for the sample *Detail/Fact*.

🍇 **Team Talk** Have students form small groups. Suggest that they focus on one quality at a time, locate all the related information in the review, and then complete that part of the chart before going on to the next quality. Review the completed charts with the class.

2. Focus on Style

- Explain that "stand-out adjectives" are adjectives that give extra life and interest to a sentence. Ask: *How do "mushy" and "mad"*

UNIT 9 ▪ STUDENT BOOK, PAGE 157

give extra life to each sentence? Help students add one more adjective to each sentence. Invite students to try adding additional stand-out adjectives to other sentences in the reviews they have read.

- Have students complete the activity individually. Review the correct answers with the class.

📘 PRACTICE BOOK ACTIVITY

See Activity G, Focus on Style, on Practice Book page 88.

WRAP UP

- Ask students to bring to class restaurant reviews that describe food. Explain that they can find these in local newspapers, in magazines, or on the Internet. Remind students that the reviews they bring in should list reasons and provide facts and details.

ANSWER KEY

Think about It: magazine or newspaper.

Focus on Organization 2: 1. convenience: You can eat oatmeal fast. This is handy if you overslept. 2. taste: It comes in many varieties. It comes in "Maple and Brown Sugar" and "cinnamon and spice." You can add raisins and nuts. 3. satisfaction: It is filling. You won't get hungry until lunch. 4. health benefits: It's nutritious. It reduces cholesterol and the risk of heart attacks. It contains calcium, fiber, iron, vitamins, and minerals.

Focus on Style 2: 1. c; 2. d; 3. b; 4. e; 5. a.

UNIT 9 ▪ STUDENT BOOK, PAGE 158

WRITING

 WRITER'S WORKSHOP — Evaluation

Imagine that you have been invited to write a review for the food section of your local newspaper.

1. Getting It Out

❶ Choose a food to review. Select something that—

- ☐ you really love to eat and eat often
- ☐ other people might not know about or have tried yet
- ☐ will be fun for others to read about

Here are some ideas.

1.

A burrito

2.

Granola bars and breakfast bars

3.

Egg rolls

4.

Papayas

 Access for All Consider having less-proficient writers work together in small groups, choosing a single food to write about. Have an instructional aide or volunteer help them as they complete the Writer's Workshop.

H WRITER'S WORKSHOP

Standards
- Use the writing process: prewriting
- Develop a multi-paragraph composition that develops an argument and provides supporting details

1. Getting It Out

WARM UP

- Ask volunteers to share the food reviews they have brought to class. Have them read sections of the reviews aloud, focusing on reasons, details, and the use of language that hooks the reader.

- Tell students that they are now going to have the chance to write food reviews, just like those that appear in the newspaper.

TEACHING TIP 💡 Make copies of reviews and display them in the classroom where students can look at them as they draft their own reviews.

TEACHING THE LESSON

- Tell students that the first step will involve choosing a food to write about (Part 1). Discuss the foods in the pictures.

- Ask a volunteer to identify one of the foods, then "think aloud" about that food in relation to each criterion.

- Help students generate additional ideas for foods. Record responses on the board.

WRITING

UNIT 9 ▪ STUDENT BOOK, PAGE 159

❷ Describe the food. Use a diagram like this. On your own, brainstorm what the food is like.

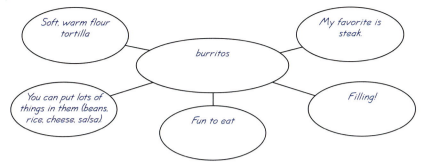

❸ Now decide which traits you will discuss. Think about your reasons then add details. Complete the chart below.

Traits	Reasons	Details/Facts
1. *taste*	*delicious*	
2. *appearance*		
3.		
4.		

Read the reviews that other teens have written at **www.teenink.com**

I Love Jell-O®!

from each other to add to their own charts.

- Point out the *Connect to the Web* note at the bottom of the page. Encourage students to read some food reviews either at home or using a school computer.

- **Using Technology** Encourage students to try using an Internet-based dictionary such as **www.YourDictionary.com**. Online dictionaries often contain lists of synonyms along with definitions and sample sentences.

WRAP UP

- Explain that during the next workshop session students will use the information from their diagrams and charts to outline and then draft their food reviews.

PB PRACTICE BOOK ACTIVITY

See Activity H, Writer's Workshop, on Practice Book page 89.

TEACHING THE LESSON

- **Think Aloud** Have students brainstorm the qualities or characteristics of the food they have selected, using a web diagram (Part 2). Students can make their own diagrams or use the diagram on Practice Book page 89.

- Remind students to write down everything that comes to mind while brainstorming and completing their diagrams, even if it seems silly or unimportant. Explain that if they stop to criticize and judge their ideas, they will miss out on a lot of good material. They can cross out the unuseable ideas later. Also tell them not to worry about spelling at this point.

- Have students begin listing the traits, reasons, details, and facts about the food they have selected on their charts.

- 🍎 **Heads Together** At this point, consider having students share their charts with a partner. Invite volunteers to share the contents of their charts with the class. Encourage students to pick up ideas

Unit 9 159

UNIT 9 ▪ STUDENT BOOK, PAGE 160

H WRITER'S WORKSHOP

Standards
- Use notes and outlining to organize writing
- Use the writing process: drafting, revising and editing for clarity and organization
- Give a short oral presentation

2. Getting It Down

WARM UP
- Have students revisit their charts. Ask volunteers to share a trait, then a reason, then a detail from their charts.

> **TEACHING TIP** 💡 Provide guided support to individuals or small groups of students whose charts reveal that they do not yet understand that their reviews need to be organized around traits.

TEACHING THE LESSON

🍎 **Shared Writing** Model the process of outlining (Part 1). Have volunteers who are reviewing the same food provide examples from their charts, as you create a partial outline on the board. First develop an opinion statement. Then identify one reason and at least one detail, written in outline form.

- Model the drafting of a paragraph, based on the outline you have generated (Part 2).

- Look at Sau-Lim's review with the class, pointing out the features or points noted in the speech bubbles. Encourage students to identify other features they notice about Sau-Lim's review.

🍎 **Mini-Lesson on Conventions** Ask students to locate the sentence-opening adverbs that are followed by commas in the *Couscous* review

(Finally) and in the *Jell-O®* review on page 150 (Normally, Cautiously, Now). Ask students to make up some original sentences beginning with these and other adverbs such as *at first, later,* and *carefully.*

WRAP UP
- Tell students that they will have a chance to revise their work during the next session. Have them locate the ChecBric for this unit in the Student Book or Practice Book. Have them prepare for Getting It Right by reviewing the ChecBric on their own, underlining indicators they're not sure about.

WRITING

UNIT 9 ▪ STUDENT BOOK, PAGE 161

3. Getting It Right Look carefully at your review. Use this guide to revise your paragraph.

Ask yourself...	How to check...	How to revise...
1. Does my review have an opinion statement?	Underline your opinion statement.	Tell the reader exactly how you feel about the food or product.
2. Do I describe the food or product?	Show your draft to a neighbor. Ask them to describe the food in their own words.	Change your description so that others will know more about the food.
3. Do I give reasons for my opinion?	Draw a wavy line under each reason.	Provide more than one reason.
4. Do I give details to back up each reason?	Put a check mark (✓) next to each detail.	Add details that will convince your reader.
5. Do I use stand-out adjectives?	Circle each adjective.	Add an adjective or two to make your review interesting.

4. Presenting It Share the page you have written with your classmates.

❶ Read your first paragraph aloud. Make sure that your classmates know how you feel about the food.

❷ Read the rest of your review aloud. Read slowly and speak clearly.

❸ Ask for feedback from your classmates.

I Love Jell-O®!

3. Getting It Right
WARM UP

- Guide students through the ChecBric for this unit. Explain that they will use the ChecBric to prepare a final draft.
- Have volunteers explain, in their own words, what each indicator in the ChecBric means.

TEACHING THE LESSON

- Have students use the chart and the ChecBric to revise their work.
- 🍇 **Group Share** Have students share their reviews in groups of four or five and give each other feedback on their articles.

WRAP UP

- Tell students to share their reviews with family members before presenting to the class.

📁 Give students time to fill out the ChecBric on Practice Book page 117. Ask them to attach it to their writing when they put it in their portfolios.

4. Presenting It
WARM UP

- Generate interest in the upcoming presentations by going around the room and having students tell the name of the food they are going to review.
- As a class, develop a simple presentation checklist. Focus on content, organization, speaking skills (poise, expression, volume, posture, eye contact), enthusiasm, use of visuals, creativity, involvement of the audience, and length of presentation.

TEACHING THE LESSON

- Have students read the instructions, then tell you in their own words what they are going to do.
- Have students present their reviews. Remind them to read slowly and clearly and to look up at the audience after each paragraph.
- After each presentation, encourage students to give each other positive feedback. Invite students to ask about and make comments on each other's work.

> **TEACHING TIP** 💡 Some students may enjoy visiting a local restaurant and writing a review. Have students go in pairs. Display the reviews in your classroom.

✓ WRAP UP

- Ask students to think of one food that they would like to try—based on the food reviews they listened to. Share and discuss.

Unit 9 161

UNIT 9 ▪ STUDENT BOOK, PAGE 162

❙ BEYOND THE UNIT

> **Standards**
> - Read a response to literature
> - Respond to a humorous poem

1. On Assignment
WARM UP

- Brainstorm with students a list of things *besides food* for which people write reviews. For example: *movies, plays, CDs, video games, and books.* Tell students they will read such reviews—each of them fun to read!

TEACHING THE LESSON

- **Team Talk** Divide students into small groups. Be sure that each group has several more-proficient students. First have them choose a review to read (Part 1). Or, consider having students go to the four corners of the room, then assigning a review to each corner.

- Ask the group to list all the vocabulary words or phrases that are difficult and may require teaching. Have them think of ways to make the meanings clear to their classmates. For example, they might use synonyms, short explanations, sample sentences, as well as gestures and pantomime. Suggest that they rehearse before giving their presentation to other groups.

- Have students take turns reading a review and explaining new vocabulary words.

- Focus special attention on the review of "Housebroken." What makes it especially fun—and funny—to read?

- Have students write their own mini-reviews, following the steps in Part 2.

❙ BEYOND THE UNIT

1. On Assignment

❶ Work in groups of three or four. Read newspaper reviews.

1. Choose one of the following reviews to read.
2. Make a list of the words nobody in your group knows. Try to guess the meaning. Use a dictionary to check your guesses.
3. Choose someone in your group to read the review aloud. Think about how you will teach your classmates the new words.
4. Which review is the most fun to read? Why?

NOW PLAYING

BAD BOYS VIII

In the silliest of plots, Miami cops try to bring down a ring of mobsters. Once again, Will Smith and Martin Lawrence play trash-talking detectives. It's hard to tell the good guys from the bad boys. (R: strong violence and action, language, and crude humor). D2

DINING OUT

Pizzeria Uno

Great pizza and surroundings that make you think you're in Italy. The menu offers a wide variety for all. Takeout is available. Two convenient locations. Highly recommended. A+

VIDEO GAMES

NFL2K1

Incredible graphics, awesome control system, and great fun factor. You'll be wondering if you are playing or watching Monday Night Football. The greatest football game ever made! A

HIP-HOP/R&B

WHAT: Housebroken

WHO: Woof Woof Dawg

GRADE: F

Woof Woof's second album makes you want to give the teen rapper up for adoption. Thirteen tracks with dumb lyrics that will make you bar your teeth. Spend your money on dog biscuits instead.

---

❷ Write your own short review.

1. Choose something to review.
2. Give it an overall grade, from A+ to F.
3. Decide why you gave it that grade. Make a list of reasons.
4. Write a review with three or four sentences.
5. Share with your classmates.

✓ WRAP UP

- Invite students to read their mini-reviews to their classmates.

2. Link to Literature

🎧 **SHARED READING** Reviews can also be about literature. Read Amy P.'s review of *Falling Up*.

Falling Up
by Shel Silverstein
Review by Amy P.

For me, poetry is a very personal thing. It makes me laugh, and sometimes even cry. I love poetry for what it says about life, about love, and about everything in this world that is worth writing about. When I think of great poetry, *Falling Up* by Shel Silverstein comes to mind. Its **humorous** poems are always what I need for a good laugh, and they help lighten my mood.

This is a collection of the silliest and **zaniest** poems you can imagine. They are **hilarious**, and good for readers of all ages. I have been reading Silverstein's poems since I was little, and I loved them even then. Some are extremely **clever**, like "The Monkey," and others are just plain funny, like "Tattooin' Ruth."

I highly recommend this book to anyone who appreciates poetry and likes to laugh. I guarantee you'll enjoy it. The book's **wacky** nature will make anyone **crack a smile**, and you can be sure that you'll be flipping through the pages for a long time to come!

Source: teenink.com

LET'S TALK Answer the questions.

1. What reasons does Amy give for liking the book?
2. Read the poem "Tattooin' Ruth." Do you agree with Amy?
3. Does the review make you want to read the book? Why or why not?

TATTOOIN' RUTH

Collars are choking,
Pants are expensive,
Jackets are itchy and hot,
So tattooin' Ruth tattooed me a suit.
Now folks think I'm *dressed*—
When I'm not.

Source: *Falling Up* by Shel Silverstein

ABOUT THE AUTHOR

 Shel Silverstein was born in Chicago, Illinois in 1930 and died in 1999. He wrote many fun stories and poems. Some of his most famous books are *The Giving Tree*, *Where the Sidewalk Ends*, and *Falling Up*.

humorous—funny
zany—funny in an unusual way
hilarious—very, very funny
clever—original
wacky—very silly
crack a smile—to begin to smile

I Love Jell-O®!

UNIT 9 ▪ STUDENT BOOK, PAGE 163

✓ **WRAP UP**

 Outcome Sentence Have students complete this sentence stem, then share:

I enjoy reading poetry that _____.

PB PRACTICE BOOK ACTIVITY

See Activity I, Responding to Literature, on Practice Book page 90.

✓ **UNIT WRAP UP**

- Have students write in their **notebooks** about what they learned to do in this unit. Consider responding to reflections.

🎧 2. Link to Literature

WARM UP

- Help students read the poem, "Tattooin' Ruth." How many students like the poem? Why? How many do not? Why not?

TEACHING THE LESSON

- Reread the poem aloud. Ask a volunteer to tell what Ruth did for the poet.

- Now have students listen to Amy P.'s review of Shel Silverstein's book of poetry *Falling Up* as they read along. Discuss glossed vocabulary items. Pause after each paragraph and ask a student to summarize what it says.

- **Let's Talk** Why does Amy like the book? Did any of the students who initially did not like the poem change their minds based on Amy's review?

Unit 10 Let's Debate!
Unit Overview

Section	At a Glance	Standards
Before You Begin	Students focus on a debate about whether or not students have too much homework.	■ Derive meaning from visual information ■ Express an opinion on an issue ■ Consider the merits of an argument
A. Connecting to Your Life	Students survey classmates on various issues, then take sides and discuss.	■ Justify a position on an issue
B. Getting Ready to Read	Students learn the language of debate, then discuss the reasons for various laws.	■ Justify a position on an issue
C. Reading to Learn	Students read an article about the pros and cons of a "courtesy law" for students. PRACTICE BOOK: Students summarize the Student Book article.	■ Identify arguments and support in persuasive text ■ Distinguish fact and opinion in text
D. Word Work	Students explore word families. PRACTICE BOOK: Students explore word families.	■ Use knowledge of roots and derivational morphology to determine word meanings ■ Use knowledge of sound/letter patterns to spell words
E. Grammar	Students learn about modals. PRACTICE BOOK: Students practice using modals to persuade.	■ Use everyday functions: express possibility, probability, certainty; give advice
F. Bridge to Writing	Students read a pro and con article about banning junk food at school. PRACTICE BOOK: Students practice taking Reading Vocabulary and Reading Comprehension tests. PRACTICE BOOK: Students identify sentences that express opinions, arguments, and disagreement.	■ Identify opposing arguments and supporting details ■ Use everyday functions: the language of discussion and debate

Section	At a Glance	Standards
G. Writing Clinic	Students learn about the critical elements of a debate. PRACTICE BOOK: Students read a pro and con article on curfews, then identify the arguments. PRACTICE BOOK: Students practice using quotation marks with direct quotes.	■ Identify structural patterns found in persuasive text ■ Trace the development of a writer's argument ■ Use direct discourse in writing
H1. Writer's Workshop: Getting It Out	Pairs of students collaborate on a feature article that argues both sides of an issue, then plan their arguments. PRACTICE BOOK: Students interview people for their "debate" articles.	■ Use the writing process: prewriting ■ Develop arguments based on fact and opinion
H2. Writer's Workshop: Getting It Down	Students make a formal outline of their articles and write a first draft.	■ Use the writing process: drafting ■ Use notes and outlining to draft writing
H3. Writer's Workshop: Getting It Right	Students revise and edit their articles.	■ Use the writing process: revising and editing for clarity and organization
H4. Writer's Workshop: Presenting It	Students share their articles with their classmates.	■ Give a persuasive presentation that states and supports a position
I. Beyond the Unit	Students assume the role of student, parent, teacher, or principal, then debate in issue. Students read the poem, "How to Successfully Persuade Your Parents to Give You More Pocket Money" by Andrea Shavick. PRACTICE BOOK: Students respond to a poem, then write an original poem based on the model.	■ Debate an issue, supporting an opinion with evidence ■ Respond to poetry

UNIT 10 ▪ STUDENT BOOK, PAGE 164

Unit 10 Let's Debate!

BEFORE YOU BEGIN

Standards
- Derive meaning from visual information
- Express an opinion on an issue
- Consider the merits of an argument

- Have students read the caption, *For and against*, under the picture. What does the phrase mean? Then have students look at the picture. What do they think is happening?

- **Building Background Knowledge** Note that the students are having a debate. Explain that a *debate* is a discussion or argument about a subject about which the *debaters* have different opinions. Tell students that people running for public office often have debates about important issues.

- **Let's Talk** Have students tell you in their own words the issue that the students in the picture are debating. Use the questions to lead a discussion.

- **Shared Quick Write** Ask students to consider the question: *Do kids get too much homework?* Have students to choose a position (yes or no) and write one or two sentences supporting their opinion on a sheet of paper. Have students dictate their sentences as you write them on the chalkboard under the headings *Yes* and *No*. Encourage students to discuss the merits of each argument.

Read...
- An article about a law that could force students to be polite.

- An article about taking junk food out of school cafeterias.

Link to Literature
- "How to Successfully Persuade Your Parents to Give You More Pocket Money," a poem by Andrea Shavick.

Objectives:

Reading:
- Evaluating feature articles that present two sides of an issue
- Strategies: Identifying facts and opinions, skimming for information
- Literature: Responding to a poem

Writing:
- Writing a feature article: A debate
- Writing an introduction that provides background information
- Using facts and quotes both to interest and convince others

Vocabulary:
- Recognizing word families
- Learning words and phrases used in discussion and debate

Listening/Speaking:
- Listening to the discussion of an issue
- Stating an opinion
- Presenting arguments to support your opinion

Grammar:
- Using modals to help persuade others

Sounds and Spelling:
- Spelling the /or/ sound as in *for* and *four*

Teacher's Edition

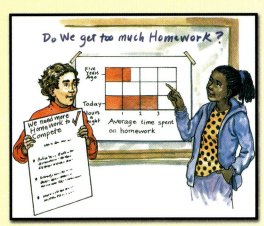

For and against

BEFORE YOU BEGIN

Talk with your classmates.

1. Look at the picture. What do you think is happening?
2. Read the words on the blackboard. What is the girl probably telling her classmates?
3. Do kids have too much homework? Should they have more?

Let's Debate!

UNIT 10 ■ STUDENT BOOK, PAGE 166

A CONNECTING TO YOUR LIFE

Standard
- Justify a position on an issue

WARM UP

- Ask students where they get their spending money. How many get an allowance? Do they have to do chores, or work around the house, for their allowance?

TEACHING THE LESSON

🎧 1. Tuning In

- Tell students they are going to hear a mother and her son discussing an important issue. As you play the tape or CD or read the script the first time, ask students to identify the issue (*Should kids have to work for their allowance?*)

- Play the tape or CD, or read the script a second time. This time, ask students to form their own opinion on the issue, jotting down the reason they hear that is most convincing. Have students share and tell why.

- Have pairs of students act out a similar discussion on this issue, one student playing the parent, the other the teen.

2. Talking It Over

- Ask students to take the short survey on their own. Have students share out, giving reasons for their responses.

- 🍎 **Let's Talk** Have students move around the room and ask each other about their opinions on one of the survey questions. Encourage students to move around quickly, talking with at least five people in five minutes.

- Have each student find someone who s/he feels *disagrees* with him/her on one of the issues. Have each student write down a good reason for his or her own

---

READING

A CONNECTING TO YOUR LIFE

🎧 **1. Tuning In** Listen to the conversation between Erik and his mother. Whose side do you take? Why?

2. Talking It Over Read the survey. Circle an answer for each question?

	YES	NO
1. Should kids have to take gym?	☺	☹
2. Should kids give themselves their own grades?	☺	☹
3. Should there be separate schools for girls and boys?	☺	☹

Find out what your classmates think. Choose one question from the survey that interests you. Ask five other people what they think.

Question: _____

Write one reason for each person's answer.

EXAMPLE:

Person 1: Answer: _yes_ Reason: *Kids need exercise for good health*
Person 2: Answer: _____ Reason: _____
Person 3: Answer: _____ Reason: _____
Person 4: Answer: _____ Reason: _____
Person 5: Answer: _____ Reason: _____

Read the title. What do you think the unit is probably about? Check (✓) the correct answer.

_____ 1. topics or questions most people agree on
_____ 2. topics or questions people often disagree about
_____ 3. topics or questions that are silly

Unit 10

---

point of view. Invite several pairs to come to the front of the room and stage a short "debate." For example:
A: *I don't think there should be separate schools for boys and girls. Then the education wouldn't be exactly the same for both.*
B: *I think there should be separate schools. We'd be able to pay attention to schoolwork better.*

- Focus on the title of the unit. Have students use finger signals to show their responses.

✓ WRAP UP

- Have students write down an additional question that is likely to spark debate among kids. Have them share their questions.

ANSWER KEY

Talking It Over: 2.

READING

UNIT 10 ▪ STUDENT BOOK, PAGE 167

B GETTING READY TO READ

1. Learning New Words Read the sentences below. Try to guess the meanings of the underlined words.

1. If you steal, you may go to jail because stealing is against the <u>law</u>.
2. Lori bumped into Sarah. She didn't even have the <u>courtesy</u> to apologize!
3. Students must take gym. It's <u>required</u>.
4. There are three good <u>arguments</u> for not cheating. First, it's wrong. Second, it's against school rules. Third, you won't learn anything.
5. We shouldn't allow skateboards at school. We should <u>ban</u> them!
6. Children can't decide if they want to go to school or stay home. They have no <u>choice</u>.
7. Juan thinks wearing bicycle helmets is a good idea because helmets save lives. That is his <u>position</u>.

Now match each word on the left with the correct definition on the right.

1. law
2. courtesy
3. required
4. argument
5. ban
6. choice
7. position

a. necessary because of a law or rule
b. an opinion about something
c. a rule in a country, state, or city that we must follow
d. the right to choose something
e. polite behavior to other people
f. an explanation you give for what you believe
g. to order that an activity must not happen

2. Talking It Over Work in groups of three or four. List three laws that you know about. Discuss why we need each law. Complete the chart below.

Laws	Why we need these laws
EXAMPLE: It's against the law to break the speed limit.	Driving too fast causes accidents.
1.	
2.	
3.	

Let's Debate! **167**

B GETTING READY TO READ

Standard
▪ Justify a position on an issue

WARM UP

- Remind students of the mini-debates they had. Ask them to identify characteristics of a debate (an issue, at least two different opinions on the issue, and one or more reasons to back up each opinion).

TEACHING THE LESSON

1. Learning New Words

- Write the new words on the board. Have students work in groups of three, trying to write a definition for each word. Have them share their definitions, then set them aside for the next step.

- Have students open their books. Have each small group read sentences 1–7, then revise their original definitions. Have them share out once again.

- Now have each group match each word to its definition, then share out. Confirm the correct answers and clarify the definitions with students.

- Have each group create an original sentence for each word, writing each on a piece of paper. Have students share out.

2. Talking It Over

- **Build Background** Explain that our *legislators*—men and women who are elected to make *laws*—often have debates before they pass (or vote down) laws.

- **Team Talk** Have small groups of students generate examples of three laws, then write the reason for each law. Have them share out.

- **Access for All** You may wish to encourage more advanced students to share an opposite point of view related to the various laws that students identify.

- **Shared Quick Write** Review the sentences in the chart by having students take turns writing one sentence each on the board. Have the student read the sentence aloud and invite other students to add their comments.

✓ WRAP UP

- Hand out copies of rules in the school handbook or point to classroom rules that are posted on the walls. Have students explain the reason for each rule and possibly point out reasons that the rule may not always be a good idea.

ANSWER KEY

Learning New Words: 1. c; 2. e; 3. a; 4. f; 5. g; 6. d; 7. b.

UNIT 10 ■ STUDENT BOOK, PAGE 168

C READING TO LEARN

Standards
- Identify arguments and support in persuasive text
- Distinguish fact and opinion in text

WARM UP
- Have students read the title of the article. Ask them to guess what a "courtesy law" might be.

TEACHING THE LESSON

1. Before You Read
- Have pairs of students discuss, then share, things students can do to be polite to teachers (raise their hands when they have a question, not interrupt when the teacher is talking, not chew gum, not come to class late).

🎧 2. Let's Read
- Tell students that when your are reading an article that describes the arguments on two sides of an issue you should pay attention to statements that are *facts* and statements that are *opinions* (Reading Strategy box). Have students tell you what a fact is, then an opinion, providing examples for both.

- 🍎 **My Turn: Real Aloud/Think Aloud** Read the article aloud. As you read, stop to comment on what you are reading.

- 🍎 **Our Turn: Interactive Reading** Read the first sentence of each paragraph. Have volunteers read the rest of the passage. As students read, focus on the glossed words, ask questions, and make comments.

- ✓ 🍎 **Question All-Write** What is one idea you have for making students be more respectful?

READING

C READING TO LEARN
Feature Articles: Debates

READING STRATEGY
Identifying Facts and Opinions: Identifying facts and opinions can help you evaluate, or analyze, an argument or point of view.

1. Before You Read Think of things that you can do to be polite to your teacher. Talk with a partner. Make a list.

🎧 **2. Let's Read** Read the article. It discusses two sides of a question that people have strong feelings about. As you read, **identify the facts and opinions.** Then decide with side you agree with most.

Do Students Need a Courtesy Law? (Debate)

Louisiana

¹In Louisiana's public schools, being polite to teachers isn't just **expected**—it's required by state law. In 1999, Louisiana passed the first student **respect** law. It requires students to address their teachers as "sir" or "ma'am," or with appropriate titles, such as "Mrs." or "Mr."
²"Just as we teach reading and writing, I think we can teach **manners**," says Donald Cravins, the state **senator** who **sponsored** the law.
³The idea has spread quickly. Several other states are **considering** similar laws. But not everyone agrees that courtesy laws are a good idea. What do you think? Should students be required by law to be polite? Read both arguments, then decide.

The argument "for" always come first.

Yes, Ma'am!
⁴Teachers don't get enough respect from students today. Courtesy laws will help students and teachers work together to create an **environment** that **fosters creativity** and learning.
⁵With courtesy laws in effect, teachers can spend less time **disciplining** their students and more time teaching them. "I've had teacher after teacher tell me that it's changed the whole experience in the classroom," says Louisiana Governor Mike Foster.
⁶Many students agree that some kids need to learn better manners. "I think a courtesy law would help some kids show respect at home," says Kurt Phelan.

expected—considered to be the thing that people should do
respect—being polite to someone because they are important
manners—polite ways of behaving
senator—a member of the Senate, one of two groups that makes laws
sponsor—to push for (a new law)

consider—to think about doing something
environment—the situation or people that affect how you live, learn, or work
foster—help something happen
creativity—using your imagination to do things
discipline—to punish for bad behavior

168 Unit 10

- **Build Fluency** Have pairs of students take turns reading aloud to each other—one person reading the "pro" side of the issue, the other reading the "con."

- 🍎 **Your Turn: Independent Reading** Have students read the debate on their own. Have them identify facts and opinions. Then have them say which side they agree with most.

- Discuss how students in other countries are expected to show respect to their teachers.

CULTURE NOTE
In some cultures, disagreement is considered extremely impolite and embarrassing. Notice any discomfort your students may be experiencing and help them understand that in the U.S. disagreement is OK.

🌈 **Access for All** Have students with linguistic intelligence engage in a role-play debate, based on the article.

168 Teacher's Edition

READING

UNIT 10 ■ STUDENT BOOK, PAGE 169

No, Sir!

7 Good manners should be taught at home by parents, not in the schools. "Teachers deserve respect because they are adults," says 17-year old Peter Lainey. "But that decision should be left up to the parents."

8 These kinds of laws only take attention away from the real problems that **plague** schools today. School districts need to build better schools, **reduce drop-out rates**, **improve** test scores, and raise teachers' salaries to really improve education.

9 "'Yes, ma'am' and 'no, ma'am' is fine, says Sue Hall, a teacher in New Orleans. "But it's pretty **superficial**. You're not getting to the **root** of the problem."

Source: *Junior Scholastic*

plague—to cause trouble again and again
reduce—to make smaller or less in number or amount
drop-out rates—the numbers of kids quitting school
improve—to make better
superficial—not very important
root—the main or basic part

❶ **Finding the Main Idea** What is the main idea of this article? Check (✓) the correct answer.

_____ 1. Most people favor courtesy laws.
_____ 2. Some people favor courtesy laws and others do not.
_____ 3. Most states will soon pass a courtesy law.

❷ **Finding Details** Listen as your teacher reads each of the statements. Point your thumb up 👍 if it is an argument **for** courtesy laws. Point your thumb down 👎 if it is an argument **against** such laws.

1. Courtesy laws will make students show more respect for their teachers.
2. Schools have more important problems to deal with than teaching manners.
3. Courtesy laws help students learn better.
4. Good manners should be taught at home, not school.
5. Teachers will have fewer discipline problems.

❸ **Think about It** Work with a partner. Think of one more argument for each position. Write down your arguments and discuss them.

❹ **Before You Move On** Work with your classmates. Write a "courtesy law" for your own classroom.

Let's Debate! 169

THINK ABOUT IT

■ **Heads Together** Have pairs of students generate additional pro and con arguments. Invite pairs to share their ideas with the class.

BEFORE YOU MOVE ON

■ **Interactive Writing** As a class, create your own courtesy law. As students suggest ideas, record on the board. Help students summarize and shape their ideas into a short, clear statement. Write the new "courtesy law" on chart paper and display it in the classroom.

WRAP UP

■ Ask students to reflect in their **notebooks** on the current state of courtesy at your school.

PB PRACTICE BOOK ACTIVITY

See Activity A, Revisit and Retell, on Practice Book page 91.

ANSWER KEY

Finding the Main Idea: 2.
Finding Details: For: 1, 3, 5; Against: 2, 4.
Think about It: Answers will vary.
Before You Move On: Answers will vary.

3. Unlocking Meaning

✓ FINDING THE MAIN IDEA

■ Have students use finger signals to identify the main idea of the article. Ask a volunteer explain why the chosen answer is correct.

✓ FINDING DETAILS

■ Read the sentences aloud. Ask students to give the thumbs up sign for arguments that support courtesy laws and the thumbs down sign for arguments against them.

✓ **Sentence Synthesis** Write these words on the board: *courtesy, respect, law*. Have students write a sentence using all three words that makes the case *for* courtesy laws. Have them share their sentences. Then, have students use the same three words in a sentence that makes the case *against* courtesy laws.

Unit 10 169

UNIT 10 ■ STUDENT BOOK, PAGE 170

D WORD WORK

Standards
- Use knowledge of roots and derivational morphology to determine word meanings
- Use knowledge of sound-letter patterns to spell words

WARM UP

- Write these sentences on the board: *The law requires students to be polite. Some people don't like this requirement. They don't think required courtesy is the answer.* Explain that the underlined words are in the same word family.

TEACHING THE LESSON

1. Word Detective

🍎 **Team Talk** Have students work in small groups as they write a noun form for each of the verbs in the activity. Explain that one of the words has the same noun form and verb form.

2. Word Study

🍎 **Heads Together** Point out the three columns in the chart and review what adjectives do. (They describe nouns.) Have students write sentences for all the words in the Word Detective activity and share out.

3. Word Play

🍎 **Heads Together** Read the directions and have students complete the activity in pairs. Then have the class help you complete the chart on the board.

Spelling and Phonics

🍎 **Heads Together** Have students listen to the words and tell you what they notice (they have different spellings for the same sound /or/).

- Have students complete the activity. Go over the answers.

READING

D WORD WORK

1. Word Detective Words that look alike, or almost alike, often belong to the same word family. Read this list of verbs. Write a noun that is a family member for each verb. Use your dictionary for help.

1. require — *requirement*
2. argue — _____
3. respect — _____
4. learn — _____
5. create — _____
6. decide — _____

2. Word Study Members of the same word family look almost alike, but they have different meanings and different jobs in a sentence. Make up another sentence for each of these words.

VERB	NOUN	ADJECTIVE
require	requirement	required
Ms. Chiu's class requires a lot of homework.	Homework is a requirement.	Science is a required class.

SPELLING AND PHONICS: To do this activity, go to page 196.

3. Word Play Work with a partner. Complete the following word family chart. Use your dictionary for help. Then choose two of the word families and write a sentence for each word (6 sentences).

Verb	Noun	Adjective
create	*creation*	creative
	decision	decisive
writing		written
respect	respect	
paint		painted
harm		harmful

✓ WRAP UP

- Have students take turns saying a word from the lesson and calling on classmates to say another word in the word family.

PB PRACTICE BOOK ACTIVITY

See Activity B, Word Work, on Practice Book page 92.

ANSWER KEY

Word Detective: 1. requirement; 2. argument; 3. respect; 4. learning; 5. creation; 6. decision.

Word Play: creation, decide, write, respected/respectful, painting, harm.

Spelling and Phonics: a. c<u>ou</u>rse b. blackb<u>oa</u>rd c. p<u>oo</u>r d. d<u>oo</u>r e. w<u>o</u>re f. p<u>o</u>pcorn g. Y<u>o</u>rk h. r<u>oa</u>r i. p<u>ou</u>r.

READING

UNIT 10 ▪ STUDENT BOOK, PAGE 171

E GRAMMAR — Using Modals to Persuade Others

1. Listen Up Listen to these sentences. Point one finger up ☝ if the sentence is strong advice. Point two fingers up ✌ if the sentence is a gentle suggestion.

✌ 1. You should obey your teacher.
✌ 2. You could try to study harder.
✌ 3. You might try to study harder.
✌ 4. If you study harder, you may get a better grade.
✌ 5. If you want others to like you, you will be kind to them.
✌ 6. You can get good grades if you study hard.

2. Learn the Rule Imagine you want to convince someone to do what you say. Certain modals can help you do this. Read the following rules, then do Activity 1 again.

USING MODALS TO PERSUADE OTHERS

1. When you want to give advice, use **should**. The advice can sometimes sound like a command:

   You **should** treat others with respect. You **shouldn't** be rude to others.

2. When you want to give someone a good reason for doing something (or not doing something), use modals like **can, may, could,** or **might**. These modals all express possibility:

   Skateboarding **can** be dangerous. If you go too fast, you **may** fall. If you fall, you **might** break a leg. If you break your leg, you **could** end up with a cast.

3. The modal **will** is stronger. It expresses strong probability or certainty:

   If your leg is in a cast, you **won't** be able to dance. You **will** catch cold if you don't put on a coat.

4. Do not use these modals (except **will**) in an *if* clause. That's because *if* already expresses possibility—

   Right: *If you break your leg, you will have to wear a cast.*   Wrong: *If you might break your leg, you will have to wear a cast.*

3. Practice the Rule Write one sentence for each modal: *can, may, could, might, will, should.*

Let's Debate! **171**

E GRAMMAR

> **Standard**
> ■ Use everyday functions: express possibility, probability, certainty; give advice

WARM UP

■ Write the following sentences on the board, underlining the modals as shown:

You should always study for tests.
If you're really worried about failing, you could study harder.
If you want to pass, you will have to study hard.

Ask students to think about how these sentences are the same and how they are different. (They are all trying to persuade someone to study for a test. They use different words [*should, can,* and *will*] to make the point.)

TEACHING THE LESSON

🎧 1. Listen Up

■ Read the sentences or play the tape or CD twice. Have students follow the instructions.

2. Learn the Rule

■ Explain how modals can be used to persuade others.

■ Write the following sentence stems on the board and have volunteers complete them, using a modal from the chart:

If you don't want to be late, _____.
If you aren't careful with a knife, _____.
If you don't hurry, _____.
If you don't take your house key, _____.
If you don't go to Carmen's party, _____.
If you don't eat breakfast, _____.

■ Repeat the Listen Up activity.

3. Practice the Rule

■ **Team Talk** Have students write sentences with the aim of persuading someone. Have them share their sentences.

✓ WRAP UP

■ Have students role play an imaginary situation involving an adult and a teenager. Have the "adult" advise or persuade the "teenager," using one or more modals.

PB PRACTICE BOOK ACTIVITY

See Activity C, Grammar, on Practice Book page 93.

ANSWER KEY

Listen Up: Strong advice: 1, 5; Gentle suggestion: 2, 3, 4, 6

Practice the Rule: Answers will vary.

UNIT 10 ■ STUDENT BOOK, PAGE 172

F BRIDGE TO WRITING

Standards
- Identify opposing arguments and supporting details
- Use everyday functions: the language of discussion and debate

WARM UP

- Have students name foods they can buy at school—either in the cafeteria or from vending machines. Record the foods on the board. Have students help you circle foods that are healthy, or good for you, and underline foods that are not as healthy.

- **Build Background** Explain that certain foods are often called "junk food" because they contain a lot of sugar or fat.

TEACHING THE LESSON

1. Before You Read

- **Heads Together** Ask students to make up their lists of five foods kids often eat for lunch. Then have them share their lists in small groups, identifying which foods to circle as healthy.

2. Let's Read

- Point to the Reading Strategy box. Remind students not to try to read every word as they skim, but just look for key words and ideas.

- Have students skim the first paragraph and list the foods that are bad for them (chips, soda, chocolate ice-cream taco). Then have them skim the rest of the article and locate which paragraph contains information about why these foods are unhealthy (paragraph 4).

- **My Turn: Read Aloud/Think Aloud** Read the passage aloud. Model correct phrasing and fluent reading. As you read, stop to comment on key vocabulary and ideas.

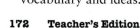

WRITING

READING STRATEGY
Skimming: When you skim, you read the whole passage quickly for general meaning. You don't read every word. This lets you know what to expect and helps you understand better.

F BRIDGE TO WRITING
Feature Articles: Debates

1. Before You Read Make a list of five common foods that kids often eat for lunch. Circle the foods on your list that are good for you (healthy).

2. Let's Read Skim the first paragraph for examples of foods that are bad for you, or junk food. Then skim for information about why these foods are unhealthy.

Ban Junk Food in School? (Debate)

1 Instead of eating a nutritious cafeteria lunch each day, Nicole Talbott grabs junk food. "Lunch for me is chips, soda, and maybe a chocolate ice-cream taco," the high-school student from Oakland, California, told The New York Times.

2 U.S. school **officials** say that students have too much sugar and fat in their diets. Many doctors agree. The number of overweight children and adolescents has more than doubled since the early 1970s.

3 As a result of such concerns, Nicole's **school district** and others across the U.S. have banned junk food. What do you think? Should junk food be banned in school?

YES

4 Junk food is especially harmful to growing kids. A recent study showed that half of the **calories** U.S. children **consume** come from fat and sugar. A can of soda, for example, **contains** 10 teaspoons of sugar!

5 "Schools should sell healthy food," says Jameela Syed, 10, a fifth-grader at Huth Road Elementary School in Grand Island, New York. "Healthy food can make you work better."

6 Banning junk food from schools—and teaching kids to eat right and exercise—will help students stay healthy.

NO

7 Making choices is an important part of learning. Deciding whether to eat junk food is one such decision.

8 "I think kids should be taught to be **responsible**, and they should learn about eating properly in health class," says Meghan Stubblebine, 14, a student at Canevin Catholic High School in Pittsburgh, Pennsylvania. "But kids should be able to choose what they eat."

9 Junk food may be bad for you, but deciding what to eat is a choice that students—not states or school districts—must make.

Source: Junior Scholastic

Facts are used to back up the argument.

Quotes help make the case, too.

The word but tells you the writer is about to disagree!

official—someone who has an important job in an agency or business
school district—an agency that runs the schools
calories—the amount of energy in food. Too many calories make you gain weight.
consume—to eat
contain—to have something inside or to include something
responsible—making good choices

172 Unit 10

- **Our Turn: Interactive Reading** Have students help you read the article. Take turns with students reading a sentence or two aloud. Focus on the glossed words, ask questions, and make comments.

- ✓ **Sentence Synthesis** Write these words on the board: *healthy, exercise, junk food*. Have students write a sentence using these words that supports a ban on junk food in school.

- **Build Fluency** Have pairs of students read the "pro" and "con" sections of the article aloud to each other.

- **Your Turn: Independent Reading** Have students read the article to themselves, focusing on this question: *Which student—Jameela or Meghan—makes the most convincing argument? Why?* Have them share out.

- **Access for All** Have students with linguistic intelligence role-play a short debate based on the article. Have students with artistic intelligence make a poster or cartoon strip to convince others of one position or the other on this issue.

172 Teacher's Edition

UNIT 10 ■ STUDENT BOOK, PAGE 173

3. Making Content Connections You have read two articles about interesting issues. Work with a partner. Compare the articles. Complete the chart below.

	Courtesy Law	Ban Junk Food
1. What is the question?	Should there be a law that requires students to be polite?	
2. What are the arguments for answering *yes*?		
3. What are the arguments for answering *no*?		
4. What is your own answer to the question? Do you agree?		

4. Expanding your vocabulary. Work with a partner. Imagine that you are discussing or debating with classmates. Match the goals with the words you might say.

Goals
1. State your position
2. Disagree with others
3. Try to understand better
4. Find out if others agree
5. Try to convince others
6. Support your position

Words You Might Say
a. That's a good point, however …
b. For example…
c. I believe that…
d. Do you agree?
e. Could you give me an example?
f. It is important that…

Let's Debate! 173

PB PRACTICE BOOK ACTIVITY

See Activity D, Test-Taking Practice, on Practice Book pages 94 and 95.

See Activity E, Using New Vocabulary, on Practice Book page 96.

✓ WRAP UP

- Have students think once again about the issue of junk food at school. Ask them to write down *one more reason*, pro or con, on this issue, then share with classmates.

3. Making Content Connections

 Heads Together Have students work in pairs, comparing the two articles and discussing their own opinions on each issue.

 Interactive Writing Copy the chart on the board. Call on volunteers to help complete the chart.

4. Expanding Your Vocabulary

 Heads Together Ask students to do the matching activity individually and then check their answers with a partner. Review the correct answers with the whole class.

- Have students work in pairs to write short dialogues, using language related to at least three functions. Have them act out their dialogues.

Unit 10   173

UNIT 10 ■ STUDENT BOOK, PAGE 174

G WRITING CLINIC

Standards
- Identify structural patterns found in persuasive text
- Trace the development of a writer's argument
- Use direct discourse in writing

WARM UP

- Ask students to think about the two articles they have read. Which was the more interesting issue to them? Why?

TEACHING THE LESSON

1. Think about It

- Ask different students to describe briefly the kinds of writing they would typically find in various sections of a newspaper. (On the front page they will usually find major news articles that *inform;* on the editorial page, they will read opinions about important issues that are meant to *persuade;* in the comics section, they'll find cartoons that *entertain.*) Ask where the two articles in this unit would probably be found (on the editorial page).

2. Focus on Organization

- Have students revisit the debate on courtesy laws, focusing on the annotations (Part 1).

  Have students identify examples of background information in the introduction. Ask: *Why does a quote make the writing more interesting?* Explain that the issue is the debate question. Explain that the word argument means "reason" not "disagreement."

WRITING

G WRITING CLINIC *Feature Articles: Debates*

1. Think about It In a newspaper, where would you most likely find articles like the ones in this unit?

☐ on the front page ☐ on the editorial page ☐ in the comics section

2. Focus on Organization

❶ Take another look at the debate about courtesy laws:

> **Do Students Need a Courtesy Law? (Debate)**
> In Louisiana's public schools, being polite to teachers isn't just expected—it's required by state law. In 1999, Louisiana passed the first student respect law. It requires students to address their teachers as "sir" or "ma'am," or with appropriate titles, such as "Mrs." or "Mr."
>
> "Just as we teach reading and writing, I think we can teach manners," says Donald Cravins, the state senator who sponsored the law.
>
> The idea has spread quickly. Several other states are considering similar laws. But not everyone agrees that courtesy laws are a good idea. What do you think? Should students be required by law to be polite? Read both arguments, then decide.
>
> **Yes, Ma'am!**
> Teachers don't get enough respect from students today. Courtesy laws will help students and teachers work together to create an environment that fosters creativity and learning.
>
> With courtesy laws in effect, teachers can spend less time disciplining their students and more time teaching them. "I've had teacher after teacher tell me that it's changed the whole experience in the classroom," says Louisiana Governor Mike Foster.
>
> Many students agree that some kids need to learn better manners. "I think a courtesy law would help some kids show respect at home," says Kurt Phelan.

Making the title a question makes me want to read the article.

The beginning of the article gives us background information.

A quote helps focus on the debate.

This paragraph states the issue.

Here is one argument.

Here is a second argument.

Here is a third argument.

174 Unit 10

PB PRACTICE BOOK ACTIVITY

See Activity F, Focus on Organization, on Practice Book page 97.

174 Teacher's Edition

WRITING

UNIT 10 ▪ STUDENT BOOK, PAGE 175

❷ Reread the other side of the debate. Outline the arguments. Add one more argument of your own.

No, Sir!

Good manners should be taught at home by parents, not in the schools. "Teachers deserve respect because they are adults," says 17-year old Peter Lainey. "But that decision should be left up the parents."

These kinds of laws only take attention away from the real problems that plague schools today. School districts need to build better schools, reduce drop-out rates, improve test scores, and raise teachers' salaries to really improve education.

"'Yes, ma'am' and 'no, ma'am' is fine, says Sue Hall, a teacher in New Orleans. "But it's pretty superficial. You're not getting to the root of the problem."

NO, there shouldn't be a law... _____.

Argument #1: _Good manners should be taught at home._

Argument #2: _____

Argument #3: _____

Your own argument: _____

3. Focus on Style

❶ People's actual words, or quotes, often help support an argument.

"Kid's should have to earn their allowance," argues one father. "It teaches responsibility."

❷ Write sentences using these people's actual words. Use quotes.

EXAMPLE: 1. Sara Chu-Smith says, "Everyone should read for an hour every day."

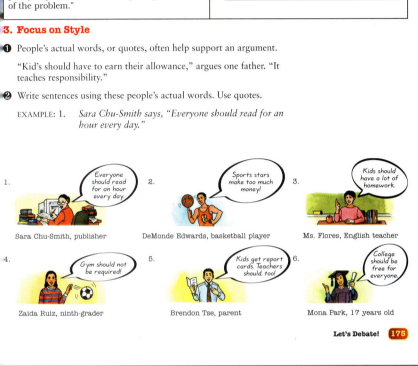

1. Sara Chu-Smith, publisher — Everyone should read for an hour every day
2. DeMonde Edwards, basketball player — Sports stars make too much money!
3. Ms. Flores, English teacher — Kids should have a lot of homework.
4. Zaida Ruiz, ninth-grader — Gym should not be required!
5. Brendon Tse, parent — Kids get report cards. Teachers should, too!
6. Mona Park, 17 years old — College should be free for everyone.

Let's Debate! **175**

PB PRACTICE BOOK ACTIVITY

See Activity G, Focus on Style, on Practice Book page 98.

✓ WRAP UP

- Have students tell you which side of the courtesy law issue is presented in a more convincing way. Why?

ANSWER KEY

Think about It: on the editorial page.

Focus on Organization 2: Argument 2: These kinds of laws take attention away from the real problems. Argument 3: It doesn't get to the root of the problem. Your own argument: Answers will vary.

Focus on Style 2: 1. Sara Chu-Smith says, "Everyone should read for an hour every day." 2. DeMonde Edwards says, "Sports stars make too much money!" 3. "Kids should have a lot of homework," says Ms. Flores. 4. "Gym should not be required!" says Zaida Ruiz. 5. Brendon Tse says, "Kids get report cards. Teachers should, too!" 6. Mona Park says, "College should be free for everyone."

🍎 **Heads Together** Ask students to read the second half of the debate and summarize the arguments individually (Part 2). Then ask them to discuss a possible fourth argument with a partner and write down their own additional arguments. Invite volunteers to share their ideas.

3. Focus on Style

- Ask students once again why articles—especially persuasive articles—often use quotations. (Quoted words often help make people believe that something is true.) Point to the quoted words. Have a volunteer tell you what the person's actual words are.

- Now have students rewrite the words in speech bubbles as quotations (Part 2). Do the first one with the class and then ask students to complete the activity on their own.

- Have students rewrite either the "yes" or "no" section of the article on courtesy laws, adding one additional (imaginary) quote to support the argument.

Unit 10   175

UNIT 10 ■ STUDENT BOOK, PAGE 176

WRITER'S WORKSHOP

> **Standards**
> - Use the writing process: prewriting
> - Develop arguments based on fact and opinion

1. Getting It Out
WARM UP

- Ask students to think about interesting debates they have heard lately. They do not have to be formal debates; they might just be discussions between friends or family members that the student overheard. Ask students to take turns briefly explaining to the class the two sides of the debate. Then have students choose debating partners.

TEACHING THE LESSON

- Remind students that both articles they have read are from *Junior Scholastic* magazine. Ask them to imagine that they are writing an article for the "Debate" feature of the magazine. Ask a volunteer to read, then explain the directions for the task to classmates. Be sure that students understand that they are to work together.

- Have students begin by choosing an issue (Part 1). They should choose an issue they both know something about and care about.

- Have partners discuss their issue and try to bring out as many different aspects of the argument and discover as many facts about it as they can. Then have them frame their issue as a question, writing it on a separate piece of paper.

- **Access for All** Consider pairing a more-proficient student to work with a less-proficient student on each side of the issue (that is, having four students work on the article). Select pairings carefully to ensure that the more-proficient students are able to guide the work of their partners.

176 Teacher's Edition

WRITING

WRITER'S WORKSHOP — Feature Articles: Debates

Work with a partner. You are going to write a feature article for the "Debate" section in *Junior Scholastic Magazine*. You will both write the introduction. Then, one of you will write the "yes" part of the article, and the other will write the "no" part.

1. Getting It Out

❶ Choose an interesting topic. Select something that both of you—
- know about.
- care about.

1.
Should schools have dress codes?

2.
Should we have a closed campus at lunch?

3.
Do students have too much homework?

4.
Your own question!

❷ Talk about the topic. What is the issue? Write a question. Your question should—
- be one that other students will be interested in.
- have a "yes" and "no" answer.
- begin with "Should …"

EXAMPLE: *Should kids have to work for an allowance?*
Your Question: _____

176 Unit 10

WRITING

UNIT 10 ■ STUDENT BOOK, PAGE 177

❸ Talk it out. Brainstorm reasons that people might answer your question "yes" and reasons people might answer "no." Make a like this one.

Our question: *Should kids have to work for their allowance?*

Yes	No
It would help kids learn good spending habits.	

❹ Decide who will write the arguments "for" and who will write the arguments "against."

❺ Find out more. Talk to others.

1. Take a survey of your classmates.

2. Interview other students. Think of two or three questions to ask. Write down the exact words that people say.

   1. Do you think kids should get an allowance? How much?
   2. Is it a good idea for kids to have to work for their allowance? Why or why not?

3. Talk to two or three adults. Get their ideas.

4. Search the Internet for information and ideas.

Let's Debate! 177

✓ WRAP UP

■ Have students share their questions (issues) and describe how they are gathering/will gather the opinions of others and other information.

■ Draw a large T-chart on the board with "yes" and "no" headings (Part 3). Focusing on the issue of allowances, model how students might brainstorm reasons under each column. Then have students brainstorm reasons related to their own issues. Check their work as they discuss.

■ Help students in each pair decide who will take which side (Part 4).

■ Tell students that they will need to gather opinions and arguments related to the position they have taken (Part 5). Help them understand the various ways they might do so—through survey, interview, or use of the Internet.

 Remind them of tips for conducting a good interview: prepare good questions; listen carefully; record exact words; ask clarifying questions; be polite.

PB PRACTICE BOOK ACTIVITY

See Activity H, Writer's Workshop, on Practice Book page 99.

UNIT 10 ■ STUDENT BOOK, PAGE 178

H WRITER'S WORKSHOP

Standards
- Use the writing process: drafting, revising, and editing for clarity and organization
- Use notes and outlining to draft writing
- Give a persuasive presentation that states and supports a position

2. Getting It Down

WARM UP
- Have volunteers share what they have learned from their interviews and other opinion research. Explain that it's now time to draft their articles.

TEACHING THE LESSON
- Have each pair prepare their outlines, following the model (Part 1). Remind them to use information from their notes. Then have them exchange their outlines with their partners, each reviewing for gaps and making suggestions.

- Have each pair turn their outlines into drafts (Part 2). Remind them that they are both responsible for writing an introduction that introduces the issue and provides background information.

- Review the article written by Suanna and Graciela. Point out the comments in the speech bubbles. Have a volunteer add one more comment about the article.

- 🍎 **Mini-Lesson on Conventions**
  Point out the Mini-Lesson box at the bottom of the page and ask students to locate the periods and commas used with each quotation in the article.

- Have a student copy a sentence with a quotation on the board. Then explain how to punctuate a direct quotation. You might say: *We start with a set of quotation marks—they curve this way—before the first word the person said. We use a second set of quotation marks after the last word the person said. This second set curves the opposite direction. And what about that comma? You put a comma or period before the second quotation mark.*

- Write some sentences containing direct quotations on the board (without the necessary punctuation) and have different students go up to the board and add the commas and quotation marks. Review their work using the same kind of monologue you used above.

WRAP UP
- Tell students that they will have a chance to revise their work during the next session. Have them locate the ChecBric for this unit in the Student Book or Practice Book. Have them prepare for Getting It Right by reviewing the ChecBric on their own, underlining indicators they're not sure about.

WRITING

UNIT 10 ▪ STUDENT BOOK, PAGE 179

3. Getting It Right Look carefully at your review. Use this guide to revise your paragraph.

Ask yourself...	How to check...	How to revise...
1. Does the title of our article use a good question?	Find out if another pair of students in class wrote about the same topic. Compare your titles (questions).	Turn your title into a question. Make your question more specific.
2. Does your introduction give the reader background information?	Reread your introduction. Highlight the sentences that set the scene.	Add new information or a quote.
3. Do we give at least three arguments "for" and "against"?	Put a number in front of each argument.	Ask if your partner has any other ideas. Add arguments.
4. Do we provide both facts and opinions? Do we use quotes?	Underline each fact. Put a wavy line under each quote.	Add a fact or a quote.

4. Presenting It Share your article with your classmates.

❶ Choose one person to read aloud the question (your title) and the background information (introduction).
❷ If you wrote the "yes" section, read your arguments aloud. Speak slowly and clearly.
❸ Now have the person who wrote the "no" side read his or her arguments.

Encourage your classmates to add their own opinions.

Let's Debate! 179

3. Getting It Right
WARM UP

- Ask students why it is especially important for them to present facts clearly in their debate articles. (You are trying to persuade people of something and possibly change their minds. You need to make it easy for your audience to follow what you are saying and to believe you.)
- Guide students through the ChecBric for this unit. Explain that they will use the ChecBric to prepare a final draft of their writing.
- Have volunteers explain, in their own words, what each indicator in the ChecBric means.

TEACHING THE LESSON

- Have students use the chart and the ChecBric to revise their work.
- Have students work in pairs to give each other feedback.

WRAP UP

- If possible, have students put their work away for a day or two and then use the ChecBric to review it again. Have them see what other improvements they can make by looking at it with fresh eyes.
- 📁 Give students time to fill out the ChecBric on Practice Book page 119. Ask them to attach it to their writing when they put it in their portfolios.

4. Presenting It
WARM UP

- It's time for students to present their articles! Remind them that they need to decide who will present the introductory/background information.
- As a class, develop a simple presentation checklist.

TEACHING THE LESSON

- Have a volunteer read the directions.
- Have pairs present their articles.
- Remind students to read in a loud clear voice and use eye contact to keep their audience interested.
- Have students take notes as they listen to each presentation, writing down "pro" and "con" arguments. Have them circle arguments they disagree with, then discuss.

✓ WRAP UP

- Post articles on the bulletin board. Have students do a gallery walk, using sticky notes to attach comments about an issue that interests them. Read selected notes aloud.

UNIT 10 ■ STUDENT BOOK, PAGE 180

I BEYOND THE UNIT

Standards
- Debate an issue, supporting an opinion with evidence
- Respond to poetry

1. On Assignment
WARM UP

- Ask students to take turns describing a formal or informal debate they have witnessed recently. The situations could range from televised political debates to a discussion between a student's parents about what color to paint the living room.

TEACHING THE LESSON

- Help students choose an issue to debate (Part 1). Discuss each issue: *Is it interesting? Do students care about the issue?* With a show of hands, have students vote to choose their debate issue.

- Tell students that they will debate the issue from one of four points of view: student, parent, teacher, or principal (Part 2). Then have students write the name of the role they have chosen for themselves on an index card.

- 🍎 **Team Talk** Have students who have chosen the same role gather in a different corner of the room (Part 3). If there are too few or too many students in any given group, ask for volunteers to join a different group to balance things out. Ask a volunteer to read the instructions, then restate them for the rest of the class.

- Have students follow each step in Part 3. Set a time limit for this activity, perhaps 20 minutes.

- Call the students together for the debate (Part 4). Have students who have chosen the same role remain together so that they can help each other formulate statements and responses during the debate.

- Discuss which side presented the strongest arguments and why (Part 5).

> **TEACHING TIP** 💡 In order not to allow one side to dominate, you may wish to limit each presentation of an idea and each response to 60 seconds. You may allow some leeway from time to time, but this format will help keep the presentations balanced and will allow more people a chance to speak.

✓ WRAP UP

🍎 **Outcome Sentence** Have students complete this sentence stem, then share:

More than ever, I am convinced that _____ because _____.

I BEYOND THE UNIT

1. On Assignment Stage a "role-play" debate.

❶ Choose an interesting issue:
  ☐ Should there be separate schools for boys and girls?
  ☐ Should schools ban chewing gum?
  ☐ Should you have to wear bicycle helmets?
  ☐ Should there be a limit on homework?
  ☐ Should schools allow students from other schools to attend school dances?

❷ Choose one of these four roles and write it on a 3" × 5" index card.

1.
Student

2.
Parent

3.
Teacher

4.
Principal

❸ Form a small group with other students who have the same role.
  1. Discuss what the person on your card would probably say about the issue.
  2. Write a position statement—for or against.
  3. List one or more arguments the person might use.

❹ As a class, have your debate. State your argument.

❺ After the debate, decide which group presented the best arguments. Discuss why.

180 Unit 10

Link to Literature

SHARED READING All teens can agree on one issue: They want and need a larger allowance. This poem will teach you how to get it! As you read, underline the verbs you do not know.

LET'S TALK

1. Look first at the verbs you have underlined. Work with a classmate to find the definitions of ten of them.
2. Choose five verbs from number 1. Write a sentence for each one.
3. How do you persuade your parents? List five verbs that work for you.

ABOUT THE AUTHOR

Andrea Shavick is an award-winning English author and poet. She has written ten books for kids as well as a number of non-fiction books for adults.

How to Successfuly Persuade Your Parents to Give You More Pocket Money
by Andrea Shavick

Ask, request, demand, suggest, cajole or charm
Ingratiate, suck up to, flatter, complement or smarm
Negotiate, debate, discuss, persuade, convince, explain
Or reason, justify, protest, object, dispute, complain
Propose, entreat, beseech, beg, plead, appeal, implore
Harass, go on about it, pester, whinge, whine, nag and bore
Annoy, insult, reproach, denounce, squeal, scream and shout
Go quiet, subdued, look worried, fret, brood, tremble, shiver, pout
Act depressed, downhearted, upset, snivel, sigh
Go all glum and plaintive, wobble bottom lip and cry
Sniff, sulk, grumble, stare at ceiling, mope, pine, stay in bed
Get cross, get angry, fume, seethe, fester, agitate, see red
Provoke, enrage, push, bully, aggravate and goad
Screech, smoke, burn up, ignite, spark, detonate, EXPLODE

And if all that doesn't work

Here are two little tricks
That should do it with ease

No 1: smile
No 2: say please.

Source: *Unzip Your Lips Again*

pocket money—(*British*) spending money

Let's Debate! **181**

> UNIT 10 ▪ STUDENT BOOK, PAGE 181

- Have students write five new words that describe how they might persuade their parents.

✓ WRAP UP

As a class, create a poem called, "How to Successfully Persuade..." on chart paper. (Have students choose the poem's topic.) Post on the bulletin board.

📘 PRACTICE BOOK ACTIVITY

See Activity I, Responding to Literature, on Practice Book page 100.

✓ UNIT WRAP UP

- Have students reflect in writing in their **notebooks** on what they learned to do in this unit. Consider responding to written reflections.

🎧 2. Link to Literature

WARM UP

🍒 **Heads Together** Ask students to share their ideas about allowance with a partner. Have students share out.

TEACHING THE LESSON

🍒 **Shared Reading** Read the poem or play the tape or CD, as students follow along. Pause after each line, commenting on difficult vocabulary.

- Ask students how they know whether this poem was written for children or adults. What words or phrases made them laugh? Which of the feelings mentioned have they experienced? Suggest that they think of words to add to the poem.

🍒 **Let's Talk** Have students work with a partner to find definitions of ten words they don't know. Then have each student write sentences using five of these words.

Mini-Unit: Note-Taking and Summarizing

Sometimes it's hard to understand and remember everything you hear or read at school. **Note-taking** and **summarizing** can help you do both.

A LISTENING AND TAKING NOTES

Always take notes when you listen to your teacher describe or explain something (unless your teacher tells you to "just listen").

1. Talk It Over Talk with a partner. Add five examples to the list below of when you might take notes in class.

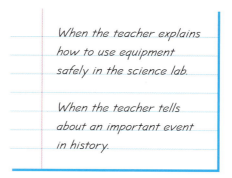

When the teacher explains how to use equipment safely in the science lab.

When the teacher tells about an important event in history.

2. Learn How to Do It Listening and note-taking is a six-step process. Read the steps below.

Step 1: Before class, make sure that you are *ready* to listen and learn. Do a quick check.
- I have done my homework and finished my assignments.
- I have reviewed yesterday's notes.
- I have my books and supplies.
- I intend, or *really mean*, to pay attention.

Step 2: Listen actively while others are talking. When you *listen*, you don't just hear words. You *think* about what the person is saying. You ask yourself questions.
- What am I learning?
- Why is this important or interesting to know?
- What do I need to remember?
- Do I understand what my teacher is explaining?

Step 3: Listen for "signal" words. They help you organize information.

First ... second ... third ... in addition ...furthermore ... finally...	For instance ... for example ... picture this ... to illustrate...	Previously ... before ... at first ... as soon as ... following ... after...
These signal that a **new idea** is coming.	These signal that an **example** is coming.	These let you know **when**.

Step 4: As you listen, write down ideas that are important. Jot down details, examples, definitions, and important facts that support each idea—

- Use your own words.
- Indent examples, details, and facts under each idea.
- Leave a wide margin on both sides of the paper.

```
  2 inches       |                                              |   2 inches
                 |   Grizzly bears are omnivores                |
                 |       -Love to eat small mammals, fish, and birds  |
                 |       -Also eat berries, roots, and other plants)  |
```

Step 5: After class, review and edit your notes. <u>Underline</u> or ==highlight== the most important ideas. Put a question mark ? next to points you don't understand. Add your own comments to your notes. Fill in missing points or define terms you need to remember.

```
  Additional Notes      |                                          |   Questions and Ideas
                        |   Grizzly bears are omnivores            |
  omnivore = eats both  |       -Love to eat small mammals, fish, and birds  |   Do grizzly bears
  animals and plants    |       -Also eat berries, roots, and other plants)  |   attack people?
```

Step 6: Ask your teacher to explain the things you didn't understand.

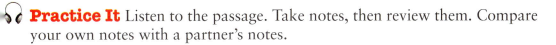

Practice It Listen to the passage. Take notes, then review them. Compare your own notes with a partner's notes.

B READING AND TAKING NOTES

When you read your textbook or are working on a report, take notes as you read to help you understand and remember what you read.

1. Talk It Over Talk with a partner. How can note-taking help you when you read? Add three ways to the list below.

> *Helps you really think about what you are reading.*

2. Learn How to Do It *Graphic organizers* can help you take good notes. Remember to use your own words.

T-Charts

Use a **T-chart** when you are reading for **information**. Complete the T-chart below.

> Sharks are carnivores. They eat all kinds of flesh. Sharks prefer tuna, mackerel, and even smaller sharks for dinner, but they will eat swimmers if the conditions are right.
>
> Sharks have very sharp senses of vision, hearing, and smell to help them find food. They can see seven times better than humans and can hear sounds over two miles away. About two-thirds of a shark's brain is used for smell, so if there is even a tiny amount of blood in the water, a shark will smell it—even if it's almost a mile away!
>
> Instead of bones, sharks have something called cartilage. Bones are hard and don't bend. Cartilage is flexible, allowing sharks to bend so their heads can reach their tails. The cartilage also allows sharks to turn very quickly. All this makes them better hunters. Humans have cartilage too, but only in places like our ears and noses.

Ideas	Details, Examples
Sharks are carnivores (meat eaters)	They mostly eat smaller fish (tuna, mackerel, sharks)

Venn Diagrams

Use a **Venn diagram** when the reading is **comparing and contrasting** two things (describing how two things are the **same or different**). Make your own Venn diagram comparing alligators and crocodiles, based on this selection.

> In many ways, alligators and crocodiles are similar. They are both large reptiles that live in water and on land. They both lay eggs. They both have huge teeth and powerful jaws.
>
> But they are also different in many ways. The biggest difference between alligators and crocodiles is the shape of their heads. The crocodile's skull and jaws are long and narrow. The alligator's snout is flat and round. Alligators and crocodiles both have thick, bumpy skin but alligators tend to be darker in color.
>
> Another difference between crocodiles and alligators is their choice of homes. Alligators live in rivers, lakes, and swamps. On the other hand, crocodiles prefer coastal, salt water habitats.

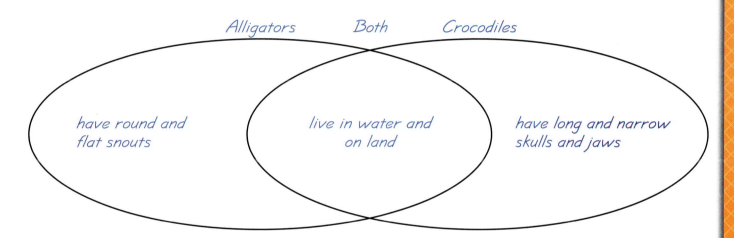

Process Diagrams

When you are learning about a **step-by-step process**—like in science or health—use a **process diagram** that shows steps or stages.

> Have you ever wondered how you get cavities? The part of the tooth that you can see is called a crown. The crown of each tooth is covered with enamel, a very hard surface. Enamel protects the tooth. You have millions of bacteria, or very tiny germs, in your mouth. When you eat foods with sugar, like candy bars, the bacteria produce acids that eat through the enamel. The bacteria then get inside the tooth and cause it to decay. The decay can spread down into the tooth and cause it to die.

We have bacteria in our mouths. When we eat foods with sugar, the bacteria makes acids.

↓

Acids eat through the enamel (hard covering) of the tooth.

↓

Bacteria get inside the tooth and cause the tooth to decay.

Now practice making your own diagram. Read about why and how snow falls.

A cloud is a mixture of air and very tiny droplets of water. When the droplets of water get very cold, they turn to ice. Ice particles start very small. As they travel through the air, more water freezes on them, and they become larger, forming ice crystals. When the ice crystals are big enough, they join together and make snow flakes. If the snow flakes are heavy enough, they fall to the ground.

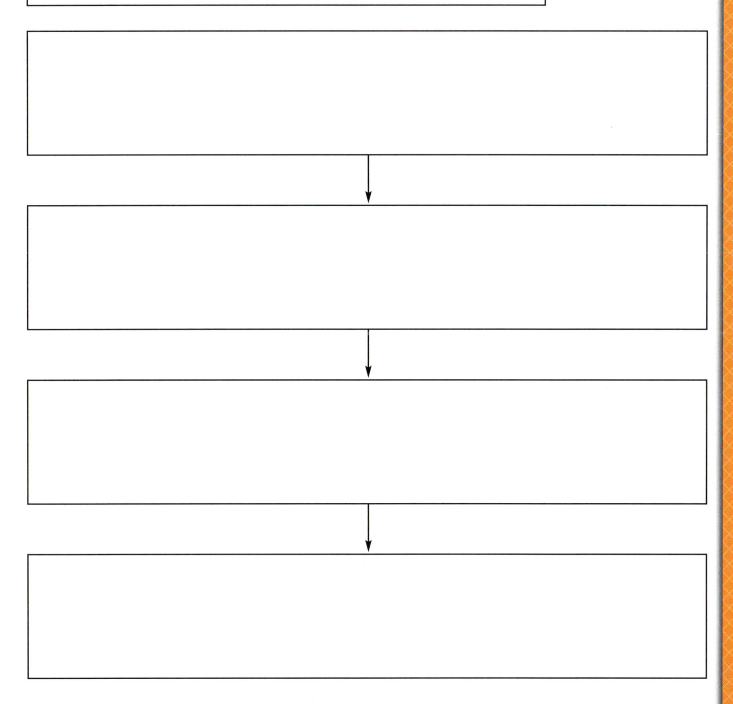

Timelines

When you are reading about an important **event in history**, make a **timeline**. Read the passage and complete the timeline below.

> It is difficult to climb Mt. Everest. Many mountain climbers have died trying to reach the summit. In 1921, the first British team tried to reach the top. They couldn't make it, but they did discover a route to the summit. Many attempts followed. In 1924, British climbers George Mallory and Andrew Irvine attempted to climb Everest and were last seen just below the summit. No one knows if they reached the top before they disappeared. The first people we know reached the top were Edmund Hillary and his Sherpa guide, Tenzing Norgay, who succeeded in 1953. Both men became heroes. In 1980, the Austrian climber Rheinhold Messner climbed Mt. Everest alone—without bottled oxygen! He is considered by many to be the greatest mountain climber of all time.

1921	The first British team tried to climb Mt. Everest. They discovered a route, but didn't reach the top.
1924	George Mallory and Andrew Irvine tried to climb Mt. Everest. No one knows what happened to them.
1953	
1980	

Mini-Unit: Note-Taking and Summarizing

3. Practice It Read these two passages. Decide which type of graphic organizer to use for each. Then take notes on a separate piece of paper. Compare your notes with a partner's.

Reading 1.

The Changing Look of America's Population

The United States is becoming more racially diverse than ever before. The most diverse group is people who are 18 years old and younger. Almost 40 percent of these people are members of a minority group, which in this case is a racial group smaller than the larger group that it belongs to.

Many Americans thought that America was becoming more diverse, but we weren't sure about it until the 2000 census was complete. A census is a count of the population of an area. Before 2000, people had to choose one race from a list of races to describe themselves in a census. But in Census 2000, people were allowed for the first time ever to choose more than one race. About 7 million people identified themselves as multiracial. Almost half of these people were 18 or younger than 18.

According to people who study population information and numbers, we are seeing increased racial diversity in the U.S. because of growing numbers of immigrants and interracial marriages here in the past several years.

Reading 2.

That volcano is about to erupt!

Do you know how and why a volcano erupts? To find out, we have to look inside the volcano. Under the ground, we find magma. Magma is hot, melted rock. Liquid magma moves around under the ground and can flow toward the surface inside a volcano. When this happens, the gas in the magma starts to bubble up, forcing the magma upward. If earthquakes happen near a volcano, you can be sure that the volcano is active because the upward movement of magma can cause earthquakes.

If you see the rocky top surface of a volcano bulging outward, run fast, because it means that gas and magma are collecting and the volcano might erupt. But before the eruption occurs, steam and gas will shoot out of cracks and holes in the volcano to release some of the pressure that's building up inside. When there is too much magma and gas to be released through these small cracks and holes, or if the top of the volcano breaks open because of an earthquake, the volcano will erupt, shooting out steam, ash, and sometimes lava, which is what magma is called when it reaches the surface.

C READING AND SUMMARIZING

When you summarize, you find the most important ideas in something you've read, then *restate* them in your own words. Writing a summary shows how well you understand something.

1. Talk It Over Talk with a partner. Write down one reason that summarizing might help you in school. Be ready to share.

2. Learn How to Do It Read the passage. Then read the summary.

Reading Passage

> **The Changing Look of America's Population**
>
> The United States is becoming more racially diverse than ever before. The most diverse group is people who are 18 years old and younger. Almost 40 percent of these people are members of a minority group, which in this case is a racial group smaller than the larger group that it belongs to.
>
> Many Americans thought that America was becoming more diverse, but we weren't sure about it until the 2000 census was complete. A census is a count of the population of an area. Before 2000, people had to choose one race from a list of races to describe themselves in a census. But in Census 2000, people were allowed for the first time ever to choose more than one race. About 7 million people identified themselves as multiracial. Almost half of these people were 18 or younger than 18.
>
> According to people who study population information and numbers, we are seeing increased racial diversity in the U.S. because of growing numbers of immigrants and interracial marriages here in the past several years.

Summary

> *More and more kids in the U.S. belong to more than one race. For the first time, in the 2000 census, people were allowed to identify themselves as members of more than one racial group. About seven million people did this. This change is the result of an increase in immigration and interracial marriages.*

How to summarize:

1. Read the passage, taking notes.
2. Review your notes, underlining the important ideas. Next, circle absolutely essential information.
3. Write a paragraph that includes the important ideas and details.

3. Practice It Summaries are short, and they are in your own words. You will need two pieces of paper for this activity. Number each one in the upper right hand corner. As you do the activity, be sure that your handwriting is the same size on each sheet.

1. Fold sheet #1 in half so you have a short, wide piece of paper. Read the passage below. Write down the most important ideas and details from the passage.
2. Fold sheet #2 in three parts so you have a very short, wide piece of paper. Study the notes on sheet #1, crossing off less important ideas or details. Then fill up sheet #2 with the notes that you think are the most important.
3. Use the notes from sheet #2 to write a short paragraph about the reading. Remember to write complete sentences and use your own words.

Why Egyptians Learned to Make Mummies

Ancient Egyptians believed that a person's soul lived on after a person died, but didn't stay near the body after death. Instead, it left its body after death and returned to find it later. The body needed its soul to go to the mythical Next World. But the *soul* couldn't return if it couldn't find or didn't recognize its body.

When Egyptians buried their dead in the sand, the hot, dry weather dried up the bodies and stopped them from rotting. But sand burials weren't good enough for wealthy Egyptians. They started to bury their family members in beautiful stone tombs. However, they soon realized that this was a horrible mistake because the bodies didn't dry up in the tombs like they did in the sand. They became skeletons. What would the Egyptians do? The souls wouldn't be able to recognize their bodies if the bodies turned into skeletons! These people would never be able to go to the Next World!

The wealthy Egyptians didn't want to go back to burying their loved ones in sand, but they had to solve this problem of bodies rotting away and becoming unrecognizable to their souls. They learned from the sand burials that bodies could be preserved if they were kept dry. They tried different things for many years until they finally discovered the perfect way to preserve bodies without burying them in the sand. They found a way to make mummies. Their techniques were so good that some of the mummified bodies still exist.

Spelling and Phonics Activities

UNIT 1

Spelling and Phonics The sound /ā/ can be spelled many ways, depending on the word it is in. Listen to the following words.

cl**ai**m   f**a**me   pl**ay**   gr**ea**t   ob**ey**

Supply the missing letters for each incomplete word. Use your dictionary to check your work.

a. The team won the g_a_me.

b. Don't be l____te!

c. I got a letter in the m____l.

d. Please w____t for me.

e. Juan took the subw____.

f. My favorite food is st____k.

g. Let's t____ke a br____k.

h. This t____stes delicious.

i. I'm filling out a surv____.

UNIT 2

Spelling and Phonics The sound /ch/ can be spelled in many ways. Listen to the following words.

cockroa**ch**   ki**tch**en   crea**tu**re

Supply the missing letters for each incomplete word. Use your dictionary to check your work.

a. What time is it? I forgot my wa_tch_.

b. Here is a pic____re of my dog.

c. A ____impanzee is a kind of monkey.

d. I got a sunburn at the bea____.

e. You should stre____ before you exercise.

f. I want to see an adven____re movie.

UNIT 3

Spelling and Phonics The sound /ō/ can be spelled in many ways. Listen to the following words.

m<u>o</u>le   b<u>ow</u>l   s<u>oa</u>p   t<u>oe</u>   th<u>ough</u>

Supply the missing letters for each incomplete word. Use your dictionary to check your work.

a. Sh _ow_ me!
b. This car g____s fast.
c. Eeek! It's a gh____st!
d. I have a sore thr____t.
e. It's sn____ing.
f. Sl____ down!
g. It's a cockr____ch!
h. I wr____te the n____te.
i. Do you kn____ any j____kes?
j. I'm watching a talk sh____.
k. What's your zip c____de?
l. Roll the d____ into a ball.

UNIT 4

Spelling and Phonics In some words the letters *-gh-* are silent, and in some words they have a /f/ sound. Listen to the example sentence. Notice how the underlined words are pronounced.

Example: I thou<u>gh</u>t my old friends weren't cool enou<u>gh</u> for me.

Say the following words. Then put each one in the correct place in the chart.

cough	straight	neighbor	eight	light	tough
taught	laugh	high	thought	might	right
caught	height	night	through	bought	enough

-gh- is silent	*-gh-* sounds like /f/
eight	*cough*

Spelling and Phonics **193**

UNIT 5

Spelling and Phonics The sound /oo/ can be spelled in many ways. Listen to the following words.

f**oo**d　　　d**u**de　　　ch**ew**　　　tr**ue**　　　wh**o**　　　s**ou**p

Supply the missing letters for each incomplete word. Use your dictionary to check your work.

a. shamp**oo** 　　d. bl____　　g. st____dent　　j. z____

b. st____　　e. r____de　　h. gr____p　　k. s____n

c. scr____　　f. gl____　　i. m____ve　　l. y____

UNIT 6

Spelling and Phonics The letters -oo- can be pronounced in different ways. Listen to the following words.

t**oo**k　　　bl**oo**d　　　ball**oo**n　　　d**oo**r

Say the following words. Then put each one in the correct place in the chart.

| flood | floor | moon | pool | look | poor |
| cookie | cool | good | school | cook | foot |

/o͝o/ as in *took*	/ŭ/ as in *blood*	/o͞o/ as in *balloon*	/ô/ as in *door*
cook			

UNIT 7

Spelling and Phonics The letters -ou- can be pronounced in different ways. Listen to the following words.

f<u>ou</u>nd   th<u>ou</u>ght   t<u>ou</u>ch   gr<u>ou</u>p

Say the following words. Then put each one in the correct place in the chart.

| cloud | country | youth | around | soup | out |
| through | pound | ground | enough | count | cough |

/ou/ as in *found*	/ŏ/ as in *thought*	/ŭ/ as in *touch*	/o͞o/ as in *group*
cloud			

UNIT 8

Spelling and Phonics The letters -ea- can be pronounced many ways. Listen to the following words.

h<u>ea</u>lth   gr<u>ea</u>t   t<u>ea</u>

Say the following words. Then put each one in the correct place in the chart.

| dead | ready | break | real | increase | headache |
| steak | beneath | creature | cheap | bread | deal |

/ĕ/ as in *health*	/ā/ as in *great*	/ē/ as in *tea*
dead		

Spelling and Phonics 195

UNIT 9

Spelling and Phonics The sound /j/ can be spelled many ways, depending on the word it is in. Listen to the following words.

jelly   gigantic   fudge   age

Supply the missing letters for each incomplete word. Use your dictionary to check your work.

a. Tan____erines are sweet.

b. The police officer wears a ba____.

c. Would you like bacon or sausa____?

d. I put ____am on my toast.

e. My favorite drink is oran____ ____uice.

f. The tallest animal in the world is a ____iraffe.

UNIT 10

Spelling and Phonics The sound /or/ can be spelled many ways, depending on the word it is in. Listen to the following words.

for   more   four   board   floor

Supply the missing letters for each incomplete word. Use your dictionary to check your work.

a. Of c____se, I'll go with you.

b. Go to the blackb____d.

c. I didn't study, so I did a p____ job on my math test.

d. Please shut the d____.

e. She w____ a black dress.

f. I love to eat popc____n.

g. I live in New Y____k.

h. I heard a r____.

i. Let me p____ some milk for you.

ChecBrics*

UNIT 1

ChecBric for Interview

Focus	Overall rating
Organization ____ My heading names the person and tells about their claim to fame. ____ I based my interview on questions and answers.	____ 4 = Wow! ____ 3 = Strong ____ 2 = Some strengths ____ 1 = Needs work
Content ____ My questions and answers are about the person's "claim to fame." ____ The interview tells facts the reader might not know about the person. ____ I used the person's exact words in each answer.	____ 4 = Wow! ____ 3 = Strong ____ 2 = Some strengths ____ 1 = Needs work
Style ____ I avoided asking questions with yes/no answers. ____ My questions were open-ended, so the person had to give details. ____ The answers sound like the person is talking to you.	____ 4 = Wow! ____ 3 = Strong ____ 2 = Some strengths ____ 1 = Needs work
Grammar and mechanics ____ I used complete sentences. ____ I used the correct word order for my questions. ____ I used helping verbs for my questions when needed. ____ I started each sentence with a capital letter and ended it with the correct punctuation.	____ 4 = Wow! ____ 3 = Strong ____ 2 = Some strengths ____ 1 = Needs work

*ChecBric name and concept created by Larry Lewin.

UNIT 2

ChecBric for Informational Report

Focus	Overall rating
Organization ____ My paragraph has a topic sentence. ____ I gave at least three details. ____ Each detail connects to the topic sentence.	____ 4 = Wow! ____ 3 = Strong ____ 2 = Some strengths ____ 1 = Needs work
Content ____ I used important information. ____ I used correct information. ____ The reader will learn new information.	____ 4 = Wow! ____ 3 = Strong ____ 2 = Some strengths ____ 1 = Needs work
Style ____ My paragraph will be easy for the reader to understand. ____ My paragraph "lives and breathes." ____ I used adjectives to paint a word picture.	____ 4 = Wow! ____ 3 = Strong ____ 2 = Some strengths ____ 1 = Needs work
Grammar and mechanics ____ I used complete sentences. ____ I made the verbs and subjects agree. ____ I indented my paragraph. ____ I used commas correctly. ____ I started each sentence with a capital letter and ended it with the correct punctuation.	____ 4 = Wow! ____ 3 = Strong ____ 2 = Some strengths ____ 1 = Needs work

UNIT 3

ChecBric for How-to Instructions

Focus	Overall rating
Organization ____ I listed the necessary materials. ____ I used numbers to connect the steps. ____ I put the steps in time order.	____ 4 = Wow! ____ 3 = Strong ____ 2 = Some strengths ____ 1 = Needs work
Content ____ Each sentence is clear. ____ Each step is accurate. ____ Each sentence gives an important detail. ____ My instructions are easy to follow.	____ 4 = Wow! ____ 3 = Strong ____ 2 = Some strengths ____ 1 = Needs work
Style ____ My sentences are short and simple. ____ I used exact words. ____ I used the same words for things in every step.	____ 4 = Wow! ____ 3 = Strong ____ 2 = Some strengths ____ 1 = Needs work
Grammar and mechanics ____ I used complete sentences. ____ I used "do-it" sentences. ____ I started each sentence with a capital letter and ended it with the correct punctuation.	____ 4 = Wow! ____ 3 = Strong ____ 2 = Some strengths ____ 1 = Needs work

UNIT 4

ChecBric for Personal Narrative

Focus	Overall rating
Organization ____ My story has a beginning that sets the scene. ____ I explained what happened. ____ I described the result.	____ 4 = Wow! ____ 3 = Strong ____ 2 = Some strengths ____ 1 = Needs work
Content ____ My story tells *who*, *what*, and *when*. ____ I explained why I did what I did. ____ I let the reader know how I felt.	____ 4 = Wow! ____ 3 = Strong ____ 2 = Some strengths ____ 1 = Needs work
Style ____ I told the story in an interesting way. ____ I talked to the reader like a friend. ____ I used casual, everyday words.	____ 4 = Wow! ____ 3 = Strong ____ 2 = Some strengths ____ 1 = Needs work
Grammar and mechanics ____ I used complete sentences. ____ I used the past tense correctly. ____ I indented my paragraphs. ____ I used commas after "when" clauses. ____ I started each sentence with a capital letter and ended it with the correct punctuation.	____ 4 = Wow! ____ 3 = Strong ____ 2 = Some strengths ____ 1 = Needs work

UNIT 5

ChecBric for Explaining a Process

Focus	Overall rating
Organization ____ I gave the main idea in the first sentence. ____ I explained the steps in the food chain process.	____ 4 = Wow! ____ 3 = Strong ____ 2 = Some strengths ____ 1 = Needs work
Content ____ My report accurately describes a food chain. ____ I named plants and animals in the food chain. ____ I used a flow diagram to help explain the information.	____ 4 = Wow! ____ 3 = Strong ____ 2 = Some strengths ____ 1 = Needs work
Style ____ I used formal, serious language. ____ I used the correct names for plants and animals. ____ I used longer sentences when they made my writing smoother.	____ 4 = Wow! ____ 3 = Strong ____ 2 = Some strengths ____ 1 = Needs work
Grammar and mechanics ____ I used complete sentences. ____ I used the present and past tenses correctly. ____ I indented my paragraphs. ____ I used commas to set off examples. ____ I started each sentence with a capital letter and ended it with the correct punctuation.	____ 4 = Wow! ____ 3 = Strong ____ 2 = Some strengths ____ 1 = Needs work

UNIT 6

ChecBric for True Story

Focus	Overall rating
Organization ____ I gave my story a creative title. ____ My story has a beginning that grabs the reader's attention. ____ I described the events in the order they happened. ____ My story has an ending.	____ 4 = Wow! ____ 3 = Strong ____ 2 = Some strengths ____ 1 = Needs work
Content ____ I named the people and gave details about the setting. ____ I explained why the situation was serious. ____ I gave important details about what the "hero" did.	____ 4 = Wow! ____ 3 = Strong ____ 2 = Some strengths ____ 1 = Needs work
Style ____ The beginning and ending of my story interest the reader. ____ I used action-packed verbs. ____ I used the hero's own words to make the story interesting.	____ 4 = Wow! ____ 3 = Strong ____ 2 = Some strengths ____ 1 = Needs work
Grammar and mechanics ____ I used complete sentences. ____ I used "when" clauses correctly. ____ I used the past tense correctly. ____ I used exclamation points at the end of some sentences, but I didn't overuse them. ____ I started each sentence with a capital letter and ended it with the correct punctuation.	____ 4 = Wow! ____ 3 = Strong ____ 2 = Some strengths ____ 1 = Needs work

UNIT 7

ChecBric for Describing an Event: Eyewitness Account

Focus	Overall rating
Organization ____ My introduction sets the scene. ____ I described the event in the order things happened. ____ I described what it was like right after the event happened (the aftermath).	____ 4 = Wow! ____ 3 = Strong ____ 2 = Some strengths ____ 1 = Needs work
Content ____ My description tells *what*, *when*, *where*, *who*, and *how*. ____ I gave a minute-by-minute description. ____ My description makes the reader feel like he or she is there.	____ 4 = Wow! ____ 3 = Strong ____ 2 = Some strengths ____ 1 = Needs work
Style ____ I used sense words (taste, touch, smell, sight, sound). ____ I used action-packed verbs. ____ I used similes to make my writing interesting.	____ 4 = Wow! ____ 3 = Strong ____ 2 = Some strengths ____ 1 = Needs work
Grammar and mechanics ____ I used complete sentences. ____ I used the past tense correctly. ____ I used commas in connected sentences. ____ I started each sentence with a capital letter and ended it with the correct punctuation.	____ 4 = Wow! ____ 3 = Strong ____ 2 = Some strengths ____ 1 = Needs work

UNIT 8

ChecBric for Persuasive Writing

Focus	Overall rating
Organization ____ My title explains what the topic is. ____ My first sentence gives my position or opinion on the topic ____ Each sentence gives information that makes my position stronger. ____ My last sentence sums up my position, telling the reader what to do.	____ 4 = Wow! ____ 3 = Strong ____ 2 = Some strengths ____ 1 = Needs work
Content ____ I gave reasons for my position. ____ I gave facts and examples. ____ I gave the names of experts. ____ I corrected the incorrect thoughts many people have about the topic.	____ 4 = Wow! ____ 3 = Strong ____ 2 = Some strengths ____ 1 = Needs work
Style ____ I used subheadings to help my reader. ____ I involved my reader by asking questions.	____ 4 = Wow! ____ 3 = Strong ____ 2 = Some strengths ____ 1 = Needs work
Grammar and mechanics ____ I used complete sentences. ____ I used gerunds correctly. ____ I started each sentence with a capital letter and ended it with the correct punctuation.	____ 4 = Wow! ____ 3 = Strong ____ 2 = Some strengths ____ 1 = Needs work

UNIT 9

ChecBric for Evaluation

Focus	Overall rating
Organization ____ I explained which food I was reviewing in my introduction and gave my opinion about it. ____ I gave several reasons for my opinion. ____ I made a recommendation to the reader in my conclusion.	____ 4 = Wow! ____ 3 = Strong ____ 2 = Some strengths ____ 1 = Needs work
Content ____ I described the food I was reviewing. ____ I gave evidence to support my opinion. ____ I explained why others might like the product.	____ 4 = Wow! ____ 3 = Strong ____ 2 = Some strengths ____ 1 = Needs work
Style ____ My introduction makes others want to read my review. ____ My readers can "hear" me talking to them. ____ I used stand-out adjectives.	____ 4 = Wow! ____ 3 = Strong ____ 2 = Some strengths ____ 1 = Needs work
Grammar and mechanics ____ I used complete sentences. ____ I used "if" clauses correctly. ____ I used commas after introductory adverbs. ____ I made sure that verbs agreed with their subjects. ____ I started each sentence with a capital letter and ended it with the correct punctuation.	____ 4 = Wow! ____ 3 = Strong ____ 2 = Some strengths ____ 1 = Needs work

UNIT 10

ChecBric for Feature Article: Debate

Focus	Overall rating
Organization ____ My title explains what the debate is about. ____ My introduction makes the reader interested in the issue and gives background. ____ I gave more than one argument for each position. ____ I gave my arguments and evidence in a logical and clear way.	____ 4 = Wow! ____ 3 = Strong ____ 2 = Some strengths ____ 1 = Needs work
Content ____ My arguments and reasons are good. ____ I gave facts and examples to support each reason. ____ I listed opinions, using quotes.	____ 4 = Wow! ____ 3 = Strong ____ 2 = Some strengths ____ 1 = Needs work
Style ____ I quoted other people to make my point stronger and to make my writing more interesting. ____ I used people's exact words.	____ 4 = Wow! ____ 3 = Strong ____ 2 = Some strengths ____ 1 = Needs work
Grammar and mechanics ____ I used complete sentences. ____ I used modals like *should*, *can*, *may*, *might*, *could*, and *will* correctly. ____ I used the right punctuation in sentences with quotes.	____ 4 = Wow! ____ 3 = Strong ____ 2 = Some strengths ____ 1 = Needs work

Glossary

UNIT 1

academic—connected to learning and studying
acting—playing someone in a movie or show
advice—an opinion about what to do or not do
be serious about—to care a lot about something
business—buying and selling things
career—a job you have trained for and will do a long time
CIA—Central Intelligence Agency
claim to fame—the main reason a person is famous
degree—proof you have finished a course of study at a school—usually a university
dreams—hopes for the future
eventually—one day
fan—a person who likes something or someone a lot
featured—having a part in (a movie or story)
handle—to deal with
in a different light—in a different way
old-timer—someone from the past
opportunity—a chance to do something that will be good for you
own[1]—to have something because you bought it
own[2]—belonging to a person
performing arts—music, dance, or drama
pursue—to do or try something
root for—to want someone (like a sports team) to win
shortstop—the position between second and third base
stallion—a male horse
stereotype—an idea about a person based only on their race, religion, ethnic group, etc.

UNIT 2

amazing—making someone feel very surprised
amazing—very surprising
appetite—hunger
attack—to try to hurt
creature—an animal
crevice—a narrow opening
dangerous—able to hurt or kill
daredevil—someone who isn't afraid to do dangerous things
dinosaur—a reptile that lived millions of years ago
disgusting—very unpleasant and sickening
equipped for—made for
exceptional—very special
feared—frightening to others
metal—a material like steel, tin, or iron
path—way
powerful—very strong
scatter—to run in different directions
scurry—to move fast
survive—to stay alive
warning—a sign of danger
withstand—to experience without damage

UNIT 3

assistant—a helper
bristle—a hair on a brush
corn syrup—a sweet syrup
cornmeal—ground, dried corn
cover—to put something on something else
dab—a tiny amount
dribble—to drip in tiny drops
gelatin—a jelly-like substance used in cooking
have (someone do something)—to ask (someone to do something for you)
lb.—pound
mix—to stir together
mole—a dark growth on the skin, like a wart
oz.—ounce
place—to put somewhere
remove—to take out of
repeat—to do again
roll—to make round
slather—to spread thickly
slump—to fall over
sob—a small cry
spread—to cover something all the way to the edges
sprinkle—to scatter tiny pieces
stretch—to make something longer or larger by pulling
tbs.—tablespoon

UNIT 4

admit—to let someone into a group
all the rage—very popular
backfire—to have a surprising negative result
backfire—to have the opposite effect of what you want
bald—having no hair on the head
brand-name—made by a well-known company
carefree—easygoing
clique—a group that hangs out together
conceited—stuck-up
cuff— to turn up the bottom of pants legs
dig—to like or understand someone or something
ditch—to get rid of someone
go out for—to try to join a team
image—what other people think about you
immature—childish
impress—to make someone think you are important
in return—by other people
in—fashionable and cool
intelligent—smart
jive—jazz music or insincere talk
jock—someone who is good at sports
jump on the bandwagon—to do what is popular with most people at the moment.
mean—nasty
motto—what somebody believes
perm—to make hair curly using a chemical treatment
popular—having lots of friends; well-liked
Raggedy Ann—a type of doll with bright red-orange hair.
silly—dumb
tortured imitation—a bad copy
transform—to change completely
varsity team—the main school sports team

UNIT 5

chain—a sequence of closely connected things
energy—a source of power or strength
cause—to make something happen
destroy—to put an end to
environment—the natural world around us
depend on—to need and rely on
caterpillar—an early stage of a butterfly; like a hairy worm
wren—a type of tiny bird
hawk—a type of meat-eating bird similar to an eagle
fuel—something that helps create energy
seaweed—a family of underwater ocean plants

UNIT 6

ambush—a surprise attack
Appalachian Mountains—a chain of mountains running from Canada to Alabama
baby-sitter—someone who cares for a young child
blacksmith—someone who makes things with iron
bus stop—a place where a bus always stops
depths—areas deep under the ground
dishwasher—a machine for washing dishes
dismay—disappointment
distract—to call attention to something else
emergency—a serious situation that needs immediate action
first aid—emergency help for an injured person
hairbrush—a brush for the hair
hero—someone who is very brave; especially who risked his/her life
lawnmower—a machine for cutting grass
life-saving—saving someone's life
lumbering crew—workers who cut down trees
ogre—a monster that often eats people
paramedic—person trained to give medical help in an emergency
physical therapy—special treatment for injuries to the body
pressure—(1) urgent problems; (2) pressing hard on the body
ravine—a deep, narrow valley
reassure—to give comfort
Red Cross—an organization that helps injured people or disaster survivors
rescue—to save from danger
rumpus—a fight
save a life—stop someone from dying
settler—someone who move into a new region
stay calm—avoid getting overexcited
tragic—a situation that causes terrible destruction or death
tussle—a fight

UNIT 7

argue—to disagree with someone
bang—boom
beast—a wild animal
bunk beds—two beds that are attached, one on top of the other
cobblestone—a paving stone
dark—black
deathly—as quiet as death
demolished—completely destroyed
ear-splitting—very, very loud
every once in a while—sometimes
explode—to blow up into many pieces
fear—to be afraid
Great Spirit—God
hymn—a religious song
noisy—loud
piling—a heavy beam that supports a building at the water's edge
quiet—peaceful
restless—not able to keep still
rubble—crumbled rock, bricks, etc.
rumble—a deep, rolling sound
shock—a strong jolt
siren—a piece of equipment on police cars and fire engines that makes very loud warning sounds
slab—a thick piece of something hard, like cement
straw—dried wheat
subside—to die down or become less
swirl—to twist
throw—to toss
trolley—a streetcar

UNIT 8

abuse—to use something in a way that it should not be used
affect—to cause a change in something
bad breath—air from your mouth that smells bad
bloodshot eyes—red eyes
blurred vision—not seeing clearly
brain function—how the brain works
cancer—a serious disease in which cells in your body do not stop copying themselves
coma—a deep sleep that you can't come out of
confusion—when you are not thinking clearly
coughing—when you push air out of your throat with a rough sound
damage—to have a bad effect on something
discreet—careful not to tell information that you want to keep secret
dislike—to not like someone or something
drop-out—a kid who leaves school
fact—something that is completely true
fatal—causing death
feeling dizzy—when you feel like you might fall over
groovy—a word used in the 1960s meaning "cool"
health—the condition of your body
illegal—against the law
incomplete—not finished
inhalant—a drug you inhale, often fumes from products like glue or paint thinner
intoxication—when you are drunk
lack of coordination—when your body doesn't move right
look to—to be attracted to
nausea—a feeling like you want to vomit
nonsmoker—someone who doesn't smoke cigarettes
oxygen—the air you breathe to stay alive
performance—the act of doing something
permanent—lasting forever
persuade—to give someone good reasons for doing something or not doing it
phlegm production—coughing up slimy mucus from the lungs
risk—the chance something bad could happen
self-control—the ability to control what you say and do
self-image—how you see yourself
trip—an experience someone has when taking an illegal drug
unpopular—not having many friends

UNIT 9

Ben and Jerry's—a popular brand of ice cream
benefit—a positive result
calcium—a type of mineral
carbonated—having many tiny bubbles
cholesterol—a substance in your blood that can cause heart disease
clever—original
Concord—a type of sweet, purple grape
crack a smile—to begin to smile
delicious—tasting good
explosion—a sudden increase in the number of something
favorite—something someone likes best
fiber—a substance in vegetables, fruits, and grains that help move food through your body
flavor—the taste of food or drink
goo—a thick and sticky substance
guarantee—to promise
hilarious—very, very funny
hooked—liking something a lot
humorous—funny
iron—a type of mineral
make a mad dash—to hurry
mineral—a substance that humans, animals, and plants need to grow
normally—usually
nutritious—having things that keep you healthy
reduce—to make less
refreshing—making someone feel less tired or hot
source—where something comes from
special—like no other
strep throat—an illness that causes a very sore throat
substance—matter or material
tingly—a slight stinging feeling
varieties—different types
vitamin—a substance in foods that helps you grow and stay healthy
wacky—very silly
yum—you say this when something tastes good.
zany—funny in an unusual way

UNIT 10

argument—an explanation you give for what you believe
ban—to order that an activity must not happen
calories—the amount of energy in food. Too many calories make you gain weight.
choice—the right to choose something
consider—to think about voting for
consume—to eat
contain—to have in it
courtesy—polite behavior to other people
creativity—using your imagination to do things
discipline—punish
drop-out rates—the numbers of kids quitting school
environment—the situation or people that affect how you live, learn, or work
expected—considered to be the thing that people should do
foster—to help something happen
improve—to make better or more
law—rules in a country, state, or city that we must follow
manners—polite ways of behaving
official—someone who has an important job in an agency or business
plague—to cause trouble again and again
pocket money—(*British*) spending money
position—an opinion about something
reduce—to make smaller or less
required—having to do something because it is a law or rule
respect—being polite to someone because they are important
responsible—making good choices
root—the main or basic part
school district—an agency that runs the schools
senator—a member of the Senate, one of two groups that makes laws
sponsor—to push for (a new law)
superficial—not very important

Glossary

Common Irregular Verbs

Simple Form	Past Form	Past Participle	Simple Form	Past Form	Past Participle
be	was/were	been	lay (= put)	laid	laid
beat	beat	beaten	lead	led	led
become	became	become	leave	left	left
begin	began	begun	let	let	let
bend	bent	bent	lie (= lie down)	lay	lain
bite	bit	bitten	lose	lost	lost
break	broke	broken	make	made	made
bring	brought	brought	mean	meant	meant
build	built	built	meet	met	met
buy	bought	bought	pay	paid	paid
catch	caught	caught	put	put	put
choose	chose	chosen	quit	quit	quit
come	came	come	read	read	read
cost	cost	cost	ride	rode	ridden
cut	cut	cut	ring	rang	rung
do	did	done	rise	rose	risen
draw	drew	drawn	run	ran	run
drink	drank	drunk	say	said	said
eat	ate	eaten	see	saw	seen
fall	fell	fallen	sell	sold	sold
feed	fed	fed	send	sent	sent
feel	felt	felt	set	set	set
fight	fought	fought	show	showed	shown
find	found	found	shut	shut	shut
fly	flew	flown	sing	sang	sung
forget	forgot	forgotten	sit	sat	sat
forgive	forgave	forgiven	sleep	slept	slept
get	got	gotten	speak	spoke	spoken
give	gave	given	spend	spent	spent
go	went	gone	stand	stood	stood
grow	grew	grown	swim	swam	swum
have	had	had	take	took	taken
hear	heard	heard	teach	taught	taught
hide	hid	hidden	tear	tore	torn
hit	hit	hit	tell	told	told
hold	held	held	think	thought	thought
hurt	hurt	hurt	throw	threw	thrown
keep	kept	kept	understand	understood	understood
know	knew	known	wake	woke	woken

Listening Script

UNIT 1

A. 1. Tuning In. (page 4)

Reporter: We're talking today to Frankie Morales, the star of the TV show, *The Adventures of Max Jones*. How does it feel to be the star of a popular TV show?

Frankie: It's always been my dream to be on a TV show.

Reporter: Do you have a favorite hobby?

Frankie: Golf is my favorite thing.

Reporter: Your TV character, Max, is a genius. What about you? Do you get good grades?

Frankie: I get straight A's, but Max gets straight A-pluses.

Reporter: Is your family anything like the wacky family on the show?

Frankie: The family on *The Adventures of Max Jones* is real. A lot of families do weird things. My family's not perfect, either.

UNIT 2

A. 1. Tuning In. (page 22)

Narrator: Listen to the description. Name the animal that we are describing. This animal is a snake—a very poisonous snake! It has a rattle at the end of its tail. When it is scared or angry, it coils its body and lifts its head and tail off the ground. The tail moves back and forth, making a rattling sound. This snake uses its rattle to scare away people or other animals. If you don't move away, it may bite you with its two sharp teeth, called *fangs*! The fangs pump poison into the victim. The poison is deadly! That means it can kill a person!

UNIT 3

A. 1. Tuning In. (page 40)

Teacher: Tomorrow is our party. Let's check to see if we're ready. Who's on the refreshments committee? Raise your hand. Juan...Lourdes...Parveen. Let's see, what are we having?

Parveen: Vampire Punch!

Juan: And Eyeball Cookies!

Teacher: I'll make the cookies tonight at home. And I'll buy the ingredients for the punch. You three will need to do the rest...Don't forget to bring in the punch bowl. And, don't forget to bring in a large plate for the cookies. We'll also need napkins and paper plates. We can make the ice for the punch in the morning. We can use the freezer in the cafeteria.

Parveen: What about decorations?

Teacher: I have a surprise! Look!

Juan: A pumpkin?

Teacher: Yes. We're going to make a Jack-o'-lantern.

Juan and Parveen: Cool!

Teacher: OK, Get ready to write down these steps. Take notes as you listen. Here's how to make a Jack-o'-lantern.

First, I'll put the pumpkin on a sheet of newspaper. This is a messy job.

Then, I'll cut out the top of the pumpkin around the stem...

Next, I'll lift off the top...

	And then, I'll scoop out the seeds. I'm just going to use my hands. Next, let's see which side of the pumpkin is the best side for the face... Maybe this side... Now, I'm cutting out the eyes...carefully. And, then the nose... And now the mouth...There!

	We'll put the Jack-o'-lantern on the refreshments table, in the center. Finally, we'll put a short candle in the bottom of the pumpkin, and light it. Then we'll turn out the lights.
Juan:	That will be fun.
Teacher:	It sure will. Remember to wear your costumes, everybody.

I.   1. On Assignment. (page 54)

See script for A.1.Tuning In. (page 40)

UNIT 4

A.   1. Tuning In. (page 58)

Lori:	Michelle! You look so...*different*!
Michelle:	Do you like it?
Lori:	Uh...it's really...uh...*different*!
Michelle:	Isn't it *cool*?
Lori:	Uh...What do your parents think?
Michelle:	They don't like it. But they say it's *my* hair and I can do what I want with it.
Lori:	But, Michelle...the color...it's so...*blue*!
Michelle:	Deep sky blue. It's called deep sky blue.
Lori:	So...what made you dye your hair?
Michelle:	All the girls are doing it...that is, all the girls who are really *cool*.
Lori:	*Really*?
Michelle:	Yeah! You should try it, Lori. You would look so cool with maybe...*green* hair...
Lori:	But I *like* my hair ...
Michelle:	Trust me. Black hair is *not* cool. You would look very cool with green hair! You'd have a lot more friends.

UNIT 5

A.   1. Tuning in. (Page 76)

There once was a flower that grew on the plain,
Where the sun helped it grow, so did the rain ...

There once was a bug who nibbled on flowers,
Nibbled on flowers for hours and hours!

The bug ate the flower that grew on the plain,
Where the sun helped it grow, so did the rain ...

There once was a bird who gobbled up bugs,
And creepies and crawlies, and slimies and slugs.

The bird ate the bug, who nibbled on flowers,
Nibbled on flowers for hours and hours!

The bug ate the flower that grew on the plain,
Where the sun helped it grow, so did the rain ...

There once was a snake who often grabbed birds,
And swallowed them whole, or so I have heard.

The snake ate the bird, who gobbled up bugs,
And creepies and crawlies, and slimies and slugs.

The bird ate the bug, who nibbled on flowers,
Nibbled on flowers for hours and hours!

The bug ate the flower that grew on the plain,
Where the sun helped it grow, so did the rain ...

There once was a fox, and I'll make a bet:
He'd eat anything he could possibly get.

The fox ate the snake, who often grabbed birds,
And swallowed them whole, or so I have heard.

The snake ate the bird, who gobbled up bugs,
And creepies and crawlies, and slimies and slugs.

The bird ate the bug, who nibbled on flowers,
Nibbled on flowers for hours and hours!

The bug ate the flower that grew on the plain,
Where the sun helped it grow, and so did the rain...

Listening Script

UNIT 6

A. 1. Tuning In. (page 94)

Amanda: My best friend Carmen and I were playing in the middle of a lake with some other friends when we heard a huge splash. Suddenly, Carmen disappeared. She just went under. I was really scared, but I couldn't just leave her!

Underwater, a huge alligator—it was at least ten or eleven feet long—was spinning Carmen around and around and it had her arm clenched in its jaws. It felt like a tornado! Suddenly the 'gator let her go, and I knew it was now or never!

The alligator started swimming toward us again. The other kids raced to the shore, screaming. I pulled Carmen onto a boogie board. We were terrified! We kicked about 150 feet back to shore.

The 'gator had broken Carmen's arm and ripped a seven-inch gash in her skin, but it could have been worse!

Carmen: If Amanda hadn't saved me, the alligator probably would have won! She's my hero!

H. 1. Getting It Out, Part 3. (page 104)

Interviewer: What's your name?
Karla: Karla Pierce.
Interviewer: What did you do, Karla?
Karla: I saved my dog's life. I saved him from drowning.
Interviewer: Where did it happen?
Karla: In my backyard. We have a stream that runs behind our house.
Interviewer: So, tell me what happened.
Karla: Well, my family had friends over. We were having a barbecue in the backyard. Suddenly, someone shouted that our dog Tucker was in the stream.
Interviewer: Does he know how to swim?
Karla: He *does*, but the stream was moving really, really fast.
Interviewer: I see. So what did you do?
Karla: I rushed to the edge of the stream and saw that Tucker was in trouble. As I said, the stream was moving really fast. He was fighting the water and kept hitting the rocks. So I stretched out on the side of the stream—it was really slippery—and hooked my foot around a tree. I reached out over the water and grabbed Tucker by the paw. I pulled him out of the water. He weighs at least 100 pounds!
Interviewer: Did everything turn out OK?
Karla: We were both cold, muddy, and wet, but we were OK.
Interviewer: You must have been scared!
Karla: I was really scared. I knew that if I didn't do something, Tucker might drown. Sometimes you have to try your hardest and not give up, you know.

H. 1. Getting It Out, Part 5. (page 105)

Interviewer: What's your name?
Aaron: Aaron Wallace.
Interviewer: And how old are you, Aaron?
Aaron: I'm 16.
Interviewer: Where do you live?
Aaron: In Virginia.
Interviewer: Tell me what happened.
Aaron: Well, I was walking home from school, and I saw Amber and her cousin playing on the train tracks.
Interviewer: How old are they?
Aaron: Amber's about two and her cousin is four.
Interviewer: Please, go on.
Aaron: I've been around trains my whole life, so I know that train tracks are a dangerous place to play. I sensed a train was coming. I told the kids to leave the track, but only Amber's cousin did.

Suddenly, I saw a train coming around the curve. I grabbed Amber in my arms. Then I heard her mom. She was yelling, "Jump! Jump!" I held Amber really tight and jumped off the tracks. The train roared by right at that second!
Interviewer: So, then what happened?
Aaron: The train company gave me an award. They said I was courageous. I don't really feel like that, though. I think anyone would have done the same thing.

UNIT 7

A. 1. Tuning In. (page 112)

Teenage Boy: It happened last summer. We were on a Boy Scout camping trip. All of a sudden, we heard the news. It was headed toward us! Soon it would hit!

    The wind started to blow. Things started flying around. The sky turned nasty gray. Everybody was running around with their ponchos flying in the wind.

    The wind got stronger. Lawn chairs started flying by. The flagpole at our camp site came down. By now, it was really raining hard. Our tents started blowing away.

    Then it was over. The sky got brighter. The wind died down, and the rain stopped.

    It was incredible!

Woman: I was making dinner when the first shock came. The house started to shake. Then it got stronger. Pictures fell off the wall. Our TV crashed to the floor. Dishes started to break. I grabbed the kids, and we ran outside. We all crawled under a picnic table. Another shock came, and we saw the chimney fall off the roof. Horrible sounds came from the house—crashing sounds, creaking, groaning. Then it was quiet. Nobody said a word. We just hoped it was over!

Girl: When I got up that morning, I saw black clouds in the sky. By noon, it was starting to rain and by late afternoon it was raining really hard. My friend Ann and I decided to walk into town. Big mistake! In the five minutes that it took us to get into town, the rain became sheets of water.

    The streets turned to rivers. Cars couldn't move, and drivers were trapped in their cars. We were standing in water up to our waists. We were trapped!

UNIT 8

A. 1. Tuning In. (page 130)

Amy: Hey, Maria, let's have a beer. It's Saturday night. My mom and dad are gone. We can do anything we want here.

Maria: Amy, I don't think we should. What if they come home? What if they find out?

Amy: Look, it's not like drugs. Our parents drink. Why shouldn't we?

Maria: Our parents are adults. We're only 16. Besides, alcohol is bad for you. It can make you sick. It can make you lose control.

Amy: Look, one beer isn't going to kill you, Maria.

Maria: Stop trying to pressure me, Amy. If you want to drink so badly, go find another friend. I'm going home.

Amy: Wait, Maria, don't go. I'm sorry. I didn't mean to pressure you.

Listening Script

UNIT 9

A. 1. Tuning In. (page 148)

Speaker Number 1
This is my favorite food! I love it with a soft and chewy crust and when it's covered with lots of stringy cheese. When it comes out of the oven, you can smell the tomato sauce and the spices.

Speaker Number 2
Instead of a candy bar or potato chips, I have one of these when I get home from school. It's sweet and tasty and crunchy to eat. And, it's healthy, too.

Speaker Number 3
I love this in desserts like pie and cake, but I wouldn't want to eat it all by itself. It can be so sour! It can make your mouth pucker!

Speaker Number 4
I love to have this on a hot, summer day. It's cold and kind of creamy. I love to make it with raspberries or bananas.

Speaker Number 5
Sometimes I put this on toast or crackers. It can be smooth or crunchy. It's fun to eat because it sticks to the roof of your mouth.

Speaker Number 6
This comes from a chicken. It's sort of round and it's runny if you break it. You can fry it, scramble it, or boil it. I have one of these nearly every morning for breakfast.

UNIT 10

A. 1. Tuning In. (page 166)

Erik: Mom, can I have an allowance?
Erik's mother: An allowance? How much do you want?
Erik: Twenty dollars a week.
Erik's mother: Twenty dollars! That's a lot!
Erik: It isn't! I need to buy things for school. All of my friends get an allowance...!
Erik's mother: Well...maybe you can have an allowance, but you'll have to earn it. You'll have to work for it.
Erik: Earn it? You mean do things around the house, like making my bed...and taking out the garbage...and clearing the table after dinner?
Erik's mother: I *expect* you to do *those* things! No, I mean special jobs. If you get an allowance, you will need to do things like wash the windows and paint the garage.
Erik: That's not fair!
Erik's mother: It *is* fair. Kids should work for their allowance. Work teaches you the value of money.
Erik: But I have so much homework! And I have sports after school. I don't have time to wash the windows or paint the garage!
Erik's mother: Too bad. Your father and I both have to work for our money. You should have to work, too.

MINI-UNIT

Let's talk about the grizzly bear.

A large grizzly bear is one of the strongest animals in the world. A full-grown male is over eight feet long from nose to tail and can weigh over 700 pounds. Grizzlies are omnivores. They eat everything from squirrels to deer, and from berries to birds. Almost any animal in grizzly country may wind up as a meal for this mighty hunter.

There is no doubt that a grizzly bear is a dangerous animal and should be left alone. If you see a bear that is far away or doesn't see you, turn around and go back. If the bear is close or does see you, remain calm. Do not run. Instead, stand tall or back away slowly and wave your hands and speak loudly. The chances are that the bear will not bother you and will disappear.

Listening Script

Index

Grammar and Mechanics
Adverbial clauses,
>of condition (*if* clauses), 153
>of time, 99

Gerunds, 135
Imperatives, 45
Modals, 171
Past tense, 63, 117
>versus present tense, 81

Present tense versus past tense, 81
Subject-verb agreement, 27
wh- questions, 9, 13

Internet, 33, 77, 87, 140, 159, 177

Listening and Speaking
Advice, 58
Comparison, 22, 59, 101, 112, 119, 148
Debate, 166
Description, 22, 89, 148
Dialog, 130
Discussions, 3, 5, 7, 11, 21, 22, 25, 39, 43, 57, 58, 61, 75, 76, 77, 79, 93, 111, 112, 113, 129, 130, 147, 149, 165
Facts, 4
Feedback (giving/receiving), 17, 35, 53, 71, 89, 161
Instructions, 40, 41
Interviews, 15, 102
Laws, 167
Opinions, 148, 179
Poem, 76
Presenting, 17, 35, 53, 71, 89, 107, 125, 143, 161, 179
Questions, 4
Ranking, 23
Rating, 58
Report (eyewitness), 112
Stories, 94, 95, 104
Surveys, 166, 177

Literature
Diary entry, 145
Poems, 19, 37, 55, 73, 91, 181
Reviews (book), 163
Stories, 109, 127

Reading and Writing Genres
Articles (feature), 168, 172
Brochures, 132
Cause and effect, 82
Description, 114, 118, 120
Diagrams, 78, 82, 84, 85, 86
Facts,
>fact sheet, 136
>true/false, 130

Fact sheet, 136
Forms, 14
Headlines, 94
Information, 24, 28, 78, 132, 136
Instructions, 42, 46
Interviews, 6, 10, 14
Narratives, 60, 64
Notes, 14, 89
Persuasive text, 132, 136
Poems, 19, 37, 55, 73, 91, 181
Process, 78
Reviews,
>book, 163
>food, 150, 154

Stories, 96, 100, 105, 106, 107, 109

Reading (Comprehension strategies, skills, text organization)
Charts, 115
Comic strips (for sequence), 68, 69
Comprehension, 11, 29, 47, 65, 83, 101, 119, 137, 155, 173
Details, 7, 25, 43, 61, 79, 97, 115, 133, 151, 169
Diagrams, 78, 82
Drawing a picture, 35, 42, 43
Elements of persuasive text (identifying), 138
Elements of plot (identifying), 102
Fact versus opinion, 168
Guessing, 46, 55, 64, 96, 100
Identifying the main idea, 7, 25, 61, 79, 97, 115, 133, 151, 169
Identifying the purpose, 43, 132
Illustrations (using), 51, 54, 55
Listing (what you know), 28
Main idea (identifying), 7, 25, 61, 79, 97, 115, 133, 151, 169
Note-taking, 24, 78, 89
Opinion (versus fact), 168
Persuasive text (elements of), 138
Photographs (to predict), 122, 147
Pictures (drawing), 35, 42, 43
Plot, elements of, 102
Predicting, 46, 64, 96, 100
>using photographs, 122, 147

Prereading, 6, 10, 24, 28, 42, 46, 60, 64, 78, 82, 96, 100, 114, 118, 132, 136, 150, 154, 168, 172
Purpose (identifying), 43, 132
Questioning the author, 60
Reading titles, 4, 22, 25, 40, 58, 64

Sequence, 43, 61, 68, , 69, 79, 98
      comic strips, 68, 69
Skimming, 6, 10, 136, 172
Summarizing, 154
Topic sentences, 30
Visualizing, 42, 114, 118, 150

Real World Applications
Award ceremony, 108
Book (class), 36
Class book, 36
Debate, 180
Interviews, 18
Narrative (submitting to online publication), 72
Newspaper reviews, 162
News report (about a disaster), 126
Parties (giving a Halloween party), 54
Research (animal chain), 90
Skits (anti-drug), 144

Spelling and Phonics
/ā/ as in *fame* and *play*, 182
-ea-, 185
-gh-, 183
/j/ as in *jam* and *badge*, 186
/ō/ as in *hole* and *boat*, 183
-oo-, 184
/o͞o/ as in *food* and *blue*, 184
/or/ as in *for* and *four*, 186
-ou-, 185
/ch/ as in *check* and *kitchen*, 182

Style
Adjectives, 31, 157
Audience (formal versus informal language), 67
Combining sentences, 124
Commas, 34, 70, 88, 124, 160, 178
Dashes, 142
Facts (using), 174, 175
Interview questions, 13
Leads, 102, 103
Narrative content, 60
Opinions, 156, 157
Punctuation,
    Commas, 34, 70, 88, 124, 160, 178
    Dashes, 142
    End of sentence, 16
    Quotes, 178
Questions (using to support a position), 139
Quotes (using), 174, 175, 178
Sequence, 48, 51, 68, 69
Similes, 121
Specific terminology, 80
Terminology (specific), 80
that clauses, 85
Titles, 102, 103, 174
Topic sentences, 120

Verbs (action-packed), 119
Word choice,
    Action-packed verbs, 119
    Exact words, 49
    Specific terminology, 80
    Verbs, 119

Visual Literacy
Charts, 13, 14, 29, 30, 33, 43, 44, 47, 59, 65, 80, 83, 101, 113, 119, 131, 137, 148, 149, 151, 155, 159, 167, 173
Comic strips, 68, 69
Diagrams, 78, 82, 84, 85, 86, 159
Illustrations, 3, 39, 41, 51, 54, 55, 57, 75, 93, 94, 129, 165, 148
Photographs, 21, 22, 29, 77, 80, 90, 111, 112, 122, 147, 158
Pictures, 35, 42, 43
Posters, 133, 149
Symbols, 52
Timeline, 51

Vocabulary, 5, 6, 10, 11, 23, 24, 28, 37, 41, 42, 46, 48, 55, 59, 60, 64, 77, 78, 82, 96, 100, 113, 114, 118, 119, 131, 132, 136, 139, 149, 150, 154, 155, 163, 167, 168, 169, 172
Accidents and emergencies, 95, 101
Adjectives, 155, 157
Animals, 29, 80
Debate, 173
Ocean plants and animals, 83
Parties, 40, 47
Personality description, 65
Sensory words, 121
Specific terminology, 80
Symptoms (of drugs and tobacco), 137
Terminology (specific), 80

Word Analysis Skills
Antonyms, 152
Compound words, 44, 98 (verb + noun)
Finding words within words, 26
    nouns/verbs in adjectives, 26
Homonyms, 8
Homophones, 8
Prefixes (non-, il-, in-, dis-), 134
Suffixes,
    -er/-or, 62
    -ing, 26
    -y, 26
Synonyms, 116
Word families, 170

Writing
Articles, 87, 88
    feature, 178, 179
Body (of interview), 12

Brochures, 140, 142, 143
Certificates, 97
Charts, 13, 14, 29, 30, 33, 43, 44, 47, 51, 59, 65, 80, 83, 101, 113, 119, 123, 131, 137, 139, 141, 148, 149, 151, 155, 159, 167, 173
Description, 120, 124, 125
Details, 34
Diagrams (flow), 79, 84, 85, 86, 159
Forms, 14
Headings, 12
Informational paragraph, 34, 35
Instructions, 48, 52, 53
Interviews, 12, 16, 17
Lists, 21, 28, 39, 51, 147
Narrative (personal), 70
Notes, 14, 24, 89, 104, 105

Opinions, 151
Outlines, 30, 31, 34, 70, 87, 106, 124, 142, 160, 175, 178
Persuasive writing, 140, 142, 143
Poems (portrait), 19
Posters, 133, 149
Prewriting, 14, 15, 32, 33, 50, 51, 68, 69, 86, 104, 105, 106, 122, 123, 140, 141, 158, 159, 176, 177
Process, 79, 87
Report, 32
Reviews, 156, 160, 161
Sequence, 48, 51, 68, 69
Stories, 102, 106, 107
Titles, 25
Topic sentences, 34

Text and Audio Credits

p. 24 From "Cockroaches," *The Unhuggables* by Victor Waldrup, Debbie Anker, and Elizabeth Blizzard. Copyright © 1988 National Wildlife Federation. Used by permission; *p. 28* "Sharks" from *Animals Nobody Loves* by Seymour Simon. Copyright © 2001 by Seymour Simon. Used with permission of Chronicle Books LLC, San Francisco. Visit Chronicle Books.com. Audio reproduced by permission of the Wendy Schmalz Agency; *p. 37* "Acro-Bat" copyright © 1997 by Kenn Nesbitt. Reprinted and reproduced by permission of the author. www.poetry4kids.com. All rights reserved. *pp. 42, 48* "Create Your Own Halloween Makeup," *National Geographic World*, October 2000. Used by permission of National Geographic Society; *p. 46* "Lose Your Head," *National Geographic Kids*, October 2002. Used by permission of National Geographic Society; *p. 54* Recipe for "Eyeballs" courtesy of BlackDog - The Site for Kids! Visit BlackDog on the World Wide Web: www.blackdog.net; *p. 55* "Best Mask?" from *Falling Up* by Shel Silverstein. Copyright © 1996 by Shel Silverstein. Used by permission of HarperCollins Publishers; *pp. 60, 64* © 2001 by Consumers Union of U.S., Inc., Yonkers, NY 10703-1057, a nonprofit organization. Reprinted and reproduced with permission from *Zillions: CONSUMER REPORTS® for Kids* Online for educational purposes only. No commercial use or reproduction permitted. www.zillions.org, http://www.zillions.org and www.ConsumerReports.org, http://www.ConsumerReports.org; *p. 73* "Motto" from *The Collected Poems of Langston Hughes* by Langston Hughes, copyright © 1994 by The Estate of Langston Hughes. Used by permission of Alfred A. Knopf, a division of Random House, Inc. and Harold Ober Associates Incorporated; *p. 78* Adapted from *Who Eats What?* by Patricia Lauber, HarperCollins, 1995; *p. 94* "Kids Did It! Real-Life Heroes" by Robin Terry from *National Geographic Kids*, October 2002. Used by permission of National Geographic Society; *p. 96*, "Calm Under Pressure" by Laura Daily from *National Geographic World*, July 2000. Used by permission of National Geographic Society; *p. 100* "'Bear-ly in Time" by Laura Daily from *National Geographic World*, July 2000. Used by permission of National Geographic Society; *pp. 105-107* "Dog Catcher" by Laura Daily from *National Geographic World*, July 2000. Used by permission of National Geographic Society; *p. 105* "Leap of Faith" by Laura Daily from *National Geographic World*, July 2000. Used by permission of National Geographic Society; *p. 109* "Paul Bunyan and the Gumberoos" from *Paul Bunyan* by Steven Kellogg. Text copyright © 1984 by Steven Kellogg. Used by permission of Harper Collins Publishers; *p. 114* "I Survived a Tornado!" from "Twister: winds of fury" by Jerry Dunn, *National Geographic World*, May 1997. Used by permission of National Geographic Society; *p. 118* Adaptation of "Thomas Jefferson Chase's account of the 1906 San Francisco earthquake," www.sfmuseum.org. Used by permission of The Virtual Museum of San Francisco; *p. 127* Adapted from "The Turtle Tale." Reprinted and reproduced with permission from *Earthquakes*, copyright © 1989, National Science Teachers Association and the Federal Emergency Management Agency; *p. 132* From the Coalition for Drug-Free City. *p. 145* Reprinted and reproduced with the permission of Simon & Schuster Books for Young Readers, an imprint of Simon & Schuster Children's Publishing Division from *Go Ask Alice* by Anonymous. Copyright © 1971 Simon & Schuster, Inc.; *p. 150* "Jello-O" by Casey D., *Teen Ink Reviews*. Reprinted and reproduced by permission from *Teen Ink* Magazine and teenink.com; *p. 154* From of "Oatmeal" by Keith R., *Teen Ink Reviews*. Reprinted and reproduced by permission from *Teen Ink* Magazine and teenink.com; *p. 163* Review of *Falling Up* by Shel Silverstein written by Amy P., *Teen Ink Book Reviews*. Reprinted and reproduced by permission from *Teen Ink* Magazine and teenink.com. Used by permission; *p. 163* "Tattooin' Ruth" from *Falling Up* by Shel Silverstein, HarperCollins, 1996; *p. 168* "Do Students Need a Courtesy Law?" from *Junior Scholastic*, March 12, 2001. © 2001 by Scholastic Inc. Reprinted and reproduced by permission of Scholastic Inc.; *p. 172* "Ban Junk Food in School?" from *Junior Scholastic*, September 6, 2002. © 2002 by Scholastic Inc. Reprinted and reproduced by permission of Scholastic Inc.; *p. 181* "How to Successfully Persuade Your Parents to Give You More Pocket Money" by Andrea Shavick . © Andrea Shavick. First published in *Unzip Your Lips Again*, Macmillan Children's Books UK , 2000. Used by permission of the author.

Photo Credits

Cover Images: All cover images courtesy of the Getty Images Royalty-Free Collection except the following: cockroaches eating crackers: David Maitland/Getty Images; tropical storm: Images produced by Hal Pierce, Laboratory for Atmospheres, NASA Goddard Space Flight Center/NOAA; interview in classroom: Barbara Stitzer/Photo Edit; Frog: Royalty-Free/CORBIS; Giraffes: Royalty-Free/CORBIS; man caught in hurricane: Royalty-Free/CORBIS; California State Capitol: Focus Group/Andre Jenny/PictureQuest.

Interior Images: From the Getty Images Royalty-Free Collection: *p.* 20, bottom; *p.* 22, top left; *p.* 22, top middle; *p.* 29, row 1, photo 1; *p.* 29, row 1, photo 2; *p.* 29, row 1, photo 3; *p.* 29, row 2, photo 3; *p.* 29, row 3, photo 1; *p.* 29, row 3, photo 2; *p.* 29, row 3, photo 3; *p.* 32, photo 1; *p.* 32, photo 4; *p.* 57; *p.* 77, photo 2; *p.* 77, photo 3; *p.* 80, photo c; *p.* 80, photo e; *p.* 80, photo f; *p.* 86, photo a; *p.* 86, photo b; *p.* 86, photo c; *p.* 86, photo d; *p.* 90, photo 1; *p.* 90, photo 2; *p.* 90, photo 5; *p.* 90, photo 6; *p.* 90, photo 7; *p.* 90, photo 8; *p.* 90, photo 9; *p.* 91; *p.* 127; *p.* 154; *p.* 158, photo 1; *p.* 158, photo 3; *p.* 158, photo 4; **From the Corbis Royalty-Free Collection:** *p.* 4, bottom right; *p.* 29, row 1, photo 4; *p.* 77, photo 1; *p.* 77, photo 4; *p.* 80, photo b; *p.* 90, photo 4; *p.* 90, photo 10; *p.* 110, top; *p.* 112, photo 2; *p.* 112, photo 3; *p.* 112, photo 4; *p.* 112, photo 5; *p.* 122, top left; *p.* 122, top right; *p.* 122, bottom left; *p.* 122, bottom right; **Other Images:** *p.* 2, top: Peter Muhly/Reuters/CORBIS; *p.* 2, bottom: Paul Fenton/ZUMA Press; *p.* 4, top left: Frank Trapper/CORBIS; *p.* 4, top right: Darren Hauck/CORBIS; *p.* 4, bottom left: Reuters/CORBIS; *p.* 6: Peter Muhly/Reuters/CORBIS; *p.* 10: Paul Fenton/ZUMA Press; *p.* 19: Photodisc/PictureQuest; *p.* 20, top: David Maitland/Getty Images; *p.* 21: Romilly Lockyer/Getty Images; *p.* 22, top right: Jeremy Woodhouse/Getty Images; *p.* 22, bottom left: Davies & Starr/Getty Images; *p.* 22, bottom middle: S. J. Vincent/Getty Images; *p.* 22, bottom right: Mike Buxton; Papilio/CORBIS ; *p.* 23: Eldad Rafaeli/CORBIS; *p.* 24: David Maitland/Getty Images; *p.* 28: Romilly Lockyer/Getty Images; *p.* 29, row 1, photo 5: Arthur Morris/CORBIS; *p.* 29, row 2, photo 1: Geoff Du Feu/Getty Images; *p.* 29, row 2, photo 2: Staffan Widstrand/CORBIS; *p.* 32, photo 2: Mike Buxton; Papilio/CORBIS ; *p.* 32, photo 3: Paul A. Zahl/Getty Images; *p.* 55: Jeff Albertson/CORBIS; *p.* 60: Digital Vision/PictureQuest; *p.* 73, left: CORBIS; *p.* 73, right: Bettmann/CORBIS; *p.* 77, top: Zigy Kaluzny/Getty Images; *p.* 78: Photodisc/PictureQuest; *p.* 78: Ingram/PictureQuest; *p.* 80, photo a: Vera Storman/Getty Images; *p.* 80, photo d: Michael & Patricia Fogden/CORBIS; *p.* 80, photo g: iStockphoto / Patti Meador; *p.* 80, photo h: Johnathan Smith; Cordaiy Photo Library Ltd./CORBIS; *p.* 82: liquidlibrary/PictureQuest; *p.* 82: Stockbyte/PictureQuest; *p.* 90, photo 3: Cameron Read/Getty Images; *p.* 96: Swim Ink/CORBIS; *p.* 98: Susan Werner/Getty Images; *p.* 100: Digital Vision/PictureQuest; *p.* 100: Creatas/PictureQuest; *p.* 109: Michael Leslie; *p.* 110, bottom: CORBIS; *p.* 111: Michael Maslan Historic Photographs/CORBIS; *p.* 112, photo 1: CORBIS; *p.* 112, photo 6: Chris Butler/Photo Researchers, Inc. ; *p.* 146, top: Paul Poplis /Getty Images; *p.* 146, bottom: Leigh Beisch/Getty Images; *p.* 147: Paul Poplis /Getty Images; *p.* 158, photo 2: Richard Jung/Getty Images; *p.* 163: Jeff Albertson/CORBIS; *p.* 172: Brand X Pictures/PictureQuest; *p.* 181: Photo courtesy of Andrea Shavick.

Practice Book Answer Key

UNIT 1

A. Revisit and Retell
Answers will vary.

B. Word Work
1. 1. f; 2. h; 3. b; 4. e; 5. a; 6. i; 7. d; 8. g; 9. c.
2. 1. or; 2. by; 3. two; 4. our; 5. hole; 6. buy; 7. here; 8. to; 9. dear; 10. bass; 11. deer; 12. hour; 13. hear; 14. whole; 15. male; 16. mail.

C. Grammar
1. When do you usually get up? 2. What do you usually have for breakfast? 3. Who usually makes breakfast? 4. How do you get to school? 5. Where do you catch the bus? 6. How much is the fare? 7. What is your first class? 8. How many kids are in your science class?

D. Test-Taking Practice
Reading Vocabulary: 1. D; 2. B; 3. B; 4. A; 5. B.
Reading Comprehension: 1. C; 2. B; 3. C; 4. D; 5. A

E. Using New Vocabulary
1. Thank you for agreeing to talk with me. 2. Could you begin by telling me about yourself? 3. Please tell me more. 4. Could you repeat that? 5. Do you agree? 6. I enjoyed talking with you.

F. Focus on Organization
Answers will vary.

G. Focus on Style
Possible answers: 1. What do you like about this school? 2. How long have you lived here? 3. What kind of hobbies do you have? 4. What sports do you play? 5. What kind of foods do you like? 6. What do you like to do in your spare time? 7. Where do you like to hang out?

H. Writer's Workshop
Answers will vary.

I. Responding to Literature
Answers will vary.

UNIT 2

A. Revisit and Retell
1. Possible answers: Title: Cockroaches; Book: <u>The Unhuggables</u>; Main Idea: Cockroaches are amazing animals.; Detail #1: They can withstand heat and cold.; Detail # 2: They can run a foot a second.; Detail # 3: They have survived more than 350 million years.
2. Answers will vary.

B. Word Work
1. salty; 2. barking; 3. speeding; 4. dazzling; 5. smiling; 6. scary; 7. sugary; 8. lucky; 9. flying; 10. dirty; 11. terrifying; 12. windy; 13. rainy; 14. exciting; 15. sleepy.

C. Grammar
1. When spiders are hungry, they bite. 2. Cockroaches run very fast. 2. A cockroach eats almost anything. 4. Rats spread dirt and disease. 5. A crocodile is a big lizard. 6. Crocodiles sometimes drown other animals. 7. Rattlesnakes are poisonous. 8. A rattlesnake makes noise to scare off other animals. 9. Tarantulas have huge, furry legs. 10. A black widow spider is very dangerous.

D. Test-Taking Practice
Reading Vocabulary: 1. B; 2. D; 3. D; 4. A; 5. C.
Reading Comprehension: 1. A; 2. C; 3. D; 4. A; 5. A.

E. Using New Vocabulary
1. a; 2. c; 3. b; 4. a; 5. c.
Possible sentences: 1. A bee's sting is painful. 2. Piranha(s) live in South American rivers. 3. A rattlesnake's bite can kill. 4. Lions are ferocious and beautiful. 5. Some parrots can talk.

F. Focus on Organization

1. D, D, T, D.
2. Answers will vary.

G. Focus on Style

Possible answers: 1. annoying; 2. needle-sharp; 3. deadly; 4. powerful; 5. dangerous; 6. huge; 7. terrifying; 8. disgusting; 9. lazy.

H. Writer's Workshop

1. a poisonous snake. 2. found in the southeastern and southwestern U.S.; likes grasslands, rocky hills, and deserts. 3. when it bites, it injects, or shoots, poison into its victim; its poison can kill animals and people. 4. has a rattle at the end of its tail; rattles its tail to warn away animals or people; has long, hollow teeth, called fangs; usually eats rats, mice, toads, and frogs; does not lay eggs; gives birth to live babies; eats about once every two weeks.

I. Responding to Literature

Answers will vary.

UNIT 3

A. Revisit and Retell

Answers will vary.

B. Word Work

1. birthday; 2. air conditioning; 3. cardboard; 4. newspaper; 5. food coloring; 6. masking tape; 7. yardstick; 8. report card; 9. notebook; 10. snowman; 11. Hand lotion; 12. home run.

C. Grammar

1: 1. O; 2. R; 3. W; 4. D; 5. W; 6. O; 7. D; 8. R.
2: Possible answers: 1. Please close the window. 2. Bake at 350-degrees for 10 minutes. 3. Please bring me some popcorn. 4. Don't cross the street now. 5. Please pass the salt. 6. Go up the stairs and turn left.

D. Test-Taking Practice

Reading Vocabulary: 1. C; 2. B; 3. C; 4. D; 5. A.
Reading Comprehension: 1. B; 2. C; 3. D; 4. A; 5. B.

E. Using New Vocabulary

Decorations: streamers, confetti, centerpiece, balloons, flowers, banners; **Refreshments:** appetizers, munchies, punch, finger food; **Games:** charades, twenty questions, scavenger hunt, musical chairs; **Entertainment:** rock band, magic act, face painting, dancing, karaoke, clown.

F. Focus on Organization

1: 1 cup vanilla ice cream, chocolate syrup, milk.
2: 1. Place 1 cup vanilla ice cream in a bowl. Let sit for 10 minutes. 2. Put the vanilla ice cream in a blender. 3. Add 1 cup cold milk to the ice cream in the blender. 4. Add 3 tablespoons chocolate syrup to the milk and ice cream. 5. Blend for 60 seconds, pour into a glass, and enjoy.

G. Focus on style

1. What kind, How, What kind, How much; 2. What kind, How much, What kind, How; 3. How much, How long, What kind, How; 4. What kind, How long, What kind, How much.

H. Writer's Workshop

Answers will vary.

I. Responding to Literature

Answers will vary.

UNIT 4

A. Revisit and Retell

2. Possible answers: Last Saturday I helped my father clean the garage. He gave me $50. I asked my girlfriend to go to the movies with me. I wanted to look good so I bought a new shirt. We had hamburgers before the movie. At the theater, I saw I didn't have enough money. I had to borrow $10 from my girlfriend. I was really embarrassed.

B. Word Work

1. translator; 2. trainer; 3. racer; 4. visitor;
5. reporter; 6. actor; 7. builder; 8. driver; 9. baker;
10. director; 11. walker; 12. educator; 13. player;
14. singer; 15. writer.

C. Grammar

1. drew; 2. didn't stay; 3. didn't cat; 4. bought; 5. saw; 6. didn't go; 7. didn't hear; 8. listened; 9. spoke; 10. helped; 11. did; 12. was

D. Test-Taking Practice

Reading Vocabulary: 1. B; 2. C; 3. D; 4. A; 5. B.
Reading Comprehension: 1. B; 2. D; 3. A; 4. A; 5. B.

E. Using New Vocabulary

Suggested answers (Other answer may also be correct): 1. immature, childish; 2. conceited, stuck up; 3. carefree, easygoing; 4. mean, nasty; 5. well-liked, popular.

F. Focus on Organization

1. Story 1: Why, What, Result; Story 2: Result, Why, What; Story 3. What, Result, Why
2. Answers will vary.

G. Focus on Style

2. Possible answers:
Dear Grandpa and Grandma,
How are you? I just got home from a soccer game and I'm very tired. I enjoy soccer, but sometimes I'd rather be spending time with my friends. Today I missed a goal and the coach got really angry. Mom and Dad said not to be upset, but they didn't see what happened.
At first my team and I weren't playing so well, but after practicing a while we got into a good rhythm. I made one or two really good shots. But running fast and keeping the ball under control is difficult for me. For a few minutes we thought we were going to win the game, but the other team beat us by three points in the end.
Well, I'm going to go now.
Love,
Miguel

H. Writer's Workshop

Answers will vary.

I. Responding to Literature

Answers will vary.

UNIT 5

A. Revisit and Retell

1. The items in the flow diagram should be in this order: wheat ⇒, grasshopper ⇒, frog ⇒, snake ⇒, owl.
2. Answers will vary.

B. Word Work

1. French poodle; 2. barn swallow; 3. house cat;
4. black bear; 5. horse fly; 6. sheep dog; 7. tiger cat;
8. field mouse; 9. blue whale 10. spider monkey;
11. tree frog; 12. rock lobster; 13. water snake;
14. mountain lion; 15. goldfish.

C. Grammar

1. ate; saw; had; killed; was/were; gave; used; went.
2. 1. used 2. saw 3. were 4. are 5. eat 6. has 7. uses 8. use 9. sees 10. go 11. gives 12. ate 13. had 14. kill 15. go.

D. Test-Taking Practice

Reading Vocabulary: 1. B; 2. B; 3. A; 4. C; 5. A.
Reading Comprehension: 1. D; 2. B; 3. C; 4. A; 5. D.

E. Using New Vocabulary

Students will supply information like this: Kelp is a plant and doesn't eat anything. Mackerel is a fish that eats shrimp, squid, and small fish such as anchovies. The octopus eats shrimp, crabs, snails, fish, and sometimes even turtles. The killer whale eats fish, squid, seals, and sea lions. Red algae is a type of seaweed and doesn't eat anything. Krill are tiny shrimp that eat very small sea plants and animals called plankton. Squid eat fish, shrimp, and other squid. Tuna eat fish including mackerel. Anchovies are small fish that eat plankton. The seal eats fish, squid, and krill. The sea lion eats fish and squid. The herring eats plankton and other small sea plants and tiny sea animals.

F. Focus on Organization

1. plankton ⇒ herring ⇒ seal ⇒ polar bear.
2. Answers will vary.

G. Focus on Style

1. The herring ate the tiny animals that lived in the ocean. 2. The sea urchins ate the kelp that grew on the ocean floor. 3. The killer whale ate the sea lion that ate the squid. 4. The hawk killed the pigeon that was pure white. 5. The anchovies ate the plankton that was floating in the seawater. 6. The cat killed the mouse that was sleeping under the chair. 7. The dog bit the cat that scratched his nose. 8. The seals ate the krill that were in the water. 9. I saw the shark that came near me. 10. The octopus ate the snails that were on the ocean floor.

H. Writer's Workshop

Answers will vary. Possible Answers: 1. Here is an example of a food chain in the ocean. 2. a. kelp, sea lettuce, algae; b. krill, anchovies; c. tuna, mackerel d. zaida 3. If one animal disappears from the food chain, all the other animals in the chain are affected.

I. Responding to Literature

1. Possible answers: flower ⇒ bug ⇒ bird ⇒ snake ⇒ fox.
2. Answers will vary.

UNIT 6

A. Revisit and Retell

Answers will vary. Possible answers. 1. Ashley Makale took a baby-sitting class. 2. She was babysitting for two children. 3 Mr. Becker saw his dog chasing the cat. 4. He crashed into the door and cut his knee. 5. Ashley dialed 911. 6. Then she stayed with Mr. Becker. 7. Later, Mr. Becker went to physical therapy. 8. Ashley got an award.

B. Word Work

1: 1. e; 2. c; 3. g; 4. f; 5. a; 6. h; 7. b; 8. d.
2: 1. doorknocker; 2. running shoes; 3. bathroom; 4. dishwasher; 5. phone call; 6. driveway; 7. bus stop; 8. bookmark.

C. Grammar

1. When Ashley Makale was 12 years old, she took a baby-sitting class. OR Ashley Makale took a baby-sitting class when she was 12 years old. 2. While Ashley was taking the baby-sitting class, she learned about first aid. Ashley learned about first aid while she was taking the baby-sitting class. 3. She didn't know a lot about first aid before she took the baby-sitting class. Before she took the baby-sitting class, she didn't know a lot about first aid. 4. After she took the class, Ashley got a baby-sitting job. Ashley got a baby-sitting job after she took the class. 5. While Ashley was watching the Becker children, Mr. Becker hurt himself. Mr. Becker hurt himself while Ashley was watching the Becker children. 6. After Mr. Becker fell, Ashley rushed to his side. Ashley rushed to Mr. Becker's side after he fell. 7. When she saw that he was badly hurt, she called 911. She called 911 when she saw that he was badly hurt. 8. She reassured the children before the paramedics arrived. Before the paramedics arrived, she reassured the children. 9. After Mr. Becker had surgery, he began physical therapy. Mr. Becker began physical therapy after he had surgery. 10. Ashley was surprised when the Sheriff's Department honored here. When the Sheriff's Department honored her, Ashley was surprised.

D. Test-Taking Practice

Reading Vocabulary: 1. C; 2. B; 3. D; 4. C; 5. B.
Reading Comprehension: 1. D; 2. D; 3. D; 4. C; 5. D.

E. Using New Vocabulary

Answers will vary. Possible answers: 1. Lee burned his hand on a pot. He applied antibiotic cream on it. 2. A strange dog bit Jim. He went to the emergency room. 3. A can hit me on the head. I applied a cold compress. 4. Mark scraped his knee. He applied pressure to the wound with a clean cloth.

F. Focus on Organization

1: 1. action; 2. ending; 3 action; 4. lead; 5. action; 6. action; 7. action.
2: Possible answers: When I woke up this morning, I heard running water. Something wasn't right! I sat up in bed and put one foot on the floor. The carpet was wet! It was soaked with water! I ran to the bathroom. The bathtub was overflowing. My sister had forgotten to turn off the water! My mother was really mad. Now we have to buy new carpet.

G. Focus on Style

Answers will vary.

H. Writer's Workshop

Answers will vary.

UNIT 7

A. Revisit and Retell

Possible answers:
    Carson, his mom, and his four sisters were all sitting around eating pancakes and getting ready to go to a school program. Then they heard sirens going off. They looked out one window, and the sky was totally clear. But Carson's mom looked out the other direction and it was really black.
    They decided to go down to the basement, where Carson's bedroom was. Then the electricity went out, and Carson's mom got scared. They got onto Carson's bunk beds, covered up with cushions from the couch, and all sang a hymn.
    They could hear this rumbling noise, like a big train. It got louder and louder and louder. They couldn't even hear themselves sing. And all of a sudden, in a second, it stopped. The tornado was gone.

B. Word Work

coming/headed; arrive/hit; blow/gust; nasty/menacing; running/scurrying; flying/flapping; stronger/more powerful; flying/sailing; came down/crashed; raining hard/pouring; stopped/ceased; interesting/exciting.

C. Grammar

1. I hid in the cellar during the storm. 2. The wind began to blow hard. 3. The wind blew the door off. 4. The dog ran away. 5. We heard a loud explosion. 6. My sister came home at midnight last night. 7. Mei spent all her money. 8. I thought that I was going to be late to class. 9. I woke up late this morning. 10. Juan rode the bus to school. 11. I knew the answer, but I didn't raise my hand. 12. The storm broke all the windows in the house.

D. Test-Taking Practice

Reading Vocabulary: 1. B; 2. C; 3. D; 4. C; 5. B.
Reading Comprehension: 1. D; 2. A; 3. C; 4. D; 5. C.

E. Using New Vocabulary

1. tumbled over; 2. ripped off; 3. swirled around; 4. swayed; 5. crashed into; 6. shattered; 7. snapped; 8. jumped.

F. Focus on Organization

Answers will vary.

G. Focus on Style

1. 1. an elephant; 2. coal; 3. a bat; 4. a lion; 5. a bee; 6. ice; 7. a flower; 8. a pancake; 9. a bird; 10. a fruitcake; 11. a church mouse; 12. molasses; 13. a mule; 14. honey; 15. a ghost; 16. an owl.
2. Answers will vary.

H. Writer's Workshop

Answers will vary.

I. Responding to Literature

Answers will vary.

UNIT 8

A. Revisit and Retell

Answers will vary.

B. Word Work

2. 1. illegible; 2. impatient; 3. irresponsible; 4. unlikely; 5. disobey; 6. inexpensive; 7. immature; 8. nonfiction.
3. 1. nonfiction 2. immature 3. inexpensive 4. disobey 5. illegible 6. irresponsible 7. impatient 8. unlikely.

C. Grammar

1. Running; 2. Seeing 3. Learning 4. Living 5. Taking 6. Riding 7. Cooking 8. Studying

D. Test-Taking Practice

Reading Vocabulary: 1. B; 2. A; 3. C; 4. D; 5. C.
Reading Comprehension: 1. A; 2. D; 3. B; 4. C; 5. C.

E. Using New Vocabulary

1. intoxication; 2. addictive; 3. cancer; 4. dizzy, nauseated; 5. lack of coordination; 6. coughing, suffocate.

F. Focus on Organization

1. 1. R; 2. F; 3. F; 4. F; 5. F; 6. R; 7. F; 8. R; 9. F.
2. Reasons may be in a different order. Opinion Statement: Using drugs and alcohol is a very bad idea.
Reason 1: Drugs are very dangerous. Fact/Details: Drugs can damage your brain and heart. Some drugs can cause sudden death.
Reason 2: Drugs don't let you do your best. Fact/Details: Drugs can interfere with your ability to concentrate in class. Drugs can interfere with your ability on the athletic field.
Reason 3: Drugs often make it harder to get along with others. Fact/Details: Drugs can make you feel separate from family and friends. Sometimes drugs start to seem more important than people.

G. Focus on Style

1. What keeps some teens from smoking? 2. What are some signs of drug abuse in teens? 3. How long do the effects of alcohol last? 4. How serious is the drug problem in the U.S.? 5. What happens when people quit smoking? 6. Why do teens start smoking?

H. Writer's Workshop

Answers will vary.

I. Responding to Literature

Answers will vary.

UNIT 9

A. Revisit and Retell

1. How it feels: refreshing, tingly, cool; How it looks: purple, sparkling; How it tastes: delicious.
2. Possible answers: You: When was the first time you tried Sparkling Grape Jell-O®? Casey D.: When I had strep throat. You: Who gave it to you? Casey D.: My mother. She bought me ice cream and Jell-O®. You: How did she make Sparkling Grape Jell-O®? Casey D.: She mixed it with carbonated water. You: Did you eat a lot at first? Casey D.: No, I just took a little spoonful. You: What was it like? Casey D.: It was like an explosion of bubbles going down my throat. You: Do you eat Sparkling Grape Jell-O® often? Casey D.: Yes, I eat it as often as possible.

B. Word Work

Answers will vary. Possible answers: 1. noisy; 2. low; 3. short; 4. rich; 5. left; 6. divide; 7. messy; 8. midnight.

C. Grammar

1. study, will get; 2. don't take, will get; 3. will stay, rains; 4. will be, walk; 5. run, will (still) be; 6. will get, are not; 7. will win, win; 8. forget, will lend; 9. will help, calls; 10. miss, will take.

D. Test-Taking Practice

Reading Vocabulary: 1. B; 2. C; 3. B; 4. C; 5. B.
Reading Comprehension: 1. C; 2. B; 3. A; 4. B; 5. B.

E. Using New Vocabulary

Possible answers: 1. enormous, covered with cheese; 2. salty, crunchy; 3. frosty, sweet; 4. bubbling hot, full of vegetables; 5. golden, crispy; 6. sour, yellow.

F. Focus on Organization

Answers will vary. Possible answers:
Opinion Statement: I highly recommend that you give Café Kennedy a try.
Reasons: It offers food that tastes good. There is a good selection of healthy food. It's clean. It's not expensive.
Details: They have sandwiches, hot dogs, hamburgers, and special lunch plates. They offer pizza with homemade sauce, salads, low-fat foods, and low-carb foods. You could eat off the floor. You can get a lot of food for just a few dollars.

G. Focus on Style

Answers will vary. Possible answers: 1. I always have a bowl of nutritious, filling oatmeal for breakfast. 2. I often have an inexpensive fast-food lunch. 3. I like crusty, spicy pizza. 4. Indian food is spicy and filling. 5. I like tingly, sparkling soft drinks. 6. I don't want that mushy old banana. 7. I want a big, filling steak for dinner. 8. I'd like a crusty piece of toast.

H. Writer's Workshop

Answers will vary.

I. Responding to Literature

Answers will vary.

UNIT 10

A. Revisit and Retell

1: Possible answers: Title: "Do students Need a Courtesy Law?" Where from: Junior Scholastic; Background: A courtesy law is a rule that says students have to respect their teachers. They have to use titles like "Mrs." or "Mr." For: 1. Courtesy laws make the classroom a better place for learning. 2. Teachers spend more time teaching and less time disciplining. 3. Courtesy laws help teach students to be more polite at home. Against: 1. Parents, not teachers, should teach children respect. 2. There are much more important problems in schools today than a lack of courtesy. 3. Being polite doesn't get to the root of the problems in schools today.
2: Answers will vary.

B. Word Work

1. creative; 2. create; 3. creation; 4. decision; 5. decide; 6. decisive; 7. requirement; 8. requires; 9. required; 10. written; 11. write; 12. writing.

C. Grammar

1: 1. C; 2. P; 3. P; 4. P; 5. C; 6. P; 7. P; 8. C; 9. P; 10. P.
2: Answers will vary. Possible answers: 1. If you miss the bus, you will be late. 2. If you forget your books, you won't be able to do the exercises. 3. If you don't start exercising, you could become overweight. 4. If you cheat, you will get detention. 5. If you forget to turn in your report, you might fail this course. 6. If you turn in your homework early, you could have some free time.

D. Test-Taking Practice

Reading Vocabulary: 1. D; 2. C; 3. A; 4. A; 5. C.
Reading Comprehension: 1. C; 2. D; 3. D; 4. B; 5. C.

E. Using New Vocabulary

Answers will vary. Possible answers:
a. 1, 3; b. 3, 6, 7, 8; c. 4; d. 2; e. 7; f. 5.

F. Focus on Organization

Answers will vary. Possible answers: Issue: Should cities and towns have curfews for kids? For: Curfews keep kids safe. Kids should be at home after dark, not on the street. Curfews teach kids about the importance of obeying rules. Against: Curfews violate our rights. Parents should decide what's best for their kids. Cities and towns should spend money on activities for kids instead of giving them curfews.

G. Focus on Style

1. "Parents should teach manners," says Mark Marin. "It's their responsibility." 2. Lisa Kingston says, "It's never too early to start teaching kids to be polite." 3. "Good manners aren't hard to learn," says William Vang. "They're just common sense." 4. "In my country, we always bow to older people," says Boun Thai. "It's our custom." 5. "You should always call a teacher by his or her last name," says Mina Lee. "First names are too informal." 6. "I like to be called Ms. Baker," says Tina Baker. "It shows respect." 7. "I don't like to be called Ms. Anderson," says Kelly Anderson. "I prefer to be called Kelly."

H. Writer's Workshop

Answers will vary.

I. Responding to Literature

Answers will vary.

References

Armbruster, B.B. (1991). Content area reading instruction. In Cooper, J.D. *Literacy, helping children construct meaning*, 3rd ed. Boston, MA: Houghton Mifflin Company.

Baker, L. & Brown, A. (1984). Cognitive monitoring in reading. In J. Flood (ed.), *Understanding Reading Comprehension* (pp. 21–44). Newark, DE: International Reading Association.

Calkins, L. (1991). *Living between the lines*. Portsmouth, NH: Heinemann.

Chamot, A. & O'Malley, M. (1994). *The CALLA handbook*. New York: Longman.

Chamot, A. & O'Malley, M. (1999). *The learning strategies handbook*. New York: Longman.

Cooper, J.D. (1993). *Literacy: Helping children construct meaning*. Boston, MA: Houghton Mifflin Company.

Cummins, James (1981). The role of primary language development in promoting educational success for language minority students. In California State Department of Education (Ed.), *Schooling and language minority students: A theoretical framework* (1st Edition), pp. 3–49. Los Angeles: Evaluation, Dissemination and Assessment Center, California State University, Los Angeles.

Danielson, L.M. (2000). The improvement of student writing: What research says. *Journal of School Improvement*, 1:1.

Dole, J.A., Duffy, G.G., Roehler, L.R., and Pearson, P.D. (1991). Moving from the old to the new: Research on reading comprehension instruction. *Review of Educational Research*, 61: 239–264.

Duke, N.K. & Pearson, P.D. (2002) Effective practices for developing reading comprehension. In A.E. Farstrup & S.J. Samuels (eds.) *What the research has to say about reading comprehension*. Newark, DE: International Reading Association.

Emig, J. (1971). *The composing processes of twelfth graders*. Urbana, IL: National Council of Teachers of English.

Graesser, A.C., NcNamara, D.S., & Louwerse, M.M. (2002). What do readers need to learn in order to process coherence relations in narrative and expository text? In A.P. Sweet and C.E. Snow (eds.) *Rethinking Reading Comprehension*. New York: The Guilford Press.

Graves, D. (1983). *Writing: teachers and children at work*. Portsmouth, NH: Heinemann.

Hiebert, E. (1999). *Text matters in learning to read*. CIERA Report 1.001. Ann Arbor: University of Michigan. Center for the Improvement of Early Reading Achievement.

Hogan, K. & Pressley, M. (1997). *Scaffolding student learning: Instructional approaches and issues*. Cambridge, MA: Brookline Books.

Jimenez, R.T. (1997). The strategic abilities and potential of five low-literacy Latina/o readers in middle school. *Reading Research Quarterly*, 32, 224–243.

Johns, A. (1997). *Text, role, and context: Developing academic literacies*. New York: Cambridge University Press.

Keene, E. and Zimmermann, S. (1997). Mosaic of thought: Teaching comprehension in a reader's workshop. Portsmouth, NH: Heinemann.

Kintsch, W. (1998). *Comprehension: A paradigm for cognition*. Cambridge: Cambridge University Press.

Klinger, J.K. & Vaughn, S. (2000). The helping behaviors of fifth graders while using collaborative strat reading during ESL content classes. *TESOL Quarterly*, 34(1), 69–98.

Krashen, S. (2004, April). The phonics debate: 2004. *Language*, 3: 8, 18–20.

National Council of Teachers of English (2004). Beliefs about the Teaching of Writing.

National Reading Panel (2000). Teaching *children to read: An evidence-based assessment of the scientific research literature on reading and it's implications for reading instruction*. Washington, DC: National Institute of Child Health and Human Development.

Padron, Y. (1992). The effect of strategy instruction on bilingual students' cognitive strategy use in reading. *Bilingual Research Journal*, 16, 35–52.

Pearson, P.D. & Fielding, L. (1991). Comprehension instruction. In R. Barr et al (eds.), *Handbook of reading research*, 2: 861–883. White Plains, NY: Longman.

RAND Reading Study Group (2002). *Reading for understanding: Toward an R&D Program in Reading Comprehension*. Santa Monica, CA: RAND Corporation.

Roehler, L. & Duffey, G. (1991). Teachers' instructional actions. In R. Barr et al (eds.), *Handbook of reading research*, 2: 861–883. White Plains, NY: Longman.

Smith, F. (1994). Understanding reading. Hillsdale, NJ: Erlbaum.

Tierney, R. (1990). Learning to connect reading and writing: Critical thinking through transactions with one's own subjectivity. In Shanahan, T. (ed.) *Reading and writing together: New perspectives for the classroom*. Norwood, MA: Christopher Gordon.

Weaver, C. (1996). Teaching grammar in context. Portsmouth, NH: Heinemann.